Recent Approaches for Wound Treatment

Recent Approaches for Wound Treatment

Editors

Cinzia Pagano
César Viseras
Luana Perioli

MDPI

Basel • Beijing • Wuhan • Barcelona • Belgrade • Novi Sad • Cluj • Manchester

Editors

Cinzia Pagano
Department of
Pharmaceutical Sciences
Università degli Studi di Perugia
Perugia
Italy

César Viseras
Department of Pharmacy and
Pharmaceutical Technology
University of Granada
Granada
Spain

Luana Perioli
Department of
Pharmaceutical Sciences
Università degli Studi di Perugia
Perugia
Italy

Editorial Office

MDPI
St. Alban-Anlage 66
4052 Basel, Switzerland

This is a reprint of articles from the Special Issue published online in the open access journal *International Journal of Molecular Sciences* (ISSN 1422-0067) (available at: www.mdpi.com/journal/ijms/special_issues/Wound_Treatment).

For citation purposes, cite each article independently as indicated on the article page online and as indicated below:

Lastname, A.A.; Lastname, B.B. Article Title. *Journal Name* **Year**, *Volume Number*, Page Range.

ISBN 978-3-0365-8697-7 (Hbk)
ISBN 978-3-0365-8696-0 (PDF)
doi.org/10.3390/books978-3-0365-8696-0

Contents

About the Editors

Cinzia Pagano

Cinzia Pagano received her Ph.D. in Chemistry and Pharmaceutical Technology in 2011 from the University of Perugia. She is Associate Professor at Department of Pharmaceutical Sciences (University of Perugia, Italy) and teaches Pharmaceutical Technology, Socio-Economy and Law for the course of Pharmacy (II level). The recent research activity focuses on the development and characterization of polymeric bioadhesive formulations for wounds treatment and on the use of active ingredients coming from natural sources including food wastes.

César Viseras

Prof. César Viseras is full professor at the Department of Pharmacy and Pharmaceutical Technology at University of Granada. He received a PhD in Pharmacy (with honours) in 1997 from the University of Granada.

The research activity is focused on: Pharmaceutical Development of Natural Resources: Crystallographic, physical and chemical characterisation of natural solids and solid surfaces; dynamic properties of powders. Mechanical and flow behaviour of concentrated dispersions. Rheology and phase behaviour. Polymers-Inorganic materials systems: Sorption studies; equilibrium and kinetics, conformation of polymers interfaces. Matrix formulations: Optimised prolonged release formulations, release kinetics, drug adsorption. Polymeric materials for drug release. Diffusion in Polymers, Composites, Mathematical Modeling. Controlled release theory and applications. Modified Drug Delivery: Modulated release using oral controlled release devices, Temperature and pH-sensitive systems, Mucoadhesive controlled release systems Biomaterials: Biointerfacial Phenomena, Bioadhesive systems.

Luana Perioli

Prof. Luana Perioli is Associate Professor at the Department of Pharmaceutical Sciences of the University of Perugia. She obtained her Ph.D. in Pharmacy in 1992 from the University of Perugia.

Her research topics are drug delivery, pharmaceutical technology, oral and topical dosage forms, regulatory, cosmetic products. Recent research activity focuses on the development and characterization of polymeric bioadhesive formulations for wounds treatment and on the use of active ingredients coming from natural sources including food wastes.

Preface

Wounds represent an unsolved serious healthcare problem. The treatments available are unsatisfactory because they do not take into account the patient-to-patient differences and need changing according to wound type as well as age, sex, etc. An efficacious therapy could be obtained by specific customized treatments developed taking into account the specific aspects of the patient.

Cinzia Pagano, César Viseras, and Luana Perioli
Editors

International Journal of
Molecular Sciences

MDPI

Editorial

Recent Approaches for Wound Treatment

Cinzia Pagano [1], César Antonio Viseras Iborra [2] and Luana Perioli [1,*]

1 Department of Pharmaceutical Sciences, University of Perugia, 06123 Perugia, Italy; cinzia.pagano@unipg.it
2 Department of Pharmacy and Pharmaceutical Technology, Faculty of Pharmacy, University of Granada, 18071 Granada, Spain; cviseras@ugr.es
* Correspondence: luana.perioli@unipg.it

Wounds are a serious global health problem. In particular, chronic wounds are the most challenging because their management remains difficult and the available treatments are often ineffective. This is responsible for a serious impact on patient quality of life as well as on healthcare systems, as in many cases, patient hospitalization is required, resulting in high costs. The total Medicare spending estimates for all wound types ranges from USD 28.1 to USD 96.8 billion [1].

The aim of this Special Issue is to present new approaches as valuable alternatives that could be useful in the treatment and management of wounds. The proposals take into account efficacy and safety and are environmentally friendly.

The strategies are varied and the treatments can be performed using many different approaches. The proposed strategies include new ingredients (e.g., A.P.I. and polymers) able to stimulate wound healing, new delivery systems and new formulations, as well as a new understanding of the stimulation of physiological biochemical pathways. New state-of-the-art technologies as well as diagnostic tools are also presented.

Effective therapies are decided after appropriate diagnoses and an assessment of the specific problems for each patient.

Curti et al. [2] suggested an automated model able to perform a deep analysis of wounds from images acquired from smartphones using an app developed *ad hoc*. This method is based on an active semi-supervised learning training of a convolutional neural network. It was proven to be a suitable instrument for clinical practice and a valuable support for clinicians in choosing the most appropriate treatment.

Sim et al. [3] evaluated the effect of pH value variation in the promotion of wound healing. In particular, they observed that the incubation of human immortalized keratinocytes (HaCaT) and human foreskin fibroblasts (HFF) with acidic buffer promotes cell proliferation and migration, fundamental processes for wound healing.

Bianchi et al. [4] purposed nano-fibrous scaffolds having anti-inflammatory, antibacterial and antioxidant activities. The scaffolds are characterized by aligned nanofibers able to mimic the tendon structure and to promote reconstruction and healing. The nanofibers were produced by electrospinning, an innovative technique, using a biodegradable and biocompatible synthetic polymer, poly(butyl cyanoacrylate) (PBCA), combined with copper oxide nanoparticles and caseinphosphopeptides (CPP).

With the aim of finding useful tools from natural sources, Gębarowski et al. [5] investigated the benefits of wound dressings made from flax fibers and observed that they are efficacious in the promotion of tissue regeneration.

Kua et al. [6] studied the potential use of human umbilical cord lining epithelial cells for treating cutaneous wounds. In vivo studies assessed their ability to promote wound healing.

Smart technologies could be useful instruments for customized treatments of wounds.

Ceccarini et al. [7] purposed functionalized silk fibers covalently linked to an arginine–glycine–aspartic acid (RGD) peptide to 3D print grid-like piezoresistors with wound healing

Citation: Pagano, C.; Viseras Iborra, C.A.; Perioli, L. Recent Approaches for Wound Treatment. *Int. J. Mol. Sci.* **2023**, *24*, 5959. https://doi.org/10.3390/ijms24065959

Received: 17 March 2023
Accepted: 20 March 2023
Published: 22 March 2023

and sensing properties. The peptide-modified silk fibroin exhibited wound healing capacity and piezoresistive properties, and additionally demonstrated a sensitivity to humidity.

Often, infections are one of the most common complications of chronic wounds. Consequently, the healing process is further delayed, with serious consequences for the patient. The resolution of infections is thus an important approach in the promotion of wound healing. However, the use of conventional antibiotics is often unsuccessful due to antibiotic resistance. In 2019, 1.27 million deaths were caused by treatment-resistant infections [8]. Thus, the search for new and effective alternatives is necessary.

Lin et al. [9], for example, developed metal–organic frameworks (MOFs), which are systems consisting of metal ions (copper in this case) coordinated to organic ligands to form one-, two-, or three-dimensional structures. As a result of their peroxidase (POD)-like activity, hydroxyl radicals are produced from hydrogen peroxide. These radicals, together with Cu, possess antibacterial activity, responsible for the fast resolution of infections and thus the acceleration of wound healing.

Bąchor et al. [10] developed new isoxazole derivatives which showed antibiofilm activity toward *Staphylococcus aureus*, representing a valuable alternative to conventional broad-spectrum antibiotics currently used in therapy which often suffer from antimicrobial resistance.

Di Lodovico et al. [11] developed graphene oxide compounds activated by light-emitting diodes, which demonstrated antimicrobial activity against *Staphylococcus aureus*- and *Pseudomonas aeruginosa*-resistant strains in a dual-species biofilm.

The necessity to evaluate the efficacy of most treatment options also poses a problem in that in vivo studies are limited and, in the case of wounds, injuries to the skin must be induced in animals. Cialdai et al. [12] purposed an ex vivo model for wound healing studies based on a human skin specimen (skin biopsies) mounted in a special chamber equipped with a device able to monitor tissues changes, avoiding the unnecessary use of animals.

Funding: This research received no external funding.

Conflicts of Interest: The authors declare no conflict of interest.

References

1. Nussbaum, S.R.; Carter, M.J.; Fife, C.E.; DaVanzo, J.; Haught, R.; Nusgart, M.; Cartwright, D. An Economic Evaluation of the Impact, Cost, and Medicare Policy Implications of Chronic Nonhealing Wounds. *Value Health* **2018**, *21*, 27–32. [CrossRef] [PubMed]
2. Curti, N.; Merli, Y.; Zengarini, C.; Giampieri, E.; Merlotti, A.; Dall'Olio, D.; Marcelli, E.; Bianchi, T.; Castellani, G. Effectiveness of Semi-Supervised Active Learning in Automated Wound Image Segmentation. *Int. J. Mol. Sci.* **2023**, *24*, 706. [CrossRef] [PubMed]
3. Sim, P.; Strudwick, X.L.; Song, Y.; Cowin, A.J.; Garg, S. Influence of Acidic pH on Wound Healing In Vivo: A Novel Perspective for Wound Treatment. *Int. J. Mol. Sci.* **2022**, *23*, 13655. [CrossRef] [PubMed]
4. Bianchi, E.; Vigani, B.; Ruggeri, M.; Del Favero, E.; Ricci, C.; Grisoli, P.; Ferraretto, A.; Rossi, S.; Viseras, C.; Sandri, G. Electrospun Scaffolds Based on Poly(butyl cyanoacrylate) for Tendon Tissue Engineering. *Int. J. Mol. Sci.* **2023**, *24*, 3172. [CrossRef] [PubMed]
5. Gębarowski, T.; Jęskowiak, I.; Wiatrak, B. Investigation of the Properties of Linen Fibers and Dressings. *Int. J. Mol. Sci.* **2022**, *23*, 10480. [CrossRef] [PubMed]
6. Kua, J.E.H.; Siow, C.W.; Lim, W.K.; Masilamani, J.; Tjin, M.S.; Yeong, J.; Lim, T.K.H.; Phan, T.T.; Chua, A.W.C. Human Umbilical Cord Lining-Derived Epithelial Cells: A Potential Source of Non-Native Epithelial Cells That Accelerate Healing in a Porcine Cutaneous Wound Model. *Int. J. Mol. Sci.* **2022**, *23*, 8918. [CrossRef] [PubMed]
7. Ceccarini, M.R.; Palazzi, V.; Salvati, R.; Chiesa, I.; De Maria, C.; Bonafoni, S.; Mezzanotte, P.; Codini, M.; Pacini, L.; Errante, F.; et al. Biomaterial Inks from Peptide-Functionalized Silk Fibers for 3D Printing of Futuristic Wound-Healing and Sensing Materials. *Int. J. Mol. Sci.* **2023**, *24*, 947. [CrossRef] [PubMed]
8. Murray, C.J.; Ikuta, K.S.; Sharara, F.; Swetschinski, L.; Robles Aguilar, G.; Gray, A.; Han, C.; Bisignano, C.; Rao, P.; Wool, E.; et al. Global burden of bacterial antimicrobial resistance in 2019: A systematic analysis. *Lancet* **2022**, *399*, 629–655. [CrossRef] [PubMed]
9. Lin, C.; Guo, X.; Mo, F.; Sun, D. Different Dimensional Copper-Based Metal–Organic Frameworks with Enzyme-Mimetic Activity for Antibacterial Therapy. *Int. J. Mol. Sci.* **2023**, *24*, 3173. [CrossRef] [PubMed]
10. Bąchor, U.; Junka, A.; Brożyna, M.; Mączyński, M. The In Vitro Impact of Isoxazole Derivatives on Pathogenic Biofilm and Cytotoxicity of Fibroblast Cell Line. *Int. J. Mol. Sci.* **2023**, *24*, 2997. [CrossRef] [PubMed]

11. Di Lodovico, S.; Diban, F.; Di Fermo, P.; Petrini, M.; Fontana, A.; Di Giulio, M.; Piattelli, A.; D'Ercole, S.; Cellini, L. Antimicrobial Combined Action of Graphene Oxide and Light Emitting Diodes for Chronic Wound Management. *Int. J. Mol. Sci.* **2022**, *23*, 6942. [CrossRef] [PubMed]
12. Cialdai, F.; Bacci, S.; Zizi, V.; Norfini, A.; Balsamo, M.; Ciccone, V.; Morbidelli, L.; Calosi, L.; Risaliti, C.; Vanhelden, L.; et al. Optimization of an Ex-Vivo Human Skin/Vein Model for Long-Term Wound Healing Studies: Ground Preparatory Activities for the 'Suture in Space' Experiment Onboard the International Space Station. *Int. J. Mol. Sci.* **2022**, *23*, 14123. [CrossRef] [PubMed]

International Journal of *Molecular Sciences*

MDPI

Article

Electrospun Scaffolds Based on Poly(butyl cyanoacrylate) for Tendon Tissue Engineering

Eleonora Bianchi [1], Barbara Vigani [1], Marco Ruggeri [1], Elena Del Favero [2], Caterina Ricci [2], Pietro Grisoli [1], Anita Ferraretto [3,4], Silvia Rossi [1], César Viseras [5] and Giuseppina Sandri [1,*]

[1] Department of Drug Sciences, University of Pavia, Viale Taramelli 12, 27100 Pavia, Italy
[2] Department of Medical Biotechnology and Translational Medicine, University of Milan, LITA Viale Fratelli Cervi 93, 20090 Segrate, Italy
[3] IRCCS Galeazzi Orthopaedical Institute, Laboratory of Experimental Biochemistry & Molecular Biology, Via R. Galeazzi 4, 20161 Milan, Italy
[4] Department of Biomedical Sciences for Health, University of Milan, LITA, Via Fratelli Cervi 93, 20090 Segrate, Italy
[5] Department of Pharmacy and Pharmaceutical Technology, Faculty of Pharmacy, University of Granada, Campus of Cartuja s/n, 18071 Granada, Spain
* Correspondence: g.sandri@unipv.it

Abstract: Tendon disorders are common medical conditions that could lead to significant disability, pain, healthcare costs, and a loss of productivity. Traditional approaches require long periods of treatment, and they largely fail due to the tissues weakening and the postoperative alterations of the normal joint mechanics. To overcome these limitations, innovative strategies for the treatment of these injuries need to be explored. The aim of the present work was the design of nano-fibrous scaffolds based on poly(butyl cyanoacrylate) (PBCA), a well-known biodegradable and biocompatible synthetic polymer, doped with copper oxide nanoparticles and caseinphosphopeptides (CPP), able to mimic the hierarchical structure of the tendon and to improve the tissue healing potential. These were developed as implants to be sutured to reconstruct the tendons and the ligaments during surgery. PBCA was synthetized, and then electrospun to produce aligned nanofibers. The obtained scaffolds were characterized for their structure and physico-chemical and mechanical properties, highlighting that CuO and CPP loading, and the aligned conformation determined an increase in the scaffold mechanical performance. Furthermore, the scaffolds loaded with CuO showed antioxidant and anti-inflammatory properties. Moreover, human tenocytes adhesion and proliferation to the scaffolds were assessed in vitro. Finally, the antibacterial activity of the scaffolds was evaluated using *Escherichia coli* and *Staphylococcus aureus* as representative of Gram-negative and Gram-positive bacteria, respectively, demonstrating that the CuO-doped scaffolds possessed a significant antimicrobial effect against *E. coli*. In conclusion, scaffolds based on PBCA and doped with CuO and CPP deserve particular attention as enhancers of the tendon tissue regeneration and able to avoid bacterial adhesion. Further investigation on the scaffold efficacy in vivo will assess their capability for enhancing the tendon ECM restoration in view of accelerating their translation to the clinic.

Keywords: tendon disorders; poly(butyl cyanoacrylate); copper oxide; caseinophosphopeptides; electrospinning; anti-inflammatory; antioxidant; antimicrobial

Citation: Bianchi, E.; Vigani, B.; Ruggeri, M.; Del Favero, E.; Ricci, C.; Grisoli, P.; Ferraretto, A.; Rossi, S.; Viseras, C.; Sandri, G. Electrospun Scaffolds Based on Poly(butyl cyanoacrylate) for Tendon Tissue Engineering. *Int. J. Mol. Sci.* **2023**, *24*, 3172. https://doi.org/10.3390/ijms24043172

Academic Editor: Emerito Carlos Rodriguez-Merchan

Received: 27 December 2022
Revised: 23 January 2023
Accepted: 26 January 2023
Published: 6 February 2023

1. Introduction

Tendon disorders are common medical conditions that could lead to significant disability, pain, healthcare costs, and a loss of productivity. A wide range of injury mechanisms exist, such as tears, which can occur in healthy tendons that are acutely overloaded or lacerated, or tendinitis or tendinosis, which can occur in tendons exposed to overuse conditions or intrinsic tissue degeneration [1,2].

In general, the healing of tendons follows the typical wound healing course, including an early inflammatory phase, which lasts about one week, followed by a proliferative phase, which lasts from three to four weeks, and finally by a remodeling phase, which lasts many months. The exact duration of each phase is highly dependent on the subject, the tendon location, and the injury type. For this reason, it is of paramount importance to provide an adequate support to the tissue during the entire regeneration process [3,4].

Numerous treatment approaches have been attempted to improve tendon healing, including surgical approaches and cell-based therapies, with specific rehabilitation protocols. However, these require long periods of treatment, and they largely fail due to the tissues weakening and the postoperative alterations of the normal joint mechanics [5,6].

To overcome these limitations, in recent years several studies have been conducted for the application of tissue engineering in the treatment of orthopedic injuries, aiming at the regeneration of damaged tissues, instead of replacing them, through the development of reparative constructs. For this purpose, poly(butyl cyanoacrylate) (PBCA) represents an interesting candidate to develop innovative platforms, as it is a well-known biodegradable and biocompatible synthetic polymer, used nowadays in the medical field as a nanocarrier for drug delivery [7,8]. Considering these premises, the aim of the present work was the design of nano-fibrous scaffolds based on PBCA, and doped with copper oxide nanoparticles (CuO) and caseinophosphopeptides (CPP), able to mimic the hierarchical structure of the tendon and to improve the tissue healing potential. These were developed as implants to be sutured to reconstruct the tendons and the ligaments during surgery.

Inorganic nanomaterials have recently gained great attention in tissue engineering, in particular to dope polymeric scaffolds [9,10]. In fact, they have unique properties, such as antimicrobial, antioxidant, and anti-inflammatory properties, and thus they have been widely used to improve polymeric scaffold mechanical properties, and to support and enhance the cell growth [9,10]. In particular, in the tissue engineering field, CuO nanoparticles proved to stimulate cell proliferation during wound healing by upregulating the vascular endothelial growth factor gene expression, promoting mesenchymal stem cell differentiation, and avoiding infections via their antibacterial properties. Moreover, they were demonstrated to increase the physico-chemical properties of biomaterials, such as the mechanical strength [11,12]. CPPs—phosphorylated peptides enzymatically released from casein due to in vitro and in vivo digestion—have been loaded in the scaffolds since they were proven to promote calcium uptake, due to their cation-binding activity, osteoblast differentiation [13], and exertion of antioxidant activity [14], and for these reasons they seemed suitable candidates to potentiate the effectiveness of CuO-doped PBCA scaffolds.

The developed scaffolds should be able to mimic the hierarchical structure of the tendon after being sutured, consequently improving the tissue reconstruction and the healing potential. Moreover, they should protect the site of inflammation from severe tissue damage and enhance cell proliferation and migration. Finally, the scaffolds, the object of this study, should also protect the surgical site from bacterial infections, which could lead to complications, such as tissue destruction, failure or extension of proper wound healing, and occasionally bacteremia, resulting in prolonged hospital stays, and increased patient costs for the healthcare system [15].

2. Results and Discussion

2.1. Synthesis and Characterization of PBCA

The polymerization process of the BCA is characterized by a yield % of 80.02% $\pm$ 7.85%, and the molecular weight and the polymerization degree of the obtained polymer are 749 Da and 4.89, respectively.

Figure 1 reports the chemical shifts and the signal assignments of BCA and PBCAs ^{1}H (Figure 1a) and ^{13}C (Figure 1b) NMR spectra. Other spectra reported in the literature for this type of structure were taken as references [16] to make the assignments. Several specific signals with clearly distinct shift differences are observed in the ^{1}H NMR spectra (Figure 1a). Proton signals corresponding to the broad multiplet of the α-methylene of the ester residue (-O–CH_2–) are found at 4.12 ppm (d, blue and green signals), while the broad multiplets of β- and γ-methylene groups (–CH_2–) are found at 1.62 and 1.41 ppm, respectively (b and c, blue and green signals). The broad triplet of the methyl group (–CH_3) is found at 0.92 ppm (a, blue and green signals).

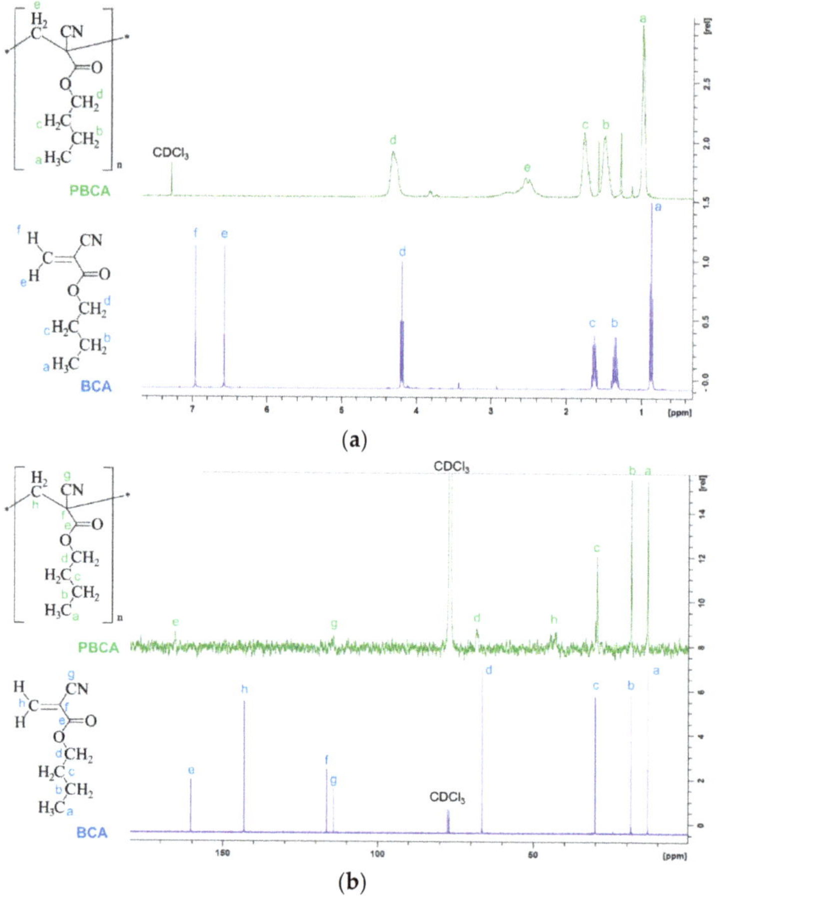

Figure 1. (**a**) ^1H and (**b**) ^{13}C NMR spectra of BCA and PBCA powders measured in deuterated chloroform ($CDCl_3$).

On the other hand, protons signals from the monomer vinyl group (at 7.0 and 6.63 ppm; e and f, blue signals) are not present in the spectra of PBCA, but a signal assigned to protons of the methylene group of the main chain of PBCA appears at 2.43 ppm (broad multiplets; e, green signal), confirming the monomer conversion into a polymer.

2.2. *Scaffold Physico-Chemical Characterization*

The PBCA optimal concentration to obtain fine nanofibers with the homogeneous morphology was 20% *w/w*. In particular, it is possible to observe that the PBCA concentration affects the fiber morphology. In fact, the increased concentration leads to the formation of irregular fibers, and knots. Moreover, the P3 blend, containing the higher polymer concentration, does not even allow to obtain a regular fiber production. On the other hand, the lower polymer concentration leads to the formation of uniform fibers with a smooth surface and nanometric dimensions (Figure S1). For this reason, the P1 blend was selected to be doped with CuO and CPP.

In Figure 2, the SEM micrographs of the random (R) and aligned (A) scaffolds are shown. The CuO and CPP doping leads to the formation of bulges, probably due to the aggregation of the nanoparticles (CuO) into the fiber structure. Despite this, the fibers maintain nano-dimensions. Moreover, the scaffolds obtained from the cylindrical collector, especially the ones loaded with the active components, shows an orderly spatial organization of the fibers.

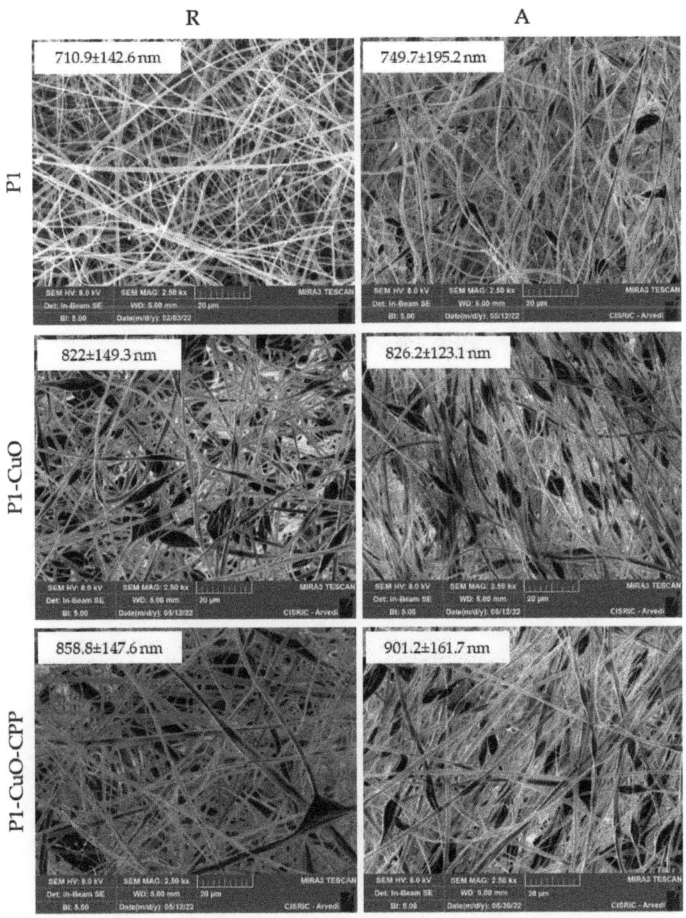

Figure 2. SEM micrographs of P1, P1-CuO, and P1-CuO-CPP scaffolds randomly collected (R) and aligned (A) at 2.5 kx magnification. In the insets, the corresponding dimensional analysis is shown (mean values ± SD, n = 30).

SEM-EDX and TEM analyses (Figure 3) were performed to evaluate the CuO incorporation into the fibers. The EDX (Figure 3a,b) underlines the presence of CuO clusters both onto the fibers and into the fiber bulges. The same trend is noted in the TEM images (Figure 3c), in which it is possible to observe the empty fibers of polymer alone, and the same CuO clusters onto the fibers and into the fiber bulges, affecting their shape and the surface roughness. The presence of CPP is not visible in the fibers, suggesting that they are homogeneously dispersed and entangled with the PBCA chains.

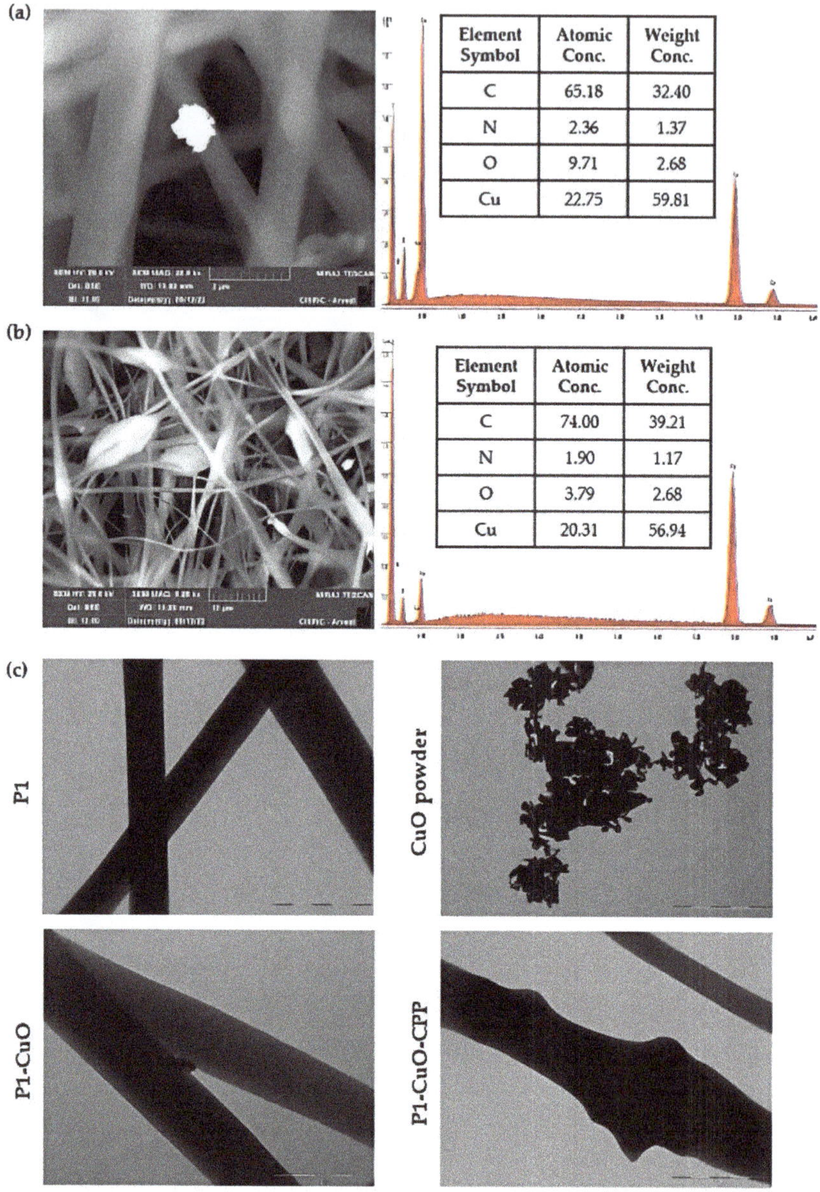

Figure 3. SEM-EDX of (**a**) P1-CuO and (**b**) P1-CuO-CPP scaffolds. (**c**) TEM micrographs of the scaffolds with and without CuO and of the CuO powder (scale bar: 1 μm).

The interfacial properties and wettability of the scaffolds, both in the aligned and random structures, were evaluated using contact angle measurements. The scaffold morphology and dimensions do not change after hydration.

Figure 4 reports the shape and the contact angle values of a 0.4 μL buffer drop released onto the scaffolds.

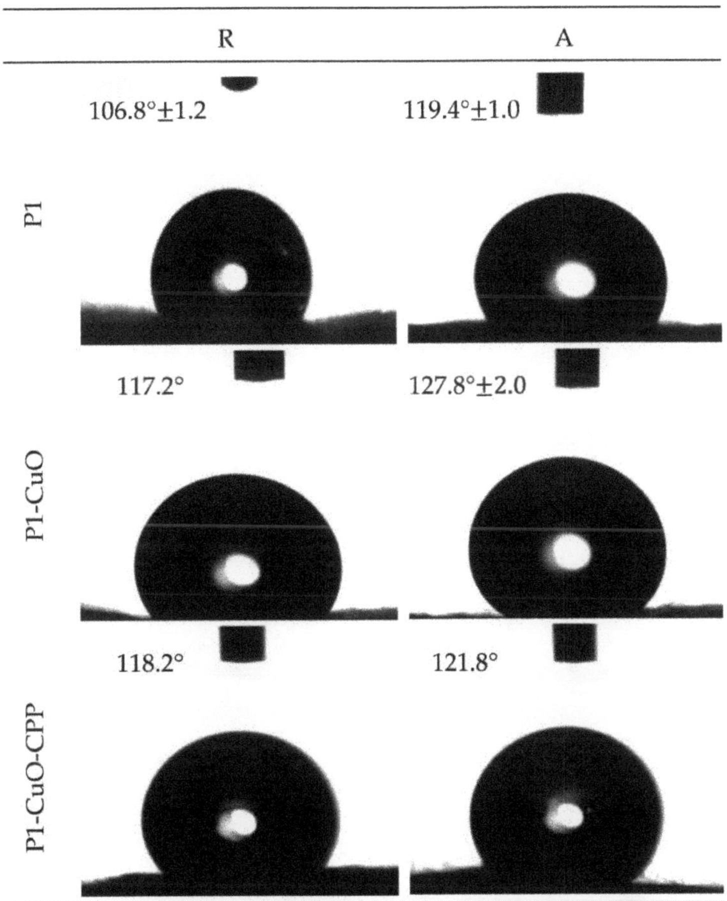

Figure 4. Images of the buffer drop onto the surface of P1, P1-CuO, and P1-CuO-CPP random (R) and aligned (A) scaffolds after 1000 ms. In each image, the value of the contact angle is reported (mean values ± SD, n = 4) (needle diameter: 0.405 mm). One-way ANOVA, Scheffé test ($p \leq 0.05$) is reported in the Supplementary Information (SI: Section S1.3.1).

It is possible to observe how the fiber orientation governs the wettability of the scaffolds, despite having the same polymeric matrix composition. In fact, the random scaffolds are characterized by contact angle values lower than the aligned ones. This could be attributable to the surface organization, which could influence the water spreading onto the scaffold surface. In particular, the inter-fiber spacing of the aligned nanofibers leads to a capillary-like force parallel to the fiber orientation, consequently preventing water spreading in the cross-direction. On the other hand, in random scaffolds, the forces induced by adjacent nanofibers are also randomly directed without any influence on hydration [17,18].

Furthermore, the presence of CuO nanoparticles into the fibrous matrix resulted in a significant increase in the contact angle of the scaffolds. This could be attributed to the hydrophobic nature of the CuO [19,20]. Moreover, the contact angle could also be affected by the surface roughness [20,21]. Therefore, these results are consistent with the increase in the surface roughness that characterizes the scaffolds containing CuO nanoparticles compared with the undoped ones.

2.3. Structural Characterization

The structural characterization of the scaffolds was studied using infrared spectroscopy, and small-angle X-ray spectroscopy. Figure 5a reports the FTIR profiles of the electrospun scaffolds. All the spectra are characteristic of the PBCA, as it is the main component of the systems (Figure S2). In fact, the bands at 1747 and 1253 cm^{-1} suggest the presence of ester groups, while the one at 2237.49 cm^{-1} is due to the stretching of the cyano group. Moreover, the absence of bands related to the stretching vibration of the vinyl group's C=C bond, usually found at 1675 cm^{-1}, as well as the absence of an absorption band at 3010 cm^{-1}, usually associated with the C–H of vinyl groups, ulteriorly confirm the polymerization reaction efficiency [22].

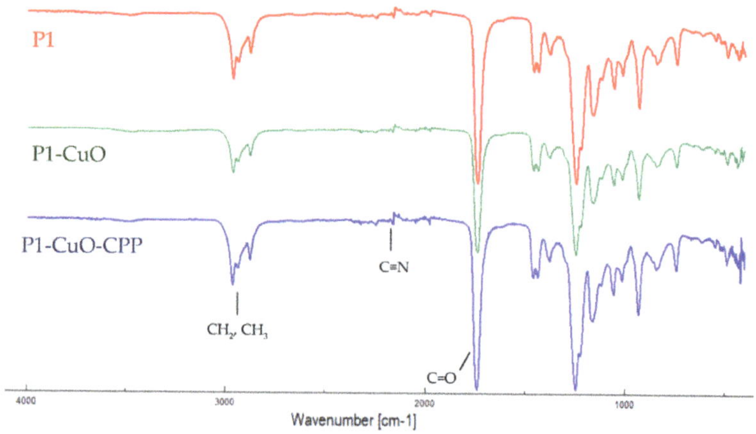

(a)

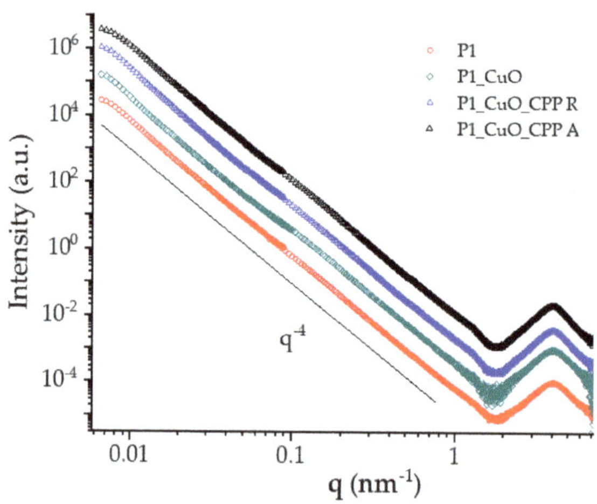

(b)

Figure 5. (**a**) FTIR spectra of P1, P1-CuO, and P1-CuO-CPP scaffolds. (**b**) SAXS spectra of P1, P1-CuO, and P1-CuO-CPP scaffolds randomly collected (R) and of P1-CuO-CPP aligned (A). The intensity profiles were vertically shifted for better visibility.

SAXS measurements were performed on scaffolds just after insertion in capillaries and full wetting to obtain structural information on the nanoscale. The SAXS spectra (I(q) vs. q) are reported in Figure 5b in the whole SAXS range, vertically shifted for better visibility. All spectra show a broad peak in the high-q region, at $q = 4\ nm^{-1}$, corresponding to a characteristic distance of $d = 1.6$ nm, due to the very local arrangement of the polymer chains within the fibers. In the region $q < 1\ nm^{-1}$, the intensity profiles follow a (q^{-4})-slope over a large q-range, covering the micro-to-nanoscale, typical of compact objects with smooth surfaces. The spectra of scaffolds in the presence of CuO nanoparticles or CPPs and CuO nanoparticles are similar to the naked one. This is conceivably due to the low-doping doses of CuO nanoparticles (1%) and CPPs (0.5%) in the fibrous matrix that does not affect the local packing of polymer chains and the compactness of the surface on the nanoscale, similarly for random and aligned scaffolds. The spectra of the two doping components are reported in Figure S3. Results indicate that CuO nanoparticles have a rod-like shape (short size = 10 nm, long size = 70 nm), while CPPs behave as gaussian polymer chains.

2.4. Mechanical Properties

The mechanical properties of both random and aligned scaffolds were evaluated in both dry (Figure 6a) and hydrated (Figure 6b) states.

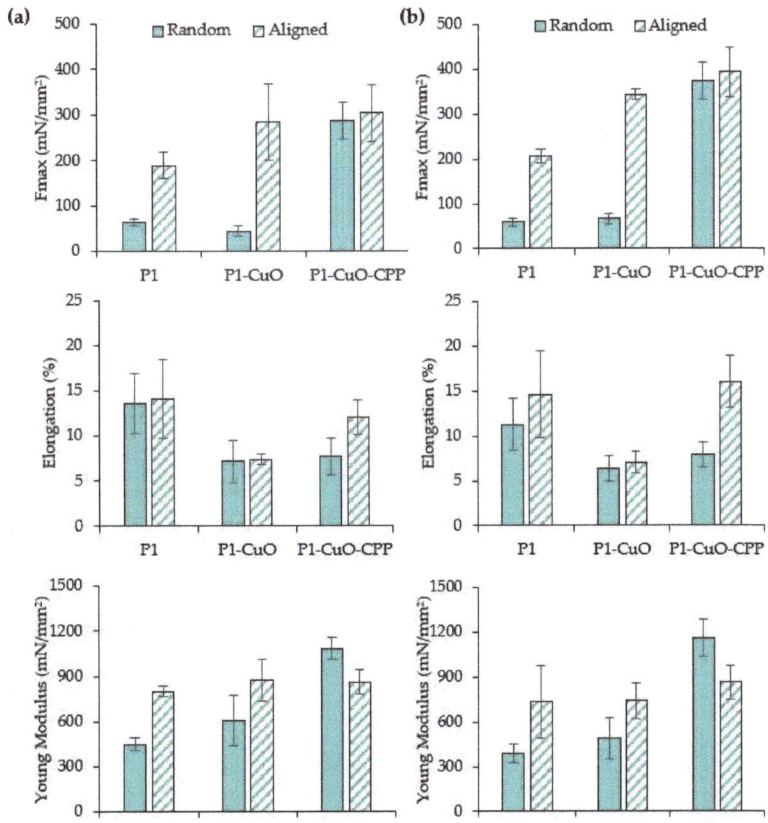

Figure 6. Maximum tensile force values (Fmax), elongation (%), and Young's modulus (mN/mm^2) evaluated for P1, P1-CuO, and P1-CuO-CPP random (full color) and aligned (shaded color) scaffolds in both (**a**) dry and (**b**) hydrated states (mean values ± SD, $n = 5$). One-way ANOVA, Scheffé test ($p \leq 0.05$) is reported in the Supplementary Information (SI: Section S1.3.2).

The aligned structure and the doping with the active components lead to a significant increase of the maximum force at break (Fmax) values, while the elongation is lower than those of the undoped scaffolds. This is principally due to the presence of the CuO nanoparticles in the fibrous matrix. In fact, the mechanical properties could be influenced by the nanoparticle distribution into the fibrous structure. In particular, they may have reduced the flexibility of the scaffolds by decreasing the free volume between the polymer chains and, consequently, their mobility [19]. The fiber orientation also plays a pivotal role in the mechanical performance since the aligned scaffolds are characterized by Fmax values significantly higher than the random ones. In fact, previous studies also highlighted that the mechanical properties could be affected by the angle between the stretching direction and the fiber orientation, significantly increasing when this was 0° [23].

2.5. DPPH Radical Scavenging Activity

Since an enhanced generation of radical oxygen species (ROS), produced by neutrophils and macrophages, at the site of inflammation could cause severe tissue damage and impair cell proliferation and migration, a scaffold with antioxidant properties could represent an important tool to effectively tackle chronic lesions. In fact, the antioxidants could guarantee the balance between the favorable ROS properties, such as angiogenesis stimulation, and the negative ones (oxidative stress and healing delay).

For this reason, these properties were characterized via the DPPH assay, evaluating the capability of the scaffolds to reduce DPPH, a standard nitrogen-concentrated free radical. Figure 7 reports the antioxidant properties of the scaffolds and the CuO powder alone as radical scavenging activity (RSA%). The results show that the incubation time of the scaffolds doped with CuO nanoparticles in PBS decreased the DPPH%, suggesting that the antioxidant activity increases over time, probably due to the release of bioactive molecules. In fact, as reported by Das et al., CuO nanoparticles have a capability to transfer their electron density towards the free radical located at the nitrogen atom in DPPH [24].

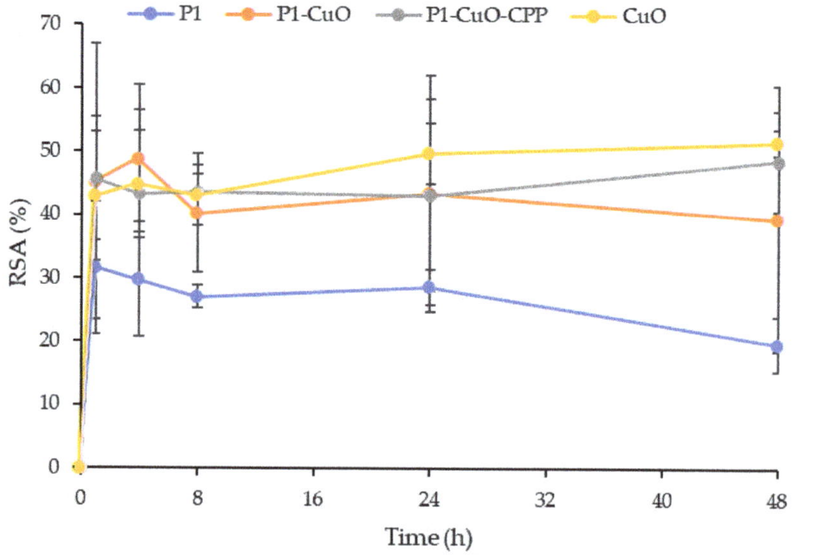

Figure 7. Radical scavenging activity (RSA%) evaluated via the DPPH assay for the P1, P1-CuO, and P1-CuO-CPP scaffolds and for the CuO and CPP powders alone (mean values ± SD, $n = 5$). One-way ANOVA, Scheffé test ($p \leq 0.05$) is reported in the Supplementary Information (SI: Section S1.3.3).

2.6. Cell Adhesion and Proliferation

In view of the application of aligned scaffolds in the repair of the tendon interface, TEN-1 cells were selected as representatives for tendon cells, and they were grown onto the scaffolds, both random and aligned, to evaluate the influence of the fiber conformation onto the cell adhesion and proliferation. Their metabolic activity, directly related to their viability, was assessed over 14 days, and it is reported in Figure 8a (fluorescence intensity (FI)). TEN-1 cells proliferate in the GM (growth medium) over the entire time interval of observation, although they show a slight decrease in viability. The same behavior is evident for the random scaffolds. On the other hand, the scaffolds with an aligned structure are able to maintain a constant cell growth over time. Moreover, the doping of CuO and CPP lead to an increase in the cell proliferation greater than that of the scaffolds of PBCA alone. The same trend was observed by means of CLSM (Figure 8b). In fact, the cells preferably adhere onto the aligned scaffolds much more than onto the random ones, and in particular, on the ones doped with both CuO and CPP, where they also assume their typical elongated shape.

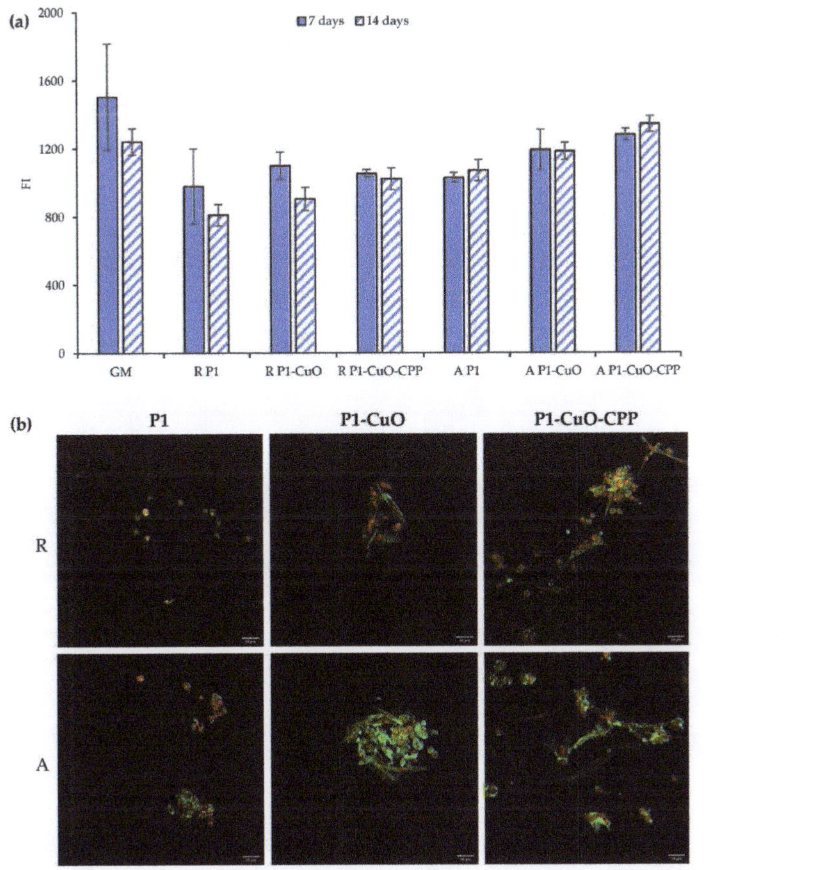

Figure 8. (**a**) Alamar Blue assay evaluated for P1, P1-CuO, and P1-CuO-CPP scaffolds, both random (R) and aligned (A), at 7 and 14 days of culture, compared to the cells grown in standard conditions (GM). (**b**) CLSM images of TEN-1 cells grown onto P1, P1-CuO, and P1-CuO-CPP scaffolds, random (R) and aligned (A), at 14 days of culture (nuclei stained in red, cytoskeleton stained in green) (mean values ± SD, $n = 5$). One-way ANOVA, Scheffé test ($p \leq 0.05$) is reported in the Supplementary Information (SI: Section S1.3.4).

2.7. Cytocompatibility of Macrophages and Pro-Inflammatory Immune Response

Recent evidence suggests that modulation of inflammation in the early stages following tendon repair may lead to improved healing. It is important to recognize that regulated inflammation is largely beneficial to tissue repair, whereas excessive or persistent inflammation can be damaging and lead to poor clinical outcomes.

For this reason, the anti-inflammatory properties were assessed. The secretion of IL-6 by macrophages stimulated by lipopolysaccharide (LPS) was assessed to evidence whether the extracts from the scaffolds were able to decrease it.

Figure 9a reports the macrophage viability in terms of optical density (OD) after the contact with the scaffold extracts, while Figure 9b reports the IL-6 cytokine concentrations secreted by the macrophages, exposed to the scaffold extracts. The extracts at every time interval are cytocompatible towards macrophages, with a cell viability superimposable to that of the positive control (GM) and the proinflammatory control (LPS), indicating that the scaffolds do not release cytotoxic components. Moreover, the scaffolds doped with CuO lead to a decrease of the IL-6 secretion after 48 h, reaching values significantly lower than those of the LPS. This suggests that the scaffolds decrease the inflammatory response of LPS over time. CuO nanoparticles are conceivably exposed in the cell medium and decorated by GM proteins, forming a protein corona around the nanostructures. This affords them a biological identity and allows them to act as a ligand for the receptors on the M2 anti-inflammatory macrophages, activating them [25].

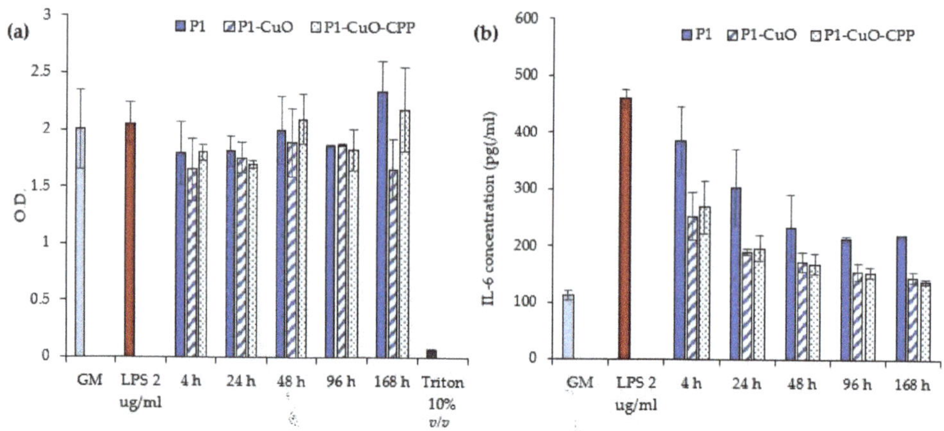

Figure 9. (**a**) Macrophages' viability after 24 h of contact with LPS and the scaffolds' extracts at different time intervals. (**b**) IL-6 cytokine concentrations (pg/mL) secreted by the macrophages exposed to different time intervals of scaffolds' extracts (GM: growth medium; LPS: lipopolysaccharide) (mean values ± SD, $n = 5$). One-way ANOVA, Scheffé test ($p \leq 0.05$) is reported in the Supplementary Information (SI: Section S1.3.5).

2.8. Antibacterial Activity Evaluation

Metal oxide nanoparticles, such as CuO, have been described as key elements for the control of bacterial growth. In fact, bacteria could develop a resistance against the most used antibiotics/chemotherapeutics. This represents a great threat to human health, and in particular surgical procedures can expose the patients to multidrug-resistant bacteria. However, inorganics, especially in nanostructures, including CuO, are generally effective against local bacterial infections [26].

Table 1 reports the microbicidal effect (ME) (log reduction) evaluated for P1-CuO and P1-CuO-CPP scaffolds at 5 and 24 h of contact with *Escherichia coli* and *Staphylococcus aureus*, used as representative strains of Gram-negative and Gram-positive bacteria, respectively. The scaffolds possess a slight antimicrobial effect against *S. aureus*, while a significant antimicrobial effect is achieved against *E. coli*, since the scaffolds decrease the bioburden by at least 100-fold (a 2-log reduction) after 24 h of contact with the bacteria. In fact, CuO nanoparticles result as mainly effective against Gram-negative bacteria, as highlighted by precedent studies [27,28].

Table 1. Microbicidal effect (ME) evaluated for P1-CuO and P1-CuO-CPP scaffolds against *E. coli* and *S. aureus* at 5 and 24 h of contact. One-way ANOVA, Scheffé test ($p \leq 0.05$) is reported in the Supplementary Information (SI: Section S1.3.6).

	E. coli		*S. aureus*	
	5 h	**24 h**	**5 h**	**24 h**
P1-CuO	0.0	2.99 ± 0.09	0.04 ± 0.03	1.01 ± 0.27
P1-CuO-CPP	0.0	1.72 ± 0.31	0.0	0.59 ± 0.27

The mechanism of action seems attributable to different pathways, such as the release of CuO^{2+} ions from the nanostructures having a prooxidant effect, and the capability of these nanomaterials to penetrate the bacterial cell membrane. In particular, such nanomaterials are more effective against Gram– bacteria, which possess a membrane mainly formed of peptidoglycans, less firm and easily crossable, while Gram+ bacteria possess a double membrane that is harder to cross [9].

To verify the antimicrobial effect and understand if CuO doping impairs the microbial adhesion onto the scaffolds, the SEM analysis of the scaffolds in contact with the *E. coli* at different time intervals (0 h of contact (t0) and 24 h of contact (t24)) was performed (Figure 10). A glass slide was used as a positive control. After 0 h of contact, it is possible to observe *E. coli* in contact with all the scaffolds (undoped and doped) on the fiber surface. Clusters of bacteria were also clearly visible, forming compact colonies with preserved morphology. On the other hand, after 24 h of contact with the scaffolds, the bacteria are no more visible onto the scaffolds, except for P1-CuO fibers, where the bacteria present are not viable, with the cell membrane visibly broken and an altered morphology. These results are in line with the ME evaluation against *E. coli*, confirming that the PBCA scaffolds doped with CuO and CPP could represent an effective tool to avoid bacteria proliferation, and depending on the strain, to also avoid bacteria adhesion and protection of the site of implants from infections after surgery.

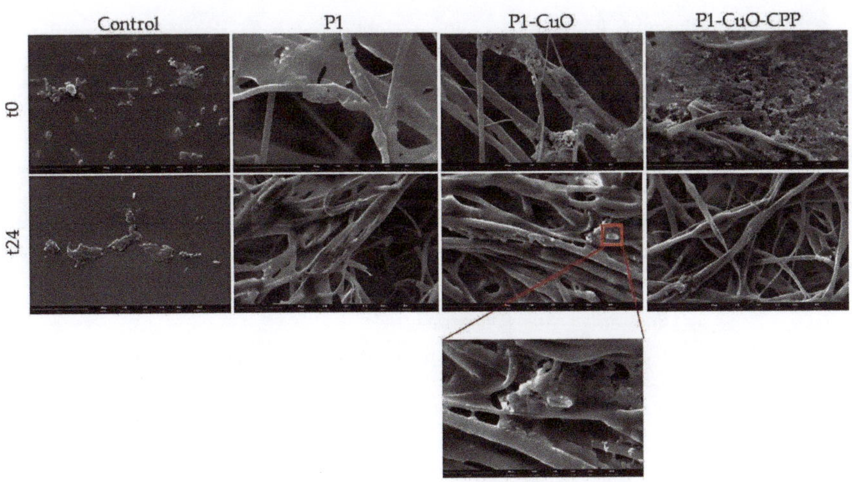

Figure 10. SEM micrographs of *E. coli* colonizing P1, P1-CuO, and P1-CuO-CPP scaffolds after 0 h of contact (t0) and 24 h of contact (t24). A glass slide was used as a control (mean values ± SD, $n = 4$) (scale bar = 15 μm).

3. Materials and Methods

3.1. Materials

Butyl(2-cyanoacrylate) (BCA) monomer (MW: 153 g/mol) (BLD Pharmatech Ltd., Shanghai, China), CuO nanoparticles (Sigma-Aldrich, Milan, Italy), with particle dimensions < 50 nm, and CPP CE90CPP enzymatically hydrolyzed casein (DMV International, Delhi, NY, USA) with a purity of 26% (w/w) were used.

3.2. Synthesis and Characterization of PBCA

The PBCA was synthesized by emulsion/polymerization of the BCA monomer, as described by Melguizo et al. [29]. This process slightly differs from mini-emulsion–polymerization since the dispersion is not ultrasonicated after stirring. Moreover, it allows some intrinsic advantages, such as a higher rate of polymerization [30,31]. A 0.3 mL acetonic solution (acetone for analysis, ISO-ACS, Carlo Erba Reagents, Milano, Italy) containing 1% w/v of monomer was prepared in a 1 mL vial. The solution was added dropwise to 3 mL of an aqueous solution containing 0.1 mN HCl (Carlo Erba Reagents, Milano, Italy) and 0.5% w/v of dextran 500 Da (Pharmacosmos A/S, Roervangsvej, Denmark) under magnetic stirring (3000 rpm). As described by Limouzin et al., dextran acts as a surfactant, both stabilizing the particles and participating in the polymerization. In fact, its counter-ion serves as an initiator of the reaction, and its headgroup forms an ion pair with the propagating species [30].

Polymerization continued for 4 h at room temperature. Then, 3 µL of a 0.1 M NaOH solution (Alfa Aesar by Thermo Fisher Scientific, Kandel, Germany) was added to neutralize the medium, ensuring the total consumption of the monomer. Finally, the solution was heated for 1 h at 60 °C to remove the acetone through evaporation, and the polymer was cleaned by 10 centrifuge cycles (10 min at 10,000 rpm; Sigma 1-14K Refrigerated microcentrifuge, Osterode am Harz, Germany) until the conductivity of the supernatants was ≤10 µS/cm. The supernatant was removed, and the precipitate was frozen at −20 °C and lyophilized for 24 h, at 0.020 mbar (Heto Drywinner sublimator, Analitica De Mori, Italia), to obtain a PBCA powder.

The process *yield* % was then determined as follows:

$$Yield\ (\%) = \frac{Wf}{Wi} \times 100 \quad (1)$$

where Wi represents the initial weight of the materials used in the synthesis and Wf is the final weight of the PBCA powder.

Proton nuclear magnetic resonance (^{1}H NMR) and carbon nuclear magnetic resonance (^{13}C NMR) spectra were recorded in deuterated chloroform ($CDCl_3$) on a FT-NMR Avance 400 MHz (Bruker, Milan, Italy) spectrometer (equipped with Z-gradient, automatic tuning and shimming, probe BBO 5 mm and BBI 5 mm, auto sampler, Topspin 3.6.1). Chemical shift (δ) was given in ppm relative to the internal standard (TMS).

The molecular weight of the obtained polymer was determined by means of a Litesizer 500 (Anton Paar, Graz, Austria) and the degree of polymerization was calculated as the ration between the polymer molecular weight and the monomer.

3.3. Preparation of the Polymeric Blends

Table 2 reports the composition of the polymeric blends used to obtain the corresponding scaffolds. PBCA was solubilized in acetone under magnetic stirring at room temperature. At first, different percentages of PBCA were used to evaluate the influence of the polymer concentration on the fiber morphology. The concentration that allowed the fine formation of nanofibers was selected for the CuO and CPP doping.

Table 2. Qualitative–quantitative composition of the polymeric blends.

Blend	PBCA % (*w/w*)	CuO % (*w/w*)	CPP % (*w/w*)
P1	20		
P2	23		
P3	30		
P1-CuO	20	0.01	
P1-CuO-CPP	20	0.01	0.25

3.4. Preparation of the Electrospun Scaffolds

Scaffolds were obtained by means of an electrospinning apparatus (STKIT-40, Linari Engineering, Pisa, Italy) equipped with a high-voltage power supply (Razel R99-E 40 kV), a 10 mL syringe with an inox 21G needle, and a volumetric pump (Razel R99-E). A static and flat collector was used to obtain the random scaffolds (namely R P1, R P1-CuO, and R P1-CuO-CPP). The lengthwise-aligned scaffolds (namely A P1, A P1-CuO, and A P1-CuO-CPP) were collected using a cylindrical stainless-steel rotating drum (dimensions: diameter: 3 cm, length: 150 mm). The distance between the needle and the collector was fixed at 15 cm, the voltage at 15 kV, the flow rate at 0.595 cc/h, and the rotation speed at 160 Hz. The relative humidity and the environmental temperature were set at 20% and 25 °C, respectively. All the obtained scaffolds were insoluble in water.

3.5. Scaffold Physico-Chemical Characterization

The scaffold morphology was assessed by means of scanning electron microscope (SEM) analysis (Tescan, Mira3XMU, Brno, Czech Republic). The samples were sputtered with graphite. Electrospun nanofiber diameters were assessed by image analysis software (ImageJ, ICY, Institut Pasteur, Paris, France). Moreover, the inclusion of the CuO nanoparticles into the fibrous structure was evaluated by means of SEM-EDX, recording an EDX spectrum, and also by means of transmission electron microscope (TEM) analysis (JEOL JEM-1200 EX II microscope; CCD camera Olympus Mega View G2, with 1376 × 1032-pixel format, Tokyo, Japan; operating HV at 100 kV, magnification 100 k). For this purpose, a thin layer of fiber was electrospun directly onto the TEM grids (formavar/carbon 300-mesh Cu, Agar Scientific, Monterotondo (RM), Italy).

The wettability of the electrospun fibers was assessed with a contact angle meter (DMe-211 Plus; FAMAS software, Kyowa, Osaka, Japan). The droplet shape (0.4 μL of PBS) was captured through the CCD camera at 1 s after the droplet touched the scaffold surface.

3.6. Structural Characterization

Fourier-transform infrared spectroscopy (FT-IR) analysis was performed using a JASCO 6200 apparatus (Tokyo, Japan) equipped with a Ge ATR. All analyses were performed from 400 to 4000 cm^{-1} with a resolution of 2 cm^{-1}, and the results were processed with Spectra Manager v2 software. The FT-IR spectra were smoothed, and the noise was removed using the Savitzky–Golay filter (OriginPro 2021b, OriginLab Corporation).

The analysis of the nanoscale structure was performed by means of small-angle X-ray scattering (SAXS) at the European Synchrotron Radiation Facility (ESRF, Grenoble, France). Experiments were carried out at the ID02 beamline (https://doi.org/10.15151/ESRF-ES-585935736, accessed on 15 July 2022). Small pieces of scaffolds (0.5 × 0.5 cm) were cut, inserted in 2 mm polycarbonate capillaries (ENKI, Milan, Italy), and fully hydrated with water. Two different sample-to-detector distances (1 and 10 m) have been used to collect the scattered radiation, reaching a wide range of $q = 4\pi sen(\vartheta/2)/\lambda$, with ϑ being the scattering angle and λ = 0.1 nm the X-ray wavelength. The intensity spectra as a function of q ($0.006 < q < 7.5$ nm^{-1}) provided information on the mesoscale arrangement of the scaffolds (hundreds of nanometers) and on the local arrangement of polymer chains (nanometer length-scale). Measurements were repeated on different samples, to check for reproducibility.

3.7. Mechanical Properties

The mechanical properties of nanofibrous scaffolds were measured using a dynamometer (TA-XT plus, Stable Microsystems, Italy) equipped with a 5.0 kg load cell. Before testing, nanofibrous scaffolds were cut to 30 × 10 mm and the strips were clamped between two tensile grips (A/TG probe), setting an initial distance between the grips of 60.0 mm. Then, the upper grip was moved forward at a constant speed of 5.0 mm/s up to break. The mechanical properties of both random and aligned scaffolds were evaluated in dry and hydrated states, and force at break vs. distance was recorded. Moreover, the elongation and Young's modulus were calculated [32].

3.8. DPPH Radical Scavenging Activity

The free radical scavenging ability (RSA%) of the scaffolds was tested by the DPPH radical scavenging assay. The ability to donate hydrogen atoms was determined by the decolorization of 2,2-diphenyl-1-picrylhydrazyl (DPPH, Sigma-Aldrich, Milan, Italy). In fact, DPPH produces a violet/purple color in methanol solution and turns yellow in the presence of antioxidants. For the time-dependent assay, 10 mg of scaffolds was placed in 2 mL of PBS at 37 °C to simulate the scaffold implant in the lesion bed [33]. At prefixed times, the supernatants were collected to quantify the DPPH activity (direct antioxidant properties). Each sample (1 mL) was mixed with 1 mL of DPPH methanol solution (8 μg/mL) and kept for 30 min in the dark. The absorbance was measured at 515 nm (FLUOstar® Omega, BMG LABTECH, Aylesbury, UK) and the results were expressed as DPPH radical scavenging activity, which was calculated as follows:

$$RSA\ (\%) = \frac{(A0 - AS)}{A0} \times 100 \quad (2)$$

where $A0$ represents the absorbance of the control (DPPH in contact with water), and AS is the absorbance of the scaffolds after the contact with DPPH [34].

3.9. Cell Adhesion and Proliferation

Proliferation and cell viability were carried out using normal human tenocytes (TEN-1) (1st–5th passages, ZenBio, Durham, NC, USA). TEN-1 were cultured in collagen (rat tail collagen coating solution, Cell Applications, Italy) coated flasks, using tenocyte growth medium (ZenBio, Durham, NC, USA) supplemented with 10% *v*/*v* fetal bovine serum (FBS, Euroclone, Milan, Italy) and with 200 IU/mL of penicillin/0.2 mg/mL of streptomycin (Sigma-Aldrich, Milan, Italy). They were grown in an incubator (CO_2 Incubator, PBI International, Milano, Italy) at 37 °C in a 5% CO_2 atmosphere with 95% relative humidity (RH).

Each scaffold (5 mm diameter, 0.2 mm thickness) was sterilized by UV radiation for 15 min and placed in a 96-well plate to perfectly cover the bottom. TEN-1 were seeded onto the scaffolds at a density of 20×10^3 cells/well and re-incubated. TEN-1 grown in standard conditions (growth medium, GM) were considered as a positive control. After 7 and 14 days of contact with the scaffolds, the medium was removed and 10% (*v*/*v*) Alamar Blue (AlamarBlue HS cell viability reagent, Invitrogen, Thermo Fisher, Monza, Italy) was diluted with the appropriate medium and added in the wells (100 μL). After 3 h of incubation in the dark at 37 °C, the Alamar Blue solution was collected from the wells and transferred to a new plate. Each well was then refilled with the culture medium and left in culture again. Alamar Blue fluorescence was recorded using a microplate reader (FLUOstar® Omega, BMG LABTECH, Aylesbury, UK), with λex = 530 nm and λem = 590 nm. Cell viability was expressed as fluorescence intensity (FI).

The cell morphology after 14 days of contact with the scaffolds was investigated using CLSM after nuclei and cytoskeleton staining. Cells grown onto the scaffolds were fixed using a 3% (*v*/*v*) glutaraldehyde solution in PBS for 2 h at room temperature. The substrates were then washed three times with PBS. The cellular cytoskeleton was stained with FITC Atto 488 phalloidin (green, Sigma-Aldrich, Milan, Italy; 50 μL at 20 μg/mL in PBS in each well, contact time 40 min), and the cell nuclei were then stained with propidium iodide (red, Sigma-Aldrich, Milano, Italy; 50 μL/sample at 25 μg/mL in PBS in each well, contact time 2 min). Scaffolds were placed onto microscope slides and imaged using a Confocal Laser Scanning Microscope (CLSM, Leica TCS SP2, Leica Microsystems, Buccinasco (MI), Italy), with λex = 535 nm and λem = 617 nm for propidium iodide, and λex = 501 nm and λem = 523 nm for FITC-phalloidin. The acquired images were processed with software (Leica Microsystem, Buccinasco (MI), Italy).

3.10. Cytocompatibility of Macrophages and Pro-Inflammatory Immune Response

The hMoCD14 + -PB-c cell line, human CD14+ monocytes derived from peripheral blood (Carlo Erba, Italy), was cultured in mononuclear cell medium (Carlo Erba, Italy) supplemented with 10% fetal bovine serum (FBS, Euroclone, Italy), and with 200 IU/mL of penicillin/0.2 mg/mL of streptomycin (Sigma-Aldrich, Italy), kept at 37 °C in a 5% CO_2 atmosphere with 95% relative humidity (RH). Each scaffold was sterilized by UV radiation for 15 min and then incubated in a serum-free DMEM medium (Dulbecco's Modified Eagle's Medium, PromoCell, WVR, Italy) for 24 h to produce extraction media of 10 mg/mL. hMoCD14 + -PB-c were seeded 20 × 10^3 cells/well in a 24-well plate and incubated for 24 h with 100 nM for 2 × 10^4 cells of phorbol 12-myristate-13-acetate (PMA, Sigma-Aldrich, Italy) to allow differentiation. After differentiation, extracted media were placed in the wells and incubated for 24 h. The cytocompatibility of the scaffold extracts was assessed using the MTT (3-(4,5-dimethylthiazol-2-yl)-2,5-diphenyltetrazolium bromide) assay. The medium in each well was removed and 100 μL of MTT solution at 1 mg/mL in DMEM w/o phenol red (Sigma-Aldrich, Milan, Italy) was added. Then, the cell substrates were placed at 37 °C for 3 h in an incubator, and finally, MTT solution was removed and 100 μL of isopropanol (Carlo Erba, Italy) was added, and the absorbance was read using the FLUOstar® Omega Microplate Reader (BMG LABTECH, Italy) at λ = 570 nm (with reference λ = 690 nm). IL-6 pro-inflammatory cytokine was assayed to evaluate the proinflammatory immune response using the ELISA kit (Thermo Fisher, Italy). Supernatants were collected from the cultures after 24 h of treatment with the scaffolds and the cytokine secretion by macrophages was assayed at 450 nm, with 570 nm as the reference wavelength. The method was linear in the concentration range from 7.8 to 500 pg/mL, with the R^2 always higher than 0.995. Lipopolysaccharide (LPS, 10 μg/mL for 24 h) was used as a positive control [35].

3.11. Antibacterial Activity Evaluation

The scaffold antibacterial activity was tested against two different microorganisms by measuring the microbicidal effect (ME): *Staphylococcus aureus* ATCC 6538 and *Escherichia coli* ATCC 10356 were used as representative strains of Gram-positive and Gram-negative bacteria, respectively. These bacteria were grown overnight at 37 °C in Tryptone Soya Broth (Oxoid, Basingstoke, Hampshire, UK). Bacterial cultures were centrifuged at 3000 rpm for 20 min to separate cells from the broth and then suspended in sterile water. The optical density of the microbial suspensions was adjusted to A = 0.3 (wavelength: 650 nm), which corresponds to a number of cells of: 1 × 10^7–1 × 10^8 CFU/mL. To measure the ME of the scaffolds, microbial suspensions (10 μL) were placed on glass slides (26 × 76 mm) and covered with the scaffolds (20 × 20 mm). This glass–scaffold system was maintained in a humid environment (with 1 mL of PBS in a Falcon test-tube) at room temperature for 5 and 24 h. The same setup was used with the undoped scaffolds (P1) as a control. After the two contact times, a volume of 9 mL of sterile water was added in each test-tube, gently shaking to obtain the detachment of the scaffold from the slides. Microbial suspensions were then placed in Tryptone Soya Agar (Oxoid; Basingstoke, Hampshire, UK) and bacterial colonies were enumerated after incubation at 37 °C for 24 h [36]. The decimal-log reduction rate, the microbicidal effect (*ME* value), was calculated for each test organism and contact time according to the following equation [37]:

$$ME = logNc - logNd \quad (3)$$

where Nc is the number of CFU of the control microbial suspension and Nd is the number of CFU of the microbial suspension in the presence of the scaffolds with CuO nanoparticles and CPP.

The antibacterial activity was also evaluated by SEM analysis, to explore the initial bacterial adhesion and progressive spreading and colonization onto the electrospun scaffolds exposed to *Escherichia coli*. Here, 10 μL of the microbial suspension was placed onto the scaffolds and covered with microscope glasses to allow the exposure of the whole surface to the bacteria. A glass slide was used as a positive control. At different time intervals of incubation (0 and 24 h), the scaffolds were put in contact with 1 mL of 3% (v/v) glutaraldehyde solution in PBS for 2 h at room temperature for bacterial fixation. Once dried, the scaffolds were mounted on SEM supports and sputtered with 5 nm of gold.

3.12. Statistical Analysis

Statistical analyses were performed using the Astatsa statistical calculator. One-way analysis of variance (ANOVA) was followed by the Scheffé test for post-hoc comparisons. Here, $p < 0.05$ was considered significant.

4. Conclusions

Nanofibrous scaffolds based on PBCA and loaded with CuO and CPP were successfully prepared by means of the electrospinning technique. Moreover, it was possible to obtain fibers in an aligned conformation able to mimic the tendon fascicles. The obtained scaffolds are characterized for their morphology, showing nanometric dimensions and an orderly structural organization.

The evaluation of the mechanical properties highlights that CuO and CPP determine an increase in the mechanical performance of the scaffolds; moreover, the aligned conformation leads to a significant increase of these properties with respect to the fibers in the random conformation. Furthermore, the CuO induces a significant increase in the hydrophobic characteristics of the scaffolds by decreasing their wettability, which could cause a slowdown in the degradation rate of the scaffolds in vivo, ensuring adequate support to the injured tissue during the entire healing process. Moreover, the scaffolds loaded with CuO also show antioxidant properties that could protect the site of inflammation from severe tissue damage and impair cell proliferation and migration.

The scaffolds prove to be biocompatible towards tenocytes and able to promote cell adhesion and proliferation. In particular, CuO and CPP seem to have a synergic effect on cell adhesion and proliferation. The scaffolds are also characterized by remarkable anti-inflammatory properties that could represent an interesting tool to overcome the poor clinical outcomes related to excessive inflammation.

The antibacterial activity evaluation demonstrates that the CuO-doped scaffolds possess a significant antimicrobial effect against *E. coli*, since they are able to decrease the bioburden by at least 100-fold (a 2-log reduction) after 24 h of contact, resulting as mainly effective against Gram-negative bacteria. The results were confirmed with SEM analysis, which highlights that the bacteria after 24 h are not present on the scaffold surface, except for P1-CuO fibers, where the bacteria are not viable, presenting the cell membrane as visibly broken.

In conclusion, scaffolds based on PBCA and doped with CuO and CPP deserve particular attention as enhancers of the tendon tissue regeneration. Further investigation of the scaffold efficacy in vivo will assess their capability for enhancing the tendon ECM restoration, and eventually accelerate their translation to the clinic.

Supplementary Materials: The following supporting information can be downloaded at: https://www.mdpi.com/article/10.3390/ijms24043172/s1.

Author Contributions: Conceptualization, G.S. and E.B.; methodology, E.B. and M.R.; software, B.V. and E.B.; formal analysis, E.B. and M.R.; investigation, E.B., M.R., P.G. and C.R.; resources, G.S., S.R., A.F. and C.V.; data curation, E.B. and M.R.; writing—original draft preparation, E.B.; writing—review and editing, E.B. and G.S.; supervision, E.B.; project administration, G.S.; funding acquisition, G.S., C.V., P.G., E.D.F. and S.R. All authors have read and agreed to the published version of the manuscript.

Funding: This research received no external funding.

Institutional Review Board Statement: Not applicable.

Informed Consent Statement: Not applicable.

Data Availability Statement: Not applicable.

Acknowledgments: The authors acknowledge ESRF (Grenoble, Fr) for beamtime allocation and financial support for X-ray experiments (doi:10.15151/ESRF-ES-585935736) and ID02 staff for their precious technical assistance. The authors also acknowledge Centro Grandi Strumenti of the University of Pavia, Teresa Recca and Massimo Boiocchi for the NMR and TEM analysis, Centro Interdipartimentale di Studi e Ricerche per la Conservazione del Patrimonio Culturale (CISRiC)—Arvedi Laboratory of the University of Pavia and Alessandro Girella for the SEM analysis, and Alfatest S.r.l. and Dario Bozzo for the SEM analysis of the bacteria.

Conflicts of Interest: The authors declare no conflict of interest.

References

1. Bianchi, E.; Ruggeri, M.; Rossi, S.; Vigani, B.; Miele, D.; Bonferoni, M.C.; Sandri, G.; Ferrari, F. Innovative Strategies in Tendon Tissue Engineering. *Pharmaceutics* **2021**, *13*, 89. [CrossRef] [PubMed]
2. Sigal, I.R.; Grande, D.A.; Dines, D.M.; Dines, J.; Drakos, M. Biologic and tissue engineering strategies for tendon repair. *Regen. Eng. Transl. Med.* **2016**, *2*, 107–125. [CrossRef]
3. Nichols, A.E.C.; Best, K.T.; Loiselle, A.E. The Cellular Basis of Fibrotic Tendon Healing: Challenges and Opportunities. *Transl. Res.* **2019**, *209*, 156–168. [CrossRef] [PubMed]
4. Thomopoulos, S.; Parks, W.C.; Rifkin, D.B.; Derwin, K.A. Mechanisms of tendon injury and repair. *J. Orthop. Res.* **2015**, *33*, 832–839. [CrossRef] [PubMed]
5. Deng, S.; Sun, Z.; Zhang, C.; Chen, G.; Li, J. Surgical Treatment Versus Conservative Management for Acute Achilles Tendon Rupture: A Systematic Review and Meta-Analysis of Randomized Controlled Trials. *J. Foot Ankle Surg.* **2017**, *6*, 1236–1243. [CrossRef]
6. Walden, G.; Liao, X.; Donell, S.; Raxworthy, M.J.; Riley, G.P.; Saeed, A. A Clinical, Biological, and Biomaterials Perspective into Tendon Injuries and Regeneration. *Tissue Eng. Part. B Rev.* **2017**, *23*, 44–58. [CrossRef]
7. Vauthier, C. A journey through the emergence of nanomedicines with poly (alkylcyanoacrylate) based nanoparticles. *J. Drug Target. Informa. Healthc.* **2019**, *27*, 502–524. [CrossRef]
8. Pascual, G.; Sotomayor, S.; Rodríguez, M.; Pérez-Köhler, B.; Kühnhardt, A.; Fernández-Gutiérrez, M.; San Román, J.; Bellón, J.M. Cytotoxicity of Cyanoacrylate-Based Tissue Adhesives and Short-Term Preclinical In Vivo Biocompatibility in Abdominal Hernia Repair. *PLoS ONE* **2016**, *11*, e0157920. [CrossRef]
9. Bianchi, E.; Vigani, B.; Viseras, C.; Ferrari, F.; Rossi, S.; Sandri, G. Inorganic Nanomaterials in Tissue Engineering. *Pharmaceutics* **2022**, *14*, 1127. [CrossRef]
10. Kim, S.-W.; Im, G.-B.; Kim, Y.-J.; Kim, Y.H.; Lee, T.-J.; Bhang, S.H. Bio-application of In-organic Nanomaterials in Tissue Engineering. In *Bioinspired Biomaterials. Advances in Experimental Medicine and Biology*; Chun, H.J., Reis, L.R., Motta, A., Khang, G., Eds.; Springer: Singapore, 2020; Volume 1, pp. 115–130. [CrossRef]
11. Wang, Y.; Zhang, W.; Yao, Q. Copper-based biomaterials for bone and cartilage tissue engineering. *J. Orthopaed. Transl.* **2021**, *29*, 60–71. [CrossRef]
12. Shi, M.; Chen, Z.; Farnaghi, S.; Friis, T.; Mao, X.; Xiao, Y.; Wu, C. Copper-doped mesoporous silica nanospheres, a promising immunomodulatory agent for inducing osteogenesis. *Acta Biomater.* **2016**, *30*, 334–344. [CrossRef] [PubMed]
13. Bottani, M.; Cattaneo, S.; Pica, V.; Stuknyte, M.; De Noni, I.; Ferraretto, A. In vitro anti-oxidant properties of digests of hydrolyzed casein and caseinophosphopeptide preparations in cell models of human intestine and osteoblasts. *J. Funct. Foods* **2020**, *64*, 103673. [CrossRef]
14. Donida, B.M.; Mrak, E.; Gravaghi, C.; Villa, I.; Cosentino, S.; Zacchi, E.; Perego, S.; Rubinacci, A.; Fiorilli, A.; Tettamanti, G.; et al. Casein phosphopeptides promote calcium uptake and modulate the differentiation pathway in human primary osteoblast-like cells. *Peptides* **2009**, *30*, 2233–2241. [CrossRef] [PubMed]
15. Barie, P.S.; Eachempati, S.R. Surgical Site Infections. *Surg. Clin. N. Am.* **2005**, *85*, 1115–1135. [CrossRef]
16. Markova, N.; Ivanova, G.; Enchev, V.; Simeonova, M. Tacticity of poly(butyl-a-cyanoacrylate) chains in nanoparticles: NMR spectroscopy and DFT calculations. *Struct. Chem.* **2012**, *23*, 815–824. [CrossRef]

17. Fan, J.; Zhang, Y.; Liu, Y.; Wang, Y.; Cao, F.; Yang, Q.; Tian, F. Explanation of the cell orientation in a nanofiber membrane by the geometric potential theory. *Results Phys.* **2019**, *15*, 102537. [CrossRef]
18. Faccendini, A.; Bianchi, E.; Ruggeri, M.; Vigani, B.; Perotti, C.; Pavesi, F.C.; Caliogna, L.; Natali, F.; Del Favero, E.; Cantù, L.; et al. Smart Device for Biologically Enhanced Functional Regeneration of Osteo–Tendon Interface. *Pharmaceutics* **2021**, *13*, 1996. [CrossRef]
19. Shankar, S.; Teng, X.; Rhim, J.W. Properties and characterization of agar/CuNP bionanocomposite films prepared with different copper salts and reducing agents. *Carbohydr. Polym.* **2014**, *114*, 484–492. [CrossRef] [PubMed]
20. Hasheminya, S.-M.; Mokarram, R.R.; Ghanbarzadeh, B.; Hamishekar, H.; Kafil, H.S. Physicochemical, mechanical, optical, microstructural and antimicrobial properties of novel kefiran-carboxymethyl cellulose biocomposite films as influenced by copper oxide nanoparticles (CuONPs). *Food Packag. Shelf Life* **2018**, *17*, 196–204. [CrossRef]
21. Noshirvani, N.; Ghanbarzadeh, B.; Rezaei Mokarram, R.; Hashemi, M.; Coma, V. Preparation and characterization of active emulsified films based on chitosan-carboxymethyl cellulose containing zinc oxide nano particles. *Int. J. Biol. Macromol.* **2017**, *99*, 530–538. [CrossRef]
22. Fard, G.C.; Mirjalili, M.; Almasian, A.; Najafi, F. PAMAM grafted α-Fe 2 O 3 nanofiber: Preparation and dye removal ability from binary system. *J. Taiwan Inst. Chem. Eng.* **2017**, *80*, 156–167. [CrossRef]
23. De Siqueira, L.; Ribeiro, N.; Paredes, M.B.A.; Grenho, L.; Cunha-Reis, C.; Trichês, E.S.; Fernandes, M.H.; Sousa, S.R.; Monteiro, F.J. Influence of PLLA/PCL/HA scaffold fiber orientation on mechanical properties and osteoblast behavior. *Materials* **2019**, *12*, 3879. [CrossRef] [PubMed]
24. Das, D.; Nath, B.C.; Phukon, P.; Dolui, S.K. Synthesis and evaluation of antioxidant and antibacterial behavior of CuO nanoparticles. *Colloids Surf. B Biointerfaces* **2013**, *101*, 430–433. [CrossRef] [PubMed]
25. Agarwal, H.; Nakara, A.; Shanmugam, V.K. Anti-inflammatory mechanism of various metal and metal oxide nanoparticles synthesized using plant extracts: A review. *Biomed. Pharmacother.* **2019**, *109*, 2561–2572. [CrossRef]
26. Prabhu, S.; Poulose, E.K. Silver nanoparticles: Mechanism of antimicrobial action, synthesis, medical applications, and toxicity effects. *Int. Nano Lett.* **2012**, *2*, 32. [CrossRef]
27. Rajamma, R.; Nair, S.G.; Abdul Khadar, F.; Baskaran, B. Antibacterial and anticancer activity of biosynthesised CuO nanoparticles. *IET Nanobiotechnol.* **2020**, *14*, 833–838. [CrossRef]
28. Ramyadevi, J.; Jeyasubramanian, K.; Marikani, A.; Rajakumar, G.; Rahuman, A.A. Synthesis and antimicrobial activity of copper nanoparticles. *Mater. Lett.* **2012**, *71*, 114–116. [CrossRef]
29. Melguizo, C.; Cabeza, L.; Prados, J.; Ortiz, R.; Caba, O.; Rama, A.R.; Delgado, A.V.; Arias, J.L. Enhanced antitumoral activity of doxorubicin against lung cancer cells using biodegradable poly(butylcyanoacrylate) nanoparticles. *Drug Des. Dev. Ther.* **2015**, *9*, 6433–6444. [CrossRef]
30. Limouzin, C.; Caviggia, A.; Gnanachaud, F.; Hémery, P. Anionic Polymerization of n-Butyl Cyanoacrylate in Emulsion and Miniemulsion. *Macromolecules* **2003**, *36*, 667–674. [CrossRef]
31. Shahmabadi, H.E.; Doun, S.K.B.; Alavi, S.E.; Mortazavi, M.; Saffari, Z.; Farahnak, M.; Akbarzadeh, A. An Investigation into the Parameters Affecting Preparation of Polybutyl Cyanoacrylate Nanoparticles by Emulsion Polymerization. *Ind. J. Clin. Biochem.* **2014**, *29*, 357–361. [CrossRef]
32. Faccendini, A.; Ruggeri, M.; Miele, D.; Rossi, S.; Bonferoni, M.C.; Aguzzi, C.; Grisoli, P.; Viseras, C.; Vigani, B.; Sandri, G.; et al. Norfloxacin-loaded electrospun scaffolds: Montmorillonite nanocomposite vs. free drug. *Pharmaceutics* **2020**, *4*, 325. [CrossRef] [PubMed]
33. Ruggeri, M.; Bianchi, E.; Rossi, S.; Boselli, C.; Icaro Cornaglia, A.; Malavasi, L.; Carzino, R.; Suarato, G.; Sánchez-Espejo, R.; Athanassiou, A.; et al. Maltodextrin-amino acids electrospun scaffolds cross-linked with Maillard-type reaction for skin tissue engineering. *Biomater Adv.* **2022**, *133*, 112593. [CrossRef] [PubMed]
34. Rahman, M.; Islam, B.; Biswas, M.; Alam, A.H.M.K. In vitro antioxidant and free radical scavenging activity of different parts of Tabebuia pallida growing in Bangladesh. *BMC Res. Notes* **2015**, *8*, 621. [CrossRef] [PubMed]
35. Lim, Y.Y.; Lim, T.T.; Tee, J.J. Antioxidant Properties of Several Tropical Fruits: A Comparative Study. *Food Chem.* **2007**, *103*, 1003–1008. [CrossRef]
36. Taglietti, A.; Dacarro, G.; Barbieri, D.; Cucca, L.; Grisoli, P.; Patrini, M.; Arciola, C.R.; Pallavicini, P. High Bactericidal Self-Assembled Nano-Monolayer of Silver Sulfadiazine on Hydroxylated Material Surfaces. *Materials* **2019**, *12*, 2761, ISSN: 1996-1944. [CrossRef]
37. Fraise, A.P.; Lambert, P.A.; Masillard, J.-Y. (Eds.) *Russell, Hugo Ayliffe's, Principles and Practice of Disinfection, Preservation & Sterilization*, 6th ed.; Wiley-Blackwell Publishing: Hoboken, NJ, USA, 2004.

International Journal of
Molecular Sciences

MDPI

Article

Different Dimensional Copper-Based Metal–Organic Frameworks with Enzyme-Mimetic Activity for Antibacterial Therapy

Chuyan Lin [1,2,†], Xiangjian Guo [1,3,†], Fayin Mo [1] and Duanping Sun [1,2,*]

1 Guangdong Provincial Key Laboratory of Pharmaceutical Bioactive Substances, Center for Drug Research and Development, Guangdong Pharmaceutical University, Guangzhou 510006, China
2 Key Specialty of Clinical Pharmacy, The First Affiliated Hospital of Guangdong Pharmaceutical University, Guangzhou 510699, China
3 The First Affiliated Hospital of Sun Yat-sen University, Guangzhou 510080, China
* Correspondence: sundp@gdpu.edu.cn or sunduanping@126.com
† These authors contributed equally to this work.

Abstract: Fighting against bacterial infection and accelerating wound healing remain important and challenging in infected wound care. Metal–organic frameworks (MOFs) have received much attention for their optimized and enhanced catalytic performance in different dimensions of these challenges. The size and morphology of nanomaterials are important in their physiochemical properties and thereby their biological functions. Enzyme-mimicking catalysts, based on MOFs of different dimensions, display varying degrees of peroxidase (POD)-like activity toward hydrogen peroxide (H_2O_2) decomposition into toxic hydroxyl radicals (•OH) for bacterial inhibition and accelerating wound healing. In this study, we investigated the two most studied representatives of copper-based MOFs (Cu-MOFs), three-dimensional (3D) HKUST-1 and two-dimensional (2D) Cu-TCPP, for antibacterial therapy. HKUST-1, with a uniform and octahedral 3D structure, showed higher POD-like activity, resulting in H_2O_2 decomposition for •OH generation rather than Cu-TCPP. Because of the efficient generation of toxic •OH, both Gram-negative Escherichia coli and Gram-positive methicillin-resistant *Staphylococcus aureus* could be eliminated under a lower concentration of H_2O_2. Animal experiments indicated that the as-prepared HKUST-1 effectively accelerated wound healing with good biocompatibility. These results reveal the multivariate dimensions of Cu-MOFs with high POD-like activity, providing good potential for further stimulation of specific bacterial binding therapies in the future.

Keywords: metal–organic frameworks; POD-like activity; antibacterial therapy; wound healing

Citation: Lin, C.; Guo, X.; Mo, F.; Sun, D. Different Dimensional Copper-Based Metal–Organic Frameworks with Enzyme-Mimetic Activity for Antibacterial Therapy. *Int. J. Mol. Sci.* **2023**, *24*, 3173. https://doi.org/10.3390/ijms24043173

Academic Editor: Salvatore G. De-Simone

Received: 13 December 2022
Revised: 20 January 2023
Accepted: 23 January 2023
Published: 6 February 2023

1. Introduction

Metal–organic frameworks (MOFs) are crystalline porous materials constructed by the coordination of metal ions or clusters with polytypic organic ligands [1,2]. They possess many promising features, such as tunable structures, active sites, rapid electron transmission, and high surface area [3,4]. Owing to their excellent physical and chemical properties, MOFs have been extensively used in electrochemical applications, gas storage, and biomedical fields, such as wound healing, enhanced cancer therapy, imaging, and antibacterial agents [5–8]. As nanozymes, MOFs have been widely explored to achieve better antibacterial efficiency due to their peroxidase (POD)-like activity [9]. They can catalyze hydrogen peroxide (H_2O_2) into hydroxyl radicals (•OH), which possess higher antibacterial activity and minimize the toxicity of higher concentrations of H_2O_2 [10]. Copper-based MOFs (Cu-MOFs) stand out among numerous MOFs due to their low cost, exceptional stability, environmental friendliness and nontoxicity [11]. On the one hand, the intrinsic antibacterial activity of Cu^{2+} renders Cu-MOFs into an antibacterial platform, either alone or in combination with other functional ligands and antibacterial composites. Shams et al. found that pure HKUST-1 displayed a notable antibacterial effect against Escherichia coli (*E. coli*) and *S. aureus* by significantly disrupting the cell membrane, discharging cell constituents, and inhibiting DNA synthesis [12]. On the other hand, the POD-like catalytic effect of Cu-MOFs could be harnessed to construct antibacterial composites. POD-like activity can kill bacteria by converting H_2O_2 into toxic •OH at low concentrations, producing bactericidal reactive oxygen species (ROS) through the Fenton-type reaction to damage the cell membrane directly [13,14]. Significantly, MOFs with more powerful POD-like activity were able to destroy the exposed bacteria, avoiding the decolonization of bacteria [10,15]. According to the differences in morphology, Cu-MOFs can be categorized into 1-dimensional (1D), two-dimensional (2D), and three-dimensional (3D) MOFs [16–18]. The size and morphology of nanomaterials are important in their physiochemical properties and thereby their biological functions [19]. For example, the uniform dimensions of MOFs are essential for their applications in drug delivery and bioassays, as their size distribution may affect the biodistribution and linear quantitative analysis of drugs [20,21]. The high surface energy of MOFs leads to their propensity to aggregate into larger and irregular sizes [19]. Cu-MOFs have excellent physicochemical properties among MOFs and excellent catalytic activity, properties which have recently attracted much attention in various biomedical applications [15,22]. The catalytic activity and substrate selectivity of the nanozyme can be reasonably tuned through prestructural design and modulation of the preparation process [15]. The catalytic activity of the nanozyme is dependent on multiple factors, such as the category, size, surface, and crystal structure of the nanomaterial; thus, the measurement and evaluation of catalytic activity are complicated. However, the comparative enzymatic catalytic activity of 2D and 3D MOFs in different dimensions for biomedical applications has rarely been reported and thus is not preferred.

Bacterial infections have been one of the most concerning issues in the clinical medicine field and have become an urgent global hazard to public health, bringing a growing challenge to healthcare systems [23,24]. Bacterial infections can cause many serious and related diseases, such as delayed wound healing, bacteremia, and even death [25,26]. In particular, acute and chronic wounds due to all kinds of injuries are accompanied by bacterial infections [24]. The two common bacteria in wound sites are the Gram-positive bacterium methicillin-resistant *Staphylococcus aureus* (MRSA) and Gram-negative bacterium Pseudomonas aeruginosa [27,28]. Currently, antibiotics are the traditional method of infection therapy. However, the abuse and prolonged use of antibiotics can result in drug resistance in bacteria and even super bacteria, threatening human health and causing a huge medical cost burden [29,30]. According to a recent study, more than 700,000 people die worldwide annually from antibiotic-resistant infections, and this number is expected to rise to 10 million a year by 2050 [31]. Thus, the development of antibacterial therapy against complex infections at the wound site is urgently essential in biomedical applications [32].

HKUST-1 and Cu-TCPP MOFs are the most widely explored 3D and 2D Cu-MOFs, respectively [18,33,34]. Here, we report the POD-like activities of Cu-MOFs, with different dimensions (Cu-TCPP/HKUST-1) for potential antimicrobial agents with low biotoxicity and high antimicrobial activity. The POD-like activity of 2D/3D Cu-MOFs in antimicrobial therapy was compared. (Scheme 1) Briefly, we developed a straightforward synthetic strategy to prepare Cu-TCPP and HKUST-1 and demonstrated their successful synthesis by characterization techniques. HKUST-1 showed better POD-like activity due to its uniform and octahedral structure for accelerating electron transportation and ROS generation. HKUST-1 could capture Gram-negative *E. coli* and Gram-positive MRSA bacteria through ROS destruction and kill some bacteria by the disintegration of H_2O_2 into toxic •OH. Moreover, HKUST-1 exhibits excellent biocompatibility. They significantly accelerate the healing of wounds infected with MRSA bacteria. We compared the bactericidal effect based on the catalytic performances of 2D and 3D Cu-MOFs and highlighted the promising potential of Cu-MOFs for POD-like antibacterial wound healing treatment. This work provides a strategy to develop multi-dimension MOFs that target bacteria, which will further inspire specific bacterial-binding therapy in the future.

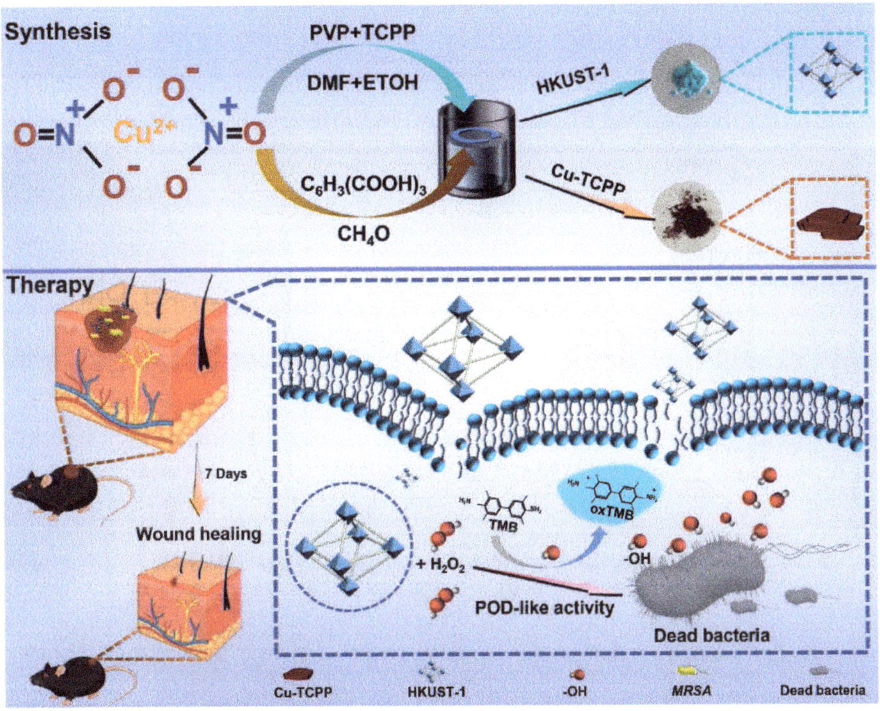

Scheme 1. Schematic illustration of the preparation of two different dimensional Cu-MOFs with POD-like activity for antibacterial and wound healing.

2. Results and Discussion

2.1. Characterization of Cu-MOFs

To study the surface morphology of Cu-MOFs, the obtained materials were characterized by scanning electron microscopy (SEM) and transmission electron microscopy (TEM). The morphology of Cu-MOFs is displayed in Figure 1. As shown in Figure 1A,B, the prepared HKUST-1 presented a uniform and 3D octahedral shape structure with an average size of 1–3 μm. A magnified SEM image reveals that the octahedral-shaped HKUST-1 possesses rough surfaces with porous structures. It reveals the possibility of providing a high surface area for substance transmission, catalysis and antibacterial applications. Similarly, the prepared Cu-TCPP was characterized by SEM and TEM, and the images are shown in Figures 1C and 1D, respectively. The obtained Cu-TCPP proved a sheet-like and layer-by-layer ultrathin 2D structure with a wrinkled film surface and folds, suggesting 2D Cu-TCPP nanosheets with a large surface area. The two kinds of Cu-MOFs were in accordance with the previous literature. Supplementary Figure S1A,B show the powders of the prepared Cu-MOFs.

The crystalline structures of the as-prepared Cu-MOFs were investigated by X-ray diffraction (XRD). The intact diffraction characteristic peak profiles of Cu-TCPP and HKUST-1 from $2\theta = 5$–$80°$. Cu-TCPP exhibited a distinguishing peak at $2\theta = 20°$, which can be indexed to the (002) crystal plane (Figure 1E). The XRD pattern of HKUST-1 was mainly composed of distinguishing peaks in the range of $2\theta = 5°$–$20°$, indicating the crystalline characteristics of the synthesized HKUST-1 samples. It revealed microporous coordination with the cubic crystalline structure and high crystallinity. The diffraction pattern was consistent with that reported in the literature, suggesting the successful synthesis of Cu-TCPP and HKUST-1. Further information about the chemical composition in terms of functional groups on Cu-MOFs was provided by Fourier transform infrared (FT-IR) spectra presented in Figure 1F.

The bands in the range of 700 to 1700 cm^{-1} were assigned to BTC, and the characteristic peak at approximately 500 cm^{-1} was contributed by Cu-O stretching vibrations. The spectra of Cu-TCPP and HKUST-1 presented two strong peaks at approximately 1400 and 1620 cm^{-1}. The most significant characteristic peak at 3500 cm^{-1} was contributed by HKUST-1. The FT-IR spectrum of HKUST-1 demonstrated an almost isobidentate behavior of the COO moiety since bands at 1645, 1620, 1570, 1550, 1445, and 1375 cm^{-1} are characteristic bands of this coordination mode. The bands at 1445 and 1645 cm^{-1} indicated –O–C–O– bonding as well as those at 1375 and 1550 cm^{-1} of C=C stretching, demonstrating the incorporation of BTC in the MOF [17]. The latter is because aniso-bidentate dicopper (II) carboxylate is a type of monomeric cluster present in the framework. X-ray photoelectron spectroscopy (XPS) was used to analyze the surface composition, chemical composition, and states of Cu-MOFs. The surface characteristics of the obtained materials were investigated by XPS. Figure 1G–J demonstrates a full survey of Cu-TCPP and HKUST-1 composed of Cu 2p3, O 1s, C 1s, and N 1s (Figure S2). In the Cu 2p3 region, the patterns of HKUST-1 and Cu-TCPP show characteristic peaks at approximately 900 eV (Figure 1H). These results suggested that two kinds of Cu-MOFs were synthesized successfully.

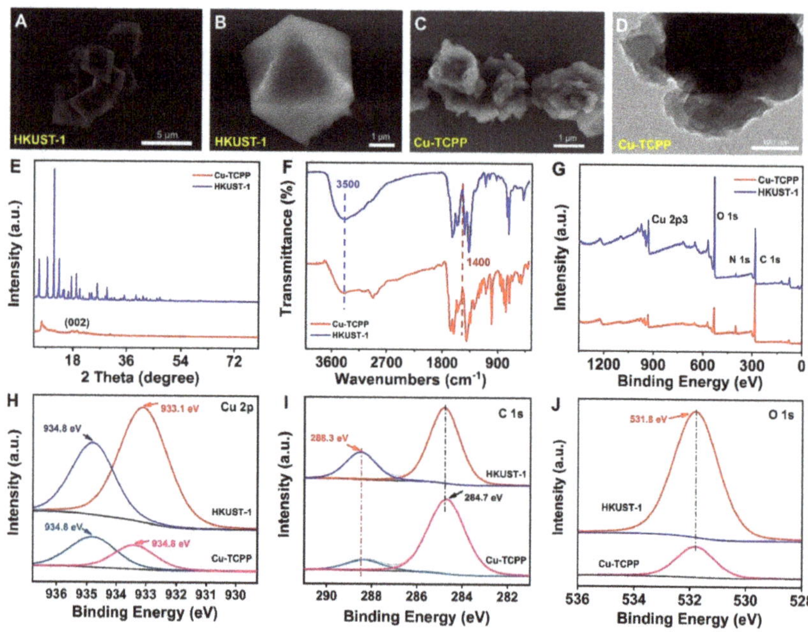

Figure 1. (**A**,**B**) SEM image of HKUST-1. (**C**) SEM image of Cu-TCPP. (**D**) TEM image of Cu–TCPP. (**E**) XRD patterns and (**F**) FT-IR spectra of HKUST-1 and Cu-TCPP. (**G**) XPS survey spectra for HKUST-1 and Cu-TCPP. High-resolution XPS spectra of (**H**) Cu 2p, (**I**) C 1s and (**J**) O 1s for HKUST-1 and Cu-TCPP.

2.2. POD-like Catalytic Activity of Cu-MOFs

In the first suite of experiments, we used H_2O_2 and 3,3′,5,5′-tetramethylbenzidine (TMB) to evaluate the catalytic ability of POD-like enzymes as substrates to challenge the catalytic ability of the prepared Cu-MOFs. The decomposition of H_2O_2 can be accelerated by catalysts to generate more oxygen, leading to gas bubble formation. Figure S3 displays a comparison of the gas bubble formation with the assistance of Cu-TCCP and HKUST-1. Both Cu-TCPP and HKUST-1 presented catalase-like activity with gas bubble formation. More gas bubbles were produced in tubes containing H_2O_2 + HKUST-1 (Figure S3-III), suggesting a higher catalase-like activity than that of Cu-TCPP. TMB is a typical chromogenic substrate serving as an indicator to determine POD-like activity. H_2O_2 could be degraded to generate •OH with the assistance of POD, which activated the cascade production of blue oxidization TMB (oxTMB) with a color change of the solutions. The POD-like catalytic activity of Cu-MOFs was studied by the colorimetric oxidation reaction system of TMB in the absence or presence of H_2O_2 (Figure 2A). Negligible color changes could be seen from the tubes in the absence of Cu-MOFs (Figure S4-II). In contrast, obvious changes from colorless to blue can be observed from the tubes containing Cu-MOFs, TMB, and H_2O_2 (Figure S4-V,VI), indicating the oxidation process with the production of oxTMB. All the results suggested that HKUST-1 with better POD-like catalytic activity can be used as a catalyst for the acceleration of TMB oxidization. Furthermore, UV–visible spectroscopy was employed to quantify TMB oxidation by H_2O_2 with the assistance of Cu-MOFs. The maximum characteristic absorption peak of oxTMB can be observed at 652 nm. Significantly, the TMB + H_2O_2 + HKUST-1 reaction system presented a higher absorption peak in comparison with TMB + H_2O_2 + Cu-TCPP, revealing the better POD-like catalytic activity of HKUST-1 than Cu-TCPP (Figure 2B). The excellent POD-like catalytic activity could be attributed to the unique 3D structure of HKUST-1 to expose more tunnel and catalytic active sites for substance exchange, which considerably enhanced the catalytic performance. We systematically explored the effect of the concentrations of catalyst and reaction time. The characteristic absorption peak value at 652 nm increased linearly with increasing HKUST-1 concentration and reaction time (Figure 2C). The TMB oxidation reaction in the presence of H_2O_2 with the assistance of HKUST-1 occurs in a catalyst concentration- and time-dependent manner (Figure S5). HKUST-1 was selected as an ideal POD-like catalyst in the following experiment based on the above results.

To analyze the POD-like catalytic activity as well as the catalytic mechanism, the kinetic parameters of HKUST-1 were further quantitatively studied using enzyme kinetics theory. Under the optimal reactive conditions, the steady-state kinetic properties of HKUST-1 were studied by changing the concentration of substrate (TMB and H_2O_2) with different reaction times. In this typical enzyme reaction kinetics, the concentration of HKUST-1 was fixed. The characteristic absorption peak value at 652 nm was recorded by fixing the concentration of TMB as well as changing the concentration of H_2O_2 in a specified range and vice versa with H_2O_2. The absorbance at 652 nm was enhanced with increasing concentrations of H_2O_2 and TMB. Figure S6 shows that the reaction rate of HKUST-1 increased obviously with increasing TMB when the concentration of H_2O_2 was fixed. With further growth of the concentration of TMB, the reaction rate increased slowly and flattens out gradually. Similarly, when the concentration of TMB was fixed, the reaction rate of HKUST-1 POD gradually increased with increasing H_2O_2. However, the reaction rate slowed down and flattened out gradually with a further extension of the concentration of H_2O_2 (Figure 2D). The results showed that the TMB oxidation reaction catalyzed by HKUST-1 followed the typical Michaelis–Menten behavior toward H_2O_2 and TMB. Table 1 lists a comparison of the K_m and V_{max} values of as-prepared HKUST-1 and several catalysts in previous reports for substrates TMB and H_2O_2. The K_m value of HKUST-1 was determined to be 2.036 mM for the H_2O_2 substrate and 0.545 mM for the TMB substrate, indicating that HKUST-1 possessed a good affinity for H_2O_2 and TMB. Compared with HKUST-1 and other reported catalysts, the K_m value of HKUST-1 with H_2O_2 as a substrate was lower than that of ZIF-67 (3.52 mM), antibody@Cu-MOFs (7.37 mM) and Cu-MOFs ($CuCl_2$) (6.41 mM), demonstrating a higher POD-like activity toward the TMB-H_2O_2 reaction system. This could benefit from the large surface areas, rough surface, pore sizes and tunnel in HKUST-1, accelerating the substance exchange. The HKUST-1 with unique 3D structure displays higher POD-like activity.

2.3. Detection of •OH

To further investigate the catalytic mechanism, a fluorescence experiment was carried out to analyze the POD-like activity of Cu-MOFs. Terephthalic acid (TA) was employed as a fluorescent indicator to further detect the generation of •OH, decomposed from H_2O_2 with the catalysis of Cu-MOFs. The detection principle says that •OH can be captured by the nonfluorescent compound TA to generate a highly fluorescent product, 2-hydroxyterephthalic acid (TAOH), with a unique characteristic fluorescence peak at 435 nm under excitation at 315 nm (Figure 2E). The fluorescence signal can be recorded by the spectrofluorometer to confirm the generation of •OH. Figure 2E shows the fluorescence spectra of Cu-MOFs, TA, H_2O_2, and their mixture in comparison with the control groups after incubation for 12 h in the dark, demonstrating the generation of •OH. Compared with the TA + H_2O_2 + HKUST-1 group, the fluorescence intensity of the TA + H_2O_2 + Cu-TCPP group displayed an unsatisfying result, with a negligible fluorescent signal as well as the result of the control group. The emission intensity of TA increased obviously with the addition of HKUST-1. The fluorescence intensity of the TA + H_2O_2 + HKUST-1 group reached approximately 550, which was 50 times higher than that of the TA + H_2O_2 + Cu-TCPP group. The results revealed that HKUST-1, with excellent POD-like activity due to its unique 3D structure, can accelerate the decomposition of H_2O_2 for •OH generation.

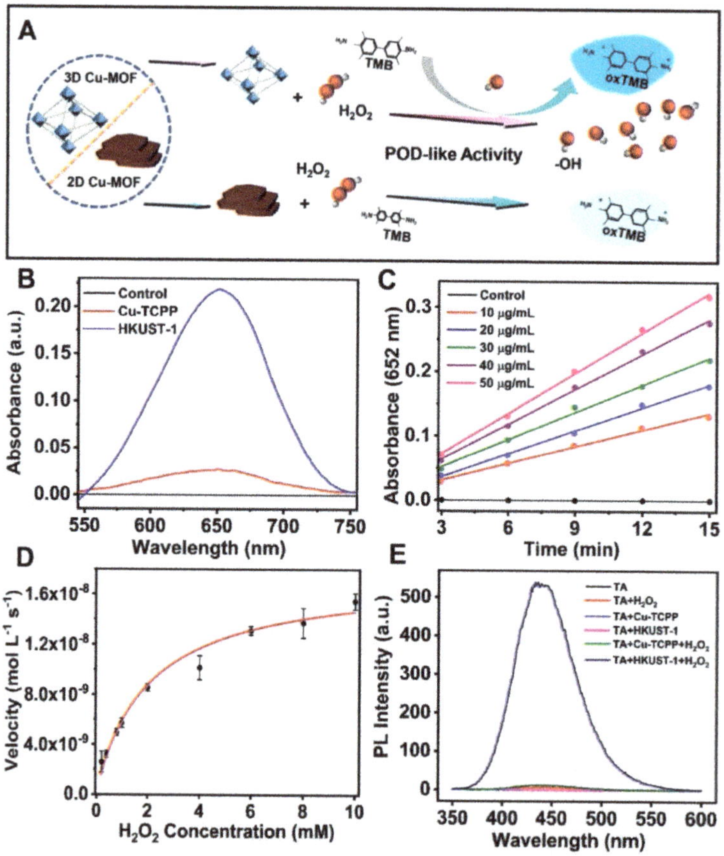

Figure 2. (**A**) Schematic diagram of the mechanism for POD-like activity in two different dimensions of MOF. (**B**) The UV–vis absorbance spectra of TMB in different reaction systems: H_2O_2 + TMB, Cu-TCPP + H_2O_2 + TMB, and HKUST-1 + H_2O_2 + TMB. (**C**) Kinetic curves of prepared Cu-MOFs artificial enzyme with varied concentrations. (**D**) Steady-state kinetic assays of HKUST-1 for H_2O_2. (**E**) Fluorescence spectra of different reaction systems: TA, TA + H_2O_2, TA + Cu-TCPP, TA + HKUST-1, TA + H_2O_2 + Cu-TCPP and TA + H_2O_2 + HKUST-1.

Table 1. Comparison of the Michaelis–Menten (K_m) constant and maximum reaction rate (V_{max}) of HKUST-1.

Catalyst	Substance	K_m (mmol L^{-1})	Vmax (mol L^{-1} s^{-1})	References
ZIF-67	TMB	13.69	3.5×10^{-7}	[35]
	H_2O_2	3.52	2.8×10^{-7}	
Antibody@Cu-MOFs	TMB	3.91	5.445×10^{-7}	[36]
	H_2O_2	7.37	1.075×10^{-7}	
Cu-MOFs ($CuCl_2$)	TMB	4.11	5.556×10^{-7}	[36]
	H_2O_2	6.41	1.02×10^{-7}	
Cu-MOFs ($Cu(NO_3)_2$)	TMB	2.56	2.5×10^{-7}	[37]
	H_2O_2	4.34	1.82×10^{-7}	
Cu-MOFs ($Cu(NO_3)_2$)	TMB	0.456	2.478×10^{-8}	[38]
	H_2O_2	28.58	5.45×10^{-8}	
Cu-MOFs (CuI)	TMB	2.4862	7.517×10^{-8}	[39]
	H_2O_2	0.163	6.736×10^{-8}	
$CuFe_2O_4$	TMB	2.26	2.07×10^{-8}	[9]
	H_2O_2	0.5	2.61×10^{-8}	
$(Ni_2Co_1)_{0.5}Cu_{0.5}$ MOFs	TMB	0.34	1.81×10^{-8}	[10]
	H_2O_2	1.08	1.29×10^{-8}	
AuNPs/Cu-MOFs	TMB	0.29	2.96×10^{-7}	[40]
	H_2O_2	0.65	2.25×10^{-7}	
HRP	TMB	0.434	10.0×10^{-8}	[41]
	H_2O_2	3.702	8.71×10^{-8}	
HKUST-1	TMB	0.545	0.833×10^{-8}	This work
	H_2O_2	2.036	1.757×10^{-8}	

2.4. Antibacterial Assay In Vitro

High concentrations of H_2O_2 have been widely used in sterilization and bacterial infectious therapy. However, it causes serious oxidative stress in tissues, which may cause unnecessary damage in tissues. In light of the impressive POD-like activity of HKUST-1 that could convert H_2O_2 into •OH, toxic •OH is much more reactive and can cause more serious oxidative damage to bacteria. We analyzed the antibacterial effects of Cu-MOFs in two dimensions against Gram-negative strains of *E. coli* and Gram-positive strains of MRSA. The antibacterial performance of the Cu-MOFs in two dimensions was evaluated by the plate counting method. Six different groups were set for exploring the antibacterial performance against both Gram-negative and Gram-positive pathogens, including (I) PBS, (II) H_2O_2, (III) Cu-TCPP, (IV) HKUST-1, (V) Cu-TCPP + H_2O_2 and (VI) HKUST-1 + H_2O_2 groups. Two kinds of bacteria were treated with different treatments before inoculation onto LB culture plates, and the PBS group was set as a parallel control. According to Figure 3A,B, HKUST-1 illustrated little antibacterial ability against *E. coli* and MRSA in the absence of H_2O_2, demonstrating that HKUST-1 has weak antibacterial activity. This could be attributed to the copper ions released from HKUST-1. As expected, both kinds of bacteria incubated with HKUST-1 + H_2O_2 treatments presented a dramatically decreasing trend, demonstrating the outstanding antibacterial activity contributed by the effect of HKUST-1 + H_2O_2. The antibacterial performance of low concentrations of H_2O_2 was greatly enhanced with the addition of HKUST-1, avoiding damage during disinfection with high concentrations of H_2O_2. In comparison, no obvious change in the number of bacterial colonies was observed after treatment with PBS, H_2O_2, Cu-TCPP and Cu-TCPP + H_2O_2, which was consistent with the results of the POD-like activity assay. These results revealed a weak antibacterial activity and poor growth inhibition of Cu-TCPP compared to HKUST-1. Benefiting from the striking POD-like activity of HKUST-1 with a unique 3D structure, H_2O_2 could generate reactive and toxic •OH to combat bacteria. These findings could be ascribed to the intrinsic bactericidal activity of •OH as a result of the effective catalysis from HKUST-1.

After displaying the antibacterial performances of Cu-MOFs with the plate counting method, we further analyzed the potential antibacterial mechanism derived from HKUST-1. We employed live/dead viability analysis using confocal fluorescence microscopy. SYTO/propidium iodide (PI) staining was used to display the live/dead assays. The SYTO dye penetrated and stained both intact membranes and broken membranes, causing fluorescent green emission, while the PI dye penetrated only the damaged cell membranes, resulting in fluorescent red emission. The bright green fluorescence obtained from the SYTO stain indicated the negligible antibacterial effect of the PBS treatment. However, upon cotreatment with HKUST-1 and H_2O_2, the sharply predominant red fluorescence intensity of PI could be recorded, indicating damaged cell membranes and bacterial apoptosis (Figure 3C). This result adequately validated the excellent antibacterial performance due to the generation of highly toxic •OH benefiting from HKUST-1 with POD-like activity. The antibacterial effect shown in these experiments illustrated the potential application of the proposed combined treatment for combating bacterial infections, which further confirmed that H_2O_2 at very low concentrations can still yield effective antibacterial efficiency with the assistance of HKUST-1.

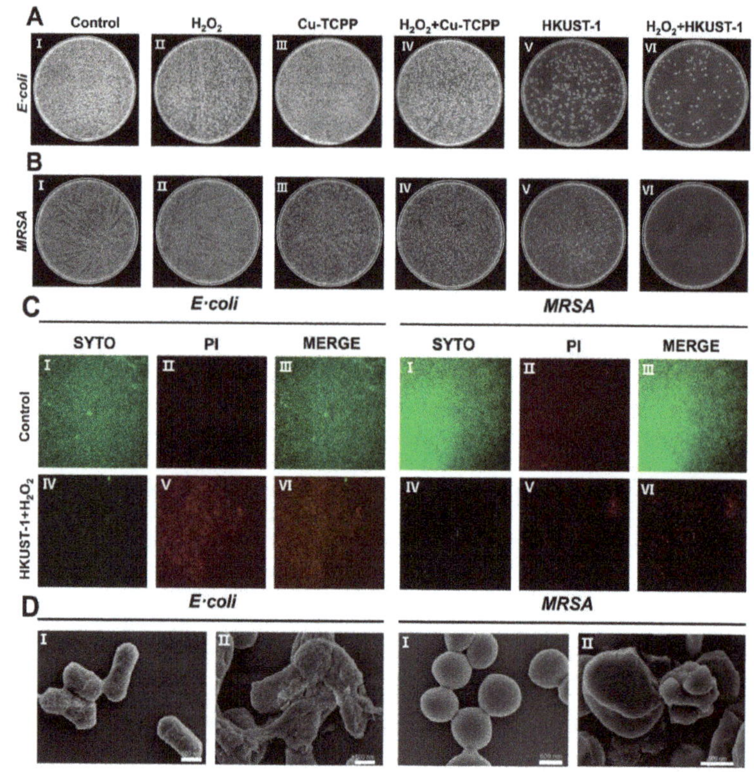

Figure 3. Photographs of the colonies against *E. coli* (**A**) and *MRSA* (**B**) with different treatments, (I) PBS (II) H_2O_2 (III) Cu-TCPP (IV) Cu-TCPP + H_2O_2 (V) HKUST-1 (VI) HKUST-1 + H_2O_2. (**C**) Fluorescence images of *E. coli* and *MRSA* that had undergone various treatments (I), (II) and (III) PBS and (IV), (V) and (VI) HKUST-1 + H_2O_2. (**D**) SEM images of *E. coli* and *MRSA* by various treatments: (I) PBS, (II) HKUST-1 + H_2O_2. Scale bar = 500 nm.

To further confirm the above results, SEM characterization was employed to visualize the morphological changes of bacteria with different treatments. As shown in Figure 3D, both Gram-negative strains of *E. coli* and Gram-positive strains of MRSA treated with PBS were typically rod-shaped and round-shaped, respectively. The smooth, uniform and intact morphologies of cells with few disruptions could be observed, indicating the negligible bactericidal function of PBS for combating bacteria. Compared to the control group, bacteria treated with HKUST-1 + H_2O_2 exhibited an obvious morphological change. The Gram-negative strains of *E. coli* displayed collapsed, split, and merged membranes, resulting in wrinkled and shrunken morphology after exposure to HKUST-1 + H_2O_2 treatment.

Similar morphological changes were also observed for MRSA, which were consistent with the results of the plate counting method and the live/dead assays. Therefore, SEM characterization of the bacteria fully confirmed the outstanding bactericidal performance of HKUST-1, leading to the severe structural deformation of the bacteria. These results suggested that HKUST-1 disrupted the bacterial membrane and induced bacterial apoptosis. HKUST-1 with excellent POD-like activity to generate •OH, revealing its highly efficient bactericidal performance under a low concentration of H_2O_2.

2.5. Evaluation of Antibacterial Activity In Vivo

Bacterial infections can result in inflammatory reactions and postpone wound healing. Inspired by the remarkable antibacterial performance of HKUST-1 in vitro, we further investigated the bactericidal efficacy of HKUST-1 in vivo to determine its potential for accelerating infectious wound healing and clinical applications. An 8 mm-diameter circular full-thickness cutaneous wound model with *MRSA* infection was constructed on the backs of mice in this experiment section. First, 50 μL 1×10^7 CFU mL^{-1} of MRSA suspension was dropped on the wound site to fabricate the infectious wound in each mouse, and the wounds were incubated with MRSA for 24 h. Subsequently, twenty C57BL/6 mice with an infectious wound on their backs were randomly divided into four groups: (I) PBS + 3% carboxymethyl cellulose sodium (CMC-Na) Hydrogels, (II) H_2O_2 + 3% CMC-Na Hydrogels, (III) HKUST-1 + 3% CMC-Na Hydrogels and (IV) HKUST-1 + H_2O_2 + 3% CMC-Na Hydrogels (Figure S7). Each group of wounds received different treatments for 7 consecutive days, and the hydrogels were changed at daily intervals after irrigation with physiological saline solution. Photographs of the wounds were taken by camera on each alternate day to demonstrate the therapeutic effects visually. As shown in Figure 4A, all wounds had obvious inflammatory reactions (red and swollen skin around the wound) after surgery, suggesting successful model construction. With the continuous process of the treatments, all groups with different treatments displayed decreased surface area of the wounds. However, the wounds treated with PBS + 3% CMC-Na hydrogels exhibited a relatively slow wound healing process. In particular, ulcers could be observed around the wound site on day 5 and day 7, indicating severe infections. A similar tendency could be seen in the treatment of H_2O_2 + 3% CMC-Na hydrogels. This result could be attributed to the negligible antibacterial effect of PBS and the low concentration of H_2O_2. Notably, HKUST-1 + H_2O_2 + 3% CMC-Na hydrogels significantly accelerated the wound closure process. The wounds almost completely healed after 7 days of treatment with scab formation. On the seventh day, the wound treated with HKUST-1 + H_2O_2 + 3% CMC-Na hydrogels displayed the best wound contraction compared with the other groups. In addition, the relative wound closure of mice with different treatments was calculated to visually assess the therapeutic effects. Figure 4B demonstrates the relative wound closure of each group in the whole therapeutic process. Importantly, the wound treated with HKUST-1 + H_2O_2 + 3% CMC-Na hydrogels illustrated the highest relative wound closure at each observation period, and the relative wound closure was 90% at day 7. Furthermore, the toxicity of HKUST-1 was studied by the weight changes in mice during the therapeutic process. Notably, no obvious weight change could be observed in each group of mice, indicating the nontoxicity of the as-prepared HKUST-1 (Figure 4C).

Histological analysis of the wound tissues was conducted to study the acceleration of the wound-healing efficiency of HKUST-1 (Figure 4D). Hematoxylin and eosin staining (H&E) and Masson staining were used to assess skin tissue repair, collagen formation, epidermis architecture and inflammation levels after different treatments. The wound tissues of each group were collected from the sacrificed mice after 7 days of treatment. As shown in Figure 4D, the H&E staining exhibited intact epidermis architecture and few inflammatory cells on the wound, with normal skin thickness in the HKUST-1 + H_2O_2 + 3% CMC-Na hydrogel group. Similar results can be observed in Masson staining, and uniform collagen fiber deposition and generation of the epithelial layer were observed in the wound treated by HKUST-1 with the assistance of a low concentration of H_2O_2, revealing commendable antibacterial effects and promotion in the healing process. In contrast, a larger number of inflammatory cells were recruited at the site of the wound in the PBS +3% CMC-Na hydrogel group than in the other groups. This may have impaired the tissue in wound sites with fibrotic repair, oxidation and inflammatory cells, suggesting severe infection. Based on the above results, we can conclude that the HKUST-1 + H_2O_2 + 3% CMC-Na hydrogel group showed an excellent wound healing effect in vivo against MRSA infection due to serious oxidative damage, induced by highly toxic •OH, benefiting from HKUST-1 with higher POD-like activity.

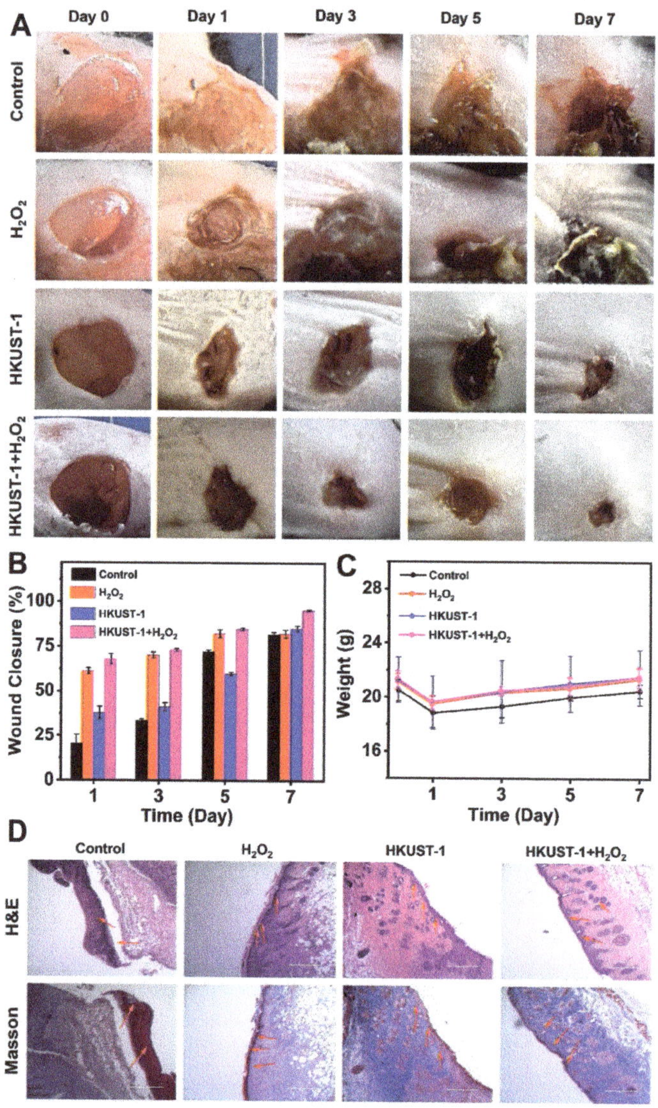

Figure 4. (**A**) Digital photos of MRSA-infected wounds on mice with therapy at different times. (**B**) Relative wound closure size of mice after different therapies. (**C**) Body weight of mice treated with different therapies for 0–7 days. (**D**) Corresponding H&E and Masson staining of skin tissue from mice with different therapies at day 7. The red arrow indicates the edge of the skin wound. Scale bar = 400 μm.

2.6. Biosafety Assay In Vivo

Biosafety and good biocompatibility are important considerations of artificial enzymes in potential biomedical and clinical applications. The toxicity assessment should be carried out first before clinical application. In this section, blood biochemistry analysis and histological analysis of major organs were further employed to assess the biosafety and biocompatibility of HKUST-1 in vivo. C57BL/6 male mice were chosen as animal models, and ten of them were randomly divided into two groups. PBS and HKUST-1 suspensions were injected into mice via the tail vein at a concentration of 0.5 mg mL^{-1} at a dose of 10 g/0.1 mL once a day for 5 days. Mice treated with PBS were used as parallel controls. After 7 days of different treatments, blood samples of the mice were collected for biochemistry analysis to study the toxicity of HKUST-1. As shown in Figure 5A, the biochemical indexes of the ratio of albumin to globulin (A/G), blood urea albumin (ALB), alanine transaminase (ALT), aspartate transaminase (AST), creatinine (CR), globulin (GLOB), total bilirubin (TBIL) and total protein (TP) were examined, demonstrating no significant difference between the PBS and HKUST-1 treatment groups. Finally, H&E staining of the major organs (heart, liver, spleen, lungs, and kidney) further confirmed the nontoxicity of HKUST-1 (Figure 5B). Taken together, HKUST-1 did not display obvious side effects on mice with biosafety and good biocompatibility, indicating its potential as an antibacterial and wound healing alternative.

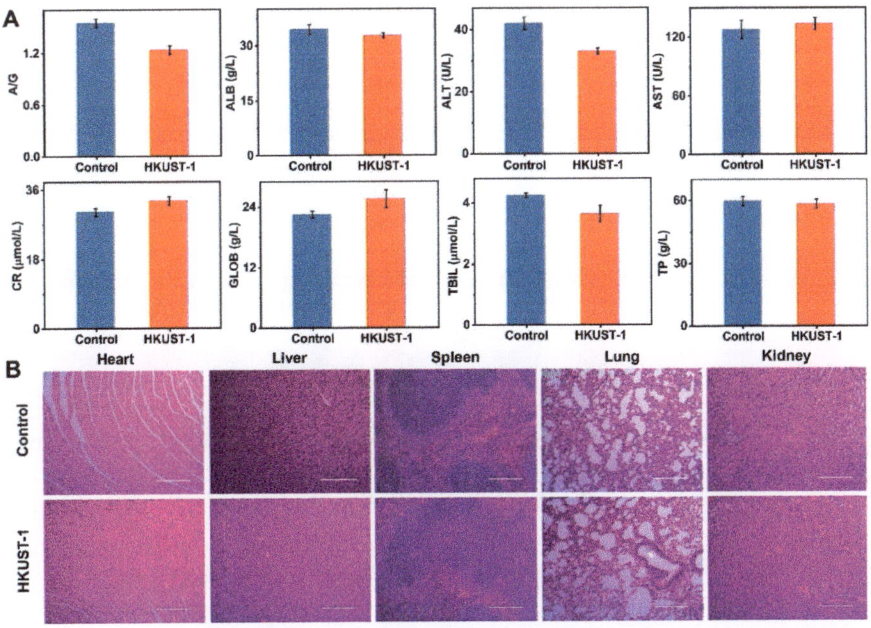

Figure 5. (**A**) Levels of different blood biochemical indexes (A/G, ALB, ALT, AST, CR, GLOB, TBIL, and TP) after intravenous injection with PBS solution or HKUST-1. (**B**) H&E staining of major organs after 7 days of treatment obtained from mice. Scale bar = 200 μm.

3. Materials and Methods

3.1. Materials

Copper nitrate hydrate [$Cu(NO_3)_2{\cdot}xH_2O$], trimesic acid [$C_6H_3(CO_2H)_3$], and TMB were obtained from Aladdin Reagent Co., Ltd. (Shanghai, China). Polyvinylpyrrolidone [PVP, molecular weight (Mw) = 40,000] was obtained from Sigma–Aldrich Co., Ltd. Tetrakis (4-carboxyphenyl) porphyrin absolute (TCPP) was obtained from Tokyo Chemical Industry Co., Ltd. Sodium chloride, disodium hydrogen phosphate (Na_2HPO_4), potassium chloride

(KCl), potassium dihydrogen phosphate (KH_2PO_4), and acetic acid (CH_3COOH) were obtained from Sinopharm Chemical Reagent Co., Ltd. (Shanghai, China). Ethanol absolute and N,N-dimethylformamide (DMF) were purchased from Tianjin Damao Chemical Reagent Co., Ltd. H_2O_2 and methanol (CH_4O) were purchased from Guangzhou Chemical Reagent Co., Ltd. (Guangzhou, China). Ultrapure water (18.2 MΩ; Millipore Co., United States) was used to prepare all solutions. All solutions were stored at room temperature at 25 ± 2 °C for further use. All reagents were of analytical grade and used without further purification.

3.2. Synthesis of Cu-MOFs

Cu-TCPP was obtained by the surfactant-assisted method [42]. First, 25 mg of copper nitrate ($Cu(NO_3)_2{\cdot}xH_2O$) and 100 mg of PVP were dispersed in a beaker containing a solution of DMF (45 mL) and absolute ethanol (15 mL) under stirring conditions to form a blue mixture. After that, 60 mg of TCPP was dissolved into the blue mixture under ultrasonication for 10 min. Then, the mixing solution was added to a Teflon autoclave and heated at 80 °C for 4 h. The resultant product was collected by centrifugation at 8000 rpm for 10 min. Finally, the red product was washed with absolute ethanol three times and dried at 60 °C.

The synthesis process of HKUST-1 was based on the previous literature [43]. Cu $(NO_3)_2{\cdot}xH_2O$ (1.82 g) and $C_6H_3(COOH)_3$ (0.875 g) were dissolved in a beaker containing 50 mL of absolute methanol with ultrasonication to obtain blue and transparent solutions, respectively. The copper nitrate solution was mixed with the trimesic acid solution under stirring. After that, the mixing solution was kept at 25 °C. After precipitating for 2 h, HKUST-1 was collected by centrifugation at 5000 rpm for 10 min. The obtained blue product was washed with methanol twice. Finally, the blue powder was dried under vacuum conditions for future use.

3.3. POD-like Catalytic Activity of Cu-MOFs

The POD-like activity of Cu-MOFs was systematically studied through the catalytic oxidation of TMB with the assistance of H_2O_2. The catalytic oxidation activity of Cu-MOFs was evaluated by gas bubble formation, the formation of a blue-colored oxTMB leading to color changes in the buffer solution and absorbance changes in oxTMB at 652 nm. In this experimental section, 20 mM acetate buffer (pH = 4.0) was used. Briefly, 1 mL HAc-NaAc buffer solution (20 mM, pH = 4.0) contained TMB, H_2O_2 and Cu-MOFs with final concentrations of 2 mM, 20 mM and 30 μg mL^{-1}, respectively. The varying concentrations of Cu-MOFs, TMB, and H_2O_2 for the POD-like activities were explored. The POD-like activities of Cu-MOFs were assessed under the same conditions. Similarly, kinetics measurements were performed to analyze the catalytic activity of HKUST-1 by changing the concentrations of TMB and H_2O_2. The kinetic parameters were assessed by the Michaelis–Menten equation: $V_0 = V_{max} \times S/(K_m + S)$, where V_{max} and V_0 correspond to the maximum velocity and initial rate, respectively. S and K_m represent the concentration of the substance and the Michaelis–Menten constant, respectively.

3.4. Detection of •OH

The generation of •OH, catalyzed by Cu-MOFs, was verified by fluorescence (FL) experiments. The hydroxyl radical assay was as follows: the solutions in the tubes including (I) TA, (II) TA + H_2O_2, (III) Cu-TCPP, (IV) HKUST-1, (V) TA + H_2O_2 + Cu-TCPP and (VI) TA + H_2O_2 + HKUST-1 were reacted for 12 h in the dark. After that, the supernatant was collected by centrifugation at 8000 rpm for 10 min. Then, the fluorescence spectra at 435 nm of the supernatant were recorded. The final concentrations of TA, H_2O_2 and Cu-MOFs were 0.5 mM, 10 mM and 30 μg mL^{-1}, respectively.

3.5. Bacterial Culture and Antibacterial Assay In Vitro

E. coli (ATCC 25922) and MRSA (ATCC 43300) bacterial cells in the log phase were used in the following experiments. The bacterial conditions were detected by measuring the OD600 nm using a UV–Vis spectrophotometer. The value of OD600 nm is approximately 0.5. Bacterial cells in the log phase can be used in the following experiments. The bacterial suspension was diluted with 0.01 M sterilized PBS to 1×10^7 CFU mL^{-1} for future use.

For the antibacterial experiments, the plate counting method was chosen to determine the sterilization effect of Cu-MOFs. The treatments were divided into six groups: (I) PBS, (II) H_2O_2, (III) Cu-TCPP, (IV) Cu-TCPP + H_2O_2, (V) HKUST-1, and (VI) HKUST-1 + H_2O_2. The mixtures of all groups were incubated for 3 h at 37 °C. Then, 100 μL mixtures of all groups were spread on LB solid medium and incubated at 37 °C for 12 h. The number of colonies was counted. All experiments were repeated three times.

Fluorescence-based live/dead bacteria staining analysis was employed to investigate the antibacterial performance of HKUST-1 with the assistance of H_2O_2. *E. coli* and MRSA, treated with PBS or HKUST-1+ H_2O_2, were stained with SYTO and PI for 30 min in the dark. Afterward, the bacteria were washed and collected by centrifugation at 12,000 rpm three times. Finally, fluorescence microscopy was employed to observe the stained bacterial cells.

The morphological changes in the bacteria were characterized by scanning electron microscopy to determine the sterilization effect of PBS or HKUST-1 + H_2O_2 treatment. First, bacteria treated with HKUST-1 + H_2O_2 were used for the treated group, and PBS treatment was used for the blank control. After incubation at 37 °C for 3 h, the bacteria were collected by washing and centrifugation and fixed with 4% paraformaldehyde. The bacteria were washed thoroughly with DI water, followed by dehydration using a series of ethanol solutions. Finally, morphological changes in treated bacteria were examined under conditions of SEM after sputter-coating with gold.

3.6. Evaluation of Antibacterial Activity In Vivo

Animal experiments were designed based on the standard protocol and approved by the Ethical Review Committee and Laboratory Animal Welfare Committee of Guangdong Pharmaceutical University (gdpulacspf2017523). A full-thickness cutaneous wound with MRSA infection model was built in male C57/BL6 mice (8–10 weeks, 25–30 g, six-ten mice per group) purchased from Guangdong Laboratory Animal Center. A round wound, with a diameter of approximately 8 mm, was created on the back of each mouse. Twenty mice were divided into four treatment groups: (I) PBS + 3% CMC-Na hydrogels, (II) H_2O_2 + 3% CMC-Na hydrogels, (III) HKUST-1 + 3% CMC-Na hydrogels and (IV) HKUST-1 + H_2O_2 + 3% CMC-Na hydrogels. The final concentrations of H_2O_2 and HKUST-1 were 10^{-3} M and 2 mg mL^{-1}, respectively. After sterilization with 75% alcohol and shaving with hair removal cream, 50 μL 1×10^7 CFU mL^{-1} of MRSA suspension was dropped on the wound site to construct the infectious wound model of the mouse. The wounds were observed and photographed by a digital camera. The hydrogels were changed at daily intervals after physiological saline solution irrigation. After 7 days of treatment, the mice were sacrificed. The related wound tissues were harvested for histological evaluation. The wound closure rate was calculated by the following equation:

$$\text{Wound closure rate} = \text{Wound Area}_{\text{(Day0-DayX)}} / \text{Wound Area}_{\text{(Day0)}} \times 100\%$$

3.7. Biosafety Assay In Vivo

Ten mice were divided into two groups: (I) HKUST-1 treatment was used for the treated group, and (II) PBS solution treatment was used for the blank control group. After 7 days of tail vein injection of HKUST-1 suspension (0.5 mg/mL) at a dose of 10 g/0.1 mL, two groups of mice were sacrificed. The main organ tissues were harvested for histological evaluation, and blood samples were collected for biochemical analysis.

4. Conclusions

In summary, we reported Cu-MOFs in different dimensions for antibacterial application and wound healing promotion. Cu-TCPP with a sheet-like and layer-by-layer ultrathin 2D structure and HKUST-1 with a uniform 3D structure in an octahedral shape were synthesized successfully. Benefiting from the uniform 3D structure, HKUST-1 exhibited higher POD-like activity than Cu-TCPP. Based on the excellent POD-like activity, HKUST-1 could greatly accelerate the generation of ROS in terms of the decomposition of H_2O_2 into highly toxic •OH. The POD-like activity studies and fluorescent experiments systematically confirmed the results. Inspired by POD-like activity and the generation of •OH, Cu-MOFs were employed to investigate the antibacterial performance and wound healing in vivo. HKUST-1 can catalyze H_2O_2 toward •OH generation for *E. coli* and MRSA disinfection in vitro, suggesting broad antimicrobial spectrum effects that could be ascribed to a large amount of •OH generation disrupting the bacterial antioxidant system. Moreover, HKUST-1 could accelerate wound healing without significant biological toxicity to major organs or side effects. Therefore, this work has provided MOFs with different structural dimensions, having variable POD-like activity as a new antimicrobial strategy, and expanded the potential applications of MOFs in biomedical and clinical fields.

Supplementary Materials: The following supporting information can be downloaded at: https://www.mdpi.com/article/10.3390/ijms24043173/s1.

Author Contributions: C.L.: Data curation; Formal analysis; Software; Visualization; Writing—original draft. X.G.: Data curation; Methodology; Software. F.M.: Validation; Software. D.S.: Conceptualization; Funding acquisition; Investigation; Project administration; Supervision; Writing—review and editing. All authors have read and agreed to the published version of the manuscript.

Funding: This work was supported by the National Natural Science Foundation of China (82003710), the Natural Science Foundation of Guangdong Province (2020A1515010075), the Project of Educational Commission of Guangdong Province (2021ZDZX2012), the National Key Clinical Specialty Construction Project (Clinical Pharmacy), and High-Level Clinical Key Specialty (Clinical Pharmacy) in Guangdong Province.

Institutional Review Board Statement: All animal procedures were performed following the Guidelines for Care and Use of Laboratory Animals of Guangdong Pharmaceutical University and approved (NO. gdpulacspf2017523) by the Animal Ethics Committee according to the principles outlined in the Declaration for all animal experimental investigations.

Informed Consent Statement: Not applicable.

Data Availability Statement: The data used to support the findings of this study are available from the corresponding author upon request.

Acknowledgments: We thank the Care and Use of Laboratory Animals of Guangdong Pharmaceutical University for excellent animal care, rigorous observations, and detailed reports.

Conflicts of Interest: The authors declare that they have no known competing financial interest or personal relationship that could have influenced the work reported in this paper.

References

1. Furukawa, H.; Cordova, K.E.; O'Keeffe, M.; Yaghi, O.M. The chemistry and applications of metal-organic frameworks. *Science* **2013**, *341*, 1230444. [CrossRef]
2. Xie, Y.; Shi, X.; Chen, L.; Lu, J.; Lu, X.; Sun, D.; Zhang, L. Direct electrodeposition of bimetallic nanostructures on Co-based MOFs for electrochemical sensing of hydrogen peroxide. *Front. Chem.* **2022**, *10*, 856003. [CrossRef] [PubMed]
3. Yang, J.; Yang, Y.W. Metal-organic frameworks for biomedical applications. *Small* **2020**, *16*, e1906846. [CrossRef] [PubMed]
4. Sun, D.P.; Yang, D.C.; Wei, P.; Liu, B.; Chen, Z.G.; Zhang, L.Y.; Lu, J. One-step electrodeposition of silver nanostructures on 2D/3D metal-organic framework ZIF-67: Comparison and application in electrochemical detection of hydrogen peroxide. *ACS Appl. Mater. Interfaces* **2020**, *12*, 41960–41968. [CrossRef] [PubMed]
5. Liu, X.; Liu, F.; Ding, S.; Shen, J.; Zhu, K. Sublethal levels of antibiotics promote bacterial persistence in epithelial cells. *Adv. Sci.* **2020**, *7*, 1900840. [CrossRef]

6. Zhang, S.; Rong, F.L.; Guo, C.P.; Duan, F.H.; He, L.H.; Wang, M.H.; Zhang, Z.H.; Kang, M.M.; Du, M. Metal-organic frameworks (MOFs) based electrochemical biosensors for early cancer diagnosis in vitro. *Coord. Chem. Rev.* **2021**, *439*, 213948. [CrossRef]
7. Dong, L.Z.; Ran, F.S.; Ying, G.C.; Cong, L.W.; Xiang, C.J.; Hong, L.B.; Qiang, L.J. Metal-organic framework (MOF)-based nanomaterials for biomedical applications. *Curr. Med. Chem.* **2019**, *26*, 3341–3369.
8. Xie, X.; Ke, R.; Cheng, C.; Wang, Y.-H.; Song, Z.; Zhang, C.D.; Wang, H.S. Multiple adsorption properties of aptamers on metal-organic frameworks for nucleic acid assay. *Biosens. Bioelectron.* **2021**, *176*, 112896. [CrossRef]
9. Fan, X.; Shi, Q.F.; Nan, Z.D. Facile synthesis of Cu-CuFeO nanozymes for sensitive assay of H_2O_2 and GSH. *Dalton Trans.* **2020**, *49*, 12780–12792.
10. Lin, C.; Guo, X.; Chen, L.; You, T.; Lu, J.; Sun, D. Ultrathin trimetallic metal–organic framework nanosheets for accelerating bacteria-infected wound healing. *J. Colloid Interface Sci.* **2022**, *628*, 731–744. [CrossRef]
11. Long, Y.; Li, L.; Xu, T.; Wu, X.; Gao, Y.; Huang, J.; He, C.; Ma, T.; Ma, L.; Cheng, C.; et al. Hedgehog artificial macrophage with atomic-catalytic centers to combat Drug-resistant bacteria. *Nat. Commun.* **2021**, *12*, 6143. [CrossRef] [PubMed]
12. Shams, S.; Ahmad, W.; Memon, A.H.; Shams, S.; Wei, Y.; Yuan, Q.; Liang, H. Cu/H3BTC MOF as a potential antibacterial therapeutic agent against *Staphylococcus aureus* and *Escherichia coli*. *New J. Chem.* **2020**, *44*, 17671–17678. [CrossRef]
13. Li, L.; Cao, L.J.; Xiang, X.; Wu, X.Z.; Ma, L.; Chen, F.; Cao, S.J.; Cheng, C.; Deng, D.W.; Qiu, L. ROS-Catalytic transition-metal-based enzymatic nanoagents for tumor and bacterial eradication. *Adv. Funct. Mater.* **2021**, *32*, 2107530. [CrossRef]
14. Chakrabarti, S.; Chattopadhyay, P.; Islam, J.; Ray, S.; Raju, P.S.; Mazumder, B. Aspects of nanomaterials in wound healing. *Curr. Drug Deliv.* **2019**, *16*, 26–41. [CrossRef]
15. Mao, Z.H.; Chen, J.; Wang, Y.D.; Xia, J.J.; Zhang, Y.J.; Zhang, W.W.; Zhu, H.; Hu, X.J.; Chen, H.X. Copper metal organic framework as natural oxidase mimic for effective killing of Gram-negative and Gram-positive bacteria. *Nanoscale* **2022**, *14*, 9474–9484. [CrossRef]
16. Guo, L.; Sun, J.; Zhang, W.; Hou, L.; Liang, L.; Liu, Y.; Yuan, C. Bottom-up fabrication of 1D Cu-based conductive metal–organic framework nanowires as a high-rate anode towards efficient lithium storage. *ChemSusChem* **2019**, *12*, 5051–5058. [CrossRef]
17. Guo, X.J.; Lin, C.Y.; Zhang, M.J.; Duan, X.W.; Dong, X.R.; Sun, D.P.; Pan, J.B.; You, T.H. 2D/3D Copper-based metal-organic frameworks for electrochemical detection of hydrogen peroxide. *Front. Chem.* **2021**, *9*, 743637. [CrossRef]
18. Zhao, M.T.; Huang, Y.; Peng, Y.W.; Huang, Z.Q.; Ma, Q.L.; Zhang, H. Two-dimensional metal-organic framework nanosheets: Synthesis and applications. *Chem. Soc. Rev.* **2018**, *47*, 6267–6295. [CrossRef]
19. Cai, X.; Xie, Z.; Li, D.; Kassymova, M.; Zang, S.-Q.; Jiang, H.-L. Nano-sized metal-organic frameworks: Synthesis and applications. *Coord. Chem. Rev.* **2020**, *417*, 213366. [CrossRef]
20. Diring, S.; Furukawa, S.; Takashima, Y.; Tsuruoka, T.; Kitagawa, S. Controlled multiscale synthesis of porous coordination polymer innano/micro regimes. *Chem. Mater.* **2010**, *22*, 4531–4538. [CrossRef]
21. Tsuruoka, T.; Furukawa, S.; Takashima, Y.; Yoshida, K.; Isoda, S.; Kitagawa, S. Nanoporous nanorods fabricated by coordination modulation and oriented attachment growth. *Angew. Chem. Int. Ed.* **2009**, *48*, 4739–4743. [CrossRef] [PubMed]
22. Cun, J.E.; Fan, X.; Pan, Q.Q.; Gao, W.X.; Luo, K.; He, B.; Pu, Y.J. Copper-based metal-organic frameworks for biomedical applications. *Adv. Colloid Interface Sci.* **2022**, *305*, 102686. [CrossRef] [PubMed]
23. Wang, S.Y.; Yan, F.; Ren, P.; Li, Y.; Wu, Q.; Fang, X.D.; Chen, F.F.; Wang, C. Incorporation of metal-organic frameworks into electrospun chitosan/poly (vinyl alcohol) nanofibrous membrane with enhanced antibacterial activity for wound dressing application. *Int. J. Biol. Macromol.* **2020**, *158*, 9–17. [CrossRef]
24. Shanmugapriya, K.; Kang, H.W. Engineering pharmaceutical nanocarriers for photodynamic therapy on wound healing: Review. *Mater. Sci. Eng. C Mater. Biol. Appl.* **2019**, *105*, 110110. [CrossRef] [PubMed]
25. Esmaeili, E.; Eslami-Arshaghi, T.; Hosseinzadeh, S.; Elahirad, E.; Jamalpoor, Z.; Hatamie, S.; Soleimani, M. The biomedical potential of cellulose acetate/polyurethane nanofibrous mats containing reduced graphene oxide/silver nanocomposites and curcumin: Antimicrobial performance and cutaneous wound healing. *Int. J. Biol. Macromol.* **2020**, *152*, 418–427. [CrossRef] [PubMed]
26. Zhang, Y.Y.; Xu, J.; Chai, Y.S.; Zhang, J.; Hu, Z.Q.; Zhou, H.Y. Nano-silver modified porcine small intestinal submucosa for the treatment of infected partial-thickness burn wounds. *Burns* **2019**, *45*, 950–956. [CrossRef] [PubMed]
27. Mihai, M.M.; Dima, M.B.; Dima, B.; Holban, A.M. Nanomaterials for wound healing and infection control. *Materials* **2019**, *12*, 2176. [CrossRef]
28. Qian, W.; Yan, C.; He, D.F.; Yu, X.Z.; Yuan, L.; Liu, M.L.; Luo, G.X.; Deng, J. pH-triggered charge-reversible of glycol chitosan conjugated carboxyl graphene for enhancing photothermal ablation of focal infection. *Acta Biomater.* **2018**, *69*, 256–264. [CrossRef]
29. Mirzahosseinipour, M.; Khorsandi, K.; Hosseinzadeh, R.; Ghazaeian, M.; Shahidi, F.K. Antimicrobial photodynamic and wound healing activity of curcumin encapsulated in silica nanoparticles. *Photodiagn. Photodyn. Ther.* **2020**, *29*, 101639. [CrossRef]
30. Wang, S.G.; Chen, Y.C.; Chen, Y.C. Antibacterial gold nanoparticle-based photothermal killing of vancomycin-resistant bacteria. *Nanomedicine* **2018**, *13*, 1405–1416. [CrossRef]
31. Yu, X.Z.; He, D.F.; Zhang, X.M.; Zhang, H.M.; Song, J.L.; Shi, D.Z.; Fan, Y.H.; Luo, G.X.; Deng, J. Surface-adaptive and initiator-loaded graphene as a light-induced generator with free radicals for drug-resistant bacteria eradication. *ACS Appl. Mater. Interfaces* **2019**, *11*, 1766–1781. [CrossRef] [PubMed]
32. Alavi, M.; Nokhodchi, A. An overview on antimicrobial and wound healing properties of ZnO nanobiofilms, hydrogels, and bionanocomposites based on cellulose, chitosan, and alginate polymers. *Carbohydr. Polym.* **2020**, *227*, 115349. [CrossRef] [PubMed]

33. Zhao, M.T.; Wang, Y.X.; Ma, Q.L.; Huang, Y.; Zhang, X.; Ping, J.F.; Zhang, Z.C.; Lu, Q.P.; Yu, Y.F.; Xu, H.; et al. Ultrathin 2D metal-organic framework nanosheets. *Adv. Mater.* **2015**, *27*, 7372–7378. [CrossRef] [PubMed]
34. Chui, S.S.Y.; Lo, S.M.F.; Charmant, J.P.H.; Orpen, A.G.; Williams, I.D. A chemically functionalizable nanoporous material Cu-3(TMA)(2)(H_2O)(3)(n). *Science* **1999**, *283*, 1148–1150. [CrossRef]
35. Wang, S.J.; Xu, D.P.; Ma, L.; Qiu, J.X.; Wang, X.; Dong, Q.L.; Zhang, Q.; Pan, J.; Liu, Q. Ultrathin ZIF-67 nanosheets as a colorimetric biosensing platform for peroxidase-like catalysis. *Anal. Bioanal. Chem.* **2018**, *410*, 7145–7152. [CrossRef]
36. Wang, C.; Gao, J.; Tan, H. Integrated antibody with catalytic metal–organic framework for colorimetric immunoassay. *ACS Appl. Mater. Interfaces* **2018**, *10*, 25113–25120. [CrossRef] [PubMed]
37. Wang, J.Y.; Li, W.Y.; Zheng, Y.Q. Nitro-functionalized metal-organic frameworks with catalase mimic properties for glutathione detection. *Analyst* **2019**, *144*, 6041–6047. [CrossRef]
38. Yu, H.; Wu, H.L.; Tian, X.M.; Zhou, Y.F.; Ren, C.G.; Wang, Z.H. A nano-sized Cu-MOF with high peroxidase-like activity and its potential application in colorimetric detection of H_2O_2 and glucose. *RSC Adv.* **2021**, *11*, 26963–26973. [CrossRef]
39. Yang, H.J.; Liu, J.; Feng, X.; Nie, F.; Yang, G.P. A novel copper-based metal-organic framework as a peroxidase-mimicking enzyme and its glucose chemiluminescence sensing application. *Anal. Bioanal. Chem.* **2021**, *413*, 4407–4416. [CrossRef]
40. Liao, X.; Xu, Q.; Sun, H.; Liu, W.; Chen, Y.; Xia, X.H.; Wang, C. Plasmonic nanozymes: Localized surface plasmonic resonance regulates reaction kinetics and antibacterial performance. *J. Phys. Chem. Lett.* **2022**, *13*, 312–323. [CrossRef]
41. Gao, L.; Zhuang, J.; Nie, L.; Zhang, J.; Zhang, Y.; Gu, N.; Wang, T.; Feng, J.; Yang, D.; Perrett, S.; et al. Intrinsic peroxidase-like activity of ferromagnetic nanoparticles. *Nat. Nanotechnol.* **2007**, *2*, 577–583. [CrossRef] [PubMed]
42. Tang, Q.; Cao, S.; Ma, T.; Xiang, X.; Luo, H.; Borovskikh, P.; Rodriguez, R.D.; Guo, Q.; Qiu, L.; Cheng, C. Engineering biofunctional enzyme-mimics for catalytic therapeutics and diagnostics. *Adv. Funct. Mater.* **2020**, *31*, 2007475. [CrossRef]
43. Wu, R.B.; Qian, X.K.; Yu, F.; Liu, H.; Zhou, K.; Wei, J.; Huang, Y.Z. MOF-templated formation of porous CuO hollow octahedra for lithium-ion battery anode materials. *J. Mater. Chem. A* **2013**, *1*, 11126–11129. [CrossRef]

International Journal of *Molecular Sciences*

MDPI

Article

The In Vitro Impact of Isoxazole Derivatives on Pathogenic Biofilm and Cytotoxicity of Fibroblast Cell Line

Urszula Bąchor [1], Adam Junka [2,*], Malwina Brożyna [2] and Marcin Mączyński [1]

1 Department of Organic Chemistry and Drug Technology, Faculty of Pharmacy, Wroclaw Medical University, 50-556 Wroclaw, Poland

2 Unique Application Model Laboratory, Department of Pharmaceutical Microbiology and Parasitology, Faculty of Pharmacy, Wroclaw Medical University, 50-556 Wroclaw, Poland

* Correspondence: adam.junka@umw.edu.pl; Tel.: +48-71-784-0675

Abstract: The microbial, biofilm-based infections of chronic wounds are one of the major challenges of contemporary medicine. The use of topically administered antiseptic agents is essential to treat wound-infecting microorganisms. Due to observed microbial tolerance/resistance against specific clinically-used antiseptics, the search for new, efficient agents is of pivotal meaning. Therefore, in this work, 15 isoxazole derivatives were scrutinized against leading biofilm wound pathogens *Staphylococcus aureus* and *Pseudomonas aeruginosa*, and against *Candida albicans* fungus. For this purpose, the minimal inhibitory concentration, biofilm reduction in microtitrate plates, modified disk diffusion methods and antibiofilm dressing activity measurement methods were applied. Moreover, the cytotoxicity and cytocompatibility of derivatives was tested toward wound bed-forming cells, referred to as fibroblasts, using normative methods. Obtained results revealed that all isoxazole derivatives displayed antimicrobial activity and low cytotoxic effect, but antimicrobial activity of two derivatives, 2-(cyclohexylamino)-1-(5-nitrothiophen-2-yl)-2-oxoethyl 5-amino-3-methyl-1,2-oxazole-4-carboxylate (**PUB9**) and 2-(benzylamino)-1-(5-nitrothiophen-2-yl)-2-oxoethyl 5-amino-3-methyl-1,2-oxazole-4-carboxylate (**PUB10**), was noticeably higher compared to the other compounds analyzed, especially **PUB9** with regard to *Staphylococcus aureus*, with a minimal inhibitory concentration more than x1000 lower compared to the remaining derivatives. The **PUB9** and **PUB10** derivatives were able to reduce more than 90% of biofilm-forming cells, regardless of the species, displaying at the same time none (**PUB9**) or moderate (**PUB10**) cytotoxicity against fibroblasts and high (**PUB9**) or moderate (**PUB10**) cytocompatibility against these wound cells. Therefore, taking into consideration the clinical demand for new antiseptic agents for non-healing wound treatment, **PUB9** seems to be a promising candidate to be further tested in advanced animal models and later, if satisfactory results are obtained, in the clinical setting.

Keywords: isoxazole; Michael addition; Passerini reaction; anti-bacterial activity; cytotoxicity; antiseptics

Citation: Bąchor, U.; Junka, A.; Brożyna, M.; Mączyński, M. The In Vitro Impact of Isoxazole Derivatives on Pathogenic Biofilm and Cytotoxicity of Fibroblast Cell Line. *Int. J. Mol. Sci.* **2023**, *24*, 2997. https://doi.org/10.3390/ijms24032997

Academic Editors: Cinzia Pagano, César Viseras and Luana Perioli

Received: 14 December 2022
Revised: 24 January 2023
Accepted: 31 January 2023
Published: 3 February 2023

1. Introduction

The non-healing wound is referred to as the discontinuity of skin and subcutaneous tissue, which does not heal in an orderly set of stages and in a predictable amount of time. It is estimated that procedures related with management and treatment of chronic wounds consume approximately 1–3% of European Union public health budgets [1]. The presence of non-healing wounds significantly increases risk of serious health loss and, in case of wound infection, even death of the patient. The non-healing wounds are frequently colonized by differentiated consortia of bacteria, of whom Gram-positive *Staphylococcus aureus* and Gram-negative *Pseudomonas aeruginosa* should be distinguished because of their particular tendency to spread in the wound bed and to cause local, biofilm-based infections, which may develop into the life-threatening systemic forms [2]. In turn, fungi, such as yeast-like *Candida albicans*, are less frequently isolated from the non-healing wounds. Nevertheless, they are an important component of so called mixed (duo- or multi-species) biofilms in this niche; therefore, their potential impact on the process of wound healing should not be neglected [3]. The present treatment algorithms for critically colonized/infected non-healing wounds consist of wound bed debridement (of surgical, chemical/enzymatical or biological nature), use of modern dressings and application of locally administered antimicrobials referred to as the antiseptics [4]. The last-mentioned measure, used for both prophylactic and treatment purposes, are compounds of rapid antimicrobial action and preferentially of low or none cytotoxicity toward cells forming the wound bed, i.e., fibroblasts and keratinocytes [5]. Nevertheless, in recent years, the phenomenon of increased microbial tolerance and/or resistance toward many of the most widespread antiseptics occurred, just to mention cases of chlorhexidine and octenidine dihydrochloride [6,7]. Because use of antiseptics in the treatment of infected non-healing wounds is a critical factor with regard to clinical success (wound closure), presently the increasing search for new compounds, which may replace or improve activity of existing antiseptics, can be observed. One of the examples of such compounds are bioactive small molecules of a molecular weight <900 Da. These low-mass molecules make up presently 90% of pharmaceutical drugs (including such common drugs as aspirin or insulin). Thanks to their low size, such drugs can be administered orally and are able to pass through cell membranes and reach intracellular targets [8].

Much attention has been paid to the synthesis of heterocycles containing both nitrogen and oxygen due to their broad spectrum of biological and pharmacological activities. Among the wide range of pharmacologically important heterocycles, isoxazoles play a significant role in the field of medicinal chemistry. This heterocycle is considered as an important class of compounds in medicinal chemistry because of its wide spectrum of targets and varied biological application such as antimicrobial [9], antiviral [10], anticancer [11], anti-inflammatory [12], immunomodulatory [13], anticonvulsant [14] or antidiabetic properties [15]. The key feature of these heterocycles is that they exhibit the typical properties of an aromatic system but the same contain a weak nitrogen-oxygen bond that can be easily cleaved under certain reaction conditions. Thus, isoxazoles are very useful substrates since the ring system stability allows the derivatization of substituents to give functionally complex derivatives. Emerging research interest on the isoxazole moiety results from fact that this moiety is a common synthetic building block in searching for new compounds exhibiting antimicrobial and antifungal activities [16,17]. Synthesis of isoxazole derivatives is widely carried out through different methods such as condensation, cyclomerization or cycloaddition. Thus, the synthesis of new isoxazole derivatives is a very attractive aspect in the research and development field for both medicinal and organic chemistry. Due to these facts as well as to its relatively easy synthesis, isoxazole rings have become an object of our interest. Inspired by these facts we planned to synthesize some more derivatives of isoxazoles using different methods of functionalization such as Passerini multicomponent reaction and Michael addition.

Of note, the presence of an isoxazole moiety translates frequently into antimicrobial potential of such low-mass molecules as antibiotics: sulfisoxazole, cloxacilin, dicloxacilin or sulfamethozaole [18]. Isoxazole derivatives obtained earlier by our team also possessed a number of biological activities, including those of immunosuppressive [19–22], antiviral [23] or anticancer character [24]. It is well-recognized that conjugation of a small molecule to the isoxazole core offers a possibility to obtain new derivatives of biological activity [25]. As an example, maleimides are one of the most widely used functional groups for 1,4-conjugate addition. Their chemistry is widely used in the site-selective modification of thiol- and amine-containing compounds [26]. Although some types of nucleophiles can be involved in such a conjugation, ubiquitous heteronucleophiles (e.g., thiols, amines, and alcohols) are used the most frequently and, therefore, they are the most scrutinized and developed. For a number of years, these conjugate additions were limited to organic chemistry. Nevertheless, in the last few decades they have been also notably used in bioorganic and polymer chemistry for bioconjugation reactions and step-growth polymerizations, respectively, thanks to their excellent efficiency and ambient reactivity [27]. The α,β-unsaturated bond presented in maleimides allows a process of easy functionalization. Moreover, the delocalization of the double bonds (two carbonyl groups and one double bond in the ring) gives maleimides electron acceptor and dienophile characteristics [28].

Thus, click nucleophilic conjugate addition via aza-Michael reaction has become one of the ways to obtain a series of new isoxazole derivatives in this work (**MAL1-5** series) (Figure 1). In these reactions, we used 5-amino-3-methyl-isoxazole-4-carbohydrazide as a substrate [29,30]. We have employed this compound because this isoxazole derivative has attracted much attention due to its known biological activity [31]. According to the earlier investigation, this compound exhibits immunomodulatory properties, which makes it useful in further research and chemical modification [32,33]. Because the different approaches of modification of substituents in position 4 of 5-amino-3-methyl-isoxazole-4-carboxylic acid allow to obtain derivatives of different biological activity [34], we decided to employ this unnatural amino acid to a Passerini three-component reaction (**PUB1-10** series) (Figure 1). This type of reaction is the oldest isocyanide-based multicomponent reaction employing isocyanide (R_2), aldehyde/ketone (R_1) and carboxylic acid to give acyclic depsipeptides [35]. This type of peptide contains one or more ester bonds in addition to the amide bonds, and has become important lead structures in the development of new synthetic drugs. One example of this class of compounds is enniatins, which are cyclohexadepsipeptides with a range of biological activities, including those of antibiotic and cytotoxic character [36].

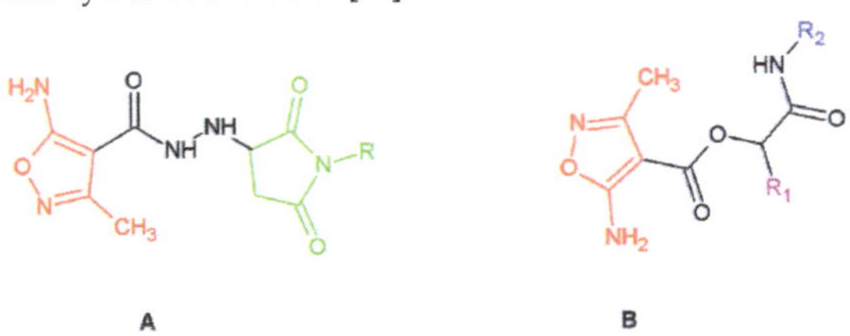

Figure 1. Designed isoxazole derivatives ((**A**) MAL1-5 series; (**B**) **PUB1-10** series: R1-aldehyde/ketone residue; R2-isocyanide residue).

Therefore, the aim of this work was to scrutinize obtained isoxazole derivatives with regard to their antimicrobial (including antibiofilm) potential, as well as their impact on fibroblast cell lines. Moreover, following the recent trends of fortification of wound dressings with antimicrobials other than antibiotics or clinically used antiseptics, we introduced the isoxazole derivatives to the experimental dressing made of polymeric bacterial cellulose and assessed its activity against biofilms [37–39]. Such a goal fits in the current trend of research aiming for introduction of new agents which can be considered an alternative for already existing antiseptic agents used in the prophylaxis and treatment of critically colonized non-healing wounds.

2. Results and Discussion

2.1. Chemistry

A series of isoxazole derivatives referred to in this work as the **PUB** series (**PUB1-8**) were obtained by our team earlier and their effects on phytohemagglutinin A (PHA)-induced proliferation of human peripheral blood mononuclear cells (PBMC), production of tumor necrosis factor alpha (TNFα) in human whole blood cultures stimulated with lipopolysaccharide (LPS) and two-way mixed lymphocyte reaction (MLR) of PBMC were investigated [25]. These compounds as well as **PUB9** and **PUB10** were obtained via Passerini three-component reaction by using methods published previously [25]. Briefly, *N′*-substituted 5-amino-3-methyl-isoxazole-4-carbohydrazide derivatives were synthesized using click nucleophilic conjugate addition via aza-Michael reaction according to Figure 2 presented below.

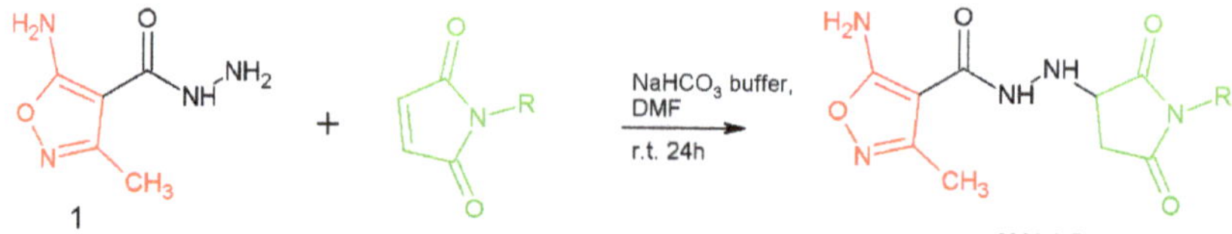

Figure 2. Synthesis of isoxazole linked maleimide conjugates (**MAL1-5**).

Maleimide is an unsaturated imide that forms pyrrole-type ring structures (1*H*-pyrrole-2,5-diones). The double bond presented in maleimides is highly electron-deficient due to the presence of two carbonyl groups, which consequently makes maleimides highly reactive and undergo nucleophilic addition reaction, called Michael addition, and is a type of "click chemistry". The Michael addition with a primary amine is faster and reaches a higher conversion rate than its reactions with thiols [19]. A new series of *N*-substituted hydrazide derivatives was obtained by reacting 5-amino-3-methyl-isoxazole-4-carbohydrazide with different commercially available maleimides. This isoxazole derivative exhibits the unique reactivity, which is due to the selectivity of reaction of the amino groups present in this compound. The maleimides react with the amine group presented in hydrazide moiety, whereas we did not observe any product of reaction between the maleimide and NH_2 group derived from the isoxazole ring. This unique property of the amino group attached to the isoxazole ring has been examined by our team in different kinds of reaction and as a result it has been shown that it remains unreactive in almost types of reactions [40,41]. The reaction is pH selective and favors primary amines in more alkaline conditions, but it unfortunately also increases the rate of hydrolysis of the maleimide group, resulting in a maleamic acid which is a non-reactive form of maleimide. Therefore, one of the most important tasks in our work was the optimalization of the reaction conditions to avoid this synthetic problem. In the course of the conducted chemical synthesis, it turned out that the most suitable pH for carrying out this reaction was pH = 7.8, which made it possible to use a bicarbonate buffer. By employing a slight excess of 5-amino-3-methyl-isoxazole-4-carbohydrazide, we ensured the full consumption of each of the used maleimides, consequently improving the yields of isolated products of conjugation to obtain a new series of isoxazole derivatives (series **MAL1-5**) (Figure 2).

2.2. *Synthesis and Structural Characterization*

The synthesis and characterization of compounds **PUB1-8** has been published previously [25]. Compounds **PUB9** and **PUB10** were obtained according to the method described previously and purified by crystallization from methanol (**PUB10**) and by column chromatography (**PUB9**) with silica gel 230–400 mesh (60 Å); mobile phase: ethyl acetate/chloroform = 3/7 (v/v), sample dissolved in chloroform. Structures of new compounds and their spectral analysis are shown in the Supplementary Material (Figures S16–S21).

2.2.1. 2-(cyclohexylamino)-1-(5-nitrothiophen-2-yl)-2-oxoethyl 5-amino-3-methyl-1,2-oxazole-4-carboxylate (**PUB9**)

30 % yield; m.p. 199–200 °C, beige solid. ^{1}H NMR (300 MHz, DMSO-d_6) δ (ppm): 1.01–1.34 (m, 5H), 1.50–1.80 (m, 6H). 2.25 (s, 3H, CH_3 group of isoxazole ring), 4.09 (q, J = 5.3 Hz, 1H), 6.34 (s, 1H), 7.26–7.31 (d, J = 4.22 Hz, 1H), 7.91 (bs, 2H, NH_2 group from isoxazole ring), 8.05 (d, J = 4.3 Hz, 1H), 8.42 (d, J = 7.8 Hz, 1H). ^{13}C NMR (75 MHz, DMSO-d_6) δ (ppm): 12.43, 24.70, 24.79, 25.52, 31.13, 32.34, 32.47, 39.15, 39.43, 39.71, 39.98, 40.26, 40.54, 40.81, 48.49, 49.05, 70.48, 84.42, 127.18, 129.91, 147.31, 161.31, 165.62, 172.65. ESI-MS: m/z calculated for formula $C_{17}H_{20}N_4O_6S$ $[M\text{-}H]^-$ 407.103, found 407.103.

2.2.2. 2-(benzylamino)-1-(5-nitrothiophen-2-yl)-2-oxoethyl 5-amino-3-methyl-1,2-oxazole-4-carboxylate (**PUB10**)

20% yield; m.p. 201–202 °C, beige solid. ^{1}H NMR (300 MHz, DMSO-d_6) δ (ppm): 2.25 (s, 3H, CH_3 groups of isoxazole ring), 4.29–4.35 (d, J = 5.8 Hz, 2H), 6.44 (s, 1H), 7.16–7.35 (m, 6H), 7.94 (bs, 2H, NH_2 group from isoxazole ring), 8.04–8.08 (d, J = 5.5 Hz, 1H), 9.02 (t, J = 5.9 Hz, 1H). ^{13}C NMR (126 MHz, DMSO-d_6) δ (ppm): 12.52, 42.80, 70.74, 84.45, 127.38, 127.46, 127.60, 128.82, 129.93, 138.98, 146.86, 151.42, 159.37, 161.40, 166.90, 172.72. ESI-MS: m/z calculated for formula $C_{18}H_{16}N_4O_6S$ $[M-H]^-$ 415.072, found 415.076.

The novel target compounds (**MAL1-5**) were synthesized according to the procedure described below using 5-amino-3-methylisoxazole-4-carbohydrazide, which was obtained by a sequence of very efficient processes described in detail in the following literature entries [29,42,43]) and different commercially available *N*-substituted maleimides as starting materials.

2.2.3. General Procedure for Preparation of a Series of Compounds (MAL1-5)

To a solution of 5-amino-3-methylisoxazole-4-carbohydrazide (**1**) (2.0 mmol) in DMF (5 mL) was added a solution of each *N*-maleimide (1.8 mmol) in 5 mL DMF with 2 mL of $NaHCO_3$ buffer (8.4 mg $NaHCO_3$ dissolved in 10 mL of water). The reaction mixture was stirred at room temperature for 24 h, then DMF was removed using a gentle stream of air. The final product was purified by crystallization from methanol. Spectral analysis of new compounds as well as their structures are shown in the Supplementary Material (Figures S1–S15).

2.2.4. 5-amino-N′-(2,5-dioxopyrrolidin-3-yl)-3-methyl-1,2-oxazole-4-carbohydrazide (MAL1)

40% yield; m.p. 220–221 °C, orange solid. ^{1}H NMR (300 MHz, DMSO-d_6) δ (ppm): 2.21 (s, 3H, CH_3 group of isoxazole ring), 2.56–2.90 (m, 2H), 3.90–4.04 (m, 1H), 5.42–5.76 (m, 1H), 7.25–7.62 (bs, 2H, NH_2 group from isoxazole ring), 8.34–8.87 (d, 1H, J = 5.5 Hz), 10.97–11.42 (s, 1H). ^{13}C NMR (75 MHz, DMSO-d_6) δ (ppm): 11.54, 35.21, 58.91, 86.23, 157.25, 163.72, 171.02, 177.24, 178.03. ESI-MS: m/z calculated for formula $C_9H_{11}N_5O_4$ $[M+H]^+$ 254.088, found 254.081.

2.2.5. 5-amino-3-methyl-N′-(1-methyl-2,5-dioxopyrrolidin-3-yl)-1,2-oxazole-4-carbohydrazide (MAL2)

55% yield; m.p. 173–174 °C, orange solid. ^{1}H NMR (300 MHz, DMSO-d_6) δ (ppm): 2.19 (s, 3H, CH_3 group of isoxazole ring), 2.54–2.64 (m, 1H), 2.82 (s, 3H, CH_3 group of maleimide moiety), 2.85–2.92 (m, 1H), 3.95–4.06 (m, 1H), 5.62–5.78 (m, 1H), 7.41–7.48 (bs, 2H, NH_2 group from isoxazole ring), 8.56–8.73 (d, 1H, J = 5.39 Hz). ^{13}C NMR (126 MHz, DMSO-d_6) δ (ppm): 11.68, 24.43, 34.22, 57.89, 86.62, 157.43, 163.88, 171.19, 176.09, 176.76. ESI-MS: m/z calculated for formula $C_{10}H_{13}N_5O_4$ $[M+H]^+$ 268.104, found 268.098.

2.2.6. 6-(3-{2-[(5-amino-3-methyl-1,2-oxazol-4-yl)carbonyl]hydrazinyl}-2,5-dioxopyrrolidin-1-yl)hexanoic acid (MAL3)

37% yield; m.p. 143–144 °C, white solid. ^{1}H NMR (300 MHz, DMSO-d_6) δ (ppm): 1.10–1.56 (m, 6H), 2.08–2.18 (m, 2H), 2.19 (s, 3H, CH_3 group of isoxazole ring), 2.54–2.67 (m, 2H), 2.80–2.93 (m, 1H), 3.93–4.08 (m, 1H), 5.63–5.82 (m, 1H), 7.37–7.55 (bs, 2H, NH_2 group from isoxazole ring), 8.56–8.70 (d, 1H, J = 4.91), 11.81–12.09 (bs, 1H, COOH group from maleimide moiety). ^{13}C NMR (75 MHz, DMSO-d_6) δ (ppm): 11.99, 24.45, 26.16, 27.34, 33.86, 34.27, 38.15, 58.00, 86.65, 157.66, 164.32, 171.54, 174.80, 176.31, 177.02. ESI-MS: m/z calculated for formula $C_{15}H_{21}N_5O_6$ $[M+Na]^+$ 390.138, found 390.132.

2.2.7. 5-amino-N′-(1-cyclohexyl-2,5-dioxopyrrolidin-3-yl)-3-methyl-1,2-oxazole-4-carbohydrazide (MAL4)

27% yield; m.p. 193–195 °C, white solid. ^{1}H NMR (300 MHz, DMSO-d_6) δ (ppm): 0.94–2.08 (m, 10H), 2.20 (s, 3H, CH_3 group of isoxazole ring), 2.51–2.61 (m, 1H), 2.74–2.88 (m,

1H), 3.72–3.86 (m, 1H), 3.89–4.00 (m, 1H), 5.62–5.73 (m, 1H), 7.37–7.49 (bs, 2H, NH_2 group from isoxazole ring), 8.53–8.73 (d, 1H, J = 5.4 Hz). ^{13}C NMR (75 MHz, DMSO-d_6) δ (ppm): 11.53, 24.81, 25.31, 28.36, 33.63, 50.53, 57.09, 86.15, 157.17, 163.85, 171.08, 175.79, 176.55. ESI-MS: m/z calculated for formula $C_{15}H_{21}N_5O_4$ $[M+H]^+$ 336.166, found 336.161.

2.2.8. 5-amino-N′-[1-(4-chlorophenyl)-2,5-dioxopyrrolidin-3-yl]-3-methyl-1,2-oxazole-4-carbohydrazide (MAL5)

45% yield; m.p. 217–220 °C, white solid. ^1H NMR (300 MHz, DMSO-d_6) δ (ppm): 2.22 (s, 3H, CH_3 group of isoxazole ring), 2.69–2.87 (m, 1H), 2.95–3.19 (m, 1H), 4.10–4.27 (m, 1H), 5.81–5.94 (m, 1H), 7.25–7.37 (d, 2H, J = 8.11 Hz), 7.44–7.53 (bs, 2H, NH_2 group from isoxazole ring), 7.51–7.64 (d, 2H, J = 8.28 Hz). ^{13}C NMR (75 MHz, DMSO-d_6) δ (ppm): 11.56, 34.23, 57.98, 86.21, 128.57, 128.96, 131.08, 132.72, 157.25, 163.87, 171.04, 174.77, 175.48. ESI-MS: m/z calculated for formula $C_{15}H_{14}ClN_5O_4$ $[M+H]^+$ 364.081, found 364.072.

2.3. Biology

In the first line of biological line of experiments, the minimal inhibitory concentrations of analyzed compounds were evaluated using a microplate model towards Gram-positive and Gram-negative reference pathogens and yeast-like fungus (Table 1). Obtained results indicate that the synthesized compounds acted in a more efficient manner against *C. albicans* than against *S. aureus* and *P. aeruginosa*. Nevertheless, two of the compounds (**PUB9** and **PUB10**) displayed a few hundred times higher activity against *S. aureus* compared to the remaining compounds, maintaining at the same time comparable (to the remaining compounds) activity against *P. aeruginosa* and *C. albicans*.

Table 1. The Minimal Inhibitory Concentration [mg/mL] of tested compounds towards *S. aureus* 6538, *P. aeruginosa* 15442 and *C. albicans* 103231 tested in microplate model.

	Minimal Inhibitory Concentration [mg/mL]		
	S. aureus	***P. aeruginosa***	***C. albicans***
PUB1	0.125	0.125	0.063
PUB2	0.125	0.125	0.063
PUB3	0.125	0.125	0.063
PUB4	0.25	0.125	0.063
PUB5	0.25	0.125	0.063
PUB6	0.125	0.125	0.063
PUB7	0.125	0.125	0.063
PUB8	0.125	0.125	0.063
PUB9	0.00012	0.125	0.063
PUB10	0.00024	0.063	0.02
MAL1	0.125	0.063	0.02
MAL2	0.125	0.063	0.63
MAL3	0.125	0.125	0.063
MAL4	0.125	0.063	0.063
MAL5	0.125	0.063	0.063

Compounds **PUB9** and **PUB10** were thus selected for further analyses. The first of them included assessment of biofilm reduction in the microplate model. Obtained results indicate strong (above 90%) reduction in biofilm, regardless of the strain applied (Figure 3) in concentration range of 0.125–0.25 mg/mL.

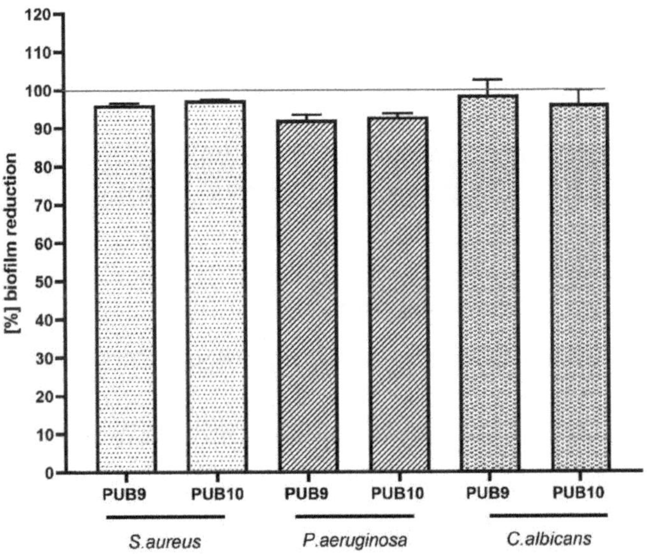

Figure 3. The [%] biofilm reduction of *S. aureus* 6538, *P. aeruginosa* 15,442 and *C. albicans* 103,231 displayed by **PUB9** and **PUB10** compounds at specific concentrations tested in microplate model. The red line shows level of 100% reduction while no reduction (0%, positive control of growth) was established for non-treated cells (maximal cellular growth).

Next, the survivability of fibroblast cells (wound bed-forming cells) was analyzed after the exposure to the range of **PUB9** and **PUB10** compounds (Figure 4). In the case of **PUB9**, the advantageous results (cytotoxicity close to none) were obtained when 0.2 mg/mL of compounds was applied, while doubling of the compound's concentration correlated with moderate level of cytotoxicity. In the case of **PUB10**, higher cytotoxicity level was observed towards fibroblasts (strong and very strong cytotoxicity when concentrations of 0.2 and 0.39 mg/mL, respectively, were applied).

The results presented in Table 1, Figures 3 and 4 allow obtaining data on the investigated compound's in vitro activity against wound pathogens and also indicate in which concentration the specific compound does not exert (or exert at the acceptable level) cytotoxicity against fibroblast cells. In the next step, another two methods assessing the impact of antimicrobials against different types of microbial consortia were performed. In the first of them, referred to as the modified disk-diffusion model, the only full inhibition of microbial growth (equal 4 mm) was observed when **PUB9** against *S. aureus* was applied (Figure 5).

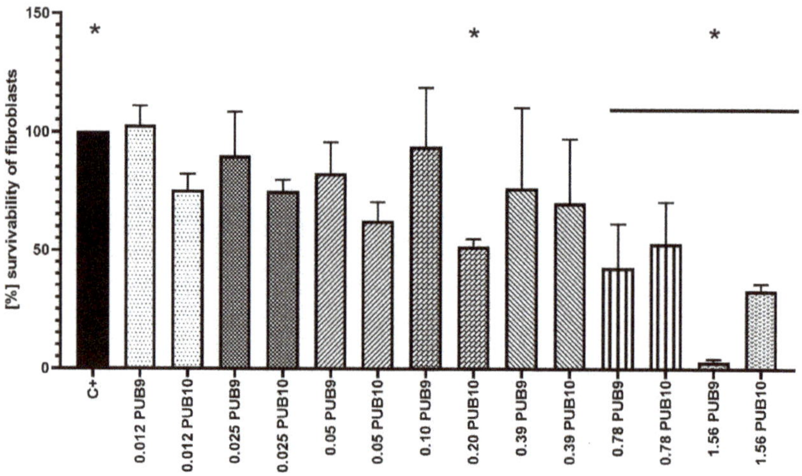

Figure 4. The survivability [%] of L929 fibroblasts exposed to the spectrum of concentrations of **PUB9** and **PUB10** compounds. The asterisks show significant ($p > 0.05$, ANOVA test with Tukey's multiple comparison test) difference in survivability between control setting (non-treated cells, considered 100% growth) and cells treated with 0.78–1.56 mg/mL of **PUB9** or **PUB10** as well as 0.20 mg/mL of **PUB10**.

Figure 5. The inhibition of staphylococcal growth zone resulting from release of **PUB9** from BC carrier in modified disk-diffusion model. The diameter of BC carrier is 18 mm.

In the case of **PUB10**, the impact was also seen only against *S. aureus*; however, within the zone of growth inhibition (equal 2 mm), distinctive microbial colonies were also observed. Therefore, it was decided to apply another experimental model to get better insight on possible activity of **PUB9** and **PUB10** against biofilm. Using a modified Antibiofilm Dressing Activity Measurement model, the reduction resulting from activity of **PUB9** and **PUB10** was assessed. In the case of **PUB9**, the [%] reduction values were 99 ± 0.1%; 99 ± 0.1%, 90.7 ± 2.4% for *S. aureus*, *C. albicans* and *P. aeruginosa*, respectively, when 0.25 mg/mL of compound was applied. In case of exposure to 0.25 mg/mL of **PUB10**, the respective values were: 72.8 ± 0.04%; 69.8 ± 0.11% and 77.7 ± 2.4%.

In turn, the cytocompatibility tests of **PUB9**- and **PUB10**-containing BC carriers toward the fibroblast cell line corresponded to the obtained data on fibroblasts' cytotoxicity, i.e., **PUB9-BC** displayed excellent cytocompatibility while **PUB10-BC** displayed the moderate cytocompatibility (Figure 6) compared to the biocompatibility of native BC.

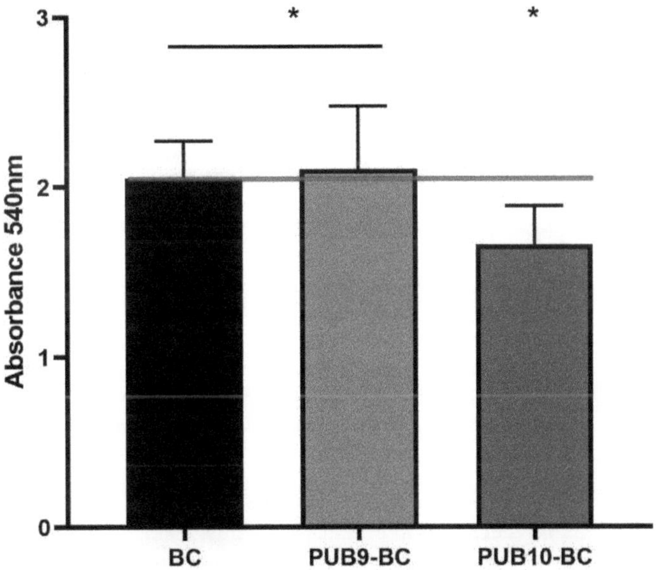

Figure 6. Comparison of cytocompatibility of isoxazole derivatives-fortified cellulosic carriers: **PUB9-BC** and **PUB10-BC** compared to control setting (cellulose carrier containing no isoxazole derivative) toward fibroblast cell line. Asterisks indicate significant differences ($p < 0.05$, ANOVA Test with Tukey's multiple comparison test) between BC vs. **PUB10-BC** and **PUB9-BC** vs. **PUB10-BC**. The red line indicates the maximal potential cellular growth (of non-fortified cellulosic carrier).

The increasing frequency of non-healing wounds occurrence in the developed populations of the Western hemisphere accelerates the search for efficient algorithms in treatment of these disease entities. Infection is considered one of the most dangerous complications of non-healing wounds, and may lead even to the patient's death. The local application of antiseptic agents is one of the pillars of modern wound treatment [44]. Nevertheless, continuous and prolonged exposure of infected wounds to antiseptics starts to induce processes analogical to those observed during application of antibiotics, namely to the rise of microbial tolerance and resistance [45]. Therefore, new classes of antiseptic agents are needed to overcome the threat of bacterial resistance and to provide wound professionals an effective tool in the fight against microbial biofilms colonizing and infecting wound beds.

The isoxazole derivatives seem to be promising candidates in this regard, thanks to their relatively easy synthesis, chemical stability, low toxicity and good bioactivity at low doses. Although numerous methods for isoxazole-containing drugs have been developed, due to their wide activity, there is still a strong need to synthesize new derivatives containing this valuable moiety with increased chemical and pharmacological properties and test their biological activity. The current research focused on the antimicrobial (including antibiofilm) activity of isoxazole derivatives and, simultaneously, on their impact on wound bed-forming cells, referred to as the fibroblasts. The general aim was thus to investigate potential applicability of isoxazole derivatives in the character of drugs for infected wound care. While the MIC evaluation and modified disk diffusion methods served, to a certain extent, as the predictors of biofilm prevention potential, the MBEC and A.D.A.M. techniques showed the performance of isoxazole derivatives in the character of drugs for biofilm treatment. In turn, tests performed on fibroblasts provided insight on potential interaction of derivatives with wound cells, especially their ability to adhere and proliferate.

The previous research on isoxazoles indicates that the substitution of various groups on the isoxazole ring imparts different activity. It was observed that the introduction of the thiophene moiety to the isoxazole ring increases its antimicrobial activity [46]. Previously, in vitro antibacterial and antifungal activity against *S. aureus, B. subtilis, E. coli, P. aeruginosa, A. niger* and *C.albicans* of 4,5-dihydro-5-(substitutedphenyl)-3-(thiophene-2-yl)isoxazole derivatives using the disc diffusion method was investigated by Gautam and Singh [47]. The obtained results clearly demonstrated high impact of the thiophene moiety on the analyzed biological activity. Another useful result was obtained by RamaRao et al. [48], who synthesized heteroarylisoxazoles and evaluated them for antibacterial activity against *E. coli, S. aureus* and *P. aeruginosa*. It was found that the isoxazoles substituted with the thiophenyl moiety displayed significant activity. The fact that the thiophene nucleus has been recognized as an important moiety in the synthesis of heterocyclic compounds with promising pharmacological characteristics prompted us to investigate such phenomena in the case of new isoxazole derivatives in the form of Passerini reaction products. In this work, 15 isoxazole derivatives were scrutinized with regard to their antimicrobial effect displayed against *S. aureus, P. aeruginosa* and *C. albicans*. The reason standing behind the choice of aforementioned species was not only different structure and composition of their cell wall, but also the fact that both *S. aureus* and *P. aeruginosa* belong to the pathogens being frequent etiological factors of non-healing wounds, while *C. albicans* is a component of mixed wound biofilms. Obtained results (Table 1) indicate that all tested compounds were able to inhibit growth of *S. aureus, P. aeruginosa* and *C. albicans* within the tested range of concentrations in the basic microplate model. Of note, in the case of 11/15 tested compounds there were no differences in Minimal Inhibitory Concentrations against *S. aureus* and *P. aeruginosa* displayed by a particular compound or these differences were on the level of just one geometric dilution, which may be related with the limitation of the method itself [49]. In turn, in the case of two compounds (**PUB9** and **PUB10**) the MIC value against *S. aureus* was more than 1000 and 260 times lower, respectively, than against *P. aeruginosa*. With regard to the chemical composition, **PUB9** and **PUB10** differed from the other analyzed compounds mainly by the presence of a thiophene ring. It was speculated by another research team that the presence of the positive charge of donor S atoms in the heteroaromatic ring was responsible for damage of the microbial cell wall/membrane, potential leakage of cytoplasmatic content to the environment and eventual cellular damage [50].

In the second line of investigation, the most promising isoxazole derivatives (**PUB9** and **PUB10**) were scrutinized with regard to their antibiofilm properties (Figure 3). The level of biofilm eradication above 90% was achieved when higher concentrations of compounds were applied (compared to the MIC values presented in Table 1). At the same time there were no significant differences in the value of reduction in biofilms formed by applied species ($p < 0.05$), which suggests the dose-dependent mode of action of tested isoxazole derivatives and the mechanism of biofilm eradication based on killing of microbial cells rather than destruction of biofilm matrix [51].

Nevertheless, such an observation confirms the well-recognized higher tolerance of biofilms against antimicrobials, compared to the tolerance displayed by their planktonic (non-adhered) counterparts [52]. Interestingly, the difference between concentrations necessary to reach MIC value vs. concentrations required to reach >90% of biofilm eradication was noticeably lower in the case of *P.aeruginosa* or *C.albicans* (two to four times) than in the case of *S.aureus* (ca. 2000–4000 times). Such a phenomenon may be related with the hypothetical mechanism of action of **PUB9** and **PUB10**, i.e., the inhibition of GTPase activity and bacterial cell division, which cause bactericidal effects [53]. The appropriate candidate for a wound antiseptic should display not only the sufficient antimicrobial (antibiofilm) activity, but also should not exert the harmful effect on the wound bed cells, such as fibroblasts [54]. Therefore, in the next analysis (Figure 4), the survivability of fibroblast cell line exposed to **PUB9** and **PUB10** activity was performed for the spectrum of concentrations, including these which proved to be sufficient to eradicate the pathogens in planktonic and biofilm forms (Table 1, Figure 3). The obtained results indicated the concentration-dependent growth of cytotoxic effects displayed by both compounds. Nevertheless, it also occurred that in the concentration range 0.2–0.4 mg/mL, **PUB9** displays acceptable (low) level of cytotoxicity, while acceptable level of cytotoxicity was recorded for **PUB10** in the concentration range 0.012–0.025 mg/mL. The exact mechanism explaining why certain isoxazole derivatives containing a thiophene ring display a cytotoxic effect toward certain cell lines but not other types still needs to be elucidated [55]. Nevertheless, in the current research two derivatives of low cytotoxicity against fibroblast cells were found, which makes them promising candidates to be investigated more thoroughly. To further analyze the impact of **PUB9** and **PUB10** on microorganisms, the modified disk diffusion test was performed (Figure 5) [56], which confirmed higher antimicrobial effect exerted by **PUB9** than **PUB10**; the coherent results were obtained in case of the A.D.A.M. test performed, i.e., the higher antibiofilm activity of **PUB9** than **PUB10**. To our knowledge it is the first time the isoxazole derivatives were introduced to the BC carrier, which paves a way to their potential application not only as antiseptic agents in the form of liquid solutions, but also as an antimicrobial component of active dressings designed to treat chronic wounds. To get deeper insight on properties of isoxazole derivatives-containing BC, we performed a cytocompatibility test in vitro (Figure 6). Obtained results revealed that excellent cytocompatibility of BC, indicated by other research teams [57], was reduced moderately (but in a statistically significant manner) by addition of **PUB10**, but not the **PUB9** compound. It may be thus assumed that the **PUB9** compound can be considered a candidate designed for treatment purposes (eradication of already formed biofilm), while **PUB10** appears to be more suitable for prophylaxis purposes (the lower, non-cytotoxic concentration of **PUB10** may be applied against planktonic forms of microorganisms, which did not develop into biofilm structure yet).

Conventional, clinically applied drugs used topically for the treatment of chronic wounds can be divided into antibiotics or antiseptics. Gentamycin is an example of an antibiotic allowed to be used topically in the treatment of chronic wounds. This antibiotic is provided in a collagen scaffold, referred to as a "gentamycin-sponge", or in a viscous hydrogel carrier. It was previously demonstrated that during the first 60 min of application of the sponge, released gentamycin reached a concentration of 1000 mg/L and during the next 4–5 days after implantation, the antibiotic concentration was at the level of 300–400 mg/L [58,59]. The indicated concentration of gentamycin sufficient to eradicate staphylococcal or pseudomonal biofilm in vitro was between 100–500 mg/L (depending on model applied) [60]. Of note, the concentration of the most efficient isoxazole derivative analyzed in the current work (**PUB9**) against *S. aureus* and *P. aeruginosa* biofilm was 125 mg/L. Such a result shows potential of **PUB9** to be applied for treatment of chronic wounds with regard to antibiofilm activity (come pared to antibiotics). The other class of products used to treat/prevent infections of chronic wounds is referred to as the antiseptics. These are mainly liquid solutions containing antimicrobial substances. The modern antiseptics include such antimicrobial compounds as octenidine dihydrochloride, povidone iodine or hypochlorous acids [54]. Due to the various mechanisms of action, the concentrations of various antiseptics necessary to eradicate pathogenic biofilm, differ significantly. The concentration of octenidine dihydrochloride (used in the current study as control of method's usability) sufficient to eradicate the in vitro staphylococcal and candida biofilm was 62.5 mg/L (Table S1, Supplementary Data). This concentration was two times lower (more favorable with regard to antimicrobial level) than the concentration of the aforementioned **PUB9** compound. In turn, with regard to the *P. aeruginosa* biofilm, **PUB9** acted more efficiently (in microtiter plate model) than octenidine dihydrochloride. Such a differentiation in antiseptics' efficacy may be applied for personalized medicine of treatment of chronic wound infections (under condition of performance of appropriate microbiological diagnostics). On the other hand, the working concentration of another common clinical antiseptic, povidone iodine, is 7.5%, and such a concentration exceeds significantly the microbiologically efficient concentrations of both **PUB9** and octenidine dihydrochloride. Therefore, the dissertations on antimicrobial efficacy should be always combined with data on compounds' cytotoxic effect/cytocompatibility. These parameters were favorable for **PUB9** as shown in Figures 4 and 6. The combined data on antimicrobial effect and cytocompatibility indicate that the **PUB9** derivative is of potential to be tested further in direction of its application as a compound for chronic wound treatment.

We are aware of the specific disadvantages of this work, derived mainly from its preliminary character, i.e., focusing on such basic parameters of obtained isoxazole derivatives as antimicrobial effect or cytotoxicity and not on, for example, such potentially important aspects as stability of derivatives introduced to the BC carrier, genotoxicity or the analysis of potential to induce antimicrobial resistance. Nevertheless, out of 15 synthesized isoxazole derivatives, two of them (**PUB9** and **PUB10**) displayed satisfactory antimicrobial effects, maintaining at the same time, acceptable level of cytotoxicity (the certain level of this feature is displayed by virtually all antiseptics [41]. These satisfactory (at this stage of research) results justify undertaking other investigation steps, including among others, testing derivatives using a *Galleria mellonella* infection animal model, performance of above-mentioned stability testing and potential of derivatives to induce antimicrobial resistance using tests as presented recently by Li et al. [61]. Taking into consideration the clinical demand for new antiseptic agents for non-healing wound treatment, the compounds presented in this work seem to be promising candidates to be further tested in more advanced animal models and later, if the satisfactory results are obtained, in the clinical setting.

3. Materials and Methods

3.1. Chemistry

Commercially available reagents, i.e., triethyl orthoacetate, cyanoacetate, hydrazine monohydrate, *N*-substituted maleimides, aldehydes and isocyanides, were purchased from Sigma-Aldrich (Merck Group, Darmstadt, Germany) or TCI (Tokyo, Japan) and were used without further purification. Thin layer chromatography (TLC) was used to assess the progress and completion of reactions and was carried out using Alugram SIL G/UV 254 nm plates (Macherey-Nagel, Düren, Germany) and the developing system ethyl acetate/chloroform = 3/7 (*v*/*v*), and visualized by ultraviolet (UV) light at 254 nm (UV A. KRÜSS Optronic GmbH, Hamburg, Germany). Melting points were determined by uniMELT 2 apparatus (LLG, Meckenheim, Germany) and were uncorrected. ^{1}H NMR and ^{13}C NMR spectra were obtained in DMSO-d_6 and recorded using a Bruker ARX 300 MHz spectrometer (using TMS as the internal standard).

All ESI-MS experiments were performed on the LCMS-9030 qTOF Shimadzu (Shimadzu, Kyoto, Japan) device, equipped with a standard ESI source and the Nexera X2 system. Analysis was performed in the positive and negative ion mode between 100–3000 *m*/*z*. LCMS-9030 parameters were the following: the nebulizing gas was nitrogen, the nebulizing gas flow was 3.0 L/min, the drying gas flow was 10 L/min, the heating gas flow was 10 L/min, interface temperature was 300 °C, desolvation line temperature was 400 °C, detector voltage was 2.02 kV, interface voltage was 4.0 kV, collision gas was argon, mobile phase (A) was H_2O + 0.1% HCOOH, (B) was MeCN + 0.1% HCOOH, and mobile phase total flow was 0.3 mL/min.

3.2. Microorganisms

For research purposes, three following reference strains from the American Type and Culture Collection (ATCC) were used: *Staphylococcus aureus* 6538, *Pseudomonas aeruginosa* 15,442 and *Candida albicans* 103,231.

3.3. Determination of Minimal Inhibitory Concentration Using Microtiter Plate Method

To determine the minimal inhibitory concentration (MIC) values of the tested compounds, the following steps were performed. Firstly, overnight cultures of the strains were prepared in TSB medium (Tryptic Soy Broth, Biomaxima, Lublin, Poland) medium.

Next, 100 μL of TBS was added to all wells of 96-well plates (Jet Bio-Filtration Co. Ltd., Guangzhou, China) and 100 μL of the tested substances or DMSO (dimethyl sulfoxide, VWR Chemicals, Radnor, PA, USA) (used as a control of the solvent's antimicrobial activity) was added to the first columns of the pates, and ten geometric dilutions were performed for each compound. Subsequently, 0.5 MacFarland of bacterial/fungal suspensions were established in 0.9% solution of sodium chloride (NaCl, Stanlab, Lublin, Poland) using a densitometer (Densilameter II Erba Lachema, Brno, the Czech Republic). The suspensions were then diluted 1000 times in TSB and 100 μL was poured to the compounds-containing wells. Control of microorganisms' growth (suspensions in TSB) and control of medium sterility (medium only) were also prepared. The absorbance of the solution was measured at 580 nm using a spectrophotometer (Multiskan Go, Thermo Fisher Scientific, Vantaa, Finland) and the plates were incubated at 37 °C for 24 h with shaking at 350 rpm (Mini-shaker PSU-2T, Biosan SIA, Riga, Latvia). The absorbance was measured after the incubation at 580 nm. The MIC values against *C. albicans* were evaluated in the first well, where no visible growth was observed. To determine MIC values against bacteria, 20 μL of 1% (*w*/*v*) TTC (2,3,5-triphenyl-tetrazolium chloride, AppliChem Gmbh, Darmstadt, Germany) in TSB was added to all wells and the plates were incubated for 2 h in the same conditions. The MIC value against bacteria was assessed in the first well where no red color was observed. There were three repetitions for each compound. The octenidine dihydrochloride-based antiseptic (Schulke Mayr, Nordstadt, Germany) served as control of method's usability.

3.4. Determination of Minimal Biofilm Eradication Concentration Using Microtiter Plate Model

The overnight cultures of the strains were prepared in TSB medium. Subsequently, 0.5 MacFarland of bacterial/fungal suspensions were established in 0.9% solution of sodium chloride using a densitometer. The suspensions were then diluted 1000 times in TSB. An amount of 100 μL of such suspension was poured to wells of the 96-well plate and incubated for 18 h/37 °C. After incubation, the medium was removed, leaving biofilm-forming cells only. Next, the 100 μL of sterile TSB was poured to each well of the plate. Subsequently, the geometrical dilutions of tested compounds were performed in the wells of the 96-well plate. The whole experimental setting was then incubated for 18 h/37 °C. Afterwards, 20 μL of 1% (*w*/*v*) TTC in TSB was added to all wells and the plates were incubated for 2 h in the same conditions. The MBEC value against bacteria was assessed in the first well where no red color was observed. In the case of *C. albicans*, 20 μL of 0.1% resazurin in TSB was added to each well and incubated for 3h in the same conditions. The MBEC value against *C. albicans* was assessed in the first well where blue color was observed. There were three repetitions performed for each compound and each compound's concentration. The formula used to determine the biofilm eradication was as follows: 100%—(value of absorbance obtained from biofilm treated with analyzed compound/absorbance value obtained from biofilm treated with saline) × 100%. These experiments were done in three repeats. The octenidine dihydrochloride-based antiseptic (Schulke Mayr, Nordstadt, Germany) served as control of method's usability.

3.5. The Cytotoxicity Assay of Analyzed Compounds towards Fibroblast Cell Line In Vitro

The Neutral Red (NR) cytotoxicity assay was performed toward fibroblast (L929 ATCC, Manassas, VA, USA) in vitro cell cultures treated with the analyzed compounds in concentration equal to their MBEC (or MIC if MBEC was beyond tested range of concentrations) value according to ISO 10993: Biological evaluation of medical devices; Part 5: Tests for in vitro cytotoxicity; Part 12: Biological evaluation of medical devices, sample preparation and reference materials (ISO 10993–5:2009 and ISO/IEC 17025:2005). The analyzed compounds were suspended in the medium for fibroblast culturing (RPMI, Sigma-Aldrich, Darmstad, Germany) and left to dry at room temperature. Next, 150 μL of a de-stain solution (50% ethanol, 96%, 49% deionized water, 1% glacial acetic acid; POCH, Lublin, Poland) was introduced to each well. The plate was shaken vigorously in a shaker (MTS4, IKA-Labortechnik, Berlin, Germany) for 30 min until NR was extracted from the cells and formed a homogenous solution. Finally, the value of NR absorbance was measured spectrometrically using a microplate reader at a wave of 540 nm length. The absorbance value of NR-dyed cells not treated with medium containing analyzed compounds was considered 100% of the potential cellular growth (positive control of growth), while cells treated with 70% EtOH (POCH, Lublin, Polska) for 30 min were considered the control of method's usability. All analyses were performed in 6 repeats.

3.6. The Synthesis and Purification of Bacterial Cellulose Carrier and Impregnation of Carrier with Tested Compounds

The *K. xylinus* strain DSM 46604, used to bio-fabricate the BC carrier, was cultivated in stationary conditions for 7 days /28 °C in a 24-well plate (VWR International, Radnor, PA, USA) using a Hestrin-Schramm (H-S) medium. To remove bacterial cells and media components, the BCs were purified in 0.1 M NaOH (POCH, Lublin, Poland) for 90 min/80 °C. Next, BC carriers were immersed in distilled water and incubated with shaking. During this process, the pH value was measured every 3 hrs, until it reached a neutral value. The wet BC carriers were weighted. These of weight equal 1000 ± 100 mg were transferred to the 24-well plate and immersed with 1 mL of solution containing analyzed compounds in a concentration equal to 2 × MIC. The plate was left for 24 h/8 °C. After this time, BC carriers were used for analyses described in the subsequent sections of Material and Methods (Sections 3.7–3.9).

3.7. The Analysis of Antimicrobial Efficacy of Analyzed Compounds Released from BC Carriers in Modified Disk-Diffusion Method

For control purposes, BC carriers introduced to 1 mL of octenidine dihydrochloride (antiseptic substance of confirmed antimicrobial activity, Schulke-Mayr, Nordstadt, Germany) or 0.9% NaCl were applied. Firstly, the *S. aureus*, *P. aeruginosa* or *C. albicans* of 0.5/0.8 McFarland density were spread over the Muller-Hinton or Sabouraud agar plates, respectively. Next, BC carriers soaked with tested compounds were placed on the plates. The whole setting was subjected to incubation at 37 °C for 24 h. After that, the growth inhibition zone (if occurred) was measured using a ruler. The tests were performed in triplicates.

3.8. The Detection of Antibiofilm Activity of Tested Compounds Using Modified Antibiofilm Dressing Activity Measurement (A.D.A.M.)

The method was described in detail in the earlier work of ours [62]. The exposure time was 24 h. After incubation of preformed biofilm with compounds, biofilm-containing agar disks were transferred to the fresh wells of a 24-well plate. Next, 1 mL of 0.1% saponin solution was subjected to vortex-mixing for 1 min to detach the biofilm cells from the agar surface. Serial dilutions of the obtained suspension in saline solution were performed and then cultured onto Sabouraud or M-H agar plates (for *C. albicans* and *S. aureus/P. aeruginosa*, respectively). The plates were incubated at 37 °C for 24 h. After incubation, the cfu number of grown colonies was counted. The formula used to determine the biofilm eradication was as follows: 100%—(value of cfu obtained from biofilm treated with cellulose carrier soaked with analyzed compound)/cfu obtained from biofilm treated with non-impregnated cellulose) × 100%. These experiments were done in three repeats. The octenidine dihydrochloride-based antiseptic (Schulke Mayr, Nordstadt, Germany) served as control of method's usability.

3.9. The Cytocompatibility of Isoxazole-Fortified BC Carriers to Fibroblast Cell Lines

One mL of culturing medium containing fibroblast cell lines of density equal 1 × 105 were seeded on the BC carriers fortified with the appropriate concentrations of **PUB9** and **PUB10** (0.25 mg/L) and cultured for 72 h at 37 °C/5% CO_2 in an incubator. Next, the procedures utilizing Neutral Red method were performed to assess the survivability of the cells. The medium for fibroblast growth was removed and 100 µL of the NR solution (40 µg/mL; Sigma-Aldrich, Dormstadt, Germany) was introduced to wells of the plate. Cells were incubated with NR for 2 h at 37 °C. After incubation, the dye was removed, wells were rinsed with phosphate buffer saline (PBS, Sigma Aldrich, Dormstadt, Germany) and left to dry at room temperature. Next, 500 μL of a de-stain solution (50% ethanol 96%, 49% deionized water, 1% glacial acetic acid; POCH, Lublin, Poland) was introduced to each well. The plate was shaken vigorously in a microtiter plate shaker (MTS4, IKA-Labortechnik, Berlin, Germany) for 30 min until NR was extracted from the cells and formed a homogenous solution. Finally, the value of NR absorbance was measured spectrometrically using a microplate reader (Multi-scan GO, Thermo Fisher Scientific, Waltham, MA, USA) at 540 nm. The absorbance value of dyed fibroblasts seeded on the BC carriers non-fortified with **PUB9** and **PUB10** was considered 100% of the potential cellular growth (positive control).

3.10. The Statistical Analysis

Statistical analyses were performed using GraphPad Prism 8.0. (GraphPad Software, San Diego, CA, USA). Normality of distribution was verified using Shapiro–Wilk's test. To evaluate statistical significance, the ANOVA test with post hoc Dunnett's multiple comparison ($\alpha = 0.05$) was performed.

Supplementary Materials: The following supporting information can be downloaded at: https://www.mdpi.com/article/10.3390/ijms24032997/s1.

Author Contributions: Conceptualization, U.B.; methodology, U.B.; formal analysis, U.B.; investigation, A.J., M.B. and U.B.; writing—original draft preparation, U.B.; writing—review and editing, A.J.; supervision, M.M.; funding acquisition, A.J. and M.M. All authors have read and agreed to the published version of the manuscript.

Funding: This research was funded by Wroclaw Medical University, grant number SUBZ.D090.23.027.

Institutional Review Board Statement: Not applicable.

Informed Consent Statement: Not applicable.

Data Availability Statement: All necessary data are presented in the manuscript and the raw data can be provided from the authors upon reasonable request.

Acknowledgments: The authors would like to thank Magdalena Korab for technical support.

Conflicts of Interest: The authors declare no conflict of interest.

References

1. Frykberg, R.G.; Banks, J. Challenges in the Treatment of Chronic Wounds. *Adv. Wound Care* **2015**, *4*, 560–582. [CrossRef] [PubMed]
2. Serra, R.; Grande, R.; Butrico, L.; Rossi, A.; Settimio, U.F.; Caroleo, B.; Amato, B.; Gallelli, L.; de Franciscis, S. Chronic wound infections: The role of *Pseudomonas aeruginosa* and *Staphylococcus aureus*. *Expert Rev. Anti Infect. Ther.* **2015**, *13*, 605–613. [CrossRef] [PubMed]
3. Durand, B.A.R.N.; Pouget, C.; Magnan, C.; Molle, V.; Lavigne, J.P.; Dunyach-Remy, C. Bacterial Interactions in the Context of Chronic Wound Biofilm: A Review. *Microorganisms* **2022**, *10*, 1500. [CrossRef] [PubMed]
4. Barrigah-Benissan, K.; Ory, J.; Sotto, A.; Salipante, F.; Lavigne, J.P.; Loubet, P. Antiseptic Agents for Chronic Wounds: A Systematic Review. *Antibiotics* **2022**, *11*, 350. [CrossRef]
5. Müller, G.; Kramer, A. Biocompatibility index of antiseptic agents by parallel assessment of antimicrobial activity and cellular cytotoxicity. *J. Antimicrob. Chemother.* **2008**, *61*, 1281–1287. [CrossRef]
6. Kampf, G. Acquired resistance to chlorhexidine—Is it time to establish an 'antiseptic stewardship' initiative? *J. Hosp. Infect.* **2016**, *94*, 213–227. [CrossRef]
7. Bock, L.J.; Ferguson, P.M.; Clarke, M.; Pumpitakkul, V.; Wand, M.E.; Fady, P.E.; Allison, L.; Fleck, R.A.; Shepherd, M.J.; Mason, A.J.; et al. *Pseudomonas aeruginosa* adapts to octenidine via a combination of efflux and membrane remodelling. *Commun. Biol.* **2021**, *4*, 1058. [CrossRef]
8. Li, Q.; Kang, C. Mechanisms of Action for Small Molecules Revealed by Structural Biology in Drug Discovery. *Int. J. Mol. Sci.* **2020**, *21*, 5262. [CrossRef]
9. Zhang, D.; Jia, J.; Meng, L.; Xu, W.; Tang, L.; Wang, J. Synthesis and Preliminary Antibacterial Evaluation of 2-Butyl Succinate-based Hydroxamate Derivatives Containing Isoxazole Rings. *Arch. Pharm. Res.* **2010**, *33*, 831–842. [CrossRef]
10. Egorova, A.; Kazakova, E.; Jahn, B.; Ekins, S.; Makarov, V.; Schmidtke, M. Novel pleconaril derivatives: Influence of substituents in the isoxazole and phenyl rings on the antiviral activity against enteroviruses. *Eur. J. Med. Chem.* **2020**, *188*, 112007. [CrossRef]
11. Arya, G.C.; Kaur, K.; Jaitak, V. Isoxazole derivatives as anticancer agent: A review on synthetic strategies, mechanism of action and SAR studies. *Eur. J. Med. Chem.* **2021**, *221*, 113511. [CrossRef]

12. Razzaq, S.; Minhas, A.M.; Qazi, N.G.; Nadeem, H.; Khan, A.-u.; Ali, F.; Hassan, S.S.u.; Bungau, S. Novel Isoxazole Derivative Attenuates Ethanol-Induced Gastric Mucosal Injury through Inhibition of H+/K+-ATPase Pump, Oxidative Stress and Inflammatory Pathways. *Molecules* **2022**, *27*, 5065. [CrossRef]
13. Sysak, A.; Obmińska-Mrukowicz, B. Isoxazole ring as a useful scaffold in a search for new therapeutic agents. *Eur. J. Med. Chem.* **2017**, *137*, 292–309. [CrossRef]
14. Huang, X.; Dong, S.; Liu, H.; Wan, P.; Wang, T.; Quan, H.; Wang, Z.; Wang, Z. Design, Synthesis, and Evaluation of Novel Benzo[*d*]isoxazole Derivatives as Anticonvulsants by Selectively Blocking the Voltage-Gated Sodium Channel $Na_V1.1$. *ACS Chem. Neurosci.* **2022**, *13*, 834–845. [CrossRef]
15. Algethami, F.K.; Saidi, I.; Abdelhamid, H.N.; Elamin, M.R.; Abdulkhair, B.Y.; Chrouda, A.; Ben Jannet, H. Trifluoromethylated Flavonoid-Based Isoxazoles as Antidiabetic and Anti-Obesity Agents: Synthesis, In Vitro α-Amylase Inhibitory Activity, Molecular Docking and Structure–Activity Relationship Analysis. *Molecules* **2021**, *26*, 5214. [CrossRef]
16. Chikkula, K.V.; Raja, S. Isoxazole-A potent pharmacophore. *Int. J. Pharm. Pharm. Sci.* **2017**, *9*, 13–24. [CrossRef]
17. Esfahani, S.N.; Damavandi, M.S.; Sadeghi, P.; Nazifi, Z.; Salari-Jazi, A.; Massah, A.R. Synthesis of some novel coumarin isoxazol sulfonamide hybrid compounds, 3D-QSAR studies, and antibacterial evaluation. *Sci. Rep.* **2021**, *11*, 20088. [CrossRef]
18. Shaik, A.; Bhandare, R.R.; Palleapati, K.; Nissankararao, S.; Kancharlapalli, V.; Shaik, S. Antimicrobial, Antioxidant, and Anticancer Activities of Some Novel Isoxazole Ring Containing Chalcone and Dihydropyrazole Derivatives. *Molecules* **2020**, *25*, 1047. [CrossRef] [PubMed]
19. Zimecki, M.; Mączyński, M.; Artym, J.; Ryng, S. Closely related isoxazoles may exhibit opposite immunological activities. *Acta Pol Pharm.—Drug Res.* **2008**, *65*, 793–794.
20. Mączyński, M.; Ryng, S.; Artym, J.; Kocięba, M.; Zimecki, M.; Brudnik, K.; Jodkowski, J.T. New lead structures in the isoxazole system: Relationship between quantum chemical parameters and immunological activity. *Acta Pol Pharm.—Drug Res.* **2014**, *71*, 71–83.
21. Mączyński, M.; Artym, J.; Kocięba, M.; Sochacka-Ćwikła, A.; Drozd-Szczygieł, E.; Ryng, S.; Zimecki, M. Synthesis and immunoregulatory properties of selected 5-amino-3-methyl-4-isoxazolecarboxylic acid benzylamides. *Acta Pol. Pharm.—Drug Res.* **2016**, *73*, 1201–1211.
22. Mączyński, M.; Regiec, A.; Sochacka-Ćwikła, A.; Kochanowska, I.; Kocięba, M.; Zaczyńska, E.; Artym, J.; Kałas, W.; Zimecki, M. Synthesis, Physicochemical Characteristics and Plausible Mechanism of Action of an Immunosuppressive Isoxazolo[5,4-*e*]-1,2,4-Triazepine Derivative (RM33). *Pharmaceuticals* **2021**, *14*, 468. [CrossRef] [PubMed]
23. Sochacka-Ćwikła, A.; Regiec, A.; Zimecki, M.; Artym, J.; Zaczyńska, E.; Kocięba, M.; Kochanowska, I.; Bryndal, I.; Pyra, A.; Mączyński, M. Synthesis and Biological Activity of New 7-Amino-oxazolo[5,4-*d*]Pyrimidine Derivatives. *Molecules* **2020**, *25*, 3558. [CrossRef]
24. Sochacka-Ćwikła, A.; Mączyński, M.; Czyżnikowska, Ż.; Wiatrak, B.; Jęśkowiak, I.; Czerski, A.; Regiec, A. New Oxazolo[5,4-*d*]pyrimidines as Potential Anticancer Agents: Their Design, Synthesis, and *In Vitro* Biological Activity Research. *Int. J. Mol. Sci.* **2022**, *23*, 11694. [CrossRef] [PubMed]
25. Bąchor, U.; Mączyński, M. Selected β2-, β3- and β2,3-Amino Acid Heterocyclic Derivatives and Their Biological Perspective. *Molecules* **2021**, *26*, 438. [CrossRef]
26. Uno, B.E.; Deibler, K.K.; Villa, C.; Raghuraman, A.; Karl, A.S. Conjugate Additions of Amines to Maleimides via Cooperative Catalysis. *Adv. Synth. Catal.* **2018**, *360*, 1719–1725. [CrossRef]
27. Worch, J.C.; Stubbs, C.J.; Matthew, J.P.; Dove, A.P. Click Nucleophilic Conjugate Additions to Activated Alkynes: Exploring Thiol-yne, Amino-yne, and Hydroxyl-yne Reactions from (Bio)Organic to Polymer Chemistry. *Chem. Rev.* **2021**, *121*, 6744–6776. [CrossRef]
28. Dolci, E.; Froidevaux, V.; Joly-Duhamel, C.; Auvergne, R.; Boutevin, B.; Caillol, S. Maleimides as a Building Block for the Synthesis of High Performance Polymers. *Polym. Rev.* **2016**, *56*, 512–556. [CrossRef]
29. Regiec, A.; Wojciechowski, P.; Pietraszko, A.; Mączyński, M. Infrared spectra and other properties predictions of 5-amino-3-methyl-4-isoxazolecarbohydrazide with electric field simulation using CPC model. *J. Mol. Struct.* **2018**, *1161*, 320–338. [CrossRef]
30. Regiec, A.; Płoszaj, P.; Ryng, S.; Wojciechowski, P. Vibrational spectroscopy of 5-amino-3-methyl-4-isoxazolecarbohydrazide and its N-deuterated isotopologue. *Vib. Spectrosc.* **2014**, *70*, 125–136. [CrossRef]
31. Płoszaj, P.; Regiec, A.; Ryng, S.; Piwowar, A.; Kruzel, M.L. Influence of 5-amino-3-methyl-4-isoxazolecarbohydrazide on selective gene expression in Caco-2 cultured cells. *Immunopharmacol. Immunotoxicol.* **2016**, *38*, 486–494. [CrossRef] [PubMed]
32. Drynda, A.; Mączyński, M.; Ryng, S.; Obmińska-Mrukowicz, B. In vitro immunomodulatory effects of 5-amino-3-methyl-4-isoxazolecarboxylic acid hydrazide on the cellular immune response. *Immunopharmacol. Immunotoxicol.* **2014**, *36*, 150–157. [CrossRef]
33. Drynda, A.; Obmińska-Mrukowicz, B.; Mączyński, M.; Ryng, S. The effect of 5-amino-3-methyl-4-isoxazolecarboxylic acid hydrazide on lymphocyte subsets and humoral immune response in SRBC-immunized mice. *Immunopharmacol. Immunotoxicol.* **2015**, *37*, 148–157. [CrossRef] [PubMed]
34. Bąchor, U.; Ryng, S.; Mączyński, M.; Artym, J.; Kocięba, M.; Zaczyńska, E.; Kochanowska, I.; Tykarska, E.; Zimecki, M. Synthesis, immunosuppressive properties, mechanism of action and X-ray analysis of a new class of isoxazole derivatives. *Acta Pol. Pharm. Drug Res.* **2019**, *76*, 251–263. [CrossRef]

35. Banfi, L.; Basso, A.; Lambruschini, C.; Moni, L.; Riva, R. The 100 facets of the Passerini reaction. *Chem. Sci.* **2021**, *12*, 15445–15472. [CrossRef]
36. Olleik, H.; Nicoletti, C.; Lafond, M.; Courvoisier-Dezord, E.; Xue, P.; Hijazi, A.; Baydoun, E.; Perrier, J.; Maresca, M. Comparative Structure–Activity Analysis of the Antimicrobial Activity, Cytotoxicity, and Mechanism of Action of the Fungal Cyclohexadepsipeptides Enniatins and Beauvericin. *Toxins* **2019**, *11*, 514. [CrossRef]
37. Zheng, L.; Li, S.; Luo, J.; Wang, X. Latest Advances on Bacterial Cellulose-Based Antibacterial Materials as Wound Dressings. *Front. Bioeng. Biotechnol.* **2020**, *23*, 593768. [CrossRef] [PubMed]
38. de Amorim, J.D.P.; da Silva Junior, C.J.G.; de Medeiros, A.D.M.; do Nascimento, H.A.; Sarubbo, M.; de Medeiros, T.P.M.; Costa, A.F.S.; Sarubbo, L.A. Bacterial Cellulose as a Versatile Biomaterial for Wound Dressing Application. *Molecules* **2022**, *27*, 5580. [CrossRef]
39. Lemnaru Popa, G.M.; Trușcă, R.D.; Ilie, C.I.; Țiplea, R.E.; Ficai, D.; Oprea, O.; Stoica-Guzun, A.; Ficai, A.; Dițu, L.M. Antibacterial Activity of Bacterial Cellulose Loaded with Bacitracin and Amoxicillin: In Vitro Studies. *Molecules* **2020**, *25*, 4069. [CrossRef]
40. Bąchor, U.; Lizak, A.; Bąchor, R.; Mączyński, M. 5-Amino-3-methyl-Isoxazole-4-carboxylic Acid as a Novel Unnatural Amino Acid in the Solid Phase Synthesis of α/β-Mixed Peptides. *Molecules* **2022**, *27*, 5612. [CrossRef]
41. Bąchor, U.; Drozd-Szczygieł, E.; Bąchor, R.; Jerzykiewicz, L.; Wieczorek, R.; Mączyński, M. New water-soluble isoxazole-linked 1,3,4-oxadiazole derivative with delocalized positive charge. *RSC Adv.* **2021**, *11*, 29668–29674. [CrossRef] [PubMed]
42. Regiec, A.; Gadziński, P. New Methods for Preparing of Esters of 2-cyano-3- alkoxy-2-butenoate acids. Polish patent- PL 216770 B1, 30 May 2014.
43. Regiec, A.; Gadziński, P.; Płoszaj, P. New methods for preparing of esters of 5-amino-3-methyl-4-isoxazolecarboxylic acid. Polish patent- PL 216764 B1, 30 May 2014.
44. Sopata, M.; Kucharzewski, M.; Tomaszewska, E. Antiseptic with modern wound dressings in the treatment of venous leg ulcers: Clinical and microbiological aspects. *J. Wound Care* **2016**, *25*, 419–426. [CrossRef]
45. Alves, P.J.; Barreto, R.T.; Barrois, B.M.; Gryson, L.G.; Meaume, S.; Monstrey, S.J. Update on the role of antiseptics in the management of chronic wounds with critical colonisation and/or biofilm. *Int Wound, J.* **2021**, *18*, 342–358. [CrossRef] [PubMed]
46. Agrawal, N.; Pradeep, M. The synthetic and therapeutic expedition of isoxazole and its analogs. *Med. Chem. Res.* **2018**, *27*, 1309–1344. [CrossRef] [PubMed]
47. Gautam, K.C.; Singh, D.P. Synthesis and antimicrobial activity of some isoxazole derivatives of thiophene. *Chem Sci Trans.* **2013**, *2*, 992–996.
48. RamaRao, R.J.; Rao, A.K.S.B.; Sreenivas, N.; Kumar, B.S.; Murthy, Y.L.N. Synthesis and antibacterial activity of novel 5-(heteroaryl)isoxazole Derivatives. *J Korean Chem Soc.* **2011**, *55*, 243–250. [CrossRef]
49. Tasse, J.; Cara, A.; Saglio, M.; Villet, R.; Laurent, F. A Steam-Based Method to Investigate Biofilm. *Sci. Rep.* **2018**, *8*, 13040. [CrossRef]
50. Ünver, H.; Cantürk, Z. New thiophene bearing dimethyl-5-hydroxy isophtalate esters and their antimicrobial activities. *Appl. Sci. Eng.* **2018**, *19*, 43–49. [CrossRef]
51. Ciecholewska-Juśko, D.; Żywicka, A.; Junka, A.; Woroszyło, M.; Wardach, M.; Chodaczek, G.; Szymczyk-Ziółkowska, P.; Migdał, P.; Fijałkowski, K. The effects of rotating magnetic field and antiseptic on in vitro pathogenic biofilm and its milieu. *Sci. Rep.* **2022**, *12*, 8836. [CrossRef]
52. Rabin, N.; Zheng, Y.; Opoku-Temeng, C.; Du, Y.; Bonsu, E.; Sintim, H.O. Biofilm Formation Mechanisms and Targets for Developing Antibiofilm Agents. *Future Med. Chem.* **2015**, *7*, 493–512. [CrossRef]
53. Fang, Z.; Li, Y.; Zheng, Y.; Li, X.; Lu, Y.J.; Yan, S.C.; Wong, W.L.; Chan, K.F.; Wong, K.Y.; Sun, N. Antibacterial activity and mechanism of action of a thiophenyl substituted pyrimidine derivative. *RSC Adv.* **2019**, *9*, 10739–10744. [CrossRef] [PubMed]
54. Kramer, A.; Dissemond, J.; Kim, S.; Willy, C.; Mayer, D.; Papke, R.; Tuchmann, F.; Assadian, O. Consensus on Wound Antisepsis: Update 2018. *Skin Pharmacol. Physiol.* **2018**, *31*, 28–58. [CrossRef] [PubMed]
55. Ghorab, M.M.; Bashandy, M.S.; Alsaid, M.S. Novel thiophene derivatives with sulfonamide, isoxazole, benzothiazole, quinoline and anthracene moieties as potential anticancer agents. *Acta Pharm.* **2014**, *64*, 419–431. [CrossRef]
56. Golonka, I.; Greber, K.E.; Oleksy-Wawrzyniak, M.; Paleczny, J.; Dryś, A.; Junka, A.; Sawicki, W.; Musiał, W. Antimicrobial and Antioxidative Activity of Newly Synthesized Peptides Absorbed into Bacterial Cellulose Carrier against *Acne vulgaris*. *Int. J. Mol. Sci.* **2021**, *22*, 7466. [CrossRef] [PubMed]
57. Abdelhamid, H.N.; Mathew, A.P. Cellulose-Based Nanomaterials Advance Biomedicine: A Review. *Int. J. Mol. Sci.* **2022**, *23*, 5405. [CrossRef] [PubMed]
58. Ruszczak, Z.; Friess, W. Collagen as a carrier for on-site delivery of antibacterial drugs. *Adv. Drug Deliv. Rev.* **2003**, *55*, 1679–1698. [CrossRef] [PubMed]
59. Brehant, O.; Sabbagh, C.; Lehert, P.; Dhahri, A.; Rebibo, L.; Regimbeau, J.M. The gentamicin–collagen sponge for surgical site infection prophylaxis in colorectal surgery: A prospective case-matched study of 606 cases. *Int. J. Colorectal Dis.* **2013**, *28*, 119–125. [CrossRef]
60. Mączyńska, B.; Secewicz, A.; Smutnicka, D.; Szymczyk, P.; Dudek-Wicher, R.; Junka, A.; Bartoszewicz, M. In vitro efficacy of gentamicin released from collagen sponge in eradication of bacterial biofilm preformed on hydroxyapatite surface. *PLoS ONE* **2019**, *14*, e0217769. [CrossRef]

61. Li, Z.; Shi, L.; Wang, B.; Wei, X.; Zhang, J.; Guo, T.; Kong, J.; Wang, M.; Xu, H. *In Vitro* Assessment of Antimicrobial Resistance Dissemination Dynamics during Multidrug-Resistant-Bacterium Invasion Events by Using a Continuous-Culture Device. *Appl. Environ. Microbiol.* **2021**, *87*, e02659-20. [CrossRef]
62. Krzyżek, P.; Gościniak, G.; Fijałkowski, K.; Migdał, P.; Dziadas, M.; Owczarek, A.; Czajkowska, J.; Aniołek, O.; Junka, A. Potential of Bacterial Cellulose Chemisorbed with Anti-Metabolites, 3-Bromopyruvate or Sertraline, to Fight against *Helicobacter pylori* Lawn Biofilm. *Int. J. Mol. Sci.* **2020**, *21*, 9507. [CrossRef]

International Journal of
Molecular Sciences

MDPI

Article

Biomaterial Inks from Peptide-Functionalized Silk Fibers for 3D Printing of Futuristic Wound-Healing and Sensing Materials

Maria Rachele Ceccarini [1], Valentina Palazzi [2], Raffaele Salvati [2], Irene Chiesa [3], Carmelo De Maria [3], Stefania Bonafoni [2], Paolo Mezzanotte [2], Michela Codini [1], Lorenzo Pacini [4], Fosca Errante [5], Paolo Rovero [5], Antonino Morabito [6], Tommaso Beccari [1], Luca Roselli [2] and Luca Valentini [7,*]

1 Department of Pharmaceutical Sciences, University of Perugia, 06123 Perugia, Italy
2 Department of Engineering, University of Perugia, 06125 Perugia, Italy
3 Department of Ingegneria dell'Informazione and Research Center E. Piaggio, University of Pisa, Largo Lucio Lazzarino 1, 56122 Pisa, Italy
4 Interdepartmental Research Unit of Peptide and Protein Chemistry and Biology, Department of Chemistry "Ugo Schiff", University of Florence, 50019 Sesto Fiorentino, Italy
5 Interdepartmental Research Unit of Peptide and Protein Chemistry and Biology, Department of NEUROFARBA, University of Florence, 50019 Sesto Fiorentino, Italy
6 Dipartimento Neuroscienze, Psicologia, Area del Farmaco e Salute del Bambino NEUROFARBA, Università degli Studi di Firenze, Viale Pieraccini 6, 50121 Firenze, Italy
7 Civil and Environmental Engineering Department, University of Perugia, Strada di Pentima 4, 05100 Terni, Italy
* Correspondence: luca.valentini@unipg.it; Tel.: +39-0744492924

Citation: Ceccarini, M.R.; Palazzi, V.; Salvati, R.; Chiesa, I.; De Maria, C.; Bonafoni, S.; Mezzanotte, P.; Codini, M.; Pacini, L.; Errante, F.; et al. Biomaterial Inks from Peptide-Functionalized Silk Fibers for 3D Printing of Futuristic Wound-Healing and Sensing Materials. *Int. J. Mol. Sci.* **2023**, *24*, 947. https://doi.org/10.3390/ijms24020947

Academic Editor: Alexander V. Ljubimov

Received: 17 December 2022
Revised: 30 December 2022
Accepted: 31 December 2022
Published: 4 January 2023

Abstract: This study illustrates the sensing and wound healing properties of silk fibroin in combination with peptide patterns, with an emphasis on the printability of multilayered grids, and envisions possible applications of these next-generation silk-based materials. Functionalized silk fibers covalently linked to an arginine–glycine–aspartic acid (RGD) peptide create a platform for preparing a biomaterial ink for 3D printing of grid-like piezoresistors with wound-healing and sensing properties. The culture medium obtained from 3D-printed silk fibroin enriched with RGD peptide improves cell adhesion, accelerating skin repair. Specifically, RGD peptide-modified silk fibroin demonstrated biocompatibility, enhanced cell adhesion, and higher wound closure rates at lower concentration than the neat peptide. It was also shown that the printing of peptide-modified silk fibroin produces a piezoresistive transducer that is the active component of a sensor based on a Schottky diode harmonic transponder encoding information about pressure. We discovered that such biomaterial ink printed in a multilayered grid can be used as a humidity sensor. Furthermore, humidity activates a transition between low and high conductivity states in this medium that is retained unless a negative voltage is applied, paving the way for utilization in non-volatile organic memory devices. Globally, these results pave the way for promising applications, such as monitoring parameters such as human wound care and being integrated in bio-implantable processors.

Keywords: regenerated silk; cytotoxicity; wound healing; peptide; RGD; 3D printing; piezoresistive biomaterials

1. Introduction

The era of the Internet of Things is driving the utilization of next-generation sensors in medical applications, where sensor performance can suffer from mechanical damage and sustainability in environmental conditions such as the presence of water, thereby restricting the practical application of such sensors in regenerative medicine. This market need makes us rethink ways to use novel materials for the fabrication of self-healing soft electronics exposed to high-moisture environments [1,2]. Natural materials (mainly proteins extracted from animals) are the most promising alternative to traditional materials, due to their non-toxicity, abundance, tunable mechanical properties, and good biocompatibility for cell activity, making them very suitable for the preparation of bio-inks [3]. Even if insect farming is still needed to achieve this objective, the valorization of proteins will be a key step in the era of green electronics.

Nowadays silk obtained from *Bombyx mori* (*B. mori*) silkworms seems a practicable way to obtain high-value opportunities from ancient materials, producing eco-friendly biodegradable materials in modern-day settings [4]. Due to its molecular structure, silk is among the strongest and toughest fibers in nature [5]. Different reverse engineering approaches to *B. mori* silk have allowed silk fibroin to be obtained, which is a promising material for novel and sustainable applications in regenerative medicine, electronics, energy harvesting and smart/edible packaging for food [6–10]. Silk fibroin brings added value in interfacing electronic devices with biological tissues [11–14]. In this regard, silk protein extracted from the wild silkworm *Antheraea pernyi* contains a high proportion of the Arg-Gly-Asp (RGD) sequence that can bind cell integrins, becoming a promising wound-dressing material due to its enhanced cell adhesion [15]. The use of natural biomaterials and the design of bio-inks has paved the way for effective wound treatment and management, including the engineering of skin and skin regeneration. Indeed, 3D printing technologies are actually the frontier for the fabrication of wound dressings, the features of the printing technology being critical for the fabrication of wound-healing materials and tissue-engineering applications [16].

Among bioinspired materials, the piezoresistivity in bioactive peptide nanotubes made using a diphenylalanine self-assembly process has been investigated [17]. They are made from biological building blocks—amino acids—and thus have intrinsic biocompatibility and a crystal structure that allows for physical effects such as piezoresistivity. More recently, tyrosine-rich peptide has also attracted great interest as a biodegradable humidity sensor and memristor [18].

In our recent work [19], a 3D-printed piezoelectric and adhesive silk-based device was interfaced with soft surfaces mimicking vital organs in the context of stimulation and electrical measurement. Recently, we reported the covalent linking of synthetic peptides to degummed silk fibers (regenerated silk, RS) to prepare ingestible devices [20]. Thus, the development of an easily extrudable material for extrusion-based bioprinting (EBB), with enhanced biocompatibility and sensing properties for the creation of electronics made entirely from "green" materials (i.e., materials that are biocompatible and biodegradable as products of insect farming) is an ambitious technological step. In this study, we apply a reverse-engineering approach to obtain peptide-functionalized RS biomaterial ink for 3D printing of multilayered grid-like piezoresistors, for promoting surface interactions with cells, and for designing a novel pressure sensor where the piezoresistor is used to vary the rectifying behavior of a Schottky diode and consequently the backscattered signal. We demonstrate that this material combines and matches its wound-dressing properties with sensing capabilities. Finally, exploiting the peculiar response of this material to humidity, we designed a novel bio-based nonvolatile sensor.

2. Results and Discussion

Multilayered grids were manufactured via EBB exploiting the RS-based solution with and without MO-07 (Figure 1A). The choice of a grid-like geometry was due to the mechanical advantages that this geometrical shape has if compared with solid structures, as we previously showed [19]. Briefly, this entails a decrease in unwanted lateral displacement, decrease in global stiffness, and decrease in stress on single grid lines, thus allowing easier conformity with the movements and deformations of the underlying substrate.

The printing occurred on a sacrificial layer made of Hydrofilm, which quickly dissolves in water [20]. This allowed the easy transfer of the grid from the Hydrofilm to the desired surface by adhering the grid to the surface and dissolving the Hydrofilm with water.

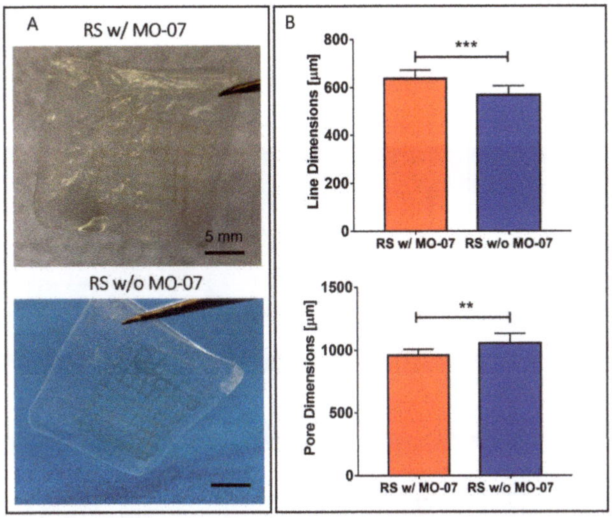

Figure 1. (**A**) Photos of the 3D-printed multilayered grids still on the Hydrofilm layer. (**B**) Morphological characterization of the grid. When the RS solution with MO-07 was used, a statistically significant increase in the line dimensions and a consequent reduction of the pore dimension was achieved. ** $p \leq 0.01$ and *** $p \leq 0.001$.

Grid line and pore dimensions were measured via image analysis. The line dimensions (e.g., the width of the printed grid lines) resulted in around 630 µm and 570 µm for the RS solution with MO-07 and for the RS solution without MO-7, respectively (Figure 1B). Statistical analysis revealed a significant increase in the line dimension when MO-07 was added to the solution ($p < 0.001$). Consequently, the pore dimension decreased when the RS solution with MO-07 was used ($p < 0.01$) (Figure 1B).

The difference in line dimension can be due to the different wettability of the Hydrofilm by the RS solution when the peptides are introduced, as we previously showed using the addition of tannin and graphene nanoplatelets [19]. Moreover, for both solutions the line dimension was more than the double the dimension of the nozzle (i.e., 210 µm). This printing performance could be improved and tuned for future applications, taking into account the increase in line dimensions during grid design and printing parameter selection (e.g., decreasing the volumetric flow). This will allow the manufacturing of grids with narrower line dimensions, up to the limit imposed by Plateau–Rayleigh instability [21,22].

Cell-based assays can be influenced by cytotoxic effects. Therefore, the side effects of MO-07 alone (Figure 2) and in combination with RS (Figure 3) on HaCaT cell viability were studied using an MTT assay. Cell survival was estimated after 24 h of treatment and results were analyzed according to the following criterion: a substance was considered safe if the viability results were more than 80% compared to the negative control (CTR). As a consequence, values lower than 80% viable cells were ascribed to cytotoxic effect and could be not suitable for wound-healing testing. Considering the abovementioned criterion, DMSO (positive control in red) tested as safe only at the lowest concentration (1%) with 82% of cell viability. Greater amounts of 2% and 4% DMSO were both cytotoxic for HaCaT and were used as positive controls to verify the cell response. MO-07, as shown in green (Figure 2), was always safe for HaCaT cells at any concentration assayed (from 7.5 to 240 µMol). In particular, two concentrations, namely 30 and 60 µMol, even showed a significant ($p< 0.01$) increment in cell viability (113.1% and 109.8%, respectively). The wound-healing assay was carried out from 7.5 to 240 µMol of MO-07.

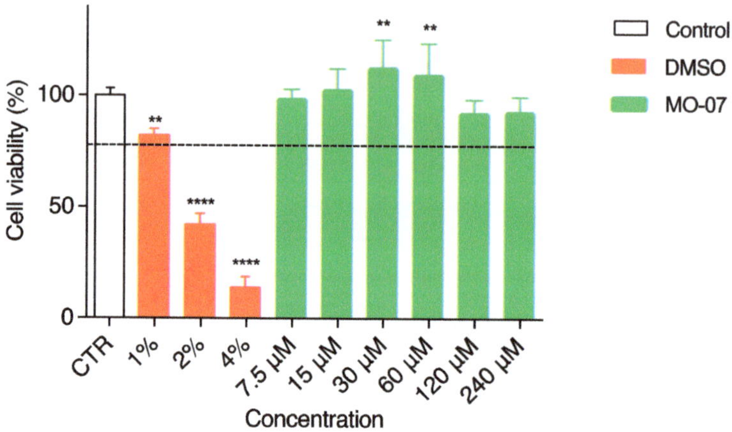

Figure 2. Viability of HaCaT cells incubated with different concentrations of MO-07 (24 h). The control is represented by untreated cells in DMEM and set at 100%; DMSO in three different percentages (1%, 2%, and 4%) was used as the positive control. The percentage of viable cells in respect to the control was reported as the mean ± SD of five independent experiments. Dotted lines indicate 80% cell viability. ** $p \leq 0.01$, and **** $p \leq 0.0001$ (one-way ANOVA test).

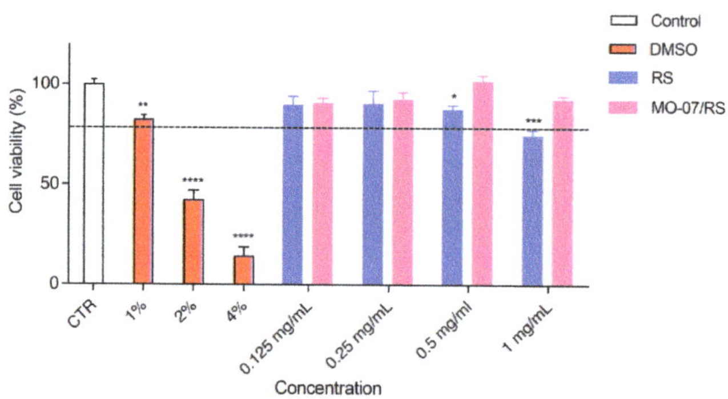

Figure 3. Viability of HaCaT cells incubated with different concentrations of RS and MO-07/RS (24 h). The control is represented by untreated cells in DMEM and set at 100%; DMSO in three different percentages (1%, 2%, and 4%) was used as the positive control. The percentage of viable cells in respect to the control was reported as the mean ± SD of five independent experiments. Dotted lines indicate 80% cell viability. * $p < 0.05$, ** $p \leq 0.01$, *** $p \leq 0.001$, and **** $p \leq 0.0001$, treatments versus control (one-way ANOVA test).

In addition, cell viability was measured (Figure 3) after RS (blue) and MO-07/RS (fuchsia) treatments. RS with/without MO-07 was diluted in complete medium. As previously described for two different cell lines [19,23], RS alone (in blue) exerted a very slight cytotoxic effect at the highest dose tested (1 mg/mL), with a cell viability of 77.4%, whereas MO-07/RS (in fuchsia) did not affect HaCaT viability. Cell survival was higher than 90% at all concentrations assayed. For this reason, all concentrations from 0.125 to 1 mg/mL of MO-07/RS could be used for the scratch test.

The most important clinical endpoint in wound management is complete epithelization, meaning 100% of wound closure in the shortest time possible. An in vitro scratch test was used to evaluate MO-07 (Figure 4) and MO-07/RS (Figure 5) effects on the wound-healing process. As a control, RS alone was also tested, but without positive results. The kit provided specific inserts that generated a defined filled wound. Firstly, the abovementioned test was carried out from 7.5 to 240 µMol of MO-07 (Figure 4a), with interesting results. The lowest concentrations, namely 7.5 and 15 µMol, did not show significant results in terms of wound closure. Migration of cells into the gap area was compared with the untreated control (CTR). After 6 h there were 22,8% migrated cells in the CTR wound field (Figure 4b in white). MO-07 at any of the concentrations assayed exerted significant effects and closed the wound to 32.6% (30 µMol, in yellow), 33.2% (60 µMol, in red), 33.7% (120 µMol, in green), and 39.2% (240 µMol, in blue). These differences grew after 12 h of treatment, where the CTR showed a 34.3% closure, whereas with 60 µMol of MO-07 we achieved the best result with a closure of up to 63.7% ($p < 0.0001$). These data were confirmed after 24 h of treatment, with 64% of closure for the CTR compared to 85,7% with 30 µMol, 92.5% with 60 µMol, 85.3% with 120 µMol, and 74.2% with 240 µMol. In conclusion, the MO-07 achieved excellent results from 30 to 240 µMol in comparison with the CTR, but without a doubt the best outcome was obtained with 60 µMol (almost complete closure).

(a)

(b)

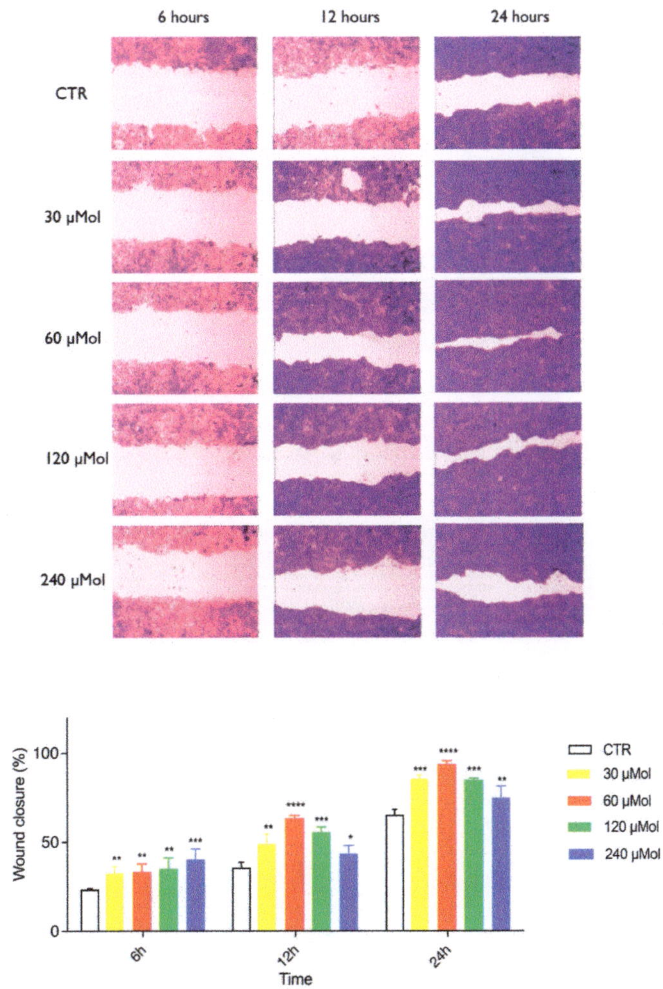

Figure 4. (**a**) Representative images of the wound field observed at 6, 12, and 24 h for untreated cells (CTR) and for cells treated with MO-07 at different concentrations (30, 60, 120, and 240 µMol). (**b**) Histogram plot together with ± SD of three independent experiments. * $p < 0.05$, ** $p \leq 0.01$, *** $p \leq 0.001$, and **** $p \leq 0.0001$, treatments versus control (one-way ANOVA test).

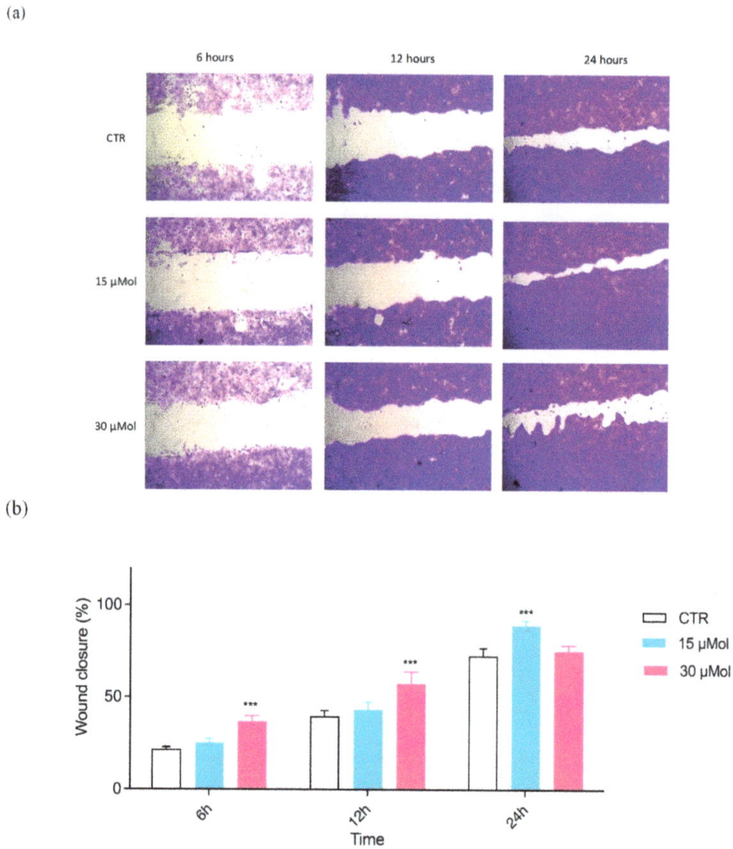

Figure 5. (**a**) Representative images of the wound field observed at 6, 12, and 24 h for untreated cells (CTR) and for cells treated with RS+MO-07 (15 and 30 μMol). (**b**) Histogram plot together with ± SD of three independent experiments. *** $p \leq 0.001$, treatments versus control (one-way ANOVA test).

Our purpose was to evaluate the level of cellular fill within the wound area in response to MO-07/RS treatments. The peptide-functionalized silk fibroin has been proven as a valuable tool to positively influence wound closure. In fact, as reported in Figure 5a, with 15 and 30 μMol of MO-07/RS we obtained really good results compared with the CTR. Specifically, after 6 and 12 h 30 μMol (Figure 5b, in fuchsia) was able to reduce the gap better than 15 μMol (in light blue), 33.9% vs. 23.9% (6 h) and 54.6% vs. 42% (12 h). However, after 24 h, 15 μMol demonstrated the best wound closure, with 88.4% vs. 73.7% with 30 μMol of treatment. We can conclude that migration of cells in the wound field is the first step in healing, and both MO-07 and MO-07/RS were able to promote this effect in comparison to the CTR. However, if we consider 24 h of treatment, MO-07 showed the best result at 60 μMol, while MO-07/RS demonstrated a good performance at 15 μMol.

Natural polymers are currently exploited as smart materials due to their intrinsic piezoresistive properties for monitoring force and deformation [24], and thus have high potential for applications in the increasing demand for sustainable and green sensors, mainly for the Internet of Things. As a first step, the 3D-printed grid's ability to sense applied pressure was tested; both the measured resistance and its reciprocal (conductance) versus the applied pressure are shown in Figure 6.

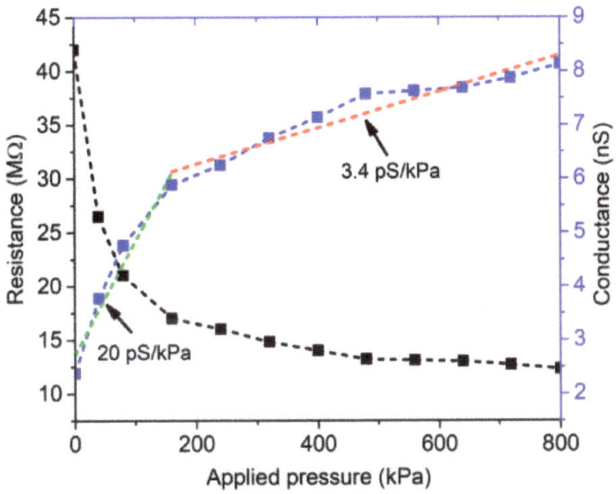

Figure 6. Measured resistance and conductance of the MO-07/RS 3D-printed grid as a function of applied pressure. Conductance = blue dot-line, Sensitivity about 20 pS/kPa and 3.4 pS/kPa = green and red line respectively; Resistance = black dot-line.

The measured resistance varied from 42 MΩ when no force was applied to 12 MΩ for a pressure of 800 kPa, clearly demonstrating the piezoresistive behavior of the 3D-printed grid. A piecewise best linear fit based on the least squares method was applied to the measured conductance. The 3D-printed grid showed a higher sensitivity, equal to about 20 pS/kPa (green dot-line), for applied pressures lower than 150 kPa, while it featured a sensitivity of about 3.4 pS/kPa (red dot-line) in the range 150–800 kPa.

In addition to its piezoresistive properties, we also demonstrated the humidity-sensitive property of the MO-07/RS grid. As shown in Figure 7a, the resistivity decreases as a function of relative humidity. This effect is a combination of the hygroscopic behavior of the peptide-functionalized silk and the activation of Ca^{2+} ion mobility due to water absorption [25]. To investigate humidity's effect on the electrical resistance of the MO-07/RS grid, we evaluated the change in current–voltage characteristics at different values of relative humidity (see Figure S3). Above 60% RH, when the voltage was increased the current abruptly increased at 1 V (Figure 7b). After this voltage threshold, the resistance state changed from high to low, known as the ON state. To recover the initial insulating state (e.g., high resistive state) we had to apply a voltage from 1 V to negative voltage values, which changed the resistance state back to an insulating state. These data suggest that peptide-modified RS has potential usage in sensor computing applications based on biological sensing [26,27].

The 3D-printed grid was also used in a radio-frequency (RF) circuit to perform wireless shock sensing. The circuit, demonstrated in ref. [28], is a passive frequency doubler, based on a series-connected low-barrier Schottky diode and two quarter-wave stubs working as harmonic filters [29]. Input- and output-matching networks were added to match the circuit to input and output impedances of 50 Ω. The circuit schematic is shown in Figure 8a. The RF signal at the circuit input (x_{in}) is distorted by the diode, which generates harmonic components. The harmonic filters are used to maximize the power of the second harmonic signal at the output port (x_{out}). By connecting one antenna working at the fundamental frequency to the input port of the doubler, and another antenna working at the second harmonic to the output port of the doubler, a passive harmonic transponder can be readily implemented [28]. One of the two copper electrodes where the 3D-printed grid is sandwiched is connected to the inductor of the output-matching network of the frequency doubler, while the other electrode is connected to ground.

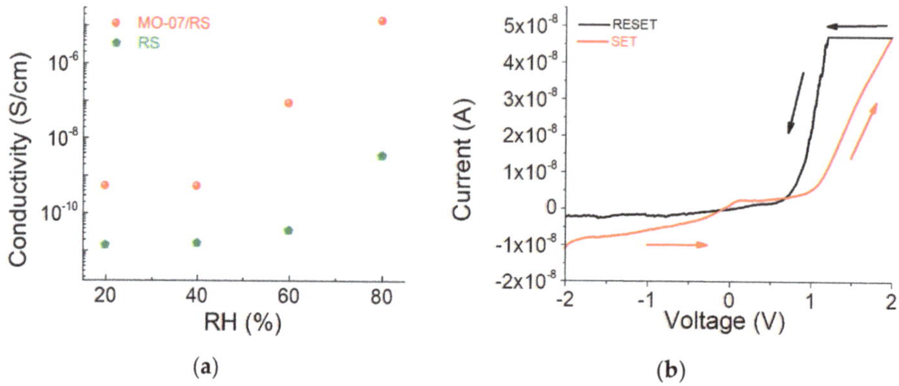

Figure 7. (**a**) Resistivity–humidity curves of RS and MO-07/RS samples. (**b**) I–V characteristic of the MO-07/RS memory device at 80% RH. The voltage sweep direction (-2 V $\rightarrow$ 2 V $\rightarrow$ 1 V $\rightarrow$ -2 V) is indicated with arrows.

(a)

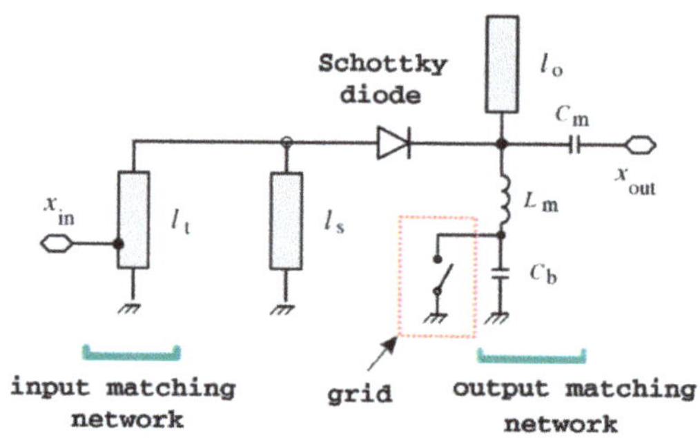

(b)

Figure 8. (**a**) Circuit schematic. Main circuit parameters: l_t = 17 mm, l_s = l_o = 21.5 mm, C_m = 0.5 pF, L_m = 1.3 nH, and C_b = 100 pF. (**b**) Photo of the shock sensor prototype.

The intrinsic visco-elastic property of RS was used to implement a mechanical switch: when a force above a specific threshold is applied to the 3D-printed grid, the RS starts to flow under pressure and the two copper electrodes are placed in contact (switch closed).

This means that the inductor is DC-connected to ground and the diode is zero-biased. When the applied pressure is below threshold, the two copper plates are separated, and no DC current can flow in the circuit. This modifies the self-bias point of the diode [29], thereby increasing the doubler's frequency conversion loss or, equivalently, reducing the power of the second harmonic signal at the output port. A bypass capacitor (C_b) is connected in parallel with the 3D-printed grid shock sensor, to avoid the RF signals being affected by the sensor parasitics.

A proof-of-concept prototype in microstrip technology was manufactured on a biodegradable PHBV substrate (photo shown in Figure 8b). The circuit was designed for a fundamental frequency of 2.25 GHz. The main circuit dimensions are reported in the caption of Figure 8b. Stereolithography was applied to a copper adhesive tape to manufacture the metal traces [30]. The obtained traces were adhered to the substrate, and the discrete circuit components (i.e., an HSMS2850 Schottky diode and two 0402 ceramic capacitors) were soldered to the traces.

The adopted experimental setup consists of an RF signal generator, a spectrum analyzer, and a dynamometer connected to a vertical stand (see Figure 9a). The RF input power was set to −10 dBm, and the compressive force was applied to the 3D-printed grid in steps of 1 N. For each step, the power of the output signal at the second harmonic was measured with the spectrum analyzer. The experimental results are illustrated in Figure 9b. The measured threshold force to place the copper electrodes in contact (switch closed) was 6 N, corresponding to a pressure of 240 kPa. The RF output power increased by 10 dB, from −35 dBm when the switch was open to −25 dBm when the switch was closed. After the pressure is released, the switch returns to the open condition (the RF output power goes back to −35 dBm) after less than one second.

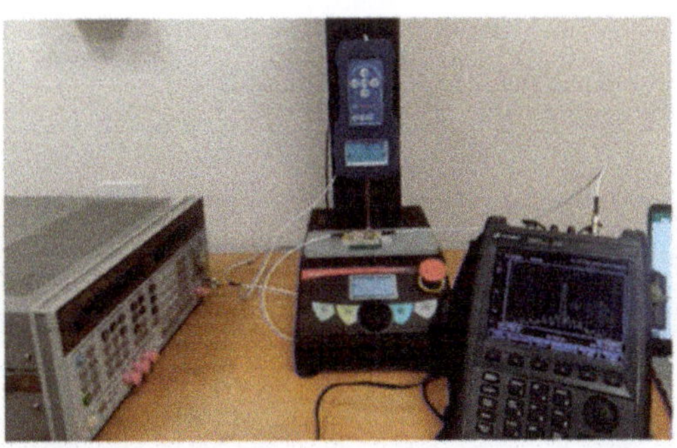

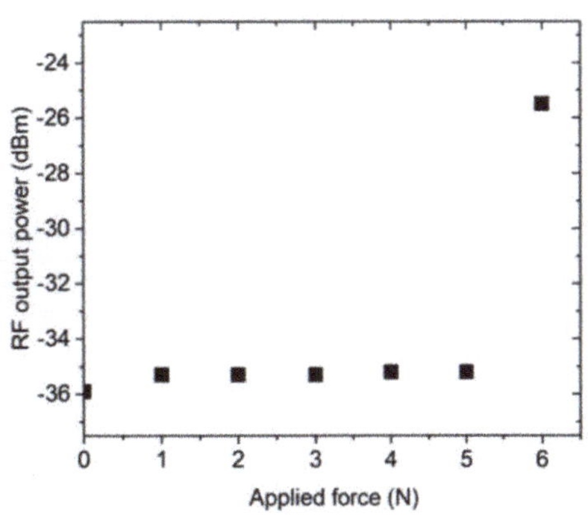

(a) (b)

Figure 9. Experimental results for the proposed shock sensor: (**a**) experimental setup and (**b**) obtained results.

3. Materials and Methods

3.1. Materials

Fmoc-Ser(tBu)-Wang resin was purchased from Iris Biotech AG (Marktredwitz, Germany). Peptide grade N,N-dimethylformamide (DMF), N,N′-diisopropylcarbodiimide (DIC) activators, Oxyma Pure, all Fmoc-L amino acids, trifluoroacetic acid (TFA), triisopropyl silane (TIS), diisopropyl ether (iPr2O), 2-propanol, and HPLC plus water were purchased from Merck

(Milan, Italy). HPLC-grade acetonitrile (ACN) was purchased from Carlo Erba (Milan, Italy). Salts used for preparing PBS buffer (NaCl, KCl, KH_2PO_4, and Na_2HPO_4) were purchased from Sigma Aldrich (Milan, Italy). EDC*HCl (N-(3-Dimethylaminopropyl)-N′-ethylcarbodiimide hydrochloride and NHS (N-Hydroxysuccinimide) used for the silk functionalization were from Sigma Aldrich (Milan, Italy). Silk cocoons were supplied from a local farm. Sodium hydrogen carbonate ($NaHCO_3$, >99.5%), calcium chloride ($CaCl_2$, anhydrous > 93%), formic acid (FA, reagent grade > 95%), gelatin from porcine skin Type A, hydrochloric acid (HCl), and sodium hydroxide (NaOH) were supplied by Merck. Hydrofilm used as a sacrificial support in the printing process was purchased from Lucart, Italy. Dulbecco's Modified Eagle Medium (DMEM) and dimethyl sulfoxide (DMSO) were purchased from Merck, Italy. Poly(3-hydroxybutyrate-*co*-3-hydroxyvalerate) (PHBV) was purchased from Merck, Italy.

3.2. Peptide Synthesis

Peptide MO-07 (YRGDS, reported in Figure S1) was prepared by induction-assisted solid-phase peptide synthesis (SPPS) in a PurePep®Chorus® instrument (Gyros Protein Technologies, Tucson, AZ, USA), using a Fmoc-L-Ser(tBu)-Wang resin (loading: 0.6 mmol/g), with a single coupling protocol, at 0.25 mmol synthesis scale. Peptide MO-07 identity was confirmed through UHPLC-MS analysis. The yield of crude peptide was 80.5%.

3.3. Silk Fiber Functionalization

Degummed silk fibers (DSF) derived from *B. mori* silk cocoons were functionalized with peptide MO-07 as previously described [31]. Briefly, *B. mori* silk cocoons were boiled at 100 °C in a solution of $NaHCO_3$, and the extracted fibers were washed and dried to be used as a solid support for the functionalization with peptide MO-07. This reaction was performed in three steps: the first one concerns the wetting of the DSF with PBS, the second one is the activation of the -COOH groups in the fibers by using EDC/NHS in PBS, and the last one is the addition of a solution of peptide MO-07 to the fibers. The functionalization degree was monitored by quantitative UHPLC analysis before and after 2.5 h of reaction. DSFs and functionalized DSFs were then dissolved in formic acid to obtain regenerated silk and regenerated silk with MO-07 solutions as previously described [19].

3.4. 3D Printing Process

Multilayered 1.5 cm × 1.5 cm × 200 μm grid structures with a 30% infill density were 3D-printed via extrusion-based bioprinting (EBB) using the regenerated silk solution with MO-07 (MO-07/RS) and the RS solution without MO-07 (RS). Briefly, the printing process occurred on a water-soluble sacrificial polymer layer (2 mg/mL of Hydrofilm) attached to an acetate foil with the following printing parameters: print speed = 5.5 $mm \cdot s^{-1}$; volumetric flow = 0.18 $mm^3 \cdot s^{-1}$; nozzle diameter = 0.21 mm; and layer height = 50 μm (four layers in total). After printing, the structures were dried at room temperature for 24 h to allow residual FA to evaporate. Then, the RS-based grids, still attached to the Hydrofilm layer, were peeled from the acetate foil and the line and pore dimensions were measured via image analysis. Images were acquired using a brightfield microscope (Leica DM 6 M) and a mean value for the line and pore dimension was obtained for both solutions.

3.5. Characterization

3.5.1. Cytotoxicity Assay In Vitro

Cell viability was evaluated by MTT test [32–34]. The experiments were performed on HaCaT cells (human immortalized keratinocyte cell line), purchased from I.Z.S.L.E.R. (Istituto Zooprofilattico Sperimentale della Lombardia e dell' Emilia Romagna) as representative of epidermis. Cells were grown in monolayer cultures, with DMEM complete medium supplemented with 10% heat-inactivated fetal bovine serum (FBS), 2 mM of L-glutamine, and antibiotics (100 U/mL penicillin and 100 μg/mL streptomycin) and incubated at 37 °C under 5% CO_2 atmosphere. When it had reached a confluence of 80–90%, the culture medium was aspirated and the cells washed with PBS 1X, as previously described [35]. Cells were seeded onto a 96-well plate with DMEM complete medium. After 24 h, fresh DMEM complete medium was replaced for treatment with different concentrations of MO-07 and RS with and without MO-07 for 24 h (the final volume in each well was required to be 180 μL). In all experiments, untreated cells were used as negative controls. Lastly, after 24 h of treatment, 20 μL of MTT (5 mg/mL) was added to each well (final concentration 0.5 mg/mL and total volume for well 200 μL). After 3 h of incubation at 37 °C, the supernatant was carefully removed and in each well was added 200 μL DMSO. After 30 min, using an automatic microplate reader (Eliza MAT 2000, DRG Instruments, GmbH), the absorbance values (optical density, OD) were measured spectrophotometrically at λ_{max} = 540 nm.

Cell viability calculation by MTT assay was performed as follows: firstly, an average of three "empty" wells, containing only MTT solution, were prepared and used as a background control (i.e., blank). The blank was used to define the baseline (no cells = zero viability) when percentages/ratios were calculated. All values were corrected for background and viability was calculated as previously reported [36]. Three independent experiments were performed in triplicate.

3.5.2. Wound Healing Assay

The scratch test was performed using a CytoSelect™ wound healing assay kit (Cell Biolabs, Inc., San Diego, CA, USA), making it possible to simulate a wound in vitro; it was used to study the effect of the prepared extracts on keratinocyte growth at different dilutions. Wound closure is a complex process involving many other cell types and it is divided in different phases. An in vitro wound healing assay is a simple and inexpensive method that mimics cell migration. It is suitable for cell types such as keratinocytes and skin fibroblasts that exhibit collective migration, also known as "sheet migration". This technique consists in performing a linear thin scratch "wound" (creating a gap) in a confluent keratinocyte monolayer. The images of cells filling the gap were taken at regular time intervals (6, 12, and 24 h).

HaCaT cells were seeded in a 24-well plate at a final concentration of 3×10^5 and incubated overnight. Inserts were removed after 24 h, leaving the wound field. After washing with PBS 1X to remove dead cells and debris [37,38], extracts, previously solubilized in DMEM complete medium, were added to the cells. Complete DMEM was used to treat control cells. After 6, 12, and 24 h the treatments were removed and 300 μL of fixing solution was added to each well for 10 min. The fixing solution was removed and each well was washed with PBS twice. Then, 500 μL of cell stain solution was added to each well to be stained; after 15 min the cell stain solution was removed and each well was washed with 500 μL of PBS X3 and deionized water twice.

Wound area was calculated by manually tracing the cell-free area in captured images using the public domain software ImageJ (NIH, Bethesda, MD, USA). The closure will increase as cells migrate over time. To measure the % closure, the migration cell surface area was determined for each experiment (migration cell surface = total surface area − cell-free area). The percent closure of the wound field was calculated for three different treatment times: 6, 12, and 24 h and using Equation (1):

$$\% \text{ closure} = \frac{(\text{total surface area} - \text{cell-free area})}{\text{total surface area}} \times 100 \quad (1)$$

where total surface area means the area immediately after removing the insert and cell-free area means the white area in the photograph.

Migration into the wound field was determined as previously described [39,40] and representative pictures of the CTR and treated cells after 6, 12, and 24 h were taken. Three independent experiments were performed in duplicate.

3.5.3. Piezoresistive Measurements

To assess the piezoresistivity of the 3D-printed grid, a square sample with an area of 5×5 mm^2 was sandwiched between two thin Cu electrodes. The Cu electrodes were connected to a digital multimeter to measure the resistance of the sample. A compressive force was applied to the sample with a dynamometer (model PCE-FB 500) connected to an automated vertical stand, as shown in Figure S2. The applied force was varied in steps of 1 N from 0 to 20 N (corresponding to an overestimated applied pressure from 0 to 800 kPa), and the resistance was recorded for each step. To monitor the effect of relative humidity (RH) on electrical conductivity, an MO-07/RS grid was fixed on a Teflon substrate with adhesive copper and then the electrical resistance was recorded by conditioning the sample in a climatic chamber at different relative humidity values (RH; i.e., from 20% RH to 80% RH) at 25 °C.

3.5.4. Characterization of Nonvolatile Memory

For electrical characterization, the 3D-printed grids were sandwiched by two adhesive Cu electrodes. A voltage bias was applied to the top electrode, while the bottom electrode was grounded. A voltage sweep from −2 V to 2 V was applied and the current–voltage characteristic was recorded using a computer-controlled Keithley 4200 Source Meter Unit (Tektronix UK Ltd., The Capitol Building, Oldbury, UK).

3.6. *Statistical Analysis*

GraphPad Prism 9.2.0.332 (GraphPad software, San Diego, CA, USA) was used to assess the statistical significance of all comparison studies in this work. In the statistical analysis for comparison between multiple groups, a two-way ANOVA with Tukey's post hoc analysis (multiple comparisons) was conducted with significance thresholds of $^{*}\ p < 0.05$, $^{**}\ p \leq 0.01$, $^{***}\ p \leq 0.001$, and $^{****}\ p \leq 0.0001$. *t*-tests were used to pinpoint statistical differences among the line and pore dimensions, with significance thresholds of $^{**}\ p \leq 0.01$ and $^{***}\ p \leq 0.001$.

4. Conclusions

We demonstrated the use of peptide-functionalized silk fibroin as a biomaterial ink for 3D printing. The RS obtained from 3D-printed grids promoted the cell proliferation and migration desired in wound healing. Accelerated wound closure resulted primarily from MO-07 peptides, with best results at 60 µMol and secondarily from MO-07/RS, with excellent results at 15 µMol. The present findings need to be confirmed in further in vivo studies.

We showed the utilization of the prepared 3D grid as a piezoresistor to sense pressure. Finally, owing to the presence of Ca^{2+} ions, we reported how the grids are able to sense humidity, and that there is a relative humidity threshold that activated a transient electronic device with memory behavior. This work suggests a broad field of applications for peptide-modified silk fibroin, ranging from wound dressings to bio-implantable processors for bio-devices.

Supplementary Materials: The following supporting information can be downloaded at: https://www.mdpi.com/article/10.3390/ijms24020947/s1.

Author Contributions: Conceptualization, L.V. and P.R.; methodology (peptide synthesis and functionalization), L.P. and F.E.; methodology (wound healing), M.R.C. and M.C.; methodology (shock sensor), V.P., R.S., S.B., P.M. and F.E.; methodology (3D printing), I.C. and C.D.M.; investigation, M.R.C., V.P., I.C. and L.V.; data curation, M.R.C., V.P., I.C. and L.V.; writing—original draft preparation, M.R.C., V.P., R.S., I.C., C.D.M., S.B., P.M., M.C., L.P., F.E., P.R., A.M., T.B., L.R. and L.V.; writing—review and editing, M.R.C., A.M., T.B. and L.V.; supervision, L.V.; funding acquisition, L.V. and L.R. All authors have read and agreed to the published version of the manuscript.

Funding: This research was received funding from the Italian Ministry of Education, University and Research (MUR) under the PRIN Project "Development and promotion of levulinic acid and carboxylate platforms by the formulation of novel and advanced PHA-based biomaterials and their exploitation for 3D-printed green-electronics applications" grant 2017FWC3WC.

Institutional Review Board Statement: Not applicable.

Informed Consent Statement: Not applicable.

Data Availability Statement: Data can be made available upon reasonable request from the corresponding author.

Acknowledgments: I.C. and C.D.M. acknowledge the support of the Crosstab Additive Manufacturing Department of Information Engineering of the University of Pisa. L.P. acknowledges MUR and EU-FSE for the financial support of the PON Research and Innovation PhD fellowship 2014–2020 (D.M 1061/2021) XXXVII Cycle in Chemical Sciences: "Greening peptide chemistry, a necessary step to the future".

Conflicts of Interest: The authors declare no conflict of interest.

References

1. He, C.L.; Liang, F.C.; Veeramuthu, L.; Cho, C.J.; Benas, J.S.; Tzeng, Y.R.; Tseng, Y.L.; Chen, W.C.; Rwei, A.; Kuo, C.C. Super Tough and Spontaneous Water-Assisted Autonomous Self-Healing Elastomer for Underwater Wearable Electronics. *Adv. Sci.* **2021**, *8*, 2102275. [CrossRef] [PubMed]
2. Liang, F.C.; Jhuang, F.C.; Fang, Y.H.; Benas, J.S.; Chen, W.C.; Yan, Z.L.; Lin, W.C.; Su, C.J.; Sato, Y.; Chiba, T.; et al. Synergistic Effect of Cation Composition Engineering of Hybrid $cs_{1-x}FA_xPbBr_3$ Nanocrystals For Self-Healing Electronics Application. *Adv. Mater.* 2022, 2207617, *accepted*. [CrossRef]
3. Su, C.; Chen, Y.; Tian, S.; Lu, C.; Lv, Q. Natural Materials for 3D Printing and Their Applications. *Gels* **2022**, *8*, 748. [CrossRef]
4. Kun, B.; Rajkhowa, R.; Kundu, S.C.; Wang, X. Silk fibroin biomaterials for tissue regenerations. *Adv. Drug Deliv. Rev.* **2013**, *65*, 457–470. [CrossRef]
5. Shao, Z.; Vollrath, F. Surprising strength of silkworm silk. *Nature* **2002**, *418*, 741. [CrossRef] [PubMed]
6. Soffer, L.; Wang, X.; Zhang, X.; Kluge, J.; Dorfmann, L.; Kaplan, D.L.; Leisk, G. Silk-based electrospun tubular scaffolds for tissue-engineered vascular grafts. *J. Biomater. Sci. Polym. Ed.* **2008**, *19*, 653–664. [CrossRef]
7. Marelli, B.; Brenckle, M.A.; Kaplan, D.L.; Omenetto, F.G. Silk Fibroin as Edible Coating for Perishable Food Preservation. *Sci. Rep.* **2016**, *6*, 25263. [CrossRef]
8. Jaramillo-Quiceno, N.; Restrepo-Osorio, A. Water-annealing treatment for edible silk fibroin coatings from fibrous waste. *J. Appl. Polym. Sci.* **2020**, *137*, 48505. [CrossRef]
9. Posati, T.; Benfenati, V.; Sagnella, A.; Pistone, A.; Nocchetti, M.; Donnadio, A.; Ruani, G.; Zamboni, R.; Muccini, M. Innovative multifunctional silk fibroin and hydrotalcite nanocomposites: A synergic effect of the components. *Biomacromolecules* **2014**, *15*, 158–168. [CrossRef]
10. Lu, S.; Wang, X.; Lu, Q.; Zhang, X.; Kluge, J.A.; Uppal, N.; Omenetto, F.; Kaplan, D.L. Insoluble and flexible silk films containing glycerol. *Biomacromolecules* **2010**, *11*, 143–150. [CrossRef]
11. Huang, W.; Ling, S.; Li, C.; Omenetto, F.G.; Kaplan, D.L. Silkworm silk-based materials and devices generated using bio-nanotechnology. *Chem. Soc. Rev.* **2018**, *47*, 6486–6504. [CrossRef]
12. Mikos, A.G.; McIntire, L.V.; Anderson, J.M.; Babensee, J.E. Host response to tissue engineered devices. *Adv. Drug Deliv. Rev.* **1998**, *33*, 111–139. [CrossRef] [PubMed]
13. Tao, H.; Kaplan, D.L.; Omenetto, F.G. Silk materials—A road to sustainable high technology. *Adv. Mater.* **2012**, *24*, 2824–2837. [CrossRef]
14. Bettinger, C.J.; Bao, Z. Biomaterials-Based Organic Electronic Devices. *Polym. Int.* **2010**, *59*, 563–567. [CrossRef] [PubMed]
15. Wang, J.; Chen, Y.; Zhou, G.; Chen, Y.; Mao, C.; Yang, M. Polydopamine-coated antheraea pernyi [a. pernyi] silk fibroin films promote cell adhesion and wound healing in skin tissue repair. *ACS Appl. Mater. Interfaces* **2019**, *11*, 34736–34743. [CrossRef]
16. Tabriz, A.G.; Douroumis, D. Recent advances in 3D printing for wound healing: A systematic review. *J. Drug Deliv. Sci. Technol.* **2022**, *74*, 103564. [CrossRef]
17. Basavalingappa, V.; Bera, S.; Xue, B.; O'Donnell, J.; Guerin, S.; Cazade, P.A.; Yuan, H.; Haq, E.U.; Silien, C.; Tao, K.; et al. Diphenylalanine-Derivative Peptide Assemblies with Increased Aromaticity Exhibit Metal-like Rigidity and High Piezoelectricity. *ACS Nano* **2020**, *14*, 7025–7037. [CrossRef] [PubMed]
18. Song, M.K.; Namgung, S.D.; Song, Y.W.; Sung, T.; Ji, W.; Lee, Y.S.; Nam, K.T.; Kwon, J.Y. Fully degradable memristors and humidity sensors based on a tyrosine-rich peptide. *ACS Appl. Electron. Mater.* **2021**, *3*, 3372–3378. [CrossRef]
19. Chiesa, I.; De Maria, C.; Ceccarini, M.R.; Mussolin, L.; Coletta, R.; Morabito, A.; Tonin, R.; Calamai, M.; Morrone, A.; Beccari, T.; et al. 3D Printing Silk-Based Bioresorbable Piezoelectric Self-Adhesive Holey Structures for In Vivo Monitoring on Soft Tissues. *ACS Appl. Mater. Interfaces* **2022**, *14*, 19253–19264. [CrossRef]

20. Carrabba, M.; De Maria, C.; Oikawa, A.; Reni, C.; Rodriguez-Arabaolaza, I.; Spencer, H.; Slater, S.; Avolio, E.; Dang, Z.; Spinetti, G.; et al. Design, fabrication and perivascular implantation of bioactive scaffolds engineered with human adventitial progenitor cells for stimulation of arteriogenesis in peripheral ischemia. *Biofabrication* **2016**, *8*, 015020. [CrossRef]
21. Bonatti, A.F.; Chiesa, I.; Vozzi, G.; De Maria, C. Open-source Cad-cam simulator of the extrusion-based bioprinting process. *Bioprinting* **2021**, *24*, e00172. [CrossRef]
22. Udofia, E.N.; Zhou, W. A guiding framework for microextrusion additive manufacturing. *J. Manuf. Sci. Eng. Trans. ASME* **2019**, *141*, 050801. [CrossRef]
23. Valentini, L.; Ceccarini, M.R.; Verdejo, R.; Tondi, G.; Beccari, T. Stretchable, Bio-Compatible, Antioxidant and Self-Powering Adhesives from Soluble Silk Fibroin and Vegetal Polyphenols Exfoliated Graphite. *Nanomaterials* **2021**, *11*, 2352. [CrossRef]
24. Oliveira, J.; Correia, V.; Castro, H.; Martins, P.; Lanceros-Mendez, S. Polymer-based smart materials by printing technologies: Improving application and integration. *Addit. Manuf.* **2018**, *21*, 269–283. [CrossRef]
25. Chiesa, I.; De Maria, C.; Tonin, R.; Ripanti, F.; Ceccarini, M.R.; Salvatori, C.; Mussolin, L.; Paciaroni, A.; Petrillo, C.; Cesprini, E.; et al. Biocompatible and Printable Ionotronic Sensing Materials Based on Silk Fibroin and Soluble Plant-Derived Polyphenols. *ACS Omega* **2022**, *7*, 43729–43737. [CrossRef] [PubMed]
26. Wang, Y.; Gong, Y.; Yang, L.; Xiong, Z.; Lu, Z.; Xing, X.; Zhou, Y.; Zhang, B.; Su, C.; Liao, Q.; et al. MXene-ZnO memristor for multimodal in-sensor computing. *Adv. Funct. Mater.* **2021**, *31*, 2100144. [CrossRef]
27. Zhang, C.; Ye, W.B.; Zhou, K.; Chen, H.-Y.; Yang, J.-Q.; Ding, G.; Chen, X.; Zhou, Y.; Zhou, L.; Li, F.; et al. Bioinspired artificial sensory nerve based on nafion memristor. *Adv. Funct. Mater.* **2019**, *29*, 1808783. [CrossRef]
28. Salvati, R.; Palazzi, V.; Cicioni, G.; Simoncini, G.; Alimenti, F.; Tentzeris, M.M.; Mezzanotte, P.; Roselli, L. Zero-power wireless pressure sensor based on backscatterer harmonic transponder in a WPT context. In Proceedings of the 2022 Wireless Power Week, Bordeaux, France, 5–8 July 2022; pp. 199–202.
29. Palazzi, V.; Roselli, L.; Tentzeris, M.M.; Mezzanotte, P.; Alimenti, F. Energy-Efficient Harmonic Transponder Based on On-Off Keying Modulation for Both Identification and Sensing. *Sensors* **2022**, *22*, 620. [CrossRef]
30. Palazzi, V.; Alimenti, F.; Zito, D.; Mezzanotte, P.; Roselli, L. A 24-GHz single-transistor oscillator on paper. *IEEE Microw. Wirel. Compon. Lett.* **2020**, *30*, 1085–1088. [CrossRef]
31. Valentini, L.; Pacini, L.; Errante, F.; Morchio, C.; Sanna, B.; Rovero, P.; Morabito, A. Peptide-Functionalized Silk Fibers as a Platform to Stabilize Gelatin for Use in Ingestible Devices. *Molecules* **2022**, *27*, 4605. [CrossRef]
32. Pagano, C.; Luzi, F.; Ricci, M.; Di Michele, A.; Puglia, D.; Ceccarini, M.R.; Beccari, T.; Blasi, F.; Cossignani, L.; Schoubben, A.; et al. Wound dressing: Combination of acacia gum/pvp/cyclic dextrin in bioadhesive patches loaded with grape seed extract. *Pharmaceutics* **2022**, *14*, 485. [CrossRef]
33. Denizot, F.; Lang, R. Rapid colorimetric assay for cell growth and survival. Modifications to the tetrazolium dye procedure giving improved sensitivity and reliability. *J. Immunol. Methods* **1986**, *89*, 271–277. [CrossRef]
34. Kumar, P.; Nagarajan, A.; Uchil, P.D. Analysis of Cell Viability by the MTT Assay. *Cold Spring Harb. Protoc.* **2018**, *2018*. [CrossRef]
35. Pagano, C.; Ceccarini, M.R.; Faieta, M.; di Michele, A.; Blasi, F.; Cossignani, L.; Beccari, T.; Oliva, E.; Pittia, P.; Sergi, M.; et al. Starch-based sustainable hydrogel loaded with Crocus sativus petals extract: A new product for wound care. *Int. J. Pharm.* **2022**, *625*, 122067. [CrossRef]
36. Ceccarini, M.R.; Puccetti, M.; Pagano, C.; Nocchetti, M.; Beccari, T.; di Michele, A.; Ricci, M.; Perioli, L. MgAl and ZnAl-Hydrotalcites as Materials for Cosmetic and Pharmaceutical Formulations: Study of Their Cytotoxicity on Different Cell Lines. *Pharmaceuticals* **2022**, *15*, 784. [CrossRef] [PubMed]
37. Pagano, C.; Marinozzi, M.; Baiocchi, C.; Beccari, T.; Calarco, P.; Ceccarini, M.R.; Chielli, M.; Orabona, C.; Orecchini, E.; Ortenzi, R.; et al. Bioadhesive Polymeric Films Based on Red Onion Skins Extract for Wound Treatment: An Innovative and Eco-Friendly Formulation. *Molecules* **2020**, *25*, 318. [CrossRef] [PubMed]
38. Pagano, C.; Puglia, D.; Luzi, F.; Michele, A.D.; Scuota, S.; Primavilla, S.; Ceccarini, M.R.; Beccari, T.; Iborra, C.A.V.; Ramella, D.; et al. Development and Characterization of Xanthan Gum and Alginate Based Bioadhesive Film for Pycnogenol Topical Use in Wound Treatment. *Pharmaceutics* **2021**, *13*, 324. [CrossRef] [PubMed]
39. Grada, A.; Otero-Vinas, M.; Prieto-Castrillo, F.; Obagi, Z.; Falanga, V. Research Techniques Made Simple: Analysis of Collective Cell Migration Using the Wound Healing Assay. *J. Investig. Dermatol.* **2017**, *137*, e11–e16. [CrossRef] [PubMed]
40. Pagano, C.; Calarco, P.; Di Michele, A.; Ceccarini, M.R.; Beccari, T.; Primavilla, S.; Scuota, S.; Marmottini, F.; Ramella, D.; Ricci, M.; et al. Development of sodium carboxymethyl cellulose based polymeric microparticles for in situ hydrogel wound dressing formation. *Int. J. Pharm.* **2021**, *602*, 120606. [CrossRef]

International Journal of
Molecular Sciences

MDPI

Article

Effectiveness of Semi-Supervised Active Learning in Automated Wound Image Segmentation

Nico Curti [1,†], Yuri Merli [2,†], Corrado Zengarini [2], Enrico Giampieri [1,*], Alessandra Merlotti [3], Daniele Dall'Olio [3], Emanuela Marcelli [1], Tommaso Bianchi [2] and Gastone Castellani [4]

1 eDIMES Lab, Department of Experimental, Diagnostic and Specialty Medicine, University of Bologna, 40138 Bologna, Italy
2 Dermatology, IRCCS Sant'Orsola-Malpighi Hospital, 40138 Bologna, Italy
3 Department of Physics and Astronomy, University of Bologna, 40127 Bologna, Italy
4 Department of Experimental, Diagnostic and Specialty Medicine, University of Bologna, 40138 Bologna, Italy
* Correspondence: enrico.giampieri@unibo.it
† These authors contributed equally to this work.

Abstract: Appropriate wound management shortens the healing times and reduces the management costs, benefiting the patient in physical terms and potentially reducing the healthcare system's economic burden. Among the instrumental measurement methods, the image analysis of a wound area is becoming one of the cornerstones of chronic ulcer management. Our study aim is to develop a solid AI method based on a convolutional neural network to segment the wounds efficiently to make the work of the physician more efficient, and subsequently, to lay the foundations for the further development of more in-depth analyses of ulcer characteristics. In this work, we introduce a fully automated model for identifying and segmenting wound areas which can completely automatize the clinical wound severity assessment starting from images acquired from smartphones. This method is based on an active semi-supervised learning training of a convolutional neural network model. In our work, we tested the robustness of our method against a wide range of natural images acquired in different light conditions and image expositions. We collected the images using an ad hoc developed app and saved them in a database which we then used for AI training. We then tested different CNN architectures to develop a balanced model, which we finally validated with a public dataset. We used a dataset of images acquired during clinical practice and built an annotated wound image dataset consisting of 1564 ulcer images from 474 patients. Only a small part of this large amount of data was manually annotated by experts (ground truth). A multi-step, active, semi-supervised training procedure was applied to improve the segmentation performances of the model. The developed training strategy mimics a continuous learning approach and provides a viable alternative for further medical applications. We tested the efficiency of our model against other public datasets, proving its robustness. The efficiency of the transfer learning showed that after less than 50 epochs, the model achieved a stable DSC that was greater than 0.95. The proposed active semi-supervised learning strategy could allow us to obtain an efficient segmentation method, thereby facilitating the work of the clinician by reducing their working times to achieve the measurements. Finally, the robustness of our pipeline confirms its possible usage in clinical practice as a reliable decision support system for clinicians.

Keywords: computer-aided diagnosis; deep learning; image analysis; wound healing; image segmentation

Citation: Curti, N.; Merli, Y.; Zengarini, C.; Giampieri, E.; Merlotti, A.; Dall'Olio, D.; Marcelli, E.; Bianchi, T.; Castellani, G. Effectiveness of Semi-Supervised Active Learning in Automated Wound Image Segmentation. *Int. J. Mol. Sci.* **2023**, 24, 706. https://doi.org/10.3390/ijms24010706

Academic Editors: César Viseras, Luana Perioli and Cinzia Pagano

Received: 22 November 2022
Revised: 18 December 2022
Accepted: 26 December 2022
Published: 31 December 2022

1. Introduction

Wound healing is a complex process where many factors, whether they are physical, chemical, or biological, work in balance to allow the repair of damaged tissue. Evaluating the impairments that may affect these factors is fundamental to ensure the greatest chances of healing acute and chronic ulcers in clinical settings [1].

A holistic approach to the patient's situation is recommended, considering social conditions such as the possibility of obtaining access to care, their age, the caregivers' presence, and a complete clinical and instrumental examination, which make it possible to recognize any comorbidities or deficits limiting the healing ability. Once an all-inclusive assessment of the wound has been performed and the correct therapy has been set, methodical and instrumental-assisted continuous monitoring becomes essential to ascertain whether the healing process is proceeding correctly or not [2].

A clinical wound follow-up involves the observation of different features in the ulcer site and leads physicians to infer data that can be used to determine prognosis and correct treatment. These parameters include the recognition of the wound margins, the bottom, the amount of exudate, the peri-wound skin, and its color, and finally, the shape and size of it [3]. Of all of them, the dimensions are the most informative values that are able to provide a numerical and objective quantification of the wound status, allowing us to plot the wound healing trajectory to determine whether it is proceeding in a correct fashion [1]. It is well known that an incorrect model of a wound assessment can lead to prolongation in wound healing [4]. Moreover, besides the clinical implications, shorter healing times due to better wound management may reduce the costs. Ulcer treatments are complex, and chronic ulcers have specific structures that need to be attended to, are more time and money consuming [5], and are known to enormously impact healthcare systems' economic burden [6]. As an example of the health costs related to ulcers, regardless of the health model and the reference population, the economic price for their management is exceptionally high, with reported values of GBP 8.3 billion for the NHS in the UK in 2013 [7] and USD 31.7 billion for the Medicare system in the USA in 2018 [8]. These conservative calculations do not take comprehensive account of the private healthcare costs and cost–benefit and cost-effectiveness outcomes, but they provide an excellent example of the numbers accounting for wound care management. Additionally, we emphasize that financial burdens are growing in most Western countries [5,9]. Therefore, it is vital to try to the costs by pursuing the best and up-to-date aids, having well-trained specialists, and using reproducible methods for ulcer assessments [10].

Given the high inter- and intra-operator variability in collecting the physical characteristics [11,12], various hardware and software models have been tested to reduce operator fluctuations in chronic wounds measurements. Based on photographic support, some of these achieved the reasonably precise sizing of the ulcer, with results that are often superior to those of manual methods [12]. Moreover, manual measurement is time-consuming. Knowing that the video-assisted estimation of wound area is becoming one of the cornerstones of chronic ulcer management [13], we wanted to develop an artificial intelligence model based on wound pictures to provide accurate and automatically reproducible measurements.

The automatic segmentation of wounds is becoming an increasingly investigated field by researchers. Related studies on digital wound measurement mainly involve using video-assistive software or the use of artificial intelligence. The first ones used software coded to recognize specific image characteristics of the wounds (differences in color and saturation, grid scales, RGB tones, etc.) and provide a numeric value. On the other hand, the latter ones offer the possibility of obtaining measurements using different models, such as those ranging from machine learning supervised by humans and based on various classification methods (Naïve-Bayes, logistic regression, etc.) to unsupervised black-box-type models.

While classical software video-assisted classification methods provide a sufficient overall accuracy [14], AI sensitivity and specificity are promising, ranging from the 81.8% accuracy of classical neural networks up to the 90% accuracy of models such as the Generative Adversarial Network (GAN) [15]. The training of an artificial neural network usually requires supervision, but it is generally difficult to obtain great quantities of manually annotated data in clinical settings. Namely, the manual segmentation of images could be indeed extremely time consuming for large datasets. Though, when it is available, manual segmentation by human experts could further suffer from imperfections which are mainly caused by inter-observer variability due to a subjective wound boundary estimation [11].

Several approaches are apt to overcome the problem of large data annotations and the consequent image segmentation [16–18]. In this work, we proposed a combination of active learning and semi-supervised learning training strategies for deep learning models, proving its effectiveness for annotating large image datasets with minimal effort from clinicians. Moreover, to the authors' knowledge, the resulting dataset, which is named *Deepskin*, represents one of the largest sets of chronic wounds used for the training of deep learning models. Therefore, the *Deepskin* dataset constitutes a novel starting point for deep learning applications in the analysis of chronic wounds and a robust benchmark for future quantitative results on this topic. Our study rationale is to develop an AI method, based on a convolutional neural network (CNN), enabling highly reproducible results thanks to its data-driven, highly representative, hierarchical image features [19]. Our future aims are to use the developed AI as a starting point to conduct more in-depth analyses of ulcer characteristics, such as the margins, wound bed, and exudation, which are used in the Bates-Jensen wound assessment tool (BWAT) score [20].

In this work, we started with a core set of 145 (less than 10% of the available samples) manually annotated images (see Section 4 for the details about the analyzed dataset). We implemented a U-Net CNN model for the automated segmentation task using an architecture that was pre-trained on the ImageNet dataset as a starting point. We repeated the active evaluation of automated segmentations until the number of training data reached (at least) 80% of the available samples. For each round of training, we divided the available image masks samples into training test sets (90–10%): in this way, we could quantify the generalization capacity of the model at each round (see Section 4 for the details about the implemented training strategy). For each round, we quantified the percentage of images that were correctly segmented on the validation according to the clinicians' evaluation. To further test the robustness of the proposed training strategy and the developed *Deepskin* dataset, we compared the results obtained by our deep learning model also on public dataset [21,22], analyzing the generalization capability of the models using different training sets (Section 2 and Supplementary Materials Table S1).

2. Results

2.1. Training with Active Learning

To reach the target of segmenting 80% of the images, we conducted four rounds of training (including the first one) with our U-Net model, incrementing the number of training images/masks at each round. We started with a set of 145 images, validating the model using the remaining samples. The training rounds that were performed with the related number of samples used at each round are reported in Table 1. In each round, the two expert dermatologists evaluated the generated masks, noting the number of correctly segmented images that would be used in the next round of the training (Table 1).

Table 1. Results obtained by the U-Net model using the active semi-supervised learning procedure at each round. We report the number of images used for the training, the number of images used for the validation, the number of correctly segmented validation images (according to the expert evaluation), and the metric scores achieved (on the test set) after 150 epochs for each round of training, respectively. The percentages of training and validation images are referred to the whole set of available samples, i.e., 1564 images. The percentage of correct segmentation is referred to the total number of validated images per each round.

	Round 0	Round 1	Round 2	Round 3
N° training images	145 (9%)	368 (24%)	916 (59%)	1365 (87%)
N° validation images	1419 (91%)	1196 (76%)	648 (41%)	199 (13%)
N° correct segmentation	223 (16%)	548 (46%)	449 (69%)	112 (56%)
DSC metric	0.95	0.98	0.97	0.96
Precision metric	0.93	0.98	0.97	0.96
Recall metric	0.96	0.98	0.97	0.96

The model was trained with the same set of hyper-parameters, resetting the initial weights in each round. We trained the model for 150 epochs, monitoring the scores described in Section 4.

2.2. Results on Deepskin Dataset

The results obtained by our training procedure at the end of the fourth round of training are shown in Figure 1a. We dichotomized the masks produced by our model according to a threshold of 0.5 (127 on the gray-level scale). The results shown in Figure 1b highlight the efficiency of the model in the wound detection and contours segmentation.

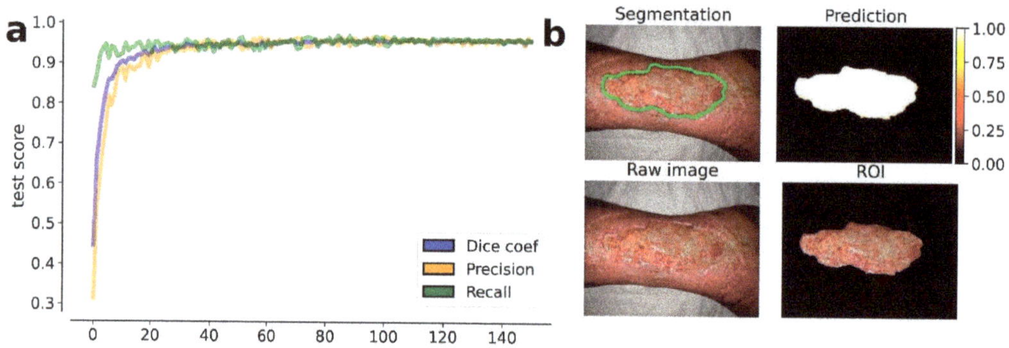

Figure 1. Results obtained by the trained U-Net model at the 4th round of training. (**a**) Evolution of the average metrics (dice coefficient, precision, and recall) during the training epochs (150). The metric values are estimated on the test set, i.e., the 10% of available images, which were excluded from the training set. On the top left image is the resulting segmentation. (**b**) On the top right image is the predicted segmentation mask. On the bottom left image is the raw (input) image. On the bottom right image is the resulting ROI of the wound area.

The results also prove the efficiency of the transfer learning procedure which was guaranteed by the EfficientNetb-3 backbone used in the U-Net model: after less than 50 epochs, the model achieved a stable DSC that was greater than 0.95. A transfer learning procedure was also proposed by Wang et al., but the model used in their work required more than 1000 training epochs, drastically increasing the computational time of the model training.

2.3. Results on Public Dataset

We tested our trained model on the FUSC public dataset without model re-training. In this way, we aimed to monitor the generalization capability of our model and its robustness against different images. The results obtained on these datasets are reported in Table 2.

Table 2. Comparison of the results obtained by the MobileNetV2 model (Wang et al.) and the U-Net model proposed in this work, on the two available datasets, (a) *Deepskin* and (b) FUSC, respectively. We re-trained the MobileNetV2 on the FUSC dataset for the reproducibility of Wang et al. results. The U-Net model was trained only on the *Deepskin* dataset as described in Section 4.

a	Mobile NetV2	Our U-Net	b	Mobile NetV2	Our U-Net
DSC	0.64	0.96	DSC	0.90	0.78
Precision	0.53	0.96	Precision	0.91	0.83
Recall	0.85	0.96	Recall	0.90	0.72
	Deepskin			FUSC	

The same dataset was also used by Wang et al. for training a MobileNetV2 model. We re-trained the same model (which is public available in [22]) on the FUSC dataset to achieve the reproducibility of the results. Furthermore, we tested the generalization capability of the Wang et al. model on our *Deepskin* dataset, allowing a direct comparison to be made between the two models and the robustness of the datasets used for their training. We report in Table 2 the results achieved by the two models on both datasets (*Deepskin* and FUSC), which are expressed in terms of the same metrics used above.

3. Discussion

The active learning strategy implemented in this work for the semi-automated annotation of a large set of images produced remarkable results. Starting with a relatively small core set of manually annotated samples, in only four rounds of training, we were able to obtain annotations for more than 90% of the available images. This procedure could drastically improve the availability of huge, annotated datasets with minimum timeframes and costs as required by expert clinicians.

We remark that the "classical" active learning involves a continuous interaction between the learning algorithm and the user. During training, the user is queried to manually label new data samples according to statistical considerations of the results proposed by the model. In our framework, we re-interpreted this procedure, requiring only a binary evaluation of the results by the user: if the generated segmentation did not satisfy the pre-determined set of criteria, it was excluded from the next training set, and vice versa. In this way, we can optimize the expert clinicians' effort, minimizing the manual annotation requirement.

The *Deepskin* dataset introduced in this work constitutes one of the largest benchmarks available in the literature for the wound segmentation task. The heterogeneity of the wound images, combined with their high resolution and image quality, guarantees the robustness of the models trained on them. All of the images were acquired using the same smartphone photo camera, providing a robust standardization of the dataset in terms of image resolution and putative artifacts. At the same time, this characteristic poses the main limitation of this dataset, since batch effects could arise in terms of the generalization capability of the model. A robust data augmentation and deep learning model is crucial to overcome this kind of issue. This limit is a direct consequence of the single-center nature of our work, which reduce the possible heterogeneity of the images, i.e., the different conditions in picture acquisition and the operators available.

Furthermore, we would stress that all of the *Deepskin* images were acquired for clinical purposes. Therefore, the focus of each image is the estimation of the clinical wound scores using the photo. In this way, the amount of background information was limited as much as possible, and the center of each image was occupied by the wound area. This was not true when we used other public datasets, such as the FUSC one used in this work, for which a pre-processing was necessary [20].

Another limitation of the *Deepskin* dataset arises from the geographical location of the Dermatology Unit which collected the data. The IRCCS Sant'Orsola-Malpighi Hospital of the University of Bologna is an Italian hospital with a strong prevalence of Caucasian people. Most of the wound segmentation studies involve US hospitals with a greater heterogeneity of ethnicities. An artificial model trained on a dataset including an unbalancing number of Caucasian samples could introduce ethnicity artifacts and biases. In conclusion, a model trained on the only *Deepskin* dataset must take care of this limitation before any practical usage.

A third limitation of the results that we reported using the *Deepskin* dataset is related to the intrinsic definition of the wound area and the boundary. For both the initial manual annotation and consequent validation of the generated masks, we forced the model to learn that the wound area is the portion of the image that includes the core of the wound, excluding the peri-wound areas. Since there is not a standardized set of criteria for the wound area definition, its specification is made according to the clinical needs.

All of the above points must be considered when one is analyzing the results obtained by our model of the FUSC public dataset. The FUSC dataset includes low-quality images, without an evident focus on the wound area and with annotations based on different criteria. Furthermore, the dataset includes only foot ulcer wounds, which were acquired by US hospitals, with heterogeneous patient ethnicity. Nevertheless, the results showed in Table 2 confirm the robustness of our *Deepskin* dataset, as much as the robustness of our U-Net model which was trained on it. An equivalent result was obtained by comparing our U-Net model to the benchmark MobileNetV2.

Despite the unfair comparison of our deeper U-Net model with the lighter MobileNetV2 one, indeed, the generalization capability obtained by our architecture confirms the complexity of the wound segmentation task and the need for a more sophisticated architecture to address it.

4. Materials and Methods

4.1. Patient Selection

The analyzed images were obtained during routine dermatological examinations in the Dermatology Unit at IRCCS Sant'Orsola-Malpighi University Hospital of Bologna. The images were retrieved from subjects who gave their voluntary consent to the research. The study was approved by the Local Ethics Committee, and it was carried out in accordance with the Declaration of Helsinki. The data acquisition protocol was approved by the Local Ethics Committee (protocol n° 4342/2020 approved on 10 December 2020) according to the Helsinki Declaration.

We collected 474 patient records over 2 years (from March 2019 to September 2021) at the center, with a total of 1564 wound images (*Deepskin* dataset). A Smartphone digital camera (Dual Sony IMX 286 12MP sensors with a 1.25 μm pixel size, 27 mm equivalent focal length, F2.2 aperture, laser-assisted AF, and DNG raw capture) acquired the raw images under uncontrolled illumination conditions, various backgrounds, and image expositions for clinical usage. The selected patients represent a heterogeneous population, and thus, the dataset includes samples with ulcers at different healing stages and in different anatomical positions.

A global description of the dataset is shown in Table 3.

Table 3. (a) Description of the patient population involved in the study. We report the number of patients, which are split according to sex and age. (b) Description of the images involved in the study. We report the number of images split according to anatomical positions. The same wound could have been acquired at different time points. We report, in the last row, the number of images associated with each anatomical position.

a	Male	Female	Tot	b	Foot	Leg	Chest	Arm	Head	Tot
N° patients	210	264	474	N° wounds	97	354	14	6	2	473
Age	71 ± 17	77 ± 17	74 ± 20	N° images	364	1142	38	13	7	1564

4.2. Data Acquisition

Two trained clinicians took the photos using a smartphone digital camera during clinical practice. No rigid or standardized protocol was used during the image acquisition. For this reason, we can classify the entire set of data as natural images with uncontrolled illumination, background, and exposition. The images were acquired in proximity to the anatomical region of interest, and the clinicians tried to put the entire wound area at the center of the picture. The photographs were taken without flash. The images were acquired according to the best judgment by each clinician, as it is standard in clinical procedure. For each visit, only one photo of each wound was collected. All of the images were captured in a raw format, i.e., RGB 8-bit, and saved in a JPEG format (1440 × 1080, 96 dpi, 24 bit).

4.3. Data Annotation

Two trained clinicians performed the manual annotation of a randomly chosen subset of images. The annotation was performed by one expert and reviewed by the second one to improve the data reliability. The manual annotation set includes a binary mask of the original image, in which only the wound area is highlighted; we intentionally did not try to define the peri-wound areas since it is not well confined, and thus, it is not representable with a binary mask. This set of image masks was used as the ground truth for our deep learning model.

Pixel-wise annotations are hard to achieve also for expert clinicians, and they are particularly time consuming. For this reason, we have chosen to minimize the number of manual annotations. This small core set of manual annotations was used as a kick starter for an active semi-supervised training procedure via a deep learning segmentation model. The initial set of segmentation masks was relatively rough, and it mostly consisting of polygonal shapes. This did not affect the following re-training procedure as it has already been observed that neural network models are able to generalize even from rough manual segmentation [23].

4.4. Training Strategy

Several machine learning and deep learning models have been proposed to address the automated wound segmentation problem in the literature [14,15,19,24]. Deep learning algorithms have provided the most promising results during this task. However, as for each segmentation task, the main issue is posed by the annotation availability. The annotation masks' reliability and quality are as essential for the robustness of the deep learning models as their quantity is. The main drawback of deep learning models is the vast amount of training data required for the convergence of its parameters.

In this work, we propose a combination of active learning [16,25–28] and semi-supervised training procedure to address the problem of annotation availability, while minimizing the effort for clinicians. Starting with a core subset of manually annotated images, we trained a deep learning segmentation model on them, keeping the unlabeled images for the validation. Since no ground truth was provided for a quantitative evaluation of the model's generalization capability, the segmentations generated by the model were submitted to the two expert clinicians. For each validation image, the clinicians determined if the generated segmentation was accurate according to the following binary criteria: (i) the mask must cover the entire wound area; (ii) the mask must cover only the wound area, i.e., the mask must not have holes or spurious parts; (iii) the mask shape must follow the correct wound boundaries. The validation images (and corresponding segmentation masks) which satisfied all of the criteria were inserted into the training set for a next round of model training. A schematic representation of the proposed training strategy is shown in Figure 2.

4.5. Segmentation Model

We tried several CNN architectures that are commonly used in segmentation tasks during the research exploration, starting with the lighter U-Net [29] variants and ending with the more complex PSPNet ones [30]. The evaluation of the model's performances must balance having both a good performance on the validation set and a greater ability to extrapolate new possible samples. We would stress that while the above requirements are commonly looked for in any deep learning clinical application, they are essential in an active learning training strategy.

All of the predicted images were carefully evaluated by the experts of the Dermatological research group of the IRCCS Sant'Orsola-Malpighi University Hospital Dermatology Unit. Their agreement, jointly with the training numerical performances, led us to choose a U-Net-like [31] model as the best model that was able to balance our needs. In our architecture we used an EfficientNet-b3 model [32] for the encoder, adapting the decoder component accordingly. The evaluation of several encoder architectures during the preliminary phase of this work leads us to this choice, aiming to balance the complexity of the model and its performance metrics. Furthermore, the use of the EfficientNet-b3 encoder allowed to use a pre-trained model (on ImageNet [33] dataset) to kick-start the training phase.

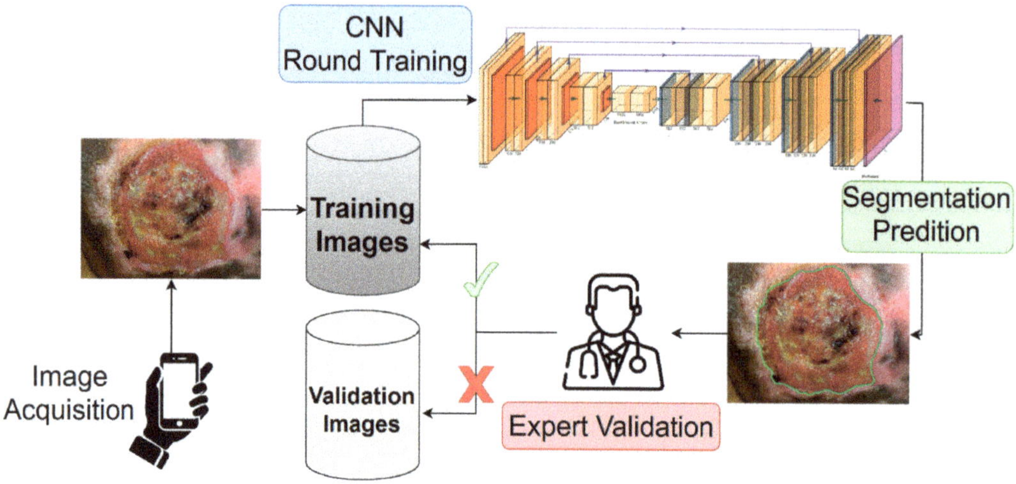

Figure 2. Representation of the active semi-supervised learning strategy implemented for the training of the wound segmentation model. The images acquired using a smartphone were stored into the training dataset. Starting with a small set of annotated images (not included into the scheme), we trained from scratch a neural network model for the wound segmentation. All of the unlabeled images were used as validation set, and the generated masks were provided by the expert. The expert analyzed the produced segmentation according to a predetermined evaluation criterion. The masks which satisfied the criteria would be added as ground truth for the next round of training.

We implemented the U-Net-like model using the Tensorflow Python library [34]. The model was trained for 150 epochs with an Adam optimizer (learning rate of 10^{-5}) and a batch size of 8 images.

For each epoch we monitored the following metrics:

$$precision = \frac{TP}{TP + FP}$$

$$recall = \frac{TP}{TP + FN}$$

$$DSC = \frac{2 \times TP}{2 \times TP + FN + FP}$$

where TP, FP, and FN are the True Positive, False Positives, and False Negative scores, respectively.

As a loss function, we used a combination of Dice score coefficient (DSC) and Binary Focal (BF) loss functions, i.e.,

$$DSC_{loss}(precision,\ recall) = 1 - \frac{\left(1 + \beta^2\right)(precision \cdot recall)}{\beta^2 \cdot precision + recall}$$

$$BF_{loss}\left(y_{true},\ y_{pred}\right) = -y_{true}\alpha\left(1 - y_{pred}\right)^{\gamma}\log(y_{pred}) - (1 - y_{true})\alpha\, y_{pred}^{\gamma}\, log(1 - y_{pred})$$

$$Loss = DSC_{loss} + BF_{loss}$$

where y_{true} and y_{pred} are the ground truth binary mask and the predicted one, respectively. In our simulations, we used values of $\alpha = 0.25$, $\beta = 1$, and $\gamma = 2$.

We performed an intensive data augmentation procedure to mimic the possible variabilities of the validation set. We provided possible vertical/horizontal flips, random rotation, and random shift with reflection for each image.

All of the simulations were performed using a 64-bit workstation machine (64 GB RAM memory and 1 CPU i9-9900K Intel®, with 8 cores, and a GeForce RTX 2070 SUPER NVIDIA GPU).

4.6. Testing on Public Dataset

Many photos are currently acquired during the clinical practice by several research laboratories and hospitals, but the availability of public annotated datasets is still limited. The number of samples required to train a deep learning model from the beginning is challenging to collect. A relevant contribution to this has been provided by the work of Wang et al. [21]. The authors proposed a novel framework for wound image segmentation based on a deep learning model, sharing a large dataset of annotated images, which had been collected over 2 years in collaboration with the Advancing the Zenith of Healthcare (AZH) Wound and Vascular Center of Milwaukee.

The dataset includes 1109 ulcer images that were taken from 889 patients and sampled at different intervals of time. The images were stored in PNG format as RGB (8-bit) and (eventually) zero-padded to a shape of 512×512. The same dataset was used also for the Foot Ulcer Segmentation Challenge (FUSC) at MICCAI 2021, and it constitutes a robust benchmark for our model.

The main difference between our dataset and the FUSC one is related to the heterogeneity of wound types. In our dataset, we collected wound images sampled in several anatomical regions (including feet), while the FUSC dataset is focused only on foot ulcer wounds. Moreover, also the image quality changes: the FUSC photos were sampled at more than $2\times$ lower resolution with a different setup, but they were stored in a lossless format. For these reasons, the FUSC dataset represents a valid benchmark for the generalization capability of our model. We performed the evaluation of the entire FUSC dataset using our model, providing the same metrics that were used by Wang et al. for a direct comparison of the results.

5. Conclusions

In this work, we introduced a fully automated pipeline for the identification and segmentation of wounds in images that were acquired using a smartphone camera. We proved the efficiency of the training strategy discussed for the creation of the *Deepskin* dataset. We remark that with a minimal effort by the expert clinicians, the proposed active semi-supervised learning strategy allowed us to obtain an efficient segmentation method and a valid benchmark dataset at the same time.

We proved the segmentation efficiency of a CNN model trained on the *Deepskin* dataset, confirming the robustness of the dataset. The results obtained in this work confirms the possible usage of the proposed pipeline in a clinical practice as a viable decision support system for dermatologists. The proposed pipeline is currently being used in the Dermatology Unit of IRCCS Sant'Orsola-Malpighi University Hospital of Bologna in Italy, and we are currently working on overcoming the issues pointed out in this work. These improvements will be the subject of future works.

Supplementary Materials: The supporting information can be downloaded at: https://www.mdpi.com/article/10.3390/ijms24010706/s1.

Author Contributions: N.C., Y.M., C.Z., E.G. and T.B. performed study concept and design; N.C., A.M., D.D. and E.G. performed development of methodology. All the authors contributing to the writing, review, and revision of the paper; Y.M., C.Z. and T.B. provided acquisition and interpretation of data; N.C. and E.G. provided statistical analysis; E.M., G.C. and T.B. provided material support. All authors have read and agreed to the published version of the manuscript.

Funding: The authors received no specific funding for this work.

Institutional Review Board Statement: The study was approved by the Local Ethics Committee, and it was carried out in accordance with the Declaration of Helsinki. The data acquisition protocol was approved by the Local Ethics Committee (protocol n° 4342/2020 approved on 10 December 2020) according to the Helsinki Declaration.

Informed Consent Statement: Informed consent was obtained from all subjects involved in the study.

Data Availability Statement: The data used during the current study are available from the corresponding author on reasonable request. The pre-trained model and parameters used for the image segmentation are available in the repository, *Deepskin* (https://github.com/Nico-Curti/Deepskin, accessed on 30 December 2022).

Conflicts of Interest: The authors declare no conflict of interest.

References

1. Gethin, G. The importance of continuous wound measuring. *Wounds UK* **2006**, *2*, 60–68.
2. Sibbald, R.; Elliot, J.A.; Persaud-jaimangal, R.; Goodman, L.; Armstrong, D.G.; Harely, C.; Coelho, S.; Xi, N.; Evans, R.; Mayer, D.O.; et al. Wound Bed Preparation 2021. *Adv. Ski. Wound Care* **2021**, *34*, 183–195. [CrossRef] [PubMed]
3. Levit, E.; Kagen, M.; Scher, R.; Grossman, M.; Altman, E. The ABC rule for clinical detection of subungual melanoma. *J. Am. Acad. Dermatol.* **2000**, *42*, 269–274. [CrossRef] [PubMed]
4. Stremitzer, S.; Wild, T.; Hoelzenbein, T. How precise is the evaluation of chronic wounds by health care professionals? *Int. Wound J.* **2007**, *4*, 156–161. [CrossRef] [PubMed]
5. Phillips, C.; Humphreys, I.; Fletcher, J.; Harding, K.; Chamberlain, G.; Macey, S. Estimating the costs associated with the management of patients with chronic wounds using linked routine data. *Int. Wound J.* **2016**, *13*, 1193–1197. [CrossRef]
6. Newton, H. Cost-effective wound management: A survey of 1717 nurses. *Br. J. Nurs.* **2017**, *26*, S44–S49. [CrossRef] [PubMed]
7. Guest, J.F.; Fuller, G.W.; Vowden, P. Cohort study evaluating the burden of wounds to the UK's National Health Service in 2017/2018: Update from 2012/2013. *BMJ Open* **2020**, *10*, e045253. [CrossRef] [PubMed]
8. Nussbaum, S.R.; Carter, M.J.; Fife, C.E.; DaVanzo, J.; Haught, R.; Nusgart, M.; Cartwright, D. An Economic Evaluation of the Impact, Cost, and Medicare Policy Implications of Chronic Nonhealing Wounds. *Value Health* **2018**, *21*, 27–32. [CrossRef]
9. Hjort, A.M.; Gottrup, F. Cost of wound treatment to increase significantly in Denmark over the next decade. *J. Wound Care* **2010**, *19*, 173–184. [CrossRef]
10. Norman, R.E.; Gibb, M.; Dyer, A.; Prentice, J.; Yelland, S.; Cheng, Q.; Lazzarini, P.A.; Carville, K.; Innes-Walker, K.; Finlayson, K. Improved wound management at lower cost: A sensible goal for Australia. *Int. Wound J.* **2016**, *13*, 303–316. [CrossRef]
11. Haghpanah, S.; Bogie, K.; Wang, X.; Banks, P.; Ho, C. Reliability of electronic versus manual measurement techniques. *Arch. Phys. Med. Rehabil.* **2006**, *87*, 1396–1402. [CrossRef] [PubMed]
12. Chan, K.S.; Lo, Z. Wound assessment, imaging and monitoring systems in diabetic foot ulcers: A systematic review. *Int. Wound J.* **2020**, *17*, 1909–1923. [CrossRef] [PubMed]
13. Ahn, C.; Salcido, S. Advances in Wound Photography and Assessment Methods. *Adv. Ski. Wound Care* **2008**, *21*, 85–93. [CrossRef] [PubMed]
14. Dhane, D.M.; Krishna, V.; Achar, A.; Bar, C.; Sanyal, K.; Chakraborty, C. Spectral Clustering for Unsupervised Segmentation of Lower Extremity Wound Beds Using Optical Images. *J. Med. Syst.* **2016**, *40*, 207. [CrossRef]
15. Sarp, S.; Kuzlu, M.; Pipattanasomporn, M.; Güler, Ö. Simultaneous wound border segmentation and tissue classification using a conditional generative adversarial network. *J. Eng.* **2021**, *2021*, 125–134. [CrossRef]
16. Zhou, J.; Cao, R.; Kang, J.; Guo, K.; Xu, Y. An Efficient High-Quality Medical Lesion Image Data Labeling Method Based on Active Learning. *IEEE Access* **2020**, *8*, 144331–144342. [CrossRef]
17. Mahapatra, D.; Schüffler, P.J.; Tielbeek, J.A.W.; Vos, F.M.; Buhmann, J.M. Semi-Supervised and Active Learning for Automatic Segmentation of Crohn's Disease. In *Medical Image Computing and Computer-Assisted Intervention—MICCAI 2013*; Lecture Notes in Computer Science; Springer: Berlin/Heidelberg, Germany, 2013; Volume 8150.
18. Zhou, T.; Li, L.; Bredell, G.; Li, J.; Unkelbach, J.; Konukoglu, E. Volumetric memory network for interactive medical image segmentation. *Med. Image Anal.* **2023**, *83*, 102599. [CrossRef]
19. Shin, H.-C.; Roth, H.R.; Gao, M.; Lu, L.; Xu, Z.; Nogues, I.; Yao, J.; Mollura, D.; Summers, R.M. Deep Convolutional Neural Networks for Computer-Aided Detection: CNN Architectures, Dataset Characteristics and Transfer Learning. *IEEE Trans. Med. Imaging* **2016**, *35*, 1285–1298. [CrossRef]
20. Harris, C.; Raizman, R.; Singh, M.; Parslow, N.; Bates-Jensen, B. Bates-Jensen Wound Assessment Tool (BWAT) Pictorial Guide Validation Project. *J. Wound Ostomy Cont. Nurs.* **2010**, *37*, 253–259. [CrossRef]

21. Wang, C.; Anisuzzaman, D.M.; Williamson, V.; Dhar, M.K.; Rostami, B.; Niezgoda, J.; Gopalakrishnan, S.; Yu, Z. Fully automatic wound segmentation with deep convolutional neural networks. *Sci. Rep.* **2020**, *10*, 21897. [CrossRef]
22. Analytics, B.D.; Lab, V. Wound Segmentation. In *GitHub Repository*; GitHub: San Francisco, CA, USA, 2021.
23. Curti, N.; Giampieri, E.; Guaraldi, F.; Bernabei, F.; Cercenelli, L.; Castellani, G.; Versura, P.; Marcelli, E. A Fully Automated Pipeline for a Robust Conjunctival Hyperemia Estimation. *Appl. Sci.* **2021**, *11*, 2978. [CrossRef]
24. Wang, C.; Yan, X.; Smith, M.; Kochhar, K.; Rubin, M.; Warren, S.M.; Wrobel, J.; Lee, H. A unified framework for automatic wound segmentation and analysis with deep convolutional neural networks. In Proceedings of the 2015 37th Annual International Conference of the IEEE Engineering in Medicine and Biology Society (EMBC), Milan, Italy, 25–29 August 2015; pp. 2415–2418. [CrossRef]
25. Camargo, G.; Bugatti, P.H.; Saito, P.T.M. Active semi-supervised learning for biological data classification. *PLoS ONE* **2020**, *15*, e0237428. [CrossRef] [PubMed]
26. Gal, Y.; Islam, R.; Ghahramani, Z. Deep Bayesian Active Learning with Image Data. In Proceedings of the 34th International Conference on Machine Learning, Sydney, Australia, 6–11 August 2017; Volume 70, pp. 1183–1192.
27. Xie, S.; Feng, Z.; Chen, Y.; Sun, S.; Ma, C.; Song, M. Deal: Difficulty-aware Active Learning for Semantic Segmentation. In Proceedings of the Asian Conference on Computer Vision (ACCV), Kyoto, Japan, 30 November–4 December 2020.
28. Zhou, T.; Wang, W.; Konukoglu, E.; Van Gool, L. Rethinking Semantic Segmentation: A Prototype View. In Proceedings of the IEEE/CVF Conference on Computer Vision and Pattern Recognition, New Orleans, LA, USA, 19–20 June 2022; pp. 2582–2593.
29. Ronneberger, O.; Fischer, P.; Brox, T. U-Net: Convolutional Networks for Biomedical Image Segmentation. In *Medical Image Computing and Computer-Assisted Intervention–MICCAI 2015*; Lecture Notes in Computer Science; Navab, N., Hornegger, J., Wells, W., Frangi, A., Eds.; Springer: Cham, Switzerland, 2015; Volume 9351.
30. Zhao, H.; Shi, J.; Qi, X.; Wang, X.; Jia, J. Pyramid Scene Parsing Network. In Proceedings of the IEEE Conference on Computer Vision and Pattern Recognition (CVPR), Honolulu, Hawaii, 22–25 July 2017; pp. 2881–2890.
31. Yakubovskiy, P. Segmentation Models. In *GitHub Repository*; GitHub: San Francisco, CA, USA, 2019.
32. Tan, M.; Le, Q.V. EfficientNet: Rethinking Model Scaling for Convolutional Neural Networks. *arXiv* **2020**, arXiv:1905.11946.
33. Deng, J.; Dong, W.; Socher, R.; Li, L.-J.; Li, K.; Li, F.-F. Imagenet: A large-scale hierarchical image database. In Proceedings of the 2009 IEEE Conference on Computer Vision and Pattern Recognition, Miami, FL, USA, 20–25 June 2009; pp. 248–255.
34. Abadi, M.; Agarwal, A.; Barham, P.; Brevdo, E.; Chen, Z.; Citro, C.; Corrado, G.S.; Davis, A.; Dean, J.; Devin, M.; et al. TensorFlow: Large-Scale Machine Learning on Heterogeneous Systems. *arXiv* **2015**, arXiv:1603.04467.

International Journal of
Molecular Sciences

MDPI

Article

Optimization of an Ex-Vivo Human Skin/Vein Model for Long-Term Wound Healing Studies: Ground Preparatory Activities for the 'Suture in Space' Experiment Onboard the International Space Station

Francesca Cialdai [1,2,†], Stefano Bacci [3,†], Virginia Zizi [3], Aleandro Norfini [4], Michele Balsamo [4], Valerio Ciccone [5], Lucia Morbidelli [5], Laura Calosi [3], Chiara Risaliti [1,2], Lore Vanhelden [3,6], Desirée Pantalone [7], Daniele Bani [3,*] and Monica Monici [1,2,*]

1 ASA Research Division, ASA Campus Joint Laboratory, 50134 Florence, Italy
2 Department of Experimental and Clinical Biomedical Sciences "Mario Serio", University of Florence, Viale Pieraccini 6, 50139 Florence, Italy
3 Imaging Platform, Department Experimental and Clinical Medicine & Joint Laboratory with Department Biology, University of Florence, Viale Pieraccini 6, 50139 Florence, Italy
4 Kayser Italia Srl, Via di Popogna 501, 57128 Livorno, Italy
5 Department Life Sciences, University of Siena, Via A. Moro 2, 53100 Siena, Italy
6 M&T Faculty, Applied Engineering and Technology, Karel de Grote University of Applied Sciences, Salesianenlaan 90, 2660 Hoboken, The Netherlands
7 Section of Surgery, Department Experimental and Clinical Medicine, University of Florence, Largo Brambilla 3, 50134 Florence, Italy
* Correspondence: daniele.bani@unifi.it (D.B.); monica.monici@unifi.it (M.M.)
† These authors contributed equally to this work.

Citation: Cialdai, F.; Bacci, S.; Zizi, V.; Norfini, A.; Balsamo, M.; Ciccone, V.; Morbidelli, L.; Calosi, L.; Risaliti, C.; Vanhelden, L.; et al. Optimization of an Ex-Vivo Human Skin/Vein Model for Long-Term Wound Healing Studies: Ground Preparatory Activities for the 'Suture in Space' Experiment Onboard the International Space Station. *Int. J. Mol. Sci.* **2022**, *23*, 14123. https://doi.org/10.3390/ijms232214123

Academic Editors: César Viseras, Luana Perioli and Cinzia Pagano

Received: 20 October 2022
Accepted: 12 November 2022
Published: 16 November 2022

Abstract: This study is preliminary to an experiment to be performed onboard the International Space Station (ISS) and on Earth to investigate how low gravity influences the healing of sutured human skin and vein wounds. Its objective was to ascertain whether these tissue explants could be maintained to be viable ex vivo for long periods of time, mimicking the experimental conditions onboard the ISS. We developed an automated tissue culture chamber, reproducing and monitoring the physiological tensile forces over time, and a culture medium enriched with serelaxin (60 ng/mL) and (Zn(PipNONO)Cl) (28 ng/mL), known to extend viability of explanted organs for transplantation. The results show that the human skin and vein specimens remained viable for more than 4 weeks, with no substantial signs of damage in their tissues and cells. As a further clue about cell viability, some typical events associated with wound repair were observed in the tissue areas close to the wound, namely remodeling of collagen fibers in the papillary dermis and of elastic fibers in the vein wall, proliferation of keratinocyte stem cells, and expression of the endothelial functional markers eNOS and FGF-2. These findings validate the suitability of this new ex vivo organ culture system for wound healing studies, not only for the scheduled space experiment but also for applications on Earth, such as drug discovery purposes.

Keywords: wound healing; human skin; human vein; serelaxin; Zn-nonoate

1. Introduction

Long-term space missions to bring astronauts beyond the Earth's orbit, to explore the closer planets, have become a feasible objective for the near future. This has prompted a surge in biomedical research in order to identify the possible risks and health issues of exposing the human body to prolonged micro/low gravity conditions and to set up appropriate countermeasures, especially taking into account the limited availability of medical resources onboard a spaceship. Studies on astronauts returning from missions onboard the International Space Station (ISS) have shown that prolonged exposure to microgravity can impair tissue homeostasis, thus negatively influencing bone and skeletal muscle, hematopoiesis and immune response. Although studies on wound healing in humans or in human tissues have never been conducted in space until now, the pathophysiological alterations caused by space flight could impair the body's resilience to injuries [1–3]. In particular, the susceptibility of astronauts to trauma due to particular working needs and conditions makes the impaired tissue response to wounds a major reason for concern [4], as well as a priority subject for biomedical research funded by the national and international space agencies. In this context, our research group is involved in an international, multidisciplinary research project to investigate how human tissues, particularly the skin and blood vessels, can adapt to microgravity conditions and how wound repair may be influenced [5]. This study was selected by the European Space Agency (ESA) to be carried out at the ISS and in parallel on Earth, tentatively in 2022 (ESA-AO-ILSRA-2014). It exploits two ex vivo human organ models, namely whole-thickness skin and saphenous vein bearing a standardized sutured wound, prepared from samples donated by volunteer patients subjected to mammary plastic or vascular bypass surgery. To ensure tissue viability throughout the experiment (4 weeks), we have developed an automated tissue culture chamber–which fits the ESA Biolab facility inside the Columbus module onboard the ISS–and a new tissue culture technique that combines biochemical and biophysical factors. The culture chamber is equipped with a device that can model physiological tensile strength in the tissues and monitor its changes throughout the experiment, thus enabling the study of tissue and suture mechanical properties. Mechanical factors are involved in the regulation of many biological processes, wound healing included, which are crucial for maintaining tissue homeostasis. Therefore, the modeling of physiological and mechanical factors improves tissue culture survival. Moreover, new long-term culture media have been created. They are based on standardized media, supplemented with substances previously used to extend the viability of explanted organs scheduled for transplantation, namely serelaxin and (Zn(PipNONO)Cl) [5]. Serelaxin, the recombinant form of human H2 relaxin hormone suitable for pharmaceutical use, has been shown to induce protection against ischemia–reperfusion injury by reducing cellular oxidative damage, apoptosis and inflammation [6,7]. By the use of similar mechanisms, serelaxin has been shown to extend the lifespan of liver and lungs to be transplanted [8]. Zn-metallononoate (Zn(PipNONO)Cl), a nitric oxide (NO)-releasing molecule (Noxamet Ltd., Milan, Italy), has been shown to promote endothelial cell survival and to induce the activation of H2S-dependent signaling pathways, resulting in potent antioxidant and tissue-trophic effects in in vitro culture [9,10]. As a mandatory preliminary step to the true experiment, we have performed the present study to ascertain whether our model is adequate to the purpose, and particularly whether the wound healing process can take place, in full or in part, even in these long-term skin and vein explants. To achieve this aim, at the end of the experimental period, key indicators of cell function and tissue remodeling were investigated in tissue regions taken either in close proximity to or at a distance from the surgical wound.

2. Results

2.1. EU Set-Upg

The Experimental Units (EU) used for the experiments are composed of a stainless steel frame, allowing the explanted skin specimens to be stitched onto micro-adjustable support brackets made of biocompatible plastic, a culture chamber filled with enriched incubation medium and a reservoir containing fresh medium to replace the exhausted medium in the culture chamber via a peristaltic pump (Figure 1), designed to prevent formation of air bubbles within the chamber. The body of the culture chamber and reservoir are made of sterilizable, biocompatible plastic. External air can readily exchange with the tissue samples via a gas-permeable silicone membrane, which also prevents bacterial contamination. In previous experiments, we observed that oxygen consumption varied depending on the tissue type, preservation conditions, time since collection, temperature and salinity. In general, oxygen consumption in tissue samples was ≤ 0.5 µmol/mL/h (with salinity ranging from 0 to 10 g/L). The thickness (0.2 mm) and exchange surface (3350 mm^2) of the membranes used in the EU has an oxygen permeability of 16.2 cm^3/h, which largely fulfills the metabolic needs of the incubated tissues [5]. The mounted skin or vein specimen is connected to a load cell (Burster Srl., Bergamo, Italy) capable of continuously measuring and recording the tensile strength in a 0–20 N range during the whole experiment by means of dedicated software developed by Kayser Italia. Electronics, including a microcontroller, are assembled within the EU in an Advanced Experiment Container (AEC), which has been sized and designed to fit and plug the Biolab slots onboard the ISS (OHB, Bremen, Germany). In this way, the EU can be interfaced with the Biolab controllers and pre-programmed software to receive commands, e.g., pump start/stop, load cell operation, data acquisition, etc. For the present experiment, the AECs were connected to a Biolab interface simulator. Both the experimental hardware and software worked properly for the entire experimental period (a minimum of 28 days), performing turnover of the incubation medium and recordings of tensile strength at the set time points with no need for external adjustments.

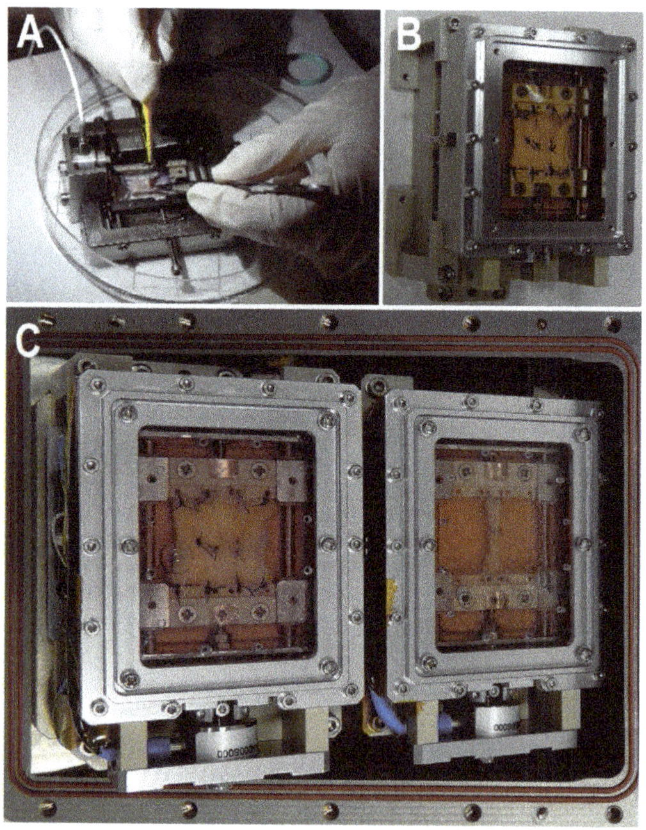

Figure 1. Representative photographs of the Experimental Unit (EU). (**A**) Detail of the stainless steel frame during surgical manipulation; (**B**) EU with a mounted skin specimen and a sutured surgical wound; (**C**) Two operating EUs assembled in an Advanced Experiment Container to be inserted into the Biolab facility of the Columbus module at the ISS.

2.2. Histology

Light microscopic examination of hematoxylin and eosin (H&E)-stained histological sections of the skin specimens after long-term incubation in the enriched incubation medium and a freeze-and-thaw cycle showed a substantially preserved architecture of the epidermis, as well as the papillary and reticular dermis (Figure 2). In all of the specimens the surgical wound was still clearly detectable, although the epidermal layer at the wound edges appeared thicker and with more pronounced ridges than it did at a distance from the wound (Figure 2A). At higher magnifications, epidermal keratinocytes showed a normal appearance, the only detectable abnormality being a slight cytoplasmic vacuolation in some supra-basal cells; in some specimens, melanin pigmentation was still visible in the basal layer. Blood microvessels and dermal stromal cells also appeared well preserved (Figure 2B). By comparison, a skin specimen incubated in a standard culture medium not enriched with serelaxin and (Zn(PipNONO)Cl) showed prominent abnormalities, namely diffuse cytoplasmic swelling of keratinocytes and detachment of the epidermis from the underlying basement membrane (Figure 2C). Dermal blood vessels were barely detectable and stromal cells often showed hyperchromatic, picnotic nuclei.

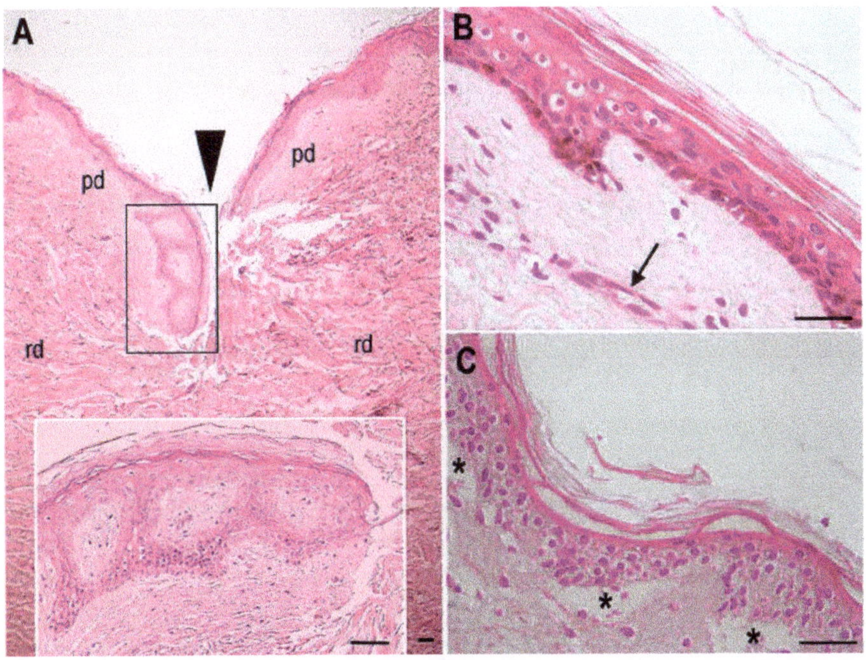

Figure 2. Representative histological features of the skin specimens after long-term incubation, freezing and thawing. (**A**) Transverse section across the surgical wound shows the epidermis nearby with pronounced rete ridges (inset); pd: papillary dermis, rd: reticular dermis. (**B**) High magnification of a skin specimen incubated in enriched medium showing a substantially normal epidermis, with brown melanin pigment in the basal layer and scattered keratinocytes with vacuolated cytoplasms, and preserved blood capillaries (arrow). (**C**) Same magnification of a skin specimen incubated in non-enriched medium showing diffuse keratinocyte vacuolation and detachment of the epidermis from the basement membrane (asterisks). H&E staining; bars = 100 μm.

Histological examination of H&E-stained saphenous vein sections subjected to the same incubation protocol also showed a substantially preserved architecture of the vascular wall layers or tunicae, the intima, media and adventitia (Figure 3). In particular, at higher magnification, a nearly continuous endothelium was observed, together with normally appearing smooth muscle and stromal cells (Figure 3B). By comparison, a vein specimen incubated in a standard non-enriched culture medium showed a nearly complete disappearance of the endothelial layer (Figure 3C).

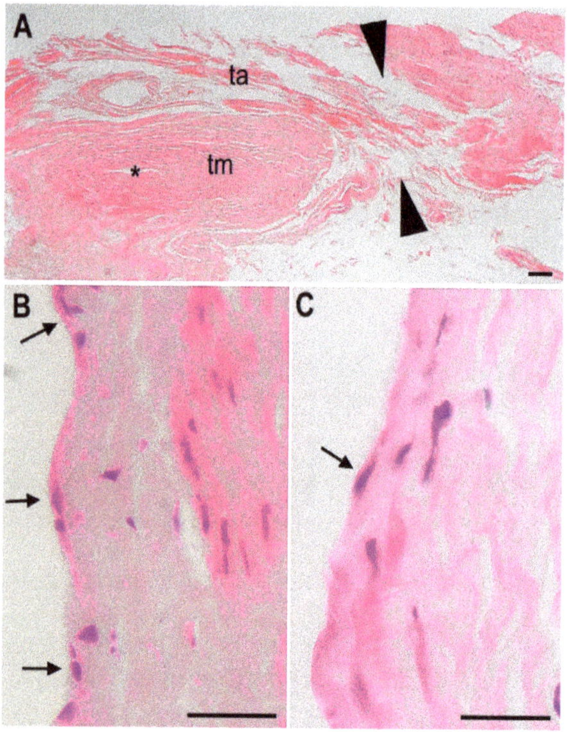

Figure 3. Representative histological features of the saphenous vein specimens after long-term incubation, freezing and thawing. (**A**) Longitudinal section across the surgical wound, indicated by arrowheads; asterisk: lumen, tm: tunica media, ta: tunica adventitia. (**B**) High magnification of a vein specimen incubated in enriched medium showing a nearly continuous layer of endothelial cells (arrows). (**C**) Same magnification of a vein specimen incubated in non-enriched medium showing diffuse endothelial loss, with only scattered residual endothelial cells (arrow). H&E staining; bars = 100 μm.

2.3. Morphometric Analysis of Connective Tissue Fibers

Histological sections of the same skin specimens were then analyzed by histochemistry and morphometry to investigate possible differences in dermal collagen and elastic fibers that could be related to the wound healing process. The percent surface area of the meshwork of picrosirius red (PSR)-stained collagen fibers was significantly decreased in the papillary dermis close to the surgical wound, compared to that at a distance from it, suggesting that collagen remodeling had occurred. On the other hand, no significant differences were found in the percent surface area of the thicker collagen fibers in the reticular dermis, regardless their proximity to the wound (Figure 4). Similarly, in the reticular dermis, no significant regional differences of paraldehyde—fuchsin (PAF)-stained elastic fibers were detected (Figure 5). In the papillary dermis, elastic fibers were too few for a reliable morphometric analysis.

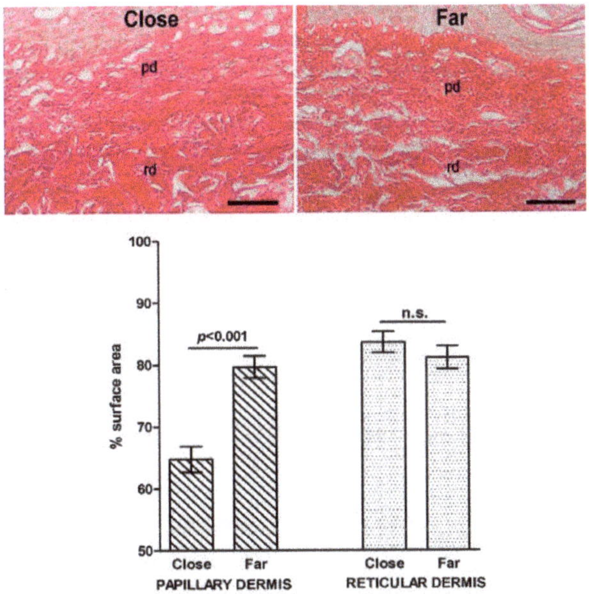

Figure 4. Light microscopic appearance and morphometry of collagen fibers from skin areas located close to and far from (3–5 mm) the surgical wound; pd: papillary dermis, rd: reticular dermis. The collagen fiber meshwork is slightly, albeit significantly, reduced in proximity to the wound. PSR staining; bars = 100 μm; values are mean ± s.e.m., $n = 4$, n.s. not significant.

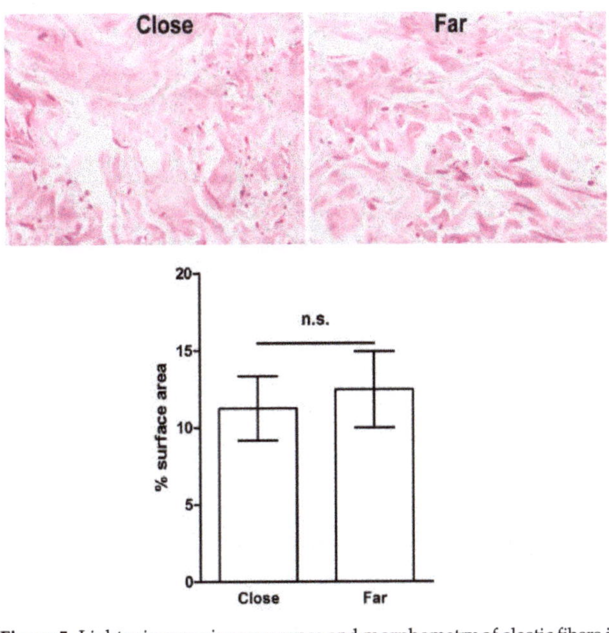

Figure 5. Light microscopic appearance and morphometry of elastic fibers in the reticular dermis from skin areas located close to and far from (3–5 mm) the surgical wound. No substantial differences can be seen or measured. PAF staining; bars = 100 μm; values are mean ± s.e.m., $n = 4$, n.s. not significant.

Histochemistry and morphometry of the vein sections showed no significant differences in the percent surface area of PSR-stained collagen fibers and PAF-stained elastic fibers between the tunica adventitia measured in tissue areas close to or far from the surgical wound (Figures 6 and 7). Instead, a slight but significant reduction of the percent surface area of the elastic fibers in the tunica media was detected in proximity to the wound (Figure 7). This finding is consistent with the occurrence of extracellular matrix remodeling.

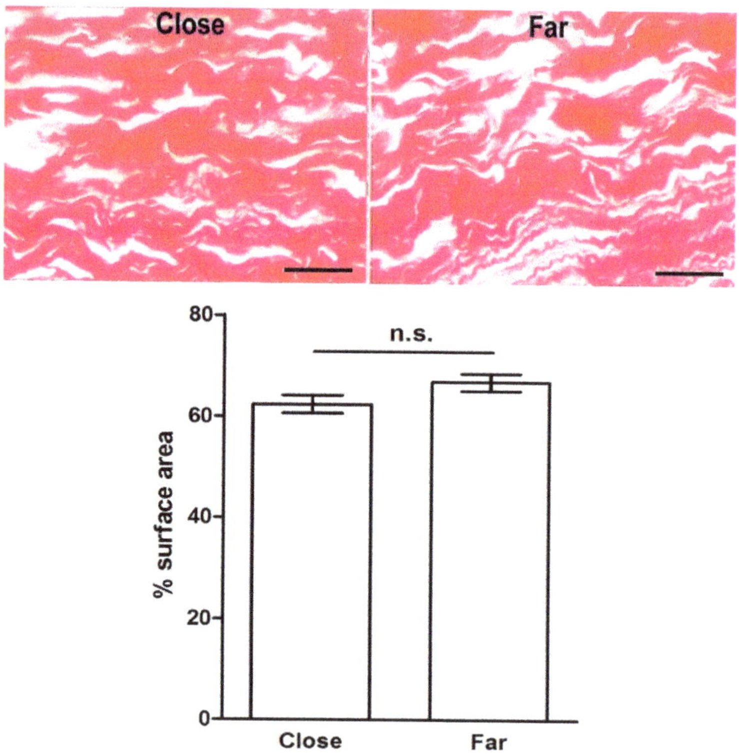

Figure 6. Light microscopic appearance and morphometry of collagen fibers from vein areas of the tunica adventitia located close to and far away (3–5 mm) the surgical wound. No substantial differences can be seen or measured. PSR staining; bars = 100 μm; values are mean ± s.e.m., $n = 4$, n.s. not significant.

2.4. *Blood Microvessels and Stromal Cells*

Small-sized blood vessels, already observed in the H&E-stained sections, were specifically identified by fluorescein isothiocyanate (FITC)-labeled *Ulex europaeus* agglutinin (UEA) lectin and anti-α-smooth muscle actin (α-SMA) antibodies (Figure 8A). They were mostly located in the papillary and upper reticular dermis and did not show any visual differences between the tissue areas close to and far from the wound. Mast cells, identified by FITC-labeled avidin, were found in the upper dermis, especially along blood vessels and around adnexa (Figure 8B,C), as well as in the tunica adventitia of the vein samples. Visually, those located in proximity to the wound appeared to contain fewer fluorescent granules, suggesting that cell activation and granule release had occurred. Both of the dermal layers harbored several spindle-shaped or stellate fibroblasts expressing the activation marker heat-shock protein 47 (HSP47), which was also expressed by epidermal keratinocytes. It was also noted that activated fibroblasts appeared to be more numerous in the dermal areas close to the wound (Figure 8D,E). On the other hand, HSP47-positive fibroblasts were only seldom encountered in the vein samples. No α-SMA-positive stromal cells identifiable as myofibroblasts were detected in any dermal or vein wall areas.

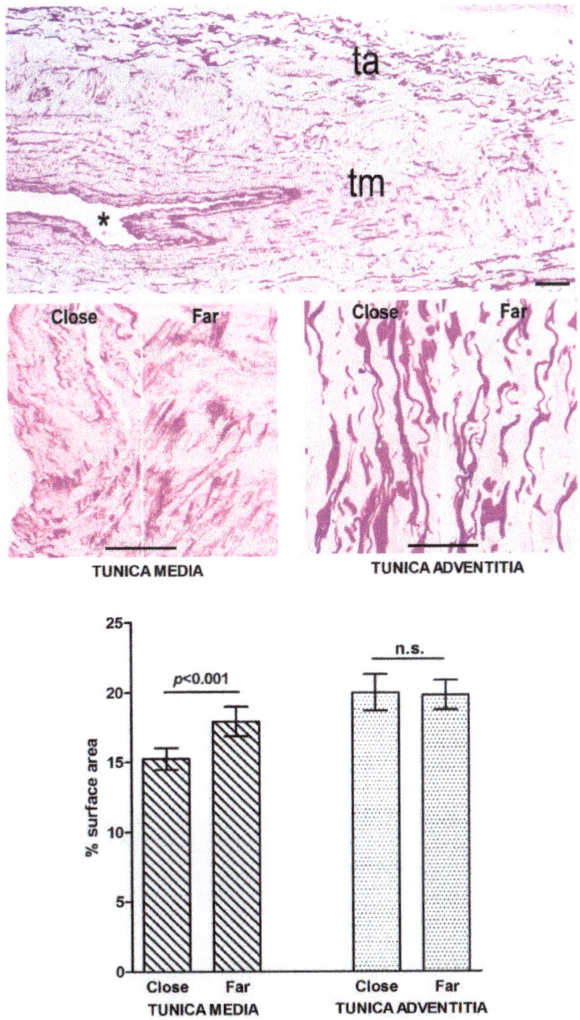

Figure 7. Light microscopic appearance and morphometry of elastic fibers from vein wall areas located close to and far from (3–5 mm) the surgical wound. No substantial differences can be seen or measured in the tunica adventitia (ta), whereas in the tunica media (tm) the elastic fiber meshwork is slightly, albeit significantly, reduced in proximity to the wound. * lumen. PAF staining; bars = 100 μm; values are mean ± s.e.m., $n = 4$, n.s. not significant.

2.5. *Proliferating Epidermal Keratinocytes*

Histological sections of the same skin specimens were then immunolabeled with anti-Ki67 antibodies to identify proliferating cells. The percentage of Ki67-positive keratinocytes over total cells was slightly, albeit significantly, higher in the epidermis of areas close to the surgical wound than at a distance from it (Figure 9). As expected, Ki67-positive cells were mainly located in the basal layer of the epidermis and at the periphery of the hair follicle sheath, likely at the level of the so-called 'bulge', which is known to harbor epidermal stem cells [11]. Scattered Ki67-positive cells were seldom found in the papillary dermis.

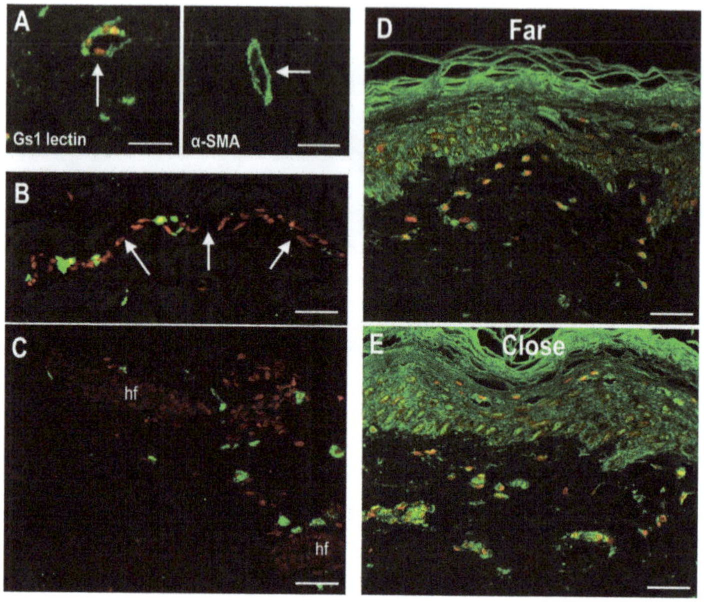

Figure 8. (**A**) Small blood vessels in the upper dermis (arrows) labeled by FITC-conjugate UEA lectin and anti-α-SMA antiserum. Mast cells, labeled by FITC-conjugated avidin, are located along blood vessels (arrows) (**B**) and around hair follicles (hf) (**C**). Visually, those located in proximity to the wound appeared to contain fewer fluorescent granules, suggesting that cell activation and granule release had occurred. (**D**,**E**) Dermal fibroblasts expressing the activation marker HSP47 appear to be more numerous in tissue areas close to the wound. HSP47 is also expressed by epidermal keratinocytes. Nuclei are counterstained in red with propidium iodide; bars = 100 μm.

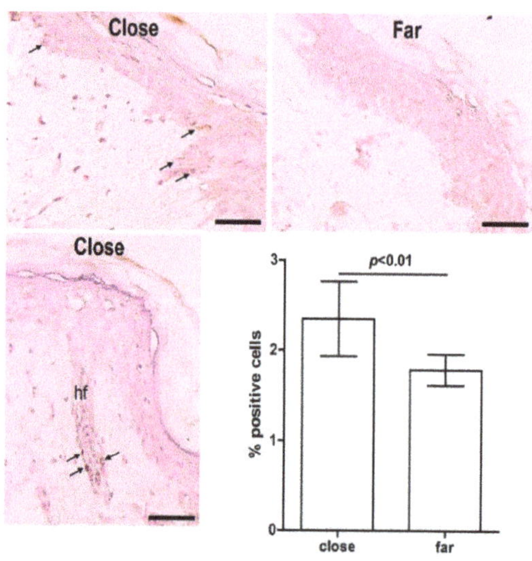

Figure 9. Immunostaining to reveal Ki67-positive proliferating cells in the skin specimens after long-term incubation in enriched medium, freezing and thawing. Positive cells (arrows) were slightly, albeit significantly, more numerous close to the wound than far (3–5 mm) from it. Some of them can be seen in the bulge of a hair follicle (hf). Ki67 immunoperoxidase staining; bars = 100 μm; values are mean ± s.e.m., $n = 4$.

2.6. Markers of Tissue Integrity and Functions

Protein lysates from skin and vein tissues taken far from or close to the surgical wound were analyzed by western blotting to evaluate the expression of two key markers of endothelial integrity and function, fibroblast growth factor 2 (FGF-2) and endothelial nitric oxide synthase (eNOS), as well as the inducible inflammatory and tissue remodeling marker inducible nitric oxide synthase (iNOS) (Figure 10). These molecules were detectable and measurable (as ADU) in all the samples, thus allowing reliable comparisons. In the skin samples, the levels of eNOS and FGF-2 were significantly higher in the specimens taken in proximity to than distant from to the wound, while iNOS was unchanged (Figure 10A,B). In the vein samples, eNOS and FGF-2 also attained higher levels in the specimens taken in proximity to than distant to the wound, the eNOS differences reaching statistical significance, whereas no substantial changes were detected for iNOS (Figure 10C,D).

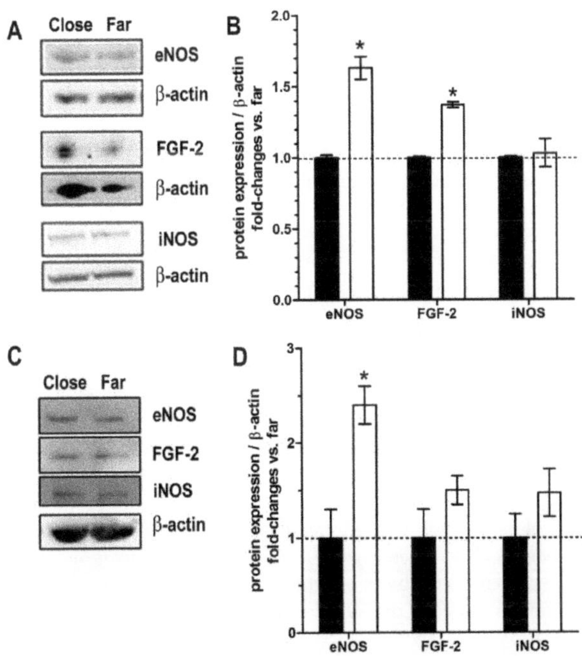

Figure 10. Western blots and densitometric quantitation for the endothelial integrity and functional markers FGF-2, eNOS and the inflammatory and tissue remodeling marker iNOS in the specimens of skin (**A**,**B**) and saphenous vein (**C**,**D**) taken in proximity to (close) or distant from (far, 3–5 mm) the surgical wound. β-actin was used as a loading invariant protein and assumed as reference control. (**A**,**C**) Representative blots of 3 independent experiments; (**B**,**D**) Bar graphs showing quantitation of the noted markers normalized to β-actin and expressed as fold-changes of the values measured in the samples taken far from the wound. Values are mean ± s.e.m., $n = 4$; * $p < 0.05$; no marks, not significant.

3. Discussion

The present study offers experimental evidence that, under the described culture conditions, ex vivo human skin and vein specimens can be maintained in a viable state for a long time, enabling them to activate some tissue-specific steps of wound healing. In particular, the findings on the epidermis and dermis from areas located in close proximity to the sutured surgical wound have shown activation of the keratinocyte stem cell compartment and of dermal fibroblasts, as judged by Ki67 and HSP47 immunofluorescent detection, accompanied by remodeling of the superficial collagen fiber network. Both of these features are typical of the wound healing process, as they predispose to epidermal cell migration from the wound margins to achieve wound closure [12–14]. In this context, the observed expression of HSP47 by both epidermal cells and dermal fibroblasts is particularly relevant: this collagen-binding chaperonin has been reported to be induced by stress conditions, when it plays a major role in the control of collagen biosynthesis by preventing the secretion of abnormal procollagen [15]. Due to its collagen regulatory properties, HSP47 has been shown to be up-regulated at both the transcriptional and translational levels during skin wound healing [16]. Its detection in the tissues of the studied skin specimens is a major piece of evidence in favor of the suitability of the present ex vivo model for wound healing studies. Finally, the fact that mast cells show signs of degranulation, accounting for cell activation, in the vicinity of the wound suggests that the activity of fibroblasts can also be influenced by their mediators [17].

The data collected from the vein model also suggest that some of the known events of vascular wall remodeling during wound healing have taken place: in particular, the reduction of the elastic fiber network in the tunica media is consistent with extracellular matrix degradation, which precedes its replacement with collagen (scarring) [18]. The slight increase in the endothelial functional markers FGF-2 and eNOS and in the smooth muscle activation marker iNOS in the specimens close to the wound also point to this conclusion.

Key features of our model that can account for its successful outcome are restoration of physiological skin and vein tensile strength and enrichment of the incubation medium with tissue protective substances. Concerning the first point, it has been demonstrated that survival of explanted tissues was impaired if free biopsies were allowed to shrink, while it was improved if biopsies were fixed onto a support to maintain the original tissue geometry [19]. Our EU allows the stitching of excised specimens onto an adjustable frame capable of restoring approximately their initial size and physiological intrinsic mechanical forces, as well as the measurement and recording of their changes during the surgical wounding, suturing and healing process. Concerning the second point, a series of studies on cellular, isolated organ and animal models of ischemia/hypoxia followed by reperfusion/reoxygenation have demonstrated that serelaxin acts at multiple levels in the complex network of the mechanisms of oxidative damage during post-ischemic reoxygenation, exerting marked protective effects [6,7]. With this background, since oxidative stress is also a key factor underlying the progressive damage and viability loss of explanted organs, serelaxin has been exploited as a protective supplement to the maintenance medium of isolated organs before transplantation, with positive results [8]. Moreover, oxidative stress has been identified as a pathogenic factor of microgravity-induced tissue damage [20]; thus, serelaxin could be beneficial in more ways for tissue maintenance in the planned experiments onboard the ISS. For the same reasons, metal–nonoates, which behave as potent antioxidants by a molecular mechanism involving NO release and H2S increase [9,10], can be helpful for this purpose. Indeed, the present findings confirm that serelaxin and (Zn(PipNONO)Cl]) are useful pharmacological tools to extend the viability of the isolated skin and blood vessel explants during the whole experimental period, as required for the planned studies onboard the ISS. More generally, by preventing oxidative damage, this culture medium, supplemented with serelaxin and and (Zn(PipNONO)Cl), could be particularly suitable for culturing biological tissue and 3D tissue constructs onboard space vehicles/stations in future deep-space missions.

A limitation of our model directly relates to the prolonged ex vivo conditions. In particular, although the EU allowed an adequate O_2 and metabolite supply for the metabolic needs of the skin and vein specimens [5], the absence of blood perfusion deprived the tissues of the substantial contribution of blood-borne inflammatory cells and mesenchymal stem cells. Together with resident cells, these play an important role in wound healing by the secretion of cytokines and growth factors that mediate inflammation and fibroblast–myofibroblast trans-differentiation [21–23]. The absence of α-SMA-positive myofibroblasts in proximity to the surgical wound can be explained by the lack of cytokine-mediated (e.g., TGF-β) induction by inflammatory cells which, in normal in vivo conditions, infiltrate the wounded tissue [24,25].

Another cause for the ostensible absence of myofibroblasts could be the lack of mechanical stresses that are normally present and continuously operating in vivo, for example, due to joint movements. It is well known that myofibroblast differentiation is strongly stimulated by mechanical forces [26] and fibrotic scars generally occur in body regions particularly exposed to mechanical stress [27]. Our future studies will focus on the application of discontinuous mechanical stresses to our ex vivo models, which also appear suitable for studying how mechanical forces may influence wound healing.

Because of the above-described limitation, as well as the fact that the remodeling phase of wound healing takes place beyond the time frame of the current ex vivo model, only part of the complex cellular and molecular mechanisms of wound healing can be investigated. However, the described ex vivo long-term human skin and vein models represent useful experimental tools to dissect and better understand the mechanisms of wound healing. For instance, the modest or absent inflammatory reaction may be an opportunity to study tissue regeneration. In fact, it has been well assessed that scarring is controlled by myofibroblasts differentiated and activated by a strong inflammatory reaction to tissue injury, while regeneration is instead associated with poor inflammation [28].

In conclusion, beside the specific goal of carrying out the planned experiment onboard the ISS, this whole-tissue human skin/vein model may represent a valuable alternative to in vitro keratinocyte/fibroblast co-cultures or in vivo rodent models for the study of wound healing and, possibly, a valuable option for drug development purposes.

4. Materials and Methods

4.1. Specimen Sampling and Handling

Skin biopsies (2 cm length) taken at surgery ($n = 4$) were carefully purged of subcutaneous fat, rinsed in PBS and stitched with 3.0 non-absorbable nylon suture onto square frames specifically developed to stretch the tissue, simulating physiological tensile strength, and to monitor its changes during wound healing (Kayser Italia Ltd., Livorno, Italy). Then, the frames with the skin biopsies were placed in transport containers filled with modified RPMI and kept at 4 °C for 17 days to simulate the time period between collection of biopsies at Careggi University Hospital (Florence, Italy) and preparation of sutured wound models at the launch site (Kennedy Space Center, Cape Canaveral, FL, USA), including the sample shipment time. A similar procedure was used to prepare saphenous vein biopsies, about 2 cm long and with a 0.5 cm diameter, which were stitched with 6.0 non-absorbable polypropylene suture onto the ends of the frames and cultured in the conditions described below. At day 18, to simulate the preparation of the wound models at the launch site, 1 cm long incisions were made on the skin biopsies with a scalpel and these were then sutured with 3.0 non-absorbable nylon thread to reproduce a surgically closed skin wound. The vein samples were cut transversely in the middle and sutured with 6.0 non-absorbable polypropylene thread to reproduce an end-to-end vascular anastomosis. Then, both of the sutured wound models were put into the in-flight experiment hardware: each sample was placed in the culture chamber of an experiment unit (EU), filled with modified DMEM incubation medium. The EUs were placed in pairs (1 skin and 1 vessel) in experimental containers (ECs) and kept at 24 °C for 6 h (to simulate the handover from the launch site to the ISS). Finally, the ECs were incubated at 32 °C for 9 to 12 days (to simulate the in-flight experiment on board the ISS). The actual in-flight experiment will last from 4 to 9 days (the various samples will be retrieved at different times to evaluate different phases of wound healing). In the present ground simulations, the longest incubation time was chosen to ensure adequate viability of the experimental models. At the end of experiment, the specimens were frozen at −80 °C directly in the medium-filled culture chambers. After 2–10 weeks (to simulate the return to Earth and trans-continental transport to the PI's laboratory) each frozen sample was cut into 2 halves, orthogonally to the surgical wound: one was gently thawed by immersion in Immunofix (Bio-Optica, Milan, Italy) formaldehyde-based fixative solution at 4 °C and then processed for conventional light microscopy, i.e., dehydrated, embedded in paraffin and cut into 5 μm-thick sections, while the other was kept frozen for molecular analyses.

4.2. Bioreactor Development

The bioreactor has been developed by Kayser Italia, following the requirements indicated by the scientific team. The culture chamber, the frame conferring mechanical support to the tissue specimens, the system including the medium reservoir and the electronically controlled peristaltic pump for medium circulation, the gas-permeable membrane, the electronically controlled load cell connected to the frame for modeling the physiological tensile strength in the tissue, and the monitoring of this throughout the culture period have been developed as previously described [5]. All of the bioreactor components in contact with the tissues and culture media are biocompatible.

4.3. Enriched Long-Term Incubation Media

Two modified incubation media were used in the experiments, namely RPMI (Sigma-Aldrich, Milan, Italy) for maintenance of the sample at 4 °C and DMEM (Sigma-Aldrich) for incubation of the samples at 24–32 °C. RPMI was supplemented with 120 μg/mL lincomycin (Pfizer, Latina, Italy), 10 μg/mL colistin (Accord Healthcare Italia S.r.l., Milan, Italy) and 50 μg/mL vancomycin (Hikma Italia S.p.a., Pavia, Italy); DMEM was supplemented with 8 μL/mL 20% bovine serum albumin, 0.4 μg/mL hydrocortisone (Sanofi S.r.l., Anagni, Italy), 0.12 UI/mL insulin (Ely Lilly, Sesto Fiorentino, Italy), 100 UI/mL G penicillin (Sigma-Aldrich), 20 μg/mL gentamycin (L.F.M., Milan, Italy), 1 μg/mL amphotericin B and 50 μg/mL ascorbic acid (Sigma-Aldrich). Both media were enriched with substances previously used to protect explanted organs for transplantation purposes, namely serelaxin (60 ng/mL) and (Zn(PipNONO)Cl) (28 ng/mL), with the aim of extending the viability of the ex vivo organ specimens during the experimental period. The currently used concentrations of serelaxin and (Zn(PipNONO)Cl) have been chosen based on those that exerted significant tissue protective effects in the above cited studies [8–10].

4.4. Histology and Morphometric Evaluation of Collagen and Elastic Fibers

Histological sections, 5 μm thick, were cut from the paraffin-embedded samples. Some of them were stained with H&E and observed using light microscopy. Histological images were acquired using a microscope equipped with a Visicam TC10 tablet camera (WWR International, Milan, Italy). Others were stained with 0.2% PSR for 60 min., a histochemical method specific for collagen fibers. Staining of the sections was performed in a single session, to minimize artifactual differences. In each skin specimen, 2 photomicrographs, including the papillary and reticular dermis, were randomly taken from areas in close proximity to or distant from (3–5 mm) the surgical wound; in each vein specimen, 2 photomicrographs of the tunica media and 2 of the tunica adventitia were randomly taken from areas in close proximity to and distant from (3–5 mm) the surgical wound. In both instances, a Nikon DS F12 CCD camera connected to a Nikon Eclipse E200 light microscope with a 40× objective (each micrograph: 57,700 μm^2) was used. On each image, 4 regions of interest (ROI), 1500 μm^2 each, were randomly chosen: here, the surface area of PSR-stained collagen fibers was selected by thresholding (to exclude the PSR-negative amorphous ground substance and cells) and measured using ImageJ 1.53 k software (http://imagej.nih.gov/ij (accessed on 2 October 2021). Values are expressed as percent area of collagen fibers over total tissue area. In the vein samples, only the tunica adventitia close to or far from the wound was selected for the measurements, since collagen fibers are chiefly present in this layer. Another series of histological sections was used to assess the percent area of elastic fibers, stained histochemically with 0.5% PAF for 5 min, applying a similar morphometrical method and sampling procedure. In the skin samples, only the reticular dermis close to or far from the wound was selected for the measurements, since elastic fibers in the papillary dermis were too few to give reliable results.

4.5. Fluorescent/Immunofluorescent Detection of Mast Cells, Blood Vessels and Fibroblasts

Histological sections (5 µm thick) were cut from te paraffin-embedded skin and vein samples and used for detection of different stromal cell types using specific fluorescent markers, as follows: FITC-labelled avidin (1:400) for mast cells [29]; FITC-labelled UEA lectin (1:10) for blood vessels [30]; rabbit polyclonal anti-HSP47 (1:50 Abcam, Milan, Italy) followed by FITC-labelled goat anti-rabbit antibodies (1:32 Abcam) for activated fibroblasts [31]; and goat polyclonal anti-α-SMA (1:400 Abcam) followed by FITC-labelled rabbit anti-goat antibodies (1:175 Abcam) for both blood vessels and myofibroblasts [32]. In some slides, nuclei were counterstained in red with propidium iodide. Before each immunolabeling, antigen retrieval was performed using 0.1 M citrate buffer at 96 °C for 10 min. The fluorescent markers and the primary antisera were applied overnight at 4 °C, and the secondary antisera for 2 h at 37 °C. Omission of the primary antibody was used as a negative control for the immunofluorescence reactions. The labelled sections were viewed and photographed using a Zeiss Axioskop UV microscope equipped with a digital camera and Axiovision 4 software (Zeiss, Jena, Germany) or a Leica TCS SP5 confocal microscope. Unless otherwise stated, all reagents were from Sigma-Aldrich.

4.6. Evaluation of Proliferating Epidermal Keratinocytes

Migration of newly formed keratinocytes to fill the skin defect is a key early step of wound healing [12,14]. To assess whether this phenomenon also occurred in our ex vivo model, a series of sections from the paraffin-embedded specimens was immunostained to reveal the Ki67 nuclear proliferation antigen. Briefly, the sections were subjected to antigen retrieval as described above, incubated overnight at 4 °C in rabbit polyclonal anti-Ki-67 antiserum (Sigma-Aldrich), and diluted at a ratio of 1:50 in PBS with 3% bovine serum albumin. An immune reaction was revealed by sequential incubation (at room temperature) in biotinylated goat anti-rabbit antiserum (Thermo Fisher Scientific, Milan, Italy; 1:600, 30 min), avidin/peroxidase complex (Thermo Fisher Scientific, 10 min), and DAB substrate kit (Abcam, Cambridge, UK; 5 min) as chromogen. Nuclei were counterstained with hematoxylin. In each skin specimen, the percentage of Ki67-positive nuclei over total nuclei of basal/suprabasal keratinocytes was counted by a trained observer directly from a light microscope with a ×40 objective, in at least 2 microscopic fields, in close proximity to or distant from the surgical wound.

4.7. Western Blotting

Western blotting analysis was performed on frozen samples of skin and vein, as described [33], taken in proximity to (close) or distant from (far, 3–5 mm) the surgical wound. Protein extraction was achieved upon disruption and homogenization of the specimens using a TissuesLyser II (Qiagen, Germantown, MD, USA). Samples were frozen/unfrozen twice in liquid nitrogen and then sonicated on ice for a total of 2 min, with a 15 s run and 15 s pause to limit heating. Tissue lysates were centrifuged at 16,000× *g* for 20 min at 4 °C and the supernatants were then collected. Protein concentration was determined using the Bradford method. Electrophoresis (50 µg of protein/sample) was carried out in 4–12% Bis-Tris Gels (Life Technologies, Carlsbad, CA, USA). Proteins were then blotted onto nitrocellulose membranes and incubated overnight with the following primary antibodies: anti-eNOS (mouse, 1:1000, cat. no. 612656, BD Transduction Laboratories, Franklin Lakes, NJ, USA), anti-iNOS (rabbit, 1: 1:500, cat. no. sc-651, Santa Cruz Biotechnology, Dallas, TX, USA), anti-FGF-2 (mouse, 1:500, cat. no. 05-118, Merck KGaA, Darmstadt, Germany), and anti-β-actin (mouse, 1:10,000, cat. no. MABT825, Merck KGaA). Immune reactions were detected by an enhanced chemiluminescence system (Biorad, Hercules, CA, USA). The results were normalized to those obtained with anti-β-actin antibodies (mouse, 1:1000, cat. no. 612656, BD Transduction Laboratories). Immunoblots were analyzed by densitometry using Fiji software (64-bit Java 1.8.0_172), and the results, expressed as arbitrary density units (ADU), were normalized to β-actin.

4.8. Statistical Analysis

The experimental values were expressed as the mean ± s.e.m. of the 4 different skin or vein specimens, each assumed as the test unit. Statistical comparison of data measured close to or far from the wound was performed by using Student's t test for unpaired values, assuming $p \leq 0.05$ as significant. Calculations and graphical rendering was carried out with Prism 5.0 software (GraphPad Dotmatics, Boston, MA, USA).

Author Contributions: Conceptualization, F.C., S.B., L.M., D.B. and M.M.; methodology, F.C., V.Z., A.N., M.B., L.C., V.C., C.R., L.V. and D.P.; software, A.N. and M.B.; data curation, F.C., S.B. and V.C.; writing—original draft preparation, D.B., M.M. and L.M.; writing—review and editing, D.B., L.M. and M.M.; supervision, D.B., L.M. and M.M.; funding acquisition, D.B., L.M., D.P. and M.M. All authors have read and agreed to the published version of the manuscript.

Funding: This research was funded by the European Space Agency (ESA) (ESA contract 4000126101/18/NL/PG and ESA contract 4000130928/20/NL/PG/pt-ESA-MAP_WHISPER) and the Italian Space Agency (ASI) (Contract ASI N.2018-14-U.0-SUTURE in SPACE).

Institutional Review Board Statement: Ethical review and approval were waived for this study because the used human tissue samples were collected during routine surgical interventions and were otherwise destined to destruction.

Informed Consent Statement: Patient consent was waived due to the reasons reported above.

Data Availability Statement: Not applicable.

Acknowledgments: The authors gratefully acknowledge Lorenzo Orzalesi and Marco Bernini from the Breast Surgery Unit, Carlo Pratesi and Pierluigi Stefano from the Cardiovascular Surgery Unit, Careggi University Hospital, Florence, Italy, for precious help in collecting human skin and vein biopsies. The authors also thank Mario Bigazzi, President of the Relaxin RRCA Foundation (Florence, Italy) for providing serelaxin, Enrico Monzani, University of Pavia, Italy, and Noxamet Ltd., Milan, Italy, for providing [Zn(PipNONO)Cl]. Thanks are also due to Leonardo Surdo (ESA), Francesca Ferranti (ASI) and Juergen Kempf (OHB) for their support and collaboration.

Conflicts of Interest: The authors declare no conflict of interest.

References

1. Sekiguchi, C. Issues of health care under weightlessness. *Acta Physiol. Scand.* **1994**, *616*, 89–97.
2. Smith, S.M.; Abrams, S.A.; Davis-Street, J.E.; Heer, M.; O'Brien, K.O.; Wastney, M.E.; Zwart, S.R. Fifty years of human space travel: Implications for bone and calcium research. *Annu. Rev. Nutr.* **2014**, *34*, 377–400. [CrossRef] [PubMed]
3. Richter, C.; Braunstein, B.; Winnard, A.; Nasser, M.; Weber, T. Human biomechanical and cardiopulmonary responses to partial gravity—A systematic review. *Front. Physiol.* **2017**, *8*, 583. [CrossRef]
4. Kirkpatrick, A.W.; Campbell, M.R.; Novinkov, O.L.; Goncharov, I.B.; Kovachevich, I.V. Blunt trauma and operative care in microgravity: A review of microgravity physiology and surgical investigations with implications for critical care and operative treatment in space. *J. Am. Coll. Surg.* **1997**, *184*, 441–453. [PubMed]
5. Monici, M.; Cialdai, F.; Bani, D.; Bacci, S.; Morbidelli, L.; Norfini, A.; Balsamo, M.; van Loon, J.; Grimm, D.; Riwaldt, S.; et al. Suture in Space: Preparation of an experiment on the healing of sutured wounds on board the ISS. In Proceedings of the 72nd International Astronautical Congress (IAC), Dubai, United Arab Emirates, 25–29 October 2021.
6. Bani, D. Recombinant human H2 relaxin (serelaxin) as a cardiovascular drug: Aiming at the right target. *Drug Discov. Today* **2020**, *25*, 1239. [CrossRef]
7. Nistri, S.; Fiorillo, C.; Becatti, M.; Bani, D. Human relaxin-2 (serelaxin) attenuates oxidative stress in cardiac muscle cells exposed in vitro to hypoxia-reoxygenation. evidence for the involvement of reduced glutathione up-regulation. *Antioxidants* **2020**, *9*, 774. [CrossRef]
8. Boehnert, M.U.; Armbruster, F.P.; Hilbig, H. Relaxin as a protective substance in preservation solutions for organ transplantation, as shown in an isolated perfused rat liver model. *Transplant. Proc.* **2008**, *40*, 978–980. [CrossRef]
9. Monti, M.; Solito, R.; Puccetti, L.; Pasotti, L.; Roggeri, R.; Monzani, E.; Casella, L.; Morbidelli, L. Protective effects of novel metal-nonoates on the cellular components of the vascular system. *J. Pharmacol. Exp. Ther.* **2014**, *351*, 500–509. [CrossRef]
10. Monti, M.; Hyseni, I.; Pacini, A.; Monzani, E.; Casella, L.; Morbidelli, L. Cross-talk between endogenous H_2S and NO accounts for vascular protective activity of the metal-nonoate Zn(PipNONO)Cl. *Biochem. Pharmacol.* **2018**, *152*, 143–152. [CrossRef]
11. Jones, P.H. Epithelial stem cells. *BioEssays* **1997**, *19*, 683–690. [CrossRef]
12. Coulombe, P.A. Towards a molecular definition of keratinocyte activation after acute injury to stratified epithelia. *Biochem. Biophys. Res. Commun.* **1997**, *236*, 231–238. [CrossRef] [PubMed]

13. Pastar, I.; Stojadinovic, O.; Yin, N.C.; Ramirez, H.; Nusbaum, A.G.; Sawaya, A.; Patel, S.B.; Khalid, L.; Isseroff, R.R.; Tomic-Canic, M. Epithelization in wound healing a comprehensive review. *Adv. Wound Care* **2014**, *3*, 445–464. [CrossRef] [PubMed]
14. Bacci, S.; Bani, D. The epidermis in microgravity and unloading conditions and their effects on wound healing. *Front. Bioeng. Biotechnol.* **2022**, *10*, 666434. [CrossRef]
15. Nagata, K. Hsp47: A collagen-specific molecular chaperone. *Trends Biochem. Sci.* **1996**, *21*, 22–26. [CrossRef]
16. Wang, J.F.; Olson, M.E.; Winkfein, R.J.; Kulyk, W.M.; Wright, J.B.; Hart, D.A. Molecular and cell biology of porcine HSP47 during wound healing: Complete cDNA sequence and regulation of gene expression. *Wound Repair Regen.* **2002**, *10*, 230–240. [CrossRef] [PubMed]
17. Bacci, S. Fine regulation during wound healing by mast cells, a physiological role not yet clarified. *Int. J. Mol. Sci.* **2022**, *23*, 1820. [CrossRef] [PubMed]
18. Owens, C.D.; Gasper, W.J.; Rahman, A.S.; Conte, M.S. Vein graft failure. *J. Vasc. Surg.* **2015**, *61*, 203–216. [CrossRef] [PubMed]
19. Hautier, A.; Sabatier, F.; Stellmann, P.; Andrac, L.; Nouaille de Gorce, Y.; Dignat-George, F.; Magalon, G. Assessment of organ culture for the conservation of human skin allografts. *Cell Tissue Bank* **2008**, *9*, 19–29. [CrossRef]
20. Goodwin, T.J.; Christofidou-Solomidou, M. Oxidative stress and space biology: An organ-based approach. *Int. J. Mol Sci.* **2018**, *19*, 959. [CrossRef]
21. Singer, A.J.; Clark, R.A. Cutaneous wound healing. *N. Engl. J. Med.* **1999**, *341*, 738–746. [CrossRef]
22. Eming, S.A.; Martin, P.; Tomic-Canic, M. Wound repair and regeneration: Mechanisms, signaling and translation. *Sci. Transl. Med.* **2014**, *6*, 265sr6. [CrossRef] [PubMed]
23. Martin, P.; Nunan, R. Cellular and molecular mechanisms of repair in acute and chronic wounds. *Br. J. Dermatol.* **2015**, *173*, 370–378. [CrossRef] [PubMed]
24. Biernacka, A.; Dobaczewski, M.; Frangogiannis, N.G. TGF-β signaling in fibrosis. *Growth Factors* **2011**, *29*, 196–202. [CrossRef] [PubMed]
25. Kim, K.K.; Sheppard, D.; Chapman, H.A. TGF-β1 signaling and tissue fibrosis. *Cold Spring Harb. Perspect. Biol.* **2018**, *10*, a022293. [CrossRef]
26. Kollmannsberger, P.; Bidan, C.M.; Dunlop, J.; Fratzl, P.; Vogel, V. Tensile forces drive a reversible fibroblast-to-myofibroblast transition during tissue growth in engineered clefts. *Sci. Adv.* **2018**, *4*, eaao4881. [CrossRef] [PubMed]
27. Tsai, C.H.; Ogawa, R. Keloid research: Current status and future directions. *Scars Burn. Heal.* **2019**, *5*, 2059513119868659. [CrossRef]
28. Cialdai, F.; Risaliti, C.; Monici, M. Role of fibroblasts in wound healing and tissue remodeling on Earth and in space. *Front. Bioeng. Biotechnol.* **2022**, *10*, 958381. [CrossRef]
29. Bergstresser, P.R.; Tigelaar, R.E.; Tharp, M.D. Conjugated avidin identifies cutaneous rodent and human mast cells. *J. Investig. Dermatol.* **1984**, *83*, 214–218. [CrossRef]
30. Greene, A.S.; Lombard, J.H.; Cowley, A.W.; Hansen-Smith, F.M. Microvessel changes in hypertension measured by Griffonia Simplicifolia I lectin. *Hypertension* **1990**, *15*, 779–783. [CrossRef]
31. Kuroda, K.; Tajima, S. HSP47 is a useful marker for skin fibroblasts in formalin-fixed, paraffin-embedded tissue specimens. *J. Cutan. Pathol.* **2004**, *31*, 241–246. [CrossRef]
32. Shinde, A.V.; Humeres, C.; Frangogiannis, N.G. The role of α-smooth muscle actin in fibroblast-mediated matrix contraction and remodeling. *Biochim. Biophys. Acta Mol. Basis Dis.* **2017**, *1863*, 298–309. [CrossRef] [PubMed]
33. Ciccone, V.; Terzuoli, E.; Ristori, E.; Filippelli, A.; Ziche, M.; Morbidelli, L.; Donnini, S. ALDH1A1 overexpression in melanoma cells promotes tumor angiogenesis by activating the IL-8/Notch signaling cascade. *Int. J. Mol. Med.* **2022**, *50*, 99. [CrossRef] [PubMed]

International Journal of *Molecular Sciences*

Article

Influence of Acidic pH on Wound Healing In Vivo: A Novel Perspective for Wound Treatment

Pivian Sim [1], Xanthe L. Strudwick [2], YunMei Song [1], Allison J. Cowin [2] and Sanjay Garg [1,*]

1 Centre for Pharmaceutical Innovation (CPI), Clinical and Health Sciences, University of South Australia, Adelaide, SA 5000, Australia
2 Regenerative Medicine, Future Industries Institute, University of South Australia, Adelaide, SA 5095, Australia
* Correspondence: sanjay.garg@unisa.edu.au; Tel.: +61-883021575

Abstract: There has been little understanding of acidification functionality in wound healing, highlighting the need to study the efficacy of wound acidification on wound closure and cellular activity in non-infected wounds. This study is focused on establishing the healing potential of wound acidification in non-infected wounds. Acidic buffers, constituting either phosphoric or citric acid, were employed to modify the physiological pH of non-infected full-thickness excisional murine wounds. Acidification of the wound by acidic buffers was found to be an effective strategy to improve wound healing. A significant improvement in wound healing parameters was observed as early as 2 days post-treatment with acidic buffers compared to controls, with faster rate of epithelialization, wound closure and higher levels of collagen at day 7. pH is shown to play a role in mediating the rate of wound healing, with acidic buffers formulated at pH 4 observed to stimulate faster recovery of wounded tissues than pH 6 buffers. Our study shows the importance of maintaining an acidic wound microenvironment at pH 4, which could be a potential therapeutic strategy for wound management.

Keywords: acidic; citric acid; phosphoric acid; pH; healing; wound; closure; re-epithelialization; collagen; excisional

Citation: Sim, P.; Strudwick, X.L.; Song, Y.; Cowin, A.J.; Garg, S. Influence of Acidic pH on Wound Healing In Vivo: A Novel Perspective for Wound Treatment. *Int. J. Mol. Sci.* **2022**, *23*, 13655. https://doi.org/10.3390/ijms232113655

Academic Editors: Cinzia Pagano, Luana Perioli and César Viseras

Received: 14 September 2022
Accepted: 4 November 2022
Published: 7 November 2022

1. Introduction

Wound healing is a complex process that can be categorized into four integrated and overlapping phases involving hemostasis, inflammation, proliferation and connective tissue remodeling as an innate response to a trauma to regenerate a functional epidermal barrier [1,2]. There are many local wound factors and systemic mediators that are known to influence this healing process [3]. The wound pH milieu is one important local factor that is often overlooked, which has been commonly described as a function for the skin barrier. The importance of regulating the pH of the wound milieu to improve wound healing is emerging. We have begun to understand its importance in mediating many biochemical processes that stimulate tissue healing properties [4–7].

The natural physiological pH of a healthy human epidermal layer is maintained at a slightly acidic milieu with the surface of the skin in the range of 4.5–5.3 and increasing pH gradient over the horny layer to 6.8 as it reaches the lower stratum corneum [8,9]. The microenvironment pH of wounds is naturally more alkaline as the presence of a trauma disturbs this acidic milieu and exposes underlying tissues that have a physiological pH of 7.4 [4,10,11]. The microenvironment pH of wounds can vary depending on the type of wound, for example, acute wounds are reported to have a mean pH of 7.44 and chronic wounds at a range from pH of 7.42 to 8.90 [4,12]. Such alkaline microenvironments are favorable for bacterial growth, thus posing as the primary strategy for many wound management regimens using acids to prevent microbial growth [13,14].

As the wound heals, physiological mechanisms begin to naturally restore an acidic milieu, progressing from a neutral pH to more acidic microenvironment throughout the healing process [10,15]. The restoration of this acidic milieu acts as a natural physiological response to mediate various internal cellular processes aimed to restore the epidermal barrier that helps facilitate wound oxygenation levels, influencing macrophage and fibroblast activity and enzymatic activity participating in wound healing [16,17]. Oxygen tension within the wound is a systemic factor that has been reported to be strongly influenced by wound pH [18–21], whereby hemoglobin releases more oxygen under acidic microenvironment due to the Bohr effect [22]. As oxygen is an essential component for the growth of fibroblast cells and collagen synthesis during wound healing [19], fibroblast cells have been reported to be more active in an acidic microenvironment expressing faster migration and proliferation behavior [23,24]. Increased activity of fibroblast cells promote rapid epithelialization, wound contraction and angiogenesis, leading to faster wound regeneration [25,26]. Such increases in fibroblast proliferation and migration behaviors under acidic conditions are thought to be strongly associated to polarity and epithelial potential (EP) between wounded and unwounded tissues, which are strongly influenced by microenvironmental pH. The fluctuation of epithelial potentials generated during wounding helps guide these cells to each other, leading to faster wound closure [27,28].

Many studies assessing wound acidification have focused primarily on modifying the physiological pH of wounds for microbial management in chronic wounds indications [29–32]. However, there has been little understanding of how acidification functionality affects wound closure and cellular activity, highlighting the need to firstly study the effect of acids in non-infected wound models to determine their efficacy in wound healing. The present study employed the use of acidic buffers to modify the physiological pH of non-infected, full-thickness, excisional murine wounds. Acidic buffers were formulated with the main constituent being either phosphoric or citric acid at different pH of 4 and 6. These acids were chosen for phosphoric acid's natural occurrence in the body and its physiological role in regulating cell division, growth and development [33,34], and citric acid, due to its physiological role in the tricarboxylic acid cycle (TCA) regulating cell proliferation and metabolism [35,36]. This study aims to demonstrate the in vivo efficacy of acidification treatment following a treatment regimen and investigate its effect on the re-epithelialization rate and collagen deposition in treated wound tissues.

2. Results

2.1. Acidic Buffers Increased Rate of Wound Closure in Murine Skin

The rate of wound closure following acidic treatment with low ionic strength (0.01 M) phosphoric acid and citric acid buffers at pH of 4 and 6 were assessed using macroscopic analysis of treated full-thickness excisional wounds on mice. Wounds treated topically with either phosphoric acid or citric acid buffer solutions were observed to have a significantly higher rate of wound closure, with p-value less than 0.0001 for all treatment groups in comparison to control solution (saline) by 7 days post-wounding (Figure 1a–c). Macroscopic evaluation of wounds, following treatment every second day with phosphoric acid pH 4 and pH 6 (PA4-2 and PA6-2), resulted in significantly smaller absolute wound size (mm^2) of 5.89 $\pm$ 3.07 and 5.48 $\pm$ 2.93, respectively, in comparison to a wound size of 13.34 $\pm$ 6.46 mm^2 from the saline control group (SAL7-2). Wound pH of saline control groups was measured at 7.52 $\pm$ 0.24 on day 0, 7.46 $\pm$ 0.27 on day 2, 7.20 $\pm$ 1.87 on day 4, 7.14 $\pm$ 0.31 on day 6 and 7.11 $\pm$ 0.28 by day 7. Increasing treatment regime to daily application (PA4-1) did not result in further reduction of wound size, with wounds maintaining at approximately 9.60 $\pm$ 3.43 mm^2. However, treatment utilizing phosphoric acid buffers, irrespective of dosing frequency, had significantly decreased the wound size in the animal model at day 7 post-treatment, with p-value less than 0.0001.

The absolute wound size (mm^2) of the animal model treated with citric acid at pH 4 once-every-second-day (CA4-2) had successfully reduced to 5.87 $\pm$ 2.29. Increasing the dosing frequency of citric acid pH 4 to once-daily (CA4-1) did not further reduce the wound size (6.09 $\pm$ 3.78). Wounds treated with pH 6 every second day (CA6-2) were slightly larger, measured at 7.37 $\pm$ 2.17. Nevertheless, citric acid buffer-treated wounds were still significantly smaller than the saline control group (SAL7-2). Statistically significant results were obtained from two-way ANOVA for PA4-2 (p-value = 0.0004), PA6-2 (p-value = 0.0344), CA4-1 (p-value < 0.0001) and CA4-2 (p-value = 0.0419) on day 2. Apart from CA6-2, all other treatment groups were statistically significant on day 4, with p-value < 0.0001 for PA4-2, PA6-2 and CA4-1, followed by PA4-1 (p-value = 0.0079) and CA4-2 (p-value = 0.0213). On day 6, PA4-2 and CA4-1 were the most statistically significant, with p-values = 0.0003 and 0.0002, respectively, followed by PA6-2 (p-value = 0.0010, CA4-2 (p-value = 0.0028) and CA6-2 (p-value = 0.00390). These results showed that buffered treatment groups improved wound healing as early as day 2 post-treatment.

Mean percentages of wound healing were calculated from initial wound size measurements at day 0 compared to the size of collected wound tissue after 7 days post-treatment, using the macroscopic analysis method. Results showed significantly better percentage healing in acid-treated wounds compared to the saline control group, as shown in Figure 1d,e. The mean percentage wound healing (% of initial) of phosphoric acid groups for PA4-1, PA4-2, PA6-2 over 7 days of treatment were measured at 78.54 $\pm$ 7.71, 84.36 $\pm$ 6.02, 86.09 $\pm$ 5.68, respectively. For citric acid, mean percentages of wound healing (% of initial) of treated groups for CA4-1, CA4-2, CA4-6 were measured at 85.53 $\pm$ 3.59, 85.74 $\pm$ 2.61, 84.79 $\pm$ 2.36, respectively. In comparison, the mean percentage wound healing for SAL7-2 control group was slower, measuring at 65.02 $\pm$ 13.83 on day 7. The p-values of measured mean percentage of wound healing for all phosphoric acid (apart from PA4-1 with p-value = 0.0265) and citric acid treatment groups were less than <0.0001.

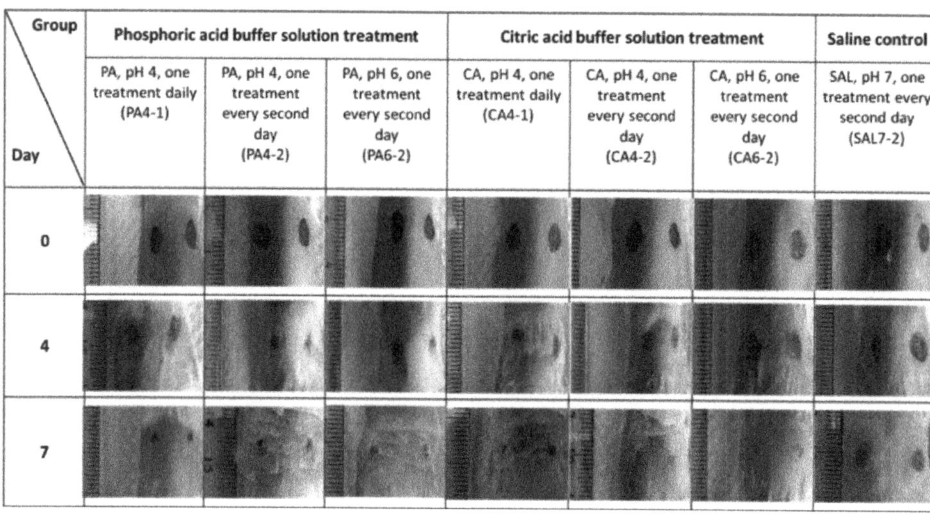

(a)

Figure 1. *Cont.*

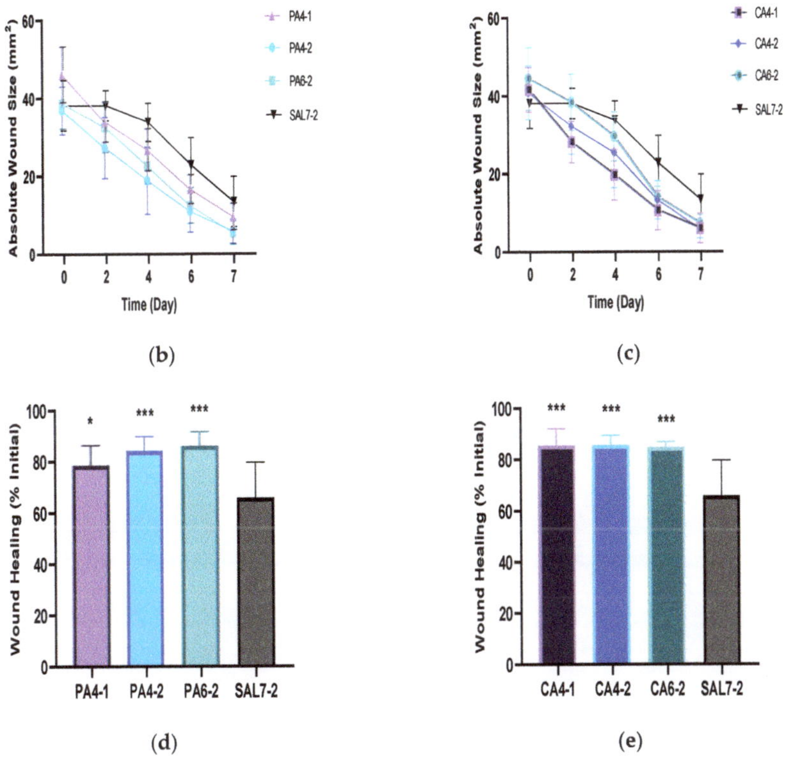

Figure 1. (**a**) Macroscopic evaluation in relation to the time course of gross wound healing after one week of topical application of phosphoric acid (PA) and citric acid (CA) buffer solutions. (**b**) Differences in absolute wound area between phosphoric acid pH 4, once-daily treatment (PA4-1), phosphoric acid pH 4 and 6, once-every-second-day treatment (PA4-2 and PA6-2), and saline control group (SAL7-2). (**c**) Time course of wound regeneration for animal model after dermal treatment with citric acid pH 4, once-daily treatment (CA4-1), citric acid pH 4 and 6, once-every-second-day treatment (CA4-2 and CA6-2) compared with saline control group (SAL7-2). (**d**) Macroscopic wound healing on day 7 when animals were topically applied with phosphoric acid with pH values of 4 and 6, and with different dosing regimens. (**e**) Topical administration of citric acid buffer solutions in comparison to saline as control group at day 7 post-treatment. Each bar represents mean $\pm$ standard deviation. * $p < 0.05$ and *** $p < 0.001$ indicates the results obtained were statistically significant from control group (SAL7-2).

2.2. Acidic Microenvironment Improves Rate of Re-Epithelialization and Wound Contraction

Histological analysis of collected wound tissue samples was performed to determine the percentage of re-epithelialization, epithelial thickness and width of panniculus gap of wound tissues collected 7 days post-wounding, stained using hematoxylin and eosin (H&E). Histological evaluation of wound re-epithelialization showed wounds treated with pH 4 phosphoric and citric acid possessed faster re-epithelialization compared to pH 6 buffers and control saline solution, as shown in Figure 2. Percentage re-epithelialization (%) of wound tissues treated with pH 4 acidic buffers following a once-daily treatment regimen (PA4-1 and CA4-1) reached 100% re-epithelialization, with *p*-value of 0.0046 and 0.0084, respectively (Figure 2b,c). In contrast, wounds that were treated following a once-every-second-day treatment regimen (PA4-2 and CA4-2) and pH 6 acidic buffers (PA6-2 and CA6-2) showed slower wound re-epithelialization. Percentage re-epithelialization of these treatment groups for PA4-2 was measured at 95.61 $\pm$ 17.58 (*p*-value = 0.0195) and PA6-2 was measured at 85.62 $\pm$ 31.37 (p-value > 0.005) from tissues collected 7 days post-operatively. For citric acid treatments, percentage re-epithelialization of wound tissues following every second day treatment regimen (CA4-2) was measured at 95.51 $\pm$ 17.97 (p-value = 0.0303) and pH 6 (CA6-2) was measured at 79.70 $\pm$ 34.66 (p-value > 0.05). The saline control group (SAL7-2) showed the slowest percentage of re-epithelialization, measured at 70.83 $\pm$ 34.36. The percentage of wounds that were fully re-epithelialized was higher in treatment groups compared to saline control, at 100% for PA4-1, 94% for PA4-2, 81% for PA6-2, 100% for CA4-1, 94% for CA4-2 and 85% for CA6-2, compared to 67% for SAL7-2 7 days post-operatively.

Wound length of tissue samples was also measured at 7 days post-wounding, as an indication of wound healing influenced by re-epithelialization and contraction. Results showed significantly smaller wound length in acid-treated wounds compared to the saline control group, as shown in Figure 2d,e. The mean wound lengths (mm) of phosphoric acid groups for PA4-1, PA4-2 and PA6-2 were measured at 3.44 $\pm$ 0.84, 2.98 $\pm$ 0.63 and 3.17 $\pm$ 0.57, respectively. For citric acid, mean wound lengths (mm) of treated groups for CA4-1, CA4-2 and CA6-2 were 2.96 $\pm$ 0.70, 2.85 $\pm$ 0.68 and 3.42 $\pm$ 0.65, respectively, when compared to wound length of saline-treated group of 4.60 $\pm$ 0.79. All acidic buffer solution treatment groups were found to be statistically significant in comparison to saline control group, with p-values less than 0.01.

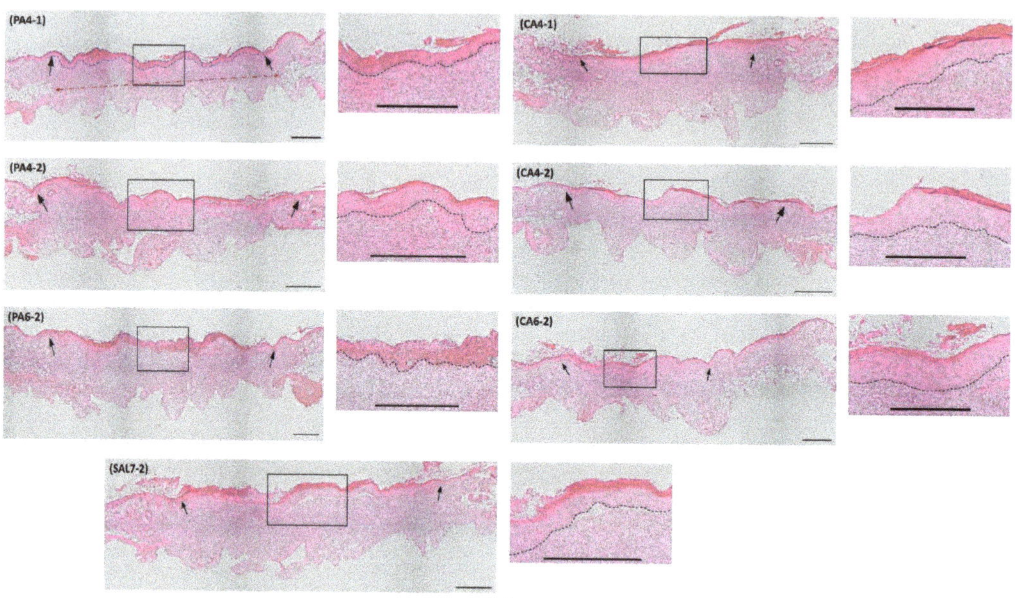

(a)

Figure 2. *Cont.*

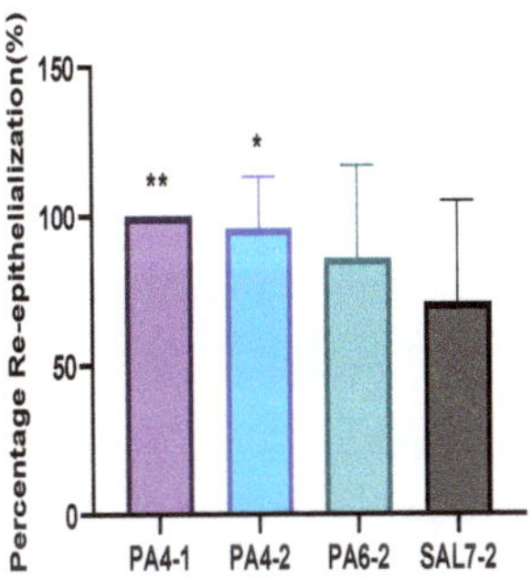

(**b**)

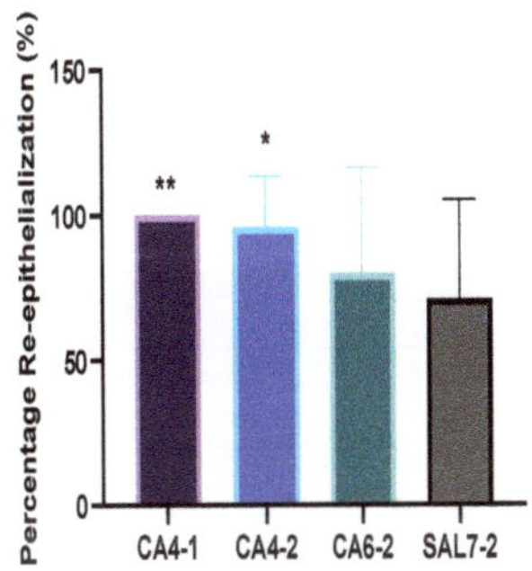

(**c**)

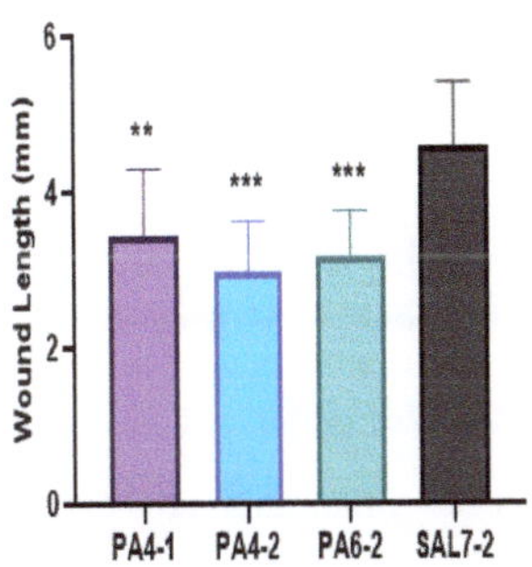

(**d**)

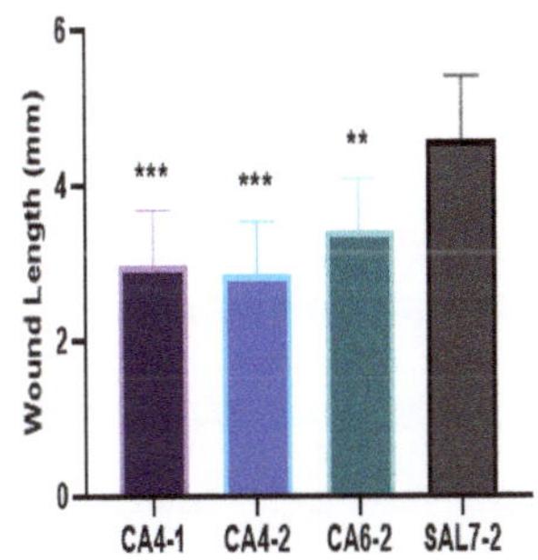

(**e**)

Figure 2. Microscopic analysis confirmed by hematoxylin and eosin (H&E) staining of percentage wound recovery after one week of topical administration of phosphoric acid (PA) and citric acid (CA) buffered solutions with different pH values and treatment regimes. (**a**) Full-thickness punch biopsy sample obtained from animal model in all acidic buffered treatment groups and saline control group at Day 7 post-injury. Original magnification 4×. Black scale bar represents 500 µm. Black arrows indicate the width of new tissue formation, blue dotted line indicate the re-epithelialized area, red dotted line indicate the panniculus gap measurement, and black dotted line indicate the base of epithelium. (**b**) Percentage re-epithelialization of animal model following topical treatment with phosphoric acid buffer solutions of pH 4 and pH 6. (**c**) Topical administration of citric acid buffer solutions or saline as control group. (**d**) Measurement of wound length at Day 7 post-injury following topical treatment with phosphoric acid buffer solutions of pH 4 and pH 6. (**e**) Wound length obtained from animal model after topically treated with citric acid buffer solutions with pH adjusted to 4 and 6 for 7 days. Each bar represents mean ± standard deviation. * $p < 0.05$, ** $p < 0.01$ and *** $p < 0.001$ indicates the results obtained were statistically significant from control group (SAL7-2).

The epithelial thickness of fully re-epithelialized wound tissues was also assessed as a defining parameter to wound recovery. Epithelial thickness of all wound tissues treated with acidic buffers displayed better recovery, showing almost complete regeneration of the epithelial layer evidence by surrounding wounded tissues, as shown in Figure 3. The epithelial thickness of treated wound tissues by phosphoric acid (PA) pH 4 treatment showed similar epithelial thickness by day 7, measuring at 0.09 ± 0.01 mm for PA4-1, 0.08 ± 0.03 mm for PA4-2 and 0.07 ± 0.02 mm for PA6-2. Both citric acid (CA) pH 4 treatments (CA4-1 and CA4-2) were measured at 0.10 ± 0.04 mm, and citric acid pH 6 (CA6-2) showed a thickness of 0.09 ± 0.03 mm. The control saline group (SAL7-2) showed the thickest epithelial layer at day 7, measuring at 0.11 ± 0.03 mm. Significantly thinner epithelial thickness was observed following treatment of PA4-2 and PA6-2, with *p*-values of 0.0384 and 0.0354, respectively.

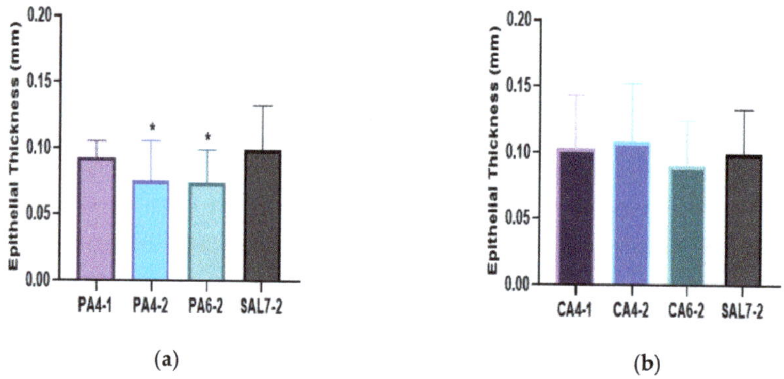

Figure 3. Comparison of epithelial thickness as an indication of the quality of regenerated wound between (**a**) phosphoric acid (PA) buffered solution treatment groups on day 7 and (**b**) citric acid (CA) buffered solution treatment groups on day 7 post-wounding with saline control group (SAL7-2). Each bar represents mean ± standard deviation. * $p < 0.05$ indicates the results obtained were statistically significant from control group (SAL7-2). PA4-1 n = 14/14, PA4-2 n = 15/16, PA6-2 n = 13/16, CA4-1 n = 16/16, CA4-2 n = 15/16, CA6-2 n = 12/14 and SAL7-2 n = 8/12.

Histological analysis of wound-contraction by measurement of the gap between the striated panniculus carnosus muscle was also assessed to understand the effect of acidic buffer solutions on wound contraction. The rate of wound contraction was significantly faster for PA4-2 (*p*-value = 0.0003), CA4-1 (*p*-value = 0.0201), CA4-2 (*p*-value = 0.0079) and CA6-2 (*p*-value = 0.0419) in comparison to control saline group. Panniculus gap measurement of phosphoric acid (PA) treated wound tissues was measured at 3.39 ± 0.55 mm (PA4-1), 2.79 ± 0.88 mm (PA4-2) and 3.27 ± 0.58 mm (PA6-2), respectively. Citric acid (CA) treatment groups were measured at 3.14 ± 0.54 mm for CA4-1, 3.06 ± 0.66 mm for CA4-2 and 3.19 ± 0.86 mm for CA6-2. Panniculus gap measurement of control saline group (SAL7-2) treatment showed the widest gap in comparison to all other acidic treatment groups measured at 3.81 ± 0.61 mm (Figure 4).

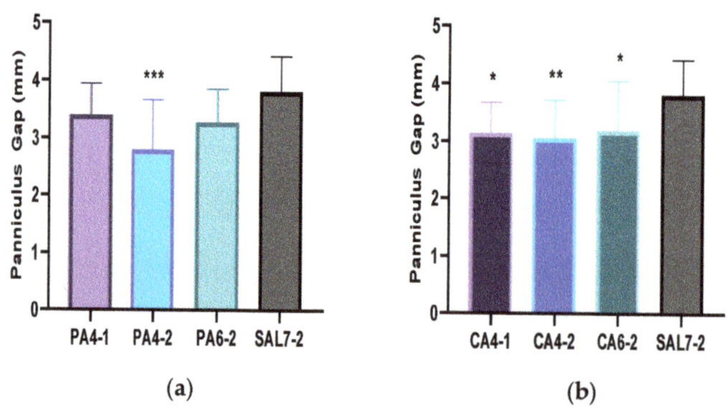

Figure 4. Panniculus carnosus muscle gap measurement during wound healing process when treated with (**a**) phosphoric acid (PA) buffered solutions of pH 4 and pH 6, (**b**) citric acid (CA) buffered solutions of pH 4 and pH 6 in comparison to saline control group (SAL7-2). Each bar represents mean ± standard deviation. * $p < 0.05$, ** $p < 0.01$ and *** $p < 0.001$ indicates the results obtained were statistically significant from control group (SAL7-2).

2.3. Acidic Treatments Promote Collagen Deposition in Wounded Tissues

Collagen fiber deposition and collagen density of collected wounded tissues were evaluated with Masson Trichrome (MT) staining technique, as shown in Figure 5. Wound tissues collected at day 7 showed a significantly higher density of collagen fibers when treated with phosphoric acid (PA) pH 4 and citric acid (CA) pH 4 once-daily treatment, showing collagen index of 0.47 ± 0.37 (PA4-1, p-value = 0.0103) and 0.52 ± 0.19 (CA4-1, p-value < 0.0001), followed by pH 4 once-every-second-day treatment with collagen index measured at 0.41 ± 0.17 (PA4-2, p-value = 0.0486) and 0.37 ± 0.11 (CA4-2, p-value = 0.0050) in comparison to control saline group (SAL7-2) measuring at 0.19 ± 0.05.

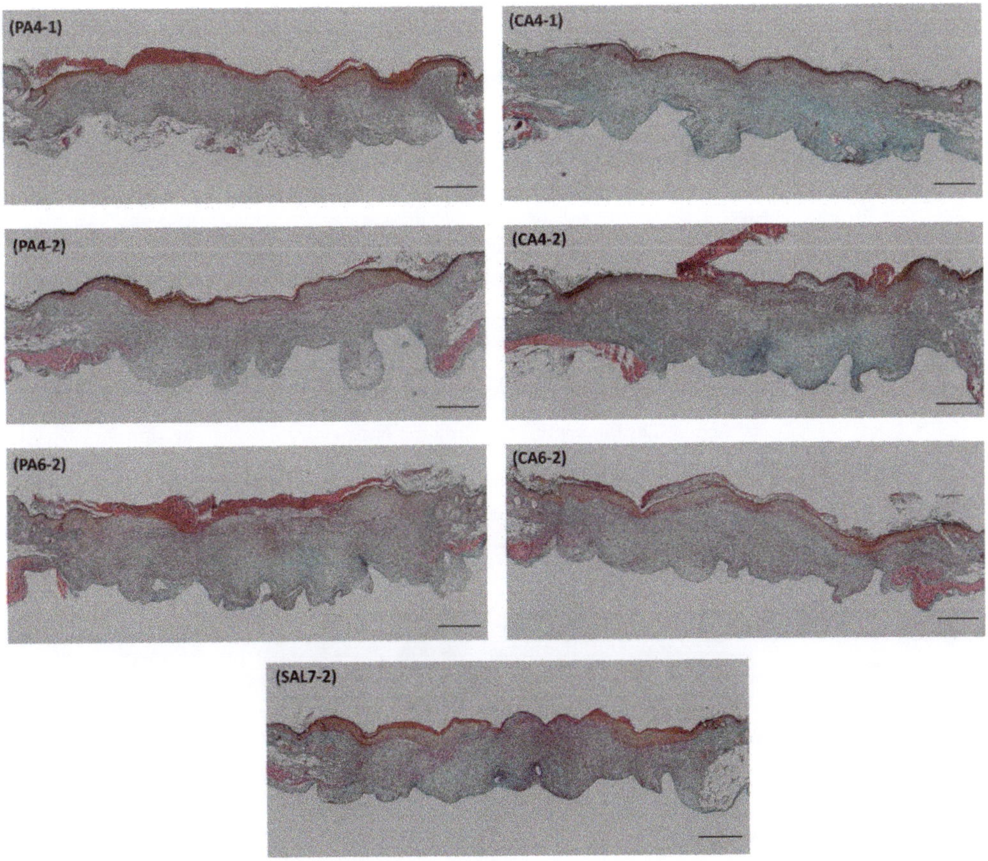

(a)

Figure 5. *Cont.*

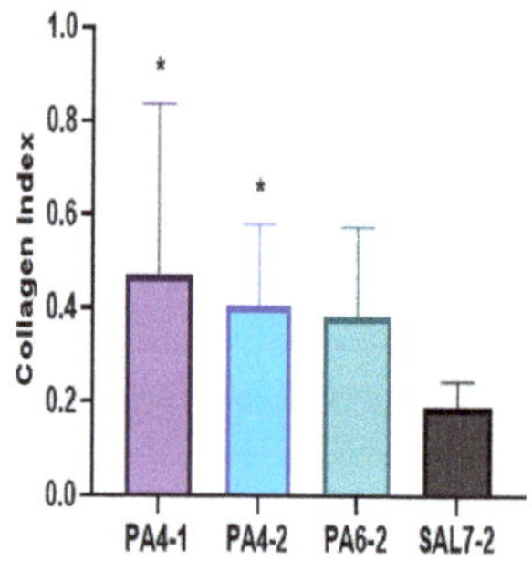

(b)

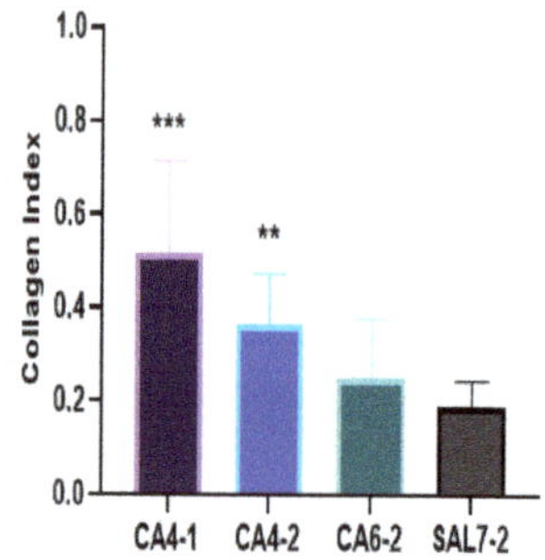

(c)

Figure 5. Evaluation of collagen deposition between phosphoric acid (PA) and citric acid (CA) treatment groups on day 7 post-wounding utilizing Masson Trichrome (MT) staining technique. (**a**) Histology analysis of skin sample obtained from all treatment groups. Original magnification 4×. Black scale bar represents 500 µm. (**b**) Collagen content evaluation between PA4-1, PA4-2, PA6-2 in comparison to SAL7-2 control group. (**c**) Differences in collagen index between CA4-1, CA4-2, CA6-2 and SAL7-2 control group. Each bar represents mean ± standard deviation. * $p < 0.05$, ** $p < 0.01$ and *** $p < 0.001$ indicates the results obtained were statistically significant from control group (SAL7-2).

3. Discussion

Wound acidification using acidic buffers was demonstrated to be an effective treatment to increase re-epithelialization, wound closure, and collagen levels of non-infected wounds, all of which are indicative of improved wound healing. A previous study by our group established that the acidification regime once-every-second-day significantly improved metabolic activity and migration of keratinocyte and fibroblast skin cells. In vitro models were studied with acidic buffers at a pH range between 3 and 7 and both skin cells were observed to be more viable and to migrate faster in acidic buffers at pH 4, 5, followed by 6, with correlation to buffer ionic strength [24]. In this study, we found wounds treated with acidic pH 4 buffers following a once-every-second-day treatment with phosphoric and citric buffers showed complete wound re-epithelialization by day 7 of the treatment period, compared to saline solution.

A faster wound re-epithelialization rate was observed in wounds treated by pH 4 buffers in both phosphoric and citric treatment groups compared to pH 6 buffers. This was evidenced from our histological analysis of epithelial thickness and wound closure measurements, showing wounds treated by pH 4 acidic buffers to have attenuated, thinner and more resolved epithelium, indicating better wound recovery. The transition of a wound epithelium thickness is evident of wound progression to the final maturation phase, due to halting migration of keratinocytes and the regeneration of a stratified epithelium, leading to a thinner epithelium [37] These wounds also showed narrower panniculus gap measurements coupled with shorter wound length by end of the treatment period, suggesting faster wound closure, potentially due to contraction by the panniculus carnosus muscle [38] compared to pH 6 treatments. Significantly shorter wound length measurements also depicted faster re-epithelialization in both acidic buffer treatment groups. We propose this contributed to the buffering capacity of the buffer systems that helps to maintain an acidic wound pH milieu to stimulate many cellular processes involving wound re-epithelialization which are enhanced by acidic pH [4–7]. The buffering capacity of a buffer system is dependent on both the acid pKa and pH value of the buffering system that allows the buffer to resist pH changes by an endogenous mechanism [39]. Therefore, this highlights the importance of acid choice in formulating a buffering system to be effective in resisting pH changes by endogenous processes to maintain an acidic wound milieu.

Overall, citric acid treatment groups (CA) were found to enhance wound healing, showing a better percentage of re-epithelialization, thinner epithelial layer, better wound contracture, and higher levels of collagen deposition in comparison to phosphoric acid (PA). This finding of slower healing by phosphoric acid treatment groups indicates that the acidic environment created by an acid with higher buffering strength slows down the healing activity of various intricate cellular processes, affecting rate of wound recovery. Interestingly, once-daily treatment by phosphoric acid (PA4-1) was observed to promote faster external epidermal wound recovery but slower internal wound contraction, evidenced from both macroscopic and histological evaluation. This is supported by the PA4-1 treatment group showing a higher percentage of re-epithelialization but larger panniculus gap measurement than other treatment groups indicative of slower wound contraction. This behavior is correlated to keratinocytes being able to tolerate more acidic conditions, which can be described by their role in the stratum corneum [7]. As the stratum corneum is constructed predominantly of keratinocytes, many studies have demonstrated that the acidic microenvironment of the skin milieu plays a key role in keratinocyte differentiation, especially during wound repair. Keratinocytes differentiation triggers an upregulation of ceramides synthesis, lipids, and aids in the restoration of lipid lamellae structure which are required to restore the epidermal layer [40–42]. Thus, this helps to explain the observed faster re-epithelization of the epidermal layer by once-daily phosphoric acid treatment at pH 4 (PA4-1), with contrasting slower internal tissue recovery. Furthermore, we also observed that wound contracture was less significant in phosphoric acid-treated groups compared to citric acid-treated wounds. This was evidenced from all citric acid groups showing significant thinner panniculus gap measurements than phosphoric acid-treated wounds, with only PA4-2 showing significant difference to the control group. We theorize faster re-epithelization can be achieved with the use of acids with stronger buffering capacity. However, cellular processes do not favor strong acid buffers and can impede wound tissue recovery rate.

The upregulation of the transforming growth factor-β (TGF-β) signaling pathway was considered as a potential mechanism by which phosphate from phosphoric acid and citrate from citric acid treatments stimulate the expression of these growth factors. Canonical activation of TGF-β occurs in the early stages of healing [43]. Upon activation, TGF-β play a crucial role in regulating fibroblast migration, proliferation and differentiation by binding to the heteromeric receptors complex transforming growth factor-β type I and type II receptors (TGFBR1 and TGFBR2) [44,45]. Phosphorylation of activin-like kinase 5 (ALK5), which is a type of TGFBR1, enables the induction of SMAD2 and SMAD3 receptor pathways that promotes differentiation of fibroblasts, resulting in increased production of myofibroblasts [46–48]. Wound closure is known to be facilitated by generated traction and contractile forces coordinated by surrounding myofibroblasts cells. This is an important step for remodeling of connective tissue to promote faster wound healing [26,49]. Our findings showed wounds treated with acidic buffers induced a faster rate of wound closure compared to the saline group. Mechanical stress by the extracellular matrix (ECM) is induced by migrating myofibroblasts and fibroblasts to the wounded site, which is also stimulated by acidification of the microenvironment that causes small tractional forces in newly formed granulation tissues [50]. Such increase in wound closure also explains our findings of high collagen levels within treated wound tissues, contributed by higher collagen synthesis by myofibroblasts cells [51,52].

Histological analysis of collected wound tissue treated by acidic buffers revealed high level of collagen deposition at the wounded site. Collagen is known to be a key component in the formation of an extracellular matrix contributing to mechanical strength and elasticity of repaired tissues [53,54]. As collected tissues were shown to be fully re-epithelialize by day 7, higher levels of collagen deposition at a later stage of the wound healing process is also evidence of increased wound closure and re-modelling activity when treated with acidic buffers, as previously described. Other studies have reported a similar increase in collagen levels at the wounded site when the wound pH microenvironment was modified using ascorbic acid treatments in murine models [55,56]. Therefore, this finding of higher collagen levels in treated tissues correlates to the increased rate of re-epithelialization and wound closure, as observed, suggesting that changing the wound environment to be more acidic leads to better wound healing.

4. Materials and Methods

4.1. Chemicals

Phosphoric acid, citric acid and sodium hydroxide were purchased from Sigma-Aldrich (Castle Hill, NSW, Australia). Sterilized saline solution was purchased from Ebos Healthcare (Kingsgrove, NSW, Australia).

4.2. Topical Buffer Preparation

The 0.01 M phosphoric acid solution (H_3PO_4) was prepared by gently pipetting 0.068 mL 85% *w*/*w* phosphoric acid to 25 mL sterile Milli-Q water. The solution was mixed thoroughly for 3 min via inversion mixing to ensure complete dissolution of the chemical, and the final volume was adjusted to 100 mL with sterile Milli-Q water. The 0.01 M citric acid solution ($C_6H_8O_7$) was prepared by adding 0.19 g crystalline citric acid to 100 mL sterile Milli-Q water. The 0.01 M sodium hydroxide solution (NaOH) was prepared by adding 0.4 g crystalline sodium hydroxide to 1 L sterile Milli-Q water followed by inversion mixing as described above.

Both phosphoric acid and citric acid buffers were prepared by adjusting pH values of 0.01 M phosphoric acid and 0.01 M citric acid with 0.01 M sodium hydroxide solution to pH values of 4 and 6, respectively. All acidic buffer solutions were incubated for 24 h and the pH values of all prepared buffers were confirmed with Orion Star A321 portable pH meter (ThermoFisher Scientific, Scoresby, VIC, Australia). All topical buffer solutions were autoclaved prior to surgery.

4.3. Murine Wound Repair Model

The murine study was carried out in compliance with current guidelines for the care of laboratory animals and the animal ethics application was approved by the University of South Australia Animal Ethics Committee (approval number U20-17). A total of 56 adult female BALB/c mice, with average age of 10 to 15 weeks and size of 19 to 25 g, were sourced from the Animal Resources Centre (ARC), and housed and acclimatized at the Core Animal Facility (CAF) for a minimum of 7 days. Animal feed was standard rat and mouse chow from Specialty Feeds. Mice were group-housed with $n = 5$ and maintained in standard laboratory conditions (temperature: 25 $\pm$ 2 °C, humidity: 55 $\pm$ 5%, 12 h/12 h light/dark cycle) prior to surgery and individually housed following wounding.

Buprenorphine was given as an analgesic 30 min pre-operation and, following anesthetic induction using isoflurane gas to achieve surgical depth anesthesia, hair from the dorsal mouse skin was shaved with a sterile electric clipper and further depilated by applying hair removal cream for 1 min. To minimize infection, the mice's skin was washed with sterile water and cleaned using 70% alcohol swabs. Two circular full-thickness skin wounds were induced using a sterilized AccuPunch 6 mm^2 punch biopsy tool. With wound size not being considered as part of randomization, a simple randomization strategy with allocation concealment was utilized prior to surgery, with mice being simultaneously randomized into seven groups according to treatment regimens ($n = 8$). Group 1—phosphoric acid pH 4 buffer solution, one treatment daily (PA4-1), Group 2—phosphoric acid pH 4 buffer solution, one treatment every second day (PA4-2), Group 3—phosphoric acid pH 6 buffer solution, one treatment every second day (PA6-2), Group 4—citric acid pH 4 buffer solution, one treatment daily (CA4-1), Group 5—citric acid pH 4 buffer solution, one treatment every second day (CA4-2), Group 6—citric acid pH 6 buffer solution, one treatment every second day (CA6-2), and Group 7—sterilized saline solution pH 7, one treatment every second day (SAL7-2). The open wounds were left open without sutures and dressed with 1 cm $\times$ 1 cm gauze dressing treated with 1 mL buffered solutions for at least 5 min. A further 3 cm $\times$ 3 cm Tegaderm dressing (3M, Australia) was applied on top to secure the treatment below. The dressings were placed on mice for the duration of the whole study and were changed daily, or once-every-second-day, according to treatment regimens, whilst mice were placed under mild anesthetic with isoflurane gas for a period no longer than 5 min during dressing change. Mice were observed and checked daily through the duration of the experiment (7 days) for signs of distress and pain, including weight, appearance (dull/ruffled coat, signs of dehydration and hunched posture), behavior (abnormal behavior and reluctance to move), appearance of wounds (infection, inflammation and swelling) and loss of dressings. Skin tissue, including the wounds, were collected from 56 mice following humane killing by carbon dioxide asphyxiation and death, confirmed by cervical dislocation on day 7.

4.4. Macroscopic Wound Size Measurement

Macroscopic wound measurement was carried out on digital photographs of the wounds taken on each day during dressing change at day 0 (initial wound) and following measurements taken on days 2, 4, 6 and 7 (actual wound) using a ruler. Actual wound area was traced and normalized by calibrating each image using Image Pro Plus Software (Maryland, USA). The percentage of wound healing (% of initial) was calculated as below:

$$\frac{Area\ of\ initial\ wound - area\ of\ actual\ wound}{Area\ of\ initial\ wound} \times 100\%$$

4.5. Histological Assessment by Hematoxylin & Eosin (H&E)

Skin tissue, including the wound and its surrounding skin tissues, were collected from mice following humane killing on day 7. Skin tissue was fixed for 24 h in 10% neutral formalin at room temperature, processed in Leica TP 1020 tissue processor (Leica Microsystems, North Ryde, NSW, Australia) and embedded in paraffin blocks. Skin tissue was sectioned at 5 μm using a microtome (Leica Microsystems, North Ryde, NSW, Australia) for histological assessment.

Paraffin sections were dewaxed by immersion in xylene, followed by ethyl alcohol and tap water. Lillie-Mayer's hematoxylin was then used to stain the sections for 6 min prior to rinsing with tap water until the water was colorless. Tissue sections were stained "blue" in 5% bicarbonate solution for 15 s prior rinsing the sections with tap water. Hematoxylin stain was differentiated in 0.25% acid alcohol before second incubation in 5% bicarbonate solution for 15 s. The sections were then stained using alcoholic eosin for 2 min, washed with ethanol prior to incubation with xylene and mounting in DPX mounting media (Sigma-Aldrich, Castle Hill, NSW, Australia).

The percentage re-epithelialization (%) was calculated based on total wound length (the area between the first hair follicle either side of the wound and above the break in the panniculus) at day 7 using the following formula:

$$\frac{Re - epithelialized\ wound\ length_{Day7}}{Total\ epithelialized + un - epithelialized\ wound\ length_{Day7}} \times 100\%$$

4.6. Histological Assessment by Masson Trichrome (MT)

The properties of connective tissues at the wound site, such as collagen, muscles and keratin, were evaluated using Masson Trichrome staining. Paraffin-embedded sections were firstly dewaxed by immersion in xylene and ethanol prior to rinsing with tap water. The sections were then placed in Bouin's Fixative solution at 60 °C for 30 min before cleaning with water. The sections were placed in celestine blue followed by Lillie-Mayer's hematoxylin for 3 min each before rinsing in running water until colorless. Prior to incubating the sections in Fuschin Ponceau for 5 min, the sections were briefly dipped in 5% bicarbonate solution for 15 s followed by washing in water. The sections were then incubated in 5% phosphotungstic acid and light green staining solution for 10 min and 3 min, respectively. All samples were briefly dipped in 1% acetic acid followed by washing in water. Dehydration of the sections was performed by briefly dipping the sections in ethanol and xylene before mounting with DPX mounting media (Sigma-Aldrich, Castle Hill, NSW, Australia).

For quantitative morphometric analysis, the slides were captured as RGB images and analyzed using Image J software (Version 1.32j, National Institutes of Health, USA). The number of blue/green pixels indicating collagen was then evaluated from the RGB images with a macro written by Kennedy et al., 2006 [57] by converting pixels of the image with substantially greater (>120%) blue than red intensity to have the new, grey scale amplitude = 1, leaving other pixels as with amplitude = 0.

4.7. Statistical Analysis

Statistical analysis was performed using GraphPad Prism v 8.0 (GraphPad Software, Inc., San Diego, CA, USA). Continuous variables were presented as a mean $\pm$ standard deviation and categorical variables as percentages. For wound healing (% initial), percentage re-epithelialization, wound length, epithelial thickness, panniculus gap measurement and collagen index, statistically significant difference were determined by one-way analysis of variance (ANOVA) with Dunnett's multiple comparisons post-hoc test. For absolute wound size over time, two-way analysis of variance (ANOVA) coupled with Dunnett's multiple comparisons post-hoc test was performed. Shapiro–Wilks was selected as the normality test for all studies. The level of statistical significance was set to $p < 0.05$.

5. Conclusions

This study has established the in vivo efficacy of acidification in promoting wound healing using acidic buffers at pH 4, following a once-every-second-day regimen in non-infected wounds. Wound acidification was demonstrated to promote a number of cellular responses, such as increasing the rate of re-epithelialization, wound closure, and collagen synthesis, inducing faster wound healing. Significant improvement to wound healing was observed as early as 2 days post-treatment. pH is shown to play a role in mediating the rate of wound healing as evidenced by faster wound healing by pH 4 buffers, compared to wounds treated by pH 6 buffers. Our study has shown the significance of acid choice, treatment frequency and duration; and the importance of maintaining an acidic wound microenvironment at pH 4 could therefore be a significant therapeutic strategy for improving wound management.

Author Contributions: Conceptualization, P.S., X.L.S., Y.S., A.J.C. and S.G.; methodology, P.S., X.L.S. and Y.S.; software, P.S. and X.L.S.; validation, P.S., X.L.S. and Y.S.; formal analysis, P.S.; investigation, P.S.; resources, A.J.C. and S.G.; data curation, P.S., X.L.S. and Y.S.; writing—original draft preparation, P.S.; writing—review and editing, P.S., X.L.S., Y.S., A.J.C. and S.G.; visualization, P.S. and X.L.S.; supervision, X.L.S., Y.S., A.J.C. and S.G.; project administration, A.J.C. and S.G.; funding acquisition, A.J.C. and S.G. All authors have read and agreed to the published version of the manuscript.

Funding: This research was funded by the Wound Management Innovation Cooperative Research Center (WMI CRC), grant number SP39-2.

Institutional Review Board Statement: The animal study protocol was approved by the Ethics Committee of the University of South Australia (protocol code U20-17 and date of approval on 16/10/2017).

Informed Consent Statement: Not applicable.

Data Availability Statement: Data is contained within the article.

Conflicts of Interest: The authors declare no conflict of interest.

References

1. Velnar, T.; Bailey, T.; Smrkolj, V. The Wound Healing Process: An Overview of the Cellular and Molecular Mechanisms. *J. Int. Med. Res.* **2009**, *37*, 1528–1542. [CrossRef] [PubMed]
2. Lodhi, S.; Singhai, A.K. Wound healing effect of flavonoid rich fraction and luteolin isolated from Martynia annua Linn. on streptozotocin induced diabetic rats. *Asian Pac. J. Trop. Med.* **2013**, *6*, 253–259. [CrossRef]

3. Guo, S.; DiPietro, L.A. Factors Affecting Wound Healing. *J. Dent. Res.* **2010**, *89*, 219–229. [CrossRef] [PubMed]
4. Schneider, L.A.; Korber, A.; Grabbe, S.; Dissemond, J. Influence of pH on wound-healing: A new perspective for wound-therapy? *Arch. Dermatol. Res.* **2006**, *298*, 413–420. [CrossRef] [PubMed]
5. Schreml, S.; Szeimies, R.-M.; Karrer, S.; Heinlin, J.; Landthaler, M.; Babilas, P. The impact of the pH value on skin integrity and cutaneous wound healing. *J. Eur. Acad. Dermatol. Venereol.* **2010**, *24*, 373–378. [CrossRef] [PubMed]
6. Sharpe, J.; Harris, K.; Jubin, K.; Bainbridge, N.; Jordan, N. The effect of pH in modulating skin cell behaviour. *Br. J. Dermatol.* **2009**, *161*, 671–673. [CrossRef]
7. Gethin, G. The significance of surface pH in chronic wounds. *Wounds* **2007**, *3*, 52.
8. Chikakane, K.; Takahashi, H. Measurement of skin pH and its significance in cutaneous diseases. *Clin. Dermatol.* **1995**, *13*, 299–306. [CrossRef]
9. Fluhr, J.W.; Elias, P.M. Stratum Corneum pH: Formation and Function of the 'Acid Mantle'. *Exog. Dermatol.* **2002**, *1*, 163–175. [CrossRef]
10. Kaufman, T.; Eichenlaub, E.; Angel, M.; Levin, M.; Futrell, J. Topical acidification promotes healing of experimental deep partial thickness skin burns: A randomized double-blind preliminary study. *Burns* **1985**, *12*, 84–90. [CrossRef]
11. Rippke, F.; Schreiner, V.; Schwanitz, H.J. The acidic milieu of the horny layer: New findings on the physiology and pathophysiology of skin pH. *Am. J. Clin. Dermatol.* **2002**, *3*, 261–272. [CrossRef] [PubMed]
12. Power, G.; Moore, Z.; O'Connor, T. Measurement of pH, exudate composition and temperature in wound healing: A systematic review. *J. Wound Care* **2017**, *26*, 381–397. [CrossRef] [PubMed]
13. Davis, C.P. Normal flora. In *Medical Microbiology*; The University of Texas Medical Branch: Galveston, TX, USA, 1996.
14. Aly, R.; Shirley, C.; Cunico, B.; Maibach, H.I. Effect of Prolonged Occlusion on the Microbial Flora, pH, Carbon Dioxide and Transepidermal Water Loss on Human Skin. *J. Investig. Dermatol.* **1978**, *71*, 378–381. [CrossRef] [PubMed]
15. Tsukada, K. The pH changes of pressure ulcers related to the healing process of wounds. *Wounds* **1992**, *4*, 16–20.
16. Nagoba, B.; Suryawanshi, N.M.; Wadher, B.; Selkar, S. Acidic Environment and Wound Healing: A Review. *Wounds Compend. Clin. Res. Pract.* **2015**, *27*, 5–11.
17. Percival, S.L.; McCarty, S.; Hunt, J.A.; Woods, E.J. The effects of pH on wound healing, biofilms, and antimicrobial efficacy. *Wound Repair Regen.* **2014**, *22*, 174–186. [CrossRef]
18. Constant, E. Chemical acidification of wounds: An adjuvant to healing and the unfavorable action of alkalinity and ammonia. *Plast. Reconstr. Surg.* **1974**, *54*, 114. [CrossRef]
19. Bishop, A. Role of oxygen in wound healing. *J. Wound Care* **2008**, *17*, 399–402. [CrossRef]
20. Hopf, H.W.; Rollins, M.D. Wounds: An Overview of the Role of Oxygen. *Antioxid. Redox Signal.* **2007**, *9*, 1183–1192. [CrossRef]
21. Schreml, S.; Szeimies, R.; Prantl, L.; Karrer, S.; Landthaler, M.; Babilas, P. Oxygen in acute and chronic wound healing. *Br. J. Dermatol.* **2010**, *163*, 257–268. [CrossRef]
22. Leveen, H.H.; Falk, G.; Borek, B.; Diaz, C.; Lynfield, Y.; Wynkoop, B.J.; Mabunda, G.A.; Rubricius, J.L.; Christoudias, G.C. Chemical acidification of wounds. An adjuvant to healing and the unfavorable action of alkalinity and ammonia. *Ann. Surg.* **1973**, *178*, 745. [CrossRef] [PubMed]
23. Lengheden, A.; Jansson, L. PH effects on experimental wound healing of human fibroblasts in vitro. *Eur. J. Oral Sci.* **1995**, *103*, 148–155. [CrossRef] [PubMed]
24. Sim, P.; Song, Y.; Yang, G.N.; Cowin, A.J.; Garg, S. In Vitro Wound Healing Properties of Novel Acidic Treatment Regimen in Enhancing Metabolic Activity and Migration of Skin Cells. *Int. J. Mol. Sci.* **2022**, *23*, 7188. [CrossRef] [PubMed]
25. Nagoba, B.S.; Gandhi, R.C.; Wadher, B.J.; Potekar, R.; Kolhe, S.M. Microbiological, histopathological and clinical changes in chronic infected wounds after citric acid treatment. *J. Med. Microbiol.* **2008**, *57*, 681–682. [CrossRef] [PubMed]
26. Grinnell, F. Fibroblasts, myofibroblasts, and wound contraction. *J. Cell Biol.* **1994**, *124*, 401–404. [CrossRef]
27. Chang, P.C.; Sulik, G.I.; Soong, H.K.; Parkinson, W.C. Galvanotropic and galvanotaxic responses of corneal endothelial cells. *J. Formos. Med. Assoc.* **1996**, *95*.
28. Soong, H.K.; Parkinson, W.C.; Bafna, S.; Sulik, G.L.; Huang, S.C. Movements of cultured corneal epithelial cells and stromal fibroblasts in electric fields. *Investig. Ophthalmol. Vis. Sci.* **1990**, *31*.
29. Nagoba, B.; Davane, M.; Gandhi, R.; Wadher, B.; Suryawanshi, N.; Selkar, S. Treatment of skin and soft tissue infections caused by Pseudomonas aeruginosa —A review of our experiences with citric acid over the past 20 years. *Wound Med.* **2017**, *19*, 5–9. [CrossRef]
30. Malu, R.G.; Nagoba, B.S.; Jaju, C.R.; Suryawanshi, N.M.; Mali, S.A.; Goyal, V.S.; Misal, N.S. Topical use of citric acid for wound bed preparation. *Int. Wound J.* **2014**, *13*, 709–712. [CrossRef]
31. Tandon, S.; Singh, B.; Kapoor, S.; Mangal, S. Comparison of Effect of pH Modulation on Wound Healing with Topical Application of Citric Acid Versus Superoxide Ions. *Niger. J. Surg.* **2020**, *26*, 122–126.
32. Prabhu, V.; Prasadi, S.; Shivani, A.; Gore, A.; Pawar, V. Does wound pH modulation with 3% citric acid solution dressing help in wound healing: A pilot study. *Saudi Surg. J.* **2014**, *2*, 38. [CrossRef]
33. Yang, Q.; Liang, H.; Maulu, S.; Ge, X.; Ren, M.; Xie, J.; Xi, B. Dietary phosphorus affects growth, glucolipid metabolism, antioxidant activity and immune status of juvenile blunt snout bream (Megalobrama amblycephala). *Anim. Feed Sci. Technol.* **2021**, *274*, 114896. [CrossRef]

34. Zhou, Q.C.; Liu, Y.J.; Mai, K.S.; Tian, L.X. Effect of dietary phosphorus levels on growth, body composition, muscle and bone mineral concentrations for orange-spotted grouper Epinephelus coioides reared in floating cages. *J. World Aquac. Soc.* **2004**, *35*, 427–435. [CrossRef]
35. Chen, X.; Lv, Q.; Liu, Y.; Deng, W. Effect of Food Additive Citric Acid on The Growth of Human Esophageal Carcinoma Cell Line EC109. *Cell J.* **2016**, *18*, 493–502. [CrossRef] [PubMed]
36. Bodner, G.M. Metabolism Part II: The tricarboxylic acid (TCA), citric acid, or Krebs cycle. *J. Chem. Educ.* **1986**, *63*. [CrossRef]
37. Pastar, I.; Stojadinovic, O.; Yin, N.C.; Ramirez, H.; Nusbaum, A.G.; Sawaya, A.; Patel, S.B.; Khalid, L.; Isseroff, R.R.; Tomic-Canic, M. Epithelialization in Wound Healing: A Comprehensive Review. *Adv. Wound Care* **2014**, *3*, 445–464. [CrossRef]
38. Chen, J.S.; Longaker, M.T.; Gurtner, G.C. Murine models of human wound healing. *Methods Mol. Biol.* **2013**, *1037*, 265–274.
39. Proksch, E. pH in nature, humans and skin. *J. Dermatol.* **2018**, *45*, 1044–1052. [CrossRef]
40. Hachem, J.-P.; Behne, M.; Aronchik, I.; Demerjian, M.; Feingold, K.; Elias, P.; Mauro, T. Extracellular pH Controls NHE1 Expression in Epidermis and Keratinocytes: Implications for Barrier Repair. *J. Investig. Dermatol.* **2005**, *125*, 790–797. [CrossRef]
41. Chan, A.; Mauro, T. Acidification in the epidermis and the role of secretory phospholipases. *Derm.-Endocrinol.* **2011**, *3*, 84–90. [CrossRef]
42. Abels, C.; Masur, C.; Daehnhardt-Pfeiffer, S.; Daehnhardt, D.; Knie, U. 413 Formulation with low pH decreases skin pH, restores disrupted epidermal barrier and improves lipid lamellae structure. *J. Investig. Dermatol.* **2017**, *137*, S71. [CrossRef]
43. Diegelmann, R.F.; Evans, M.C. Wound healing: An overview of acute, fibrotic and delayed healing. *Front. Biosci.* **2004**, *9*, 283–289. [CrossRef] [PubMed]
44. Hosokawa, R.; Urata, M.M.; Ito, Y.; Bringas, P.; Chai, Y. Functional Significance of Smad2 in Regulating Basal Keratinocyte Migration During Wound Healing. *J. Investig. Dermatol.* **2005**, *125*, 1302–1309. [CrossRef]
45. Miscianinov, V.; Martello, A.; Rose, L.; Parish, E.; Cathcart, B.; Mitić, T.; Gray, G.A.; Meloni, M.; Zen, A.A.H.; Caporali, A. MicroRNA-148b Targets the TGF-β Pathway to Regulate Angiogenesis and Endothelial-to-Mesenchymal Transition during Skin Wound Healing. *Mol. Ther.* **2018**, *26*, 1996–2007. [CrossRef] [PubMed]
46. Bergmeier, V.; Etich, J.; Pitzler, L.; Frie, C.; Koch, M.; Fischer, M.; Rappl, G.; Abken, H.; Tomasek, J.J.; Brachvogel, B. Identification of a myofibroblast-specific expression signature in skin wounds. *Matrix Biol.* **2018**, *65*, 59–74. [CrossRef]
47. Zhang, Y.E. Mechanistic insight into contextual TGF-β signaling. *Curr. Opin. Cell Biol.* **2018**, *51*, 1–7. [CrossRef]
48. Helary, C.; Ovtracht, L.; Coulomb, B.; Godeau, G.; Giraudguille, M. Dense fibrillar collagen matrices: A model to study myofibroblast behaviour during wound healing. *Biomaterials* **2006**, *27*, 4443–4452. [CrossRef]
49. Hinz, B.; Gabbiani, G. Mechanisms of force generation and transmission by myofibroblasts. *Curr. Opin. Biotechnol.* **2003**, *14*, 538–546. [CrossRef]
50. Tomasek, J.J.; Gabbiani, G.; Hinz, B.; Chaponnier, C.; Brown, R.A. Myofibroblasts and mechano-regulation of connective tissue remodelling. *Nat. Rev. Mol. Cell Biol.* **2002**, *3*, 349–363. [CrossRef]
51. Sinha, M.; Sen, C.K.; Singh, K.; DAS, A.; Ghatak, S.; Rhea, B.; Blackstone, B.; Powell, H.M.; Khanna, S.; Roy, S. Direct conversion of injury-site myeloid cells to fibroblast-like cells of granulation tissue. *Nat. Commun.* **2018**, *9*, 1–19. [CrossRef]
52. Thangavel, P.; Vilvanathan, S.P.; Kuttalam, I.; Lonchin, S. Topical administration of pullulan gel accelerates skin tissue regeneration by enhancing collagen synthesis and wound contraction in rats. *Int. J. Biol. Macromol.* **2020**, *149*, 395–403. [CrossRef] [PubMed]
53. Mathew-Steiner, S.S.; Roy, S.; Sen, C.K. Collagen in Wound Healing. *Bioengineering* **2021**, *8*, 63. [CrossRef] [PubMed]
54. Avizheh, L.; Peirouvi, T.; Diba, K.; Fathi-Azarbayjani, A. Electrospun wound dressing as a promising tool for the therapeutic delivery of ascorbic acid and caffeine. *Ther. Deliv.* **2019**, *10*, 757–767. [CrossRef] [PubMed]
55. Jagetia, G.C.; Rajanikant, G.; Rao, K.M. Ascorbic acid increases healing of excision wounds of mice whole body exposed to different doses of γ-radiation. *Burns* **2007**, *33*, 484–494. [CrossRef]
56. Shu, D.Y.; Lovicu, F.J. Myofibroblast transdifferentiation: The dark force in ocular wound healing and fibrosis. *Prog. Retin. Eye Res.* **2017**, *60*, 44–65. [CrossRef]
57. Kennedy, D.J.; Vetteth, S.; Periyasamy, S.M.; Kanj, M.; Fedorova, L.; Khouri, S.; Kahaleh, M.B.; Xie, Z.; Malhotra, D.; Kolodkin, N.I.; et al. Central Role for the Cardiotonic Steroid Marinobufagenin in the Pathogenesis of Experimental Uremic Cardiomyopathy. *Hypertension* **2006**, *47*, 488–495. [CrossRef]

International Journal of
Molecular Sciences

Article

Investigation of the Properties of Linen Fibers and Dressings

Tomasz Gębarowski [1,*], Izabela Jęśkowiak [2] and Benita Wiatrak [2]

1 Department of Biostructure and Animal Physiology, The Wroclaw University of Environmental and Life Sciences, Kożuchowska 1/3, 51-631 Wroclaw, Poland
2 Department of Pharmacology, Faculty of Medicine, Wroclaw Medical University, Mikulicza-Radeckiego 2, 50-345 Wroclaw, Poland
* Correspondence: tomasz.gebarowski@upwr.edu.pl

Abstract: In antiquity, flax was used as a dressing for healing wounds. Currently, work is underway on the genetic modification of flax fibers to improve their properties. Genetic modifications have resulted in an increased content of antioxidants and more favorable mechanical properties. The works published so far have presented independent tests of fibers and dressings after appropriate technological treatments in cell cultures. This study aimed to compare the properties of the fibers and the dressing produced in cell cultures—hamster fibroblasts—V79. The research material was traditional NIKE fibers; genetically modified M, B, and MB fibers; and linen dressings obtained from these fibers. The extract from 48-h incubation of 40 mg of fiber in the culture medium, which was desolved into 10, 20, and 30 mg, was administered to the cell culture. On the other hand, a linen dressing was placed on cells with an area of 0.5 cm^2, 1 cm^2, 1.5 cm^2, and 2 cm^2. Cells with fiber or dressing were incubated for 48 h, and then, biological tests were performed, including cell viability (in propidium iodide staining), cell proliferation (in the SRB assay), evaluation of the intracellular free radical level (in the DCF-DA assay), genotoxicity (in the comet assay), assessment of the apoptotic and necrotic cells (in staining anexin-V and iodide propidium), the course of the cell cycle, and the scratch test. The correlation between apoptosis and genotoxicity and the levels of free radicals and genotoxicity were determined for the tested linen fibers and fabrics. The tests presented that the fibers are characterized by the ability to eliminate damaged cells in the elimination phase. However, the obtained fabrics gain different properties during the technological processing of the fibers into linen dressings. Linen fabrics have better regenerative properties for cells than fibers. The linseed dressing made of MB fiber has the most favorable regenerative properties.

Keywords: flax; fiber; fibroblast

Citation: Gębarowski, T.; Jęśkowiak, I.; Wiatrak, B. Investigation of the Properties of Linen Fibers and Dressings. *Int. J. Mol. Sci.* **2022**, 23, 10480. https://doi.org/10.3390/ijms231810480

Academic Editors: César Viseras, Luana Perioli and Cinzia Pagano

Received: 31 July 2022
Accepted: 5 September 2022
Published: 9 September 2022

1. Introduction

Serious skin wounds caused by injuries, burns, or diabetes predispose patients to severe disability and even death. In addition, wound healing may slow down during pathological conditions or aging, and wounds may become chronic [1]. Traditional wound dressings (e.g., cotton bandages and gauze) are the first type of commonly used wound dressings [2]. However, chronic wounds are insufficient to ensure effective healing and can significantly delay wound closure [3].

Solutions are sought among linen products. Common flax (Latin Linum usitatissimum) is a plant that has been used for thousands of years. The health benefits of flax seeds are mainly attributed to the omega-3 fatty acids and fiber they contain. It should not be forgotten that flax is also a valuable source of antioxidant ligands that are widespread in various parts of plants as glycoside conjugates associated with a fibrous plant component. Lignans prevent the toxic effects of oxidation by sequestering free radicals. This process involves inhibiting the attack of lipid peroxidation. In addition, phenolic compounds stimulate the synthesis of collagen, one of the main components of the skin's connective tissue [4]. Flax fibers also contain many active substances, such as unsaturated fatty acids,

4-hydroxybenzoic acid, sterols (campesterol and β-sitosterol), ferulic acid, and polyhydroxy butyrate (PHB). Cannabidiol (CBD), contained in fibers, exerts an analgesic effect. Flax fibers are characterized by two very important properties, such as the ability to sweep up moisture, which is used for oozing wounds, and being hypoallergenic—thanks to which, a dressing made of such material is also available to people suffering from an overactive immune system manifested by a tendency toward allergic reactions [5].

Processed flax fibers are characterized by good mechanical properties, low density, and tensile strength from 264 to 2000 MPa [6–10]. Obtaining transgenic flax varieties improves the mechanical properties of Linum raw materials and increases the wound-healing capacity of fabrics obtained from flax fibers with more favorable properties [3,6]. In addition, the resulting flax fiber dressings are fully biodegradable.

A narrow team of researchers researched flax fabrics in cell cultures and humans. The most important conclusions from the research conducted so far are presented in Table 1.

Table 1. The results of the research on the influence of flax dressings.

Research Group	Material	Results
Skórkowska-Telichowska Katarzyna et al. [11]	Balb/3T3 cell line 30 patients with wounds that had lasted at least 2 years	- Modified linen dressings do not cause cytotoxicity and do not adversely affect the growth and morphology of Balb/3T3 cells. - After a 12-week application of a modified linen dressing, it follows accelerates healing and reduces exudate and wound size - Modified flax dressing reduced the pain associated with chronic venous ulceration.
Paladini et al. [12]	Balb/3T3 cell line	- The technology of silver nanophase deposition in flax dressings has proven to be effective and can be transferred from the laboratory scale to the macro scale - Linen dressings with nanosilver have antibacterial properties against G+ and G− be bacteria due to a loss of influence on cell viability.
Skórkowska-Telichowska Katarzyna et al. [13]	V79 cell line	- Linen fabrics from genetically modified flax W92 and M reduce DNA damage in V79 cells and produce fewer free radicals.
Gębarowski Tomasz et al. [14]	NHDF cell line	- Modified flax fiber and fabric extracts M, B, and M + B are not cytotoxic to NHDF cells and do not cause the growth of apoptotic cells in cell cultures. - Linseed dressings increase the proliferation of fibroblasts. - B and M + B flax dressings are the strongest activators of NHDF and are the most recommended dressings.
Gąsiorowski Kazimierz et al. [15]	NHEK, NHDF, HUVEC, THP-1 cell lines	- Dressings made of modified flax with an overexpression of phenolic acids and flavonoids (W92) and polyhydroxybutyrate (M48) release these substances from the cell culture dressings, giving better properties to the dressings. - Modified linen fabrics increase the proliferation of keratinocytes and fibroblasts.
Gębarowski Tomasz et al. [16]	Balb/3T3, NHDF, THP-1, NHEK, HMVEK, A431 cell lines	- Modified flax fibers increase the proliferation of fibroblasts and keratinocytes, reducing the number of free radicals. - Linen fibers do not stimulate the proliferation of cancer cells.
Skórkowska-Telichowska Katarztna et al. [5]	NHDF cell line 22 patients suffered from chronic non-healing ulcerations	- Modified flax dressing supports the removal of necrotic remnants from the wound, absorbs exudate, and provides an appropriate environment for the healing of exudative and infected wounds.
Gębarowski Tomasz et al. [17]	NHEK, Balb 3T3, HMCEV, THP-1 cell lines	- Linen dressings do not increase the number of necrotic cells. - Modified flax dressings reduce the amount of proteins in cancer cells. - All linen dressings did not lose their wound-healing properties under the influence of technological processes of processing flax fibers.

In this study, we prepared flax fibers and fabrics based on genetically modified flax fibers to evaluate their properties using Chinese Hamster Lung (V79) fibroblast cells, commonly used to test DNA damage, mutagenicity, and toxicity. V79 cells are immortal, easily mutagenized, and have a shortened cell cycles [18,19]. The V79 lineage can also be used to detect structural and numerical chromosomal damage by measuring the micronucleus formation in mitotic-divided interphase cells. In addition, V79 is well-established in toxicology studies. The stability of the karyotype and morphology makes them suitable for gene toxicity tests with low background aberrations. Ford and Yerganian developed this cell line in 1958 from the lung tissue of a young male Chinese hamster.

The study aimed to compare the properties of traditional flax fibers and NIKE dressings with the M, B, and MB-modified flax in the V79 model line.

2. Results

2.1. Cell Viability

The study compared the cell survival of V79 cultures after 24-h incubation at 37 °C of four types of flax fibers and NIKE, M, B, and MB fabrics. Increased cell viability was observed after incubation with flax fabrics compared to flax fibers. The highest viability values of the cultured V79 cells were observed after incubation with linen fabric, depending on its tested fabric size. The highest viability of V79 cells for the fabric 0.5 cm was observed for the M fabric (95.96% live cells ± 2.89) and slightly lower for the B fabric (95.04% live cells ± 0.86), 1 cm for the B fabric (94.76% live cells ± 1.07), 1.5 cm for the NIKE fabric (94.60% live cells ± 1.17), slightly smaller for B (94.20% live cells ± 1.09), and 2 cm for B (93.66% live cells ± 1.42). Based on these results, it can be concluded that the B-type flax variety fabric had the best effect on cell viability.

When analyzing the cell survival rate only for the flax fibers alone, inconclusive results were obtained (Figure 1). The highest survival of V79 cells for the 10 mg sample of fiber was obtained for the M fiber (94.08% live cells ± 3.18) and for the 20 mg sample for the B fiber (92.00% live cells ± 1.18). In contrast, for samples above 30 mg, the highest cell survival was obtained for the NIKE fiber (30 mg—90.96% live cells ± 1.29; 40 mg—89.09% live cells ± 2.13), but these were lower values compared to the cell survival after treating V79 cells with fibers weighing 10 and 20 mg of the transgenic flax varieties. The greatest vitality was obtained for B.

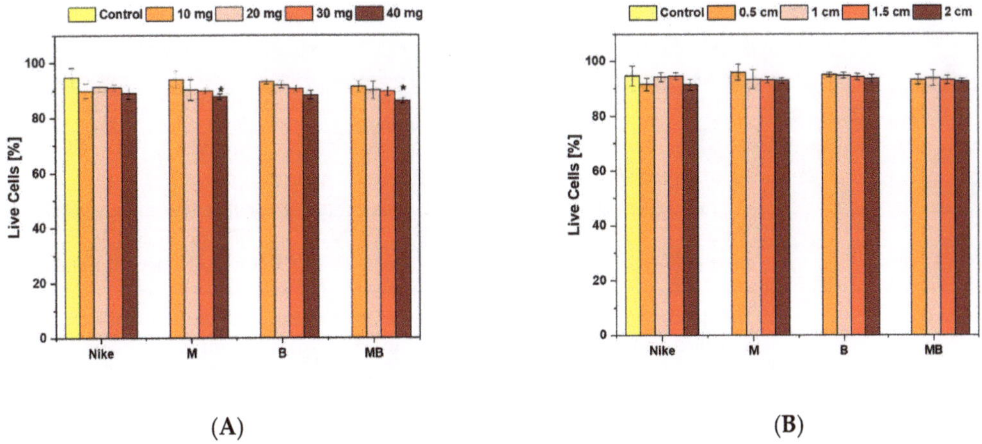

Figure 1. V79 cell viability after 48 h of incubation with fiber (**A**) and linen dressings (**B**) in the trypan blue cell staining assay (* $p < 0.05$).

Co-culture micrograph of V79 fibroblasts with linen fabric obtained from B-type plants. The number of living cells that fluoresce green predominates compared to dead cells with fluoresce red (Figure 2). The microphotograph also presented a red-dyed flax fiber.

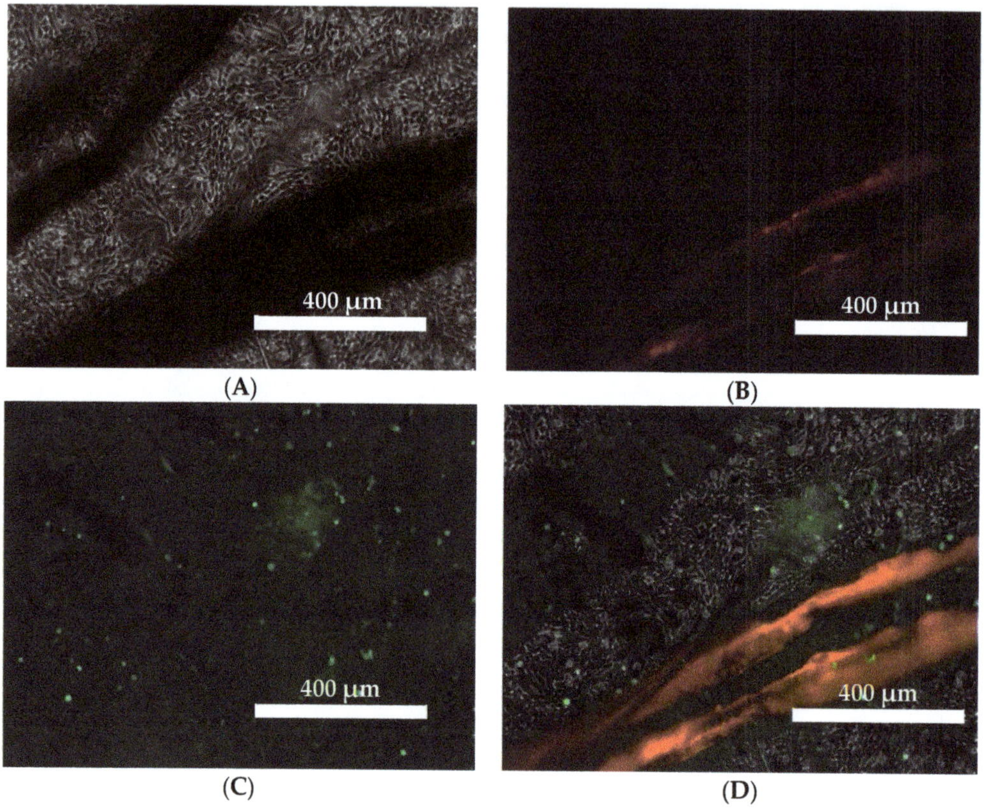

Figure 2. Microphotograph of a co-culture of V79 fibroblasts with linen fabric obtained in type-B plants. Cells were stained with the live dead cell staining kit (live cells fluoresce green and dead cells fluoresce red). Images were taken at 10x objective magnification with an EVOS FL microscope. (**A**). phase contrast, (**B**). GFP fluorescence, (**C**) RGB fluorescence, and (**D**) merging of three images.

2.2. Cell Proliferation

The highest proliferation of V79 cells occurred for flax fibers compared to fabrics (Figure 3). All fabrics and flax fibers from the M, B, and MB-modified flax varieties cause greater cell proliferation than the control NIKE flax fabric and fiber. In the case of linen fabrics, B-flax (0.5 cm—104.66 cell grown ± 7.94, 1.5 cm—113.54 cell grown ± 4.26, and 2 cm—109.29 cell grown ± 5.03) causes the greatest cell proliferation. For 1 cm, the highest cell proliferation occurs for MB flax fabric (115.06 cells grown ± 4.75). For flax fibers, the highest proliferation values of 10 mg (114.27 cells grown ± 8.47) and 20 mg (125.06 cells grown ± 5.94) are found for MB fibers. In contrast, the highest proliferation appeared for B fiber for 30 mg (123.54 cells grown ± 5.33) and 40 mg (119.29 cell grown ± 6.29) fibers. However, at 40 mg fiber weight, V79 cell proliferation significantly decreased for all fibers. The highest values of cell proliferation were obtained for the MB fiber and fabric.

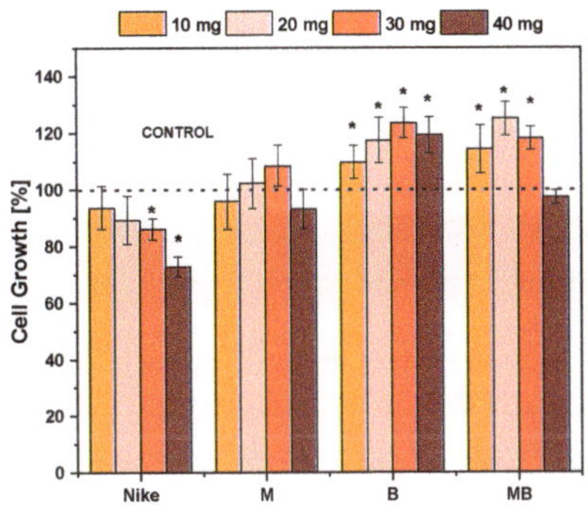

(A)

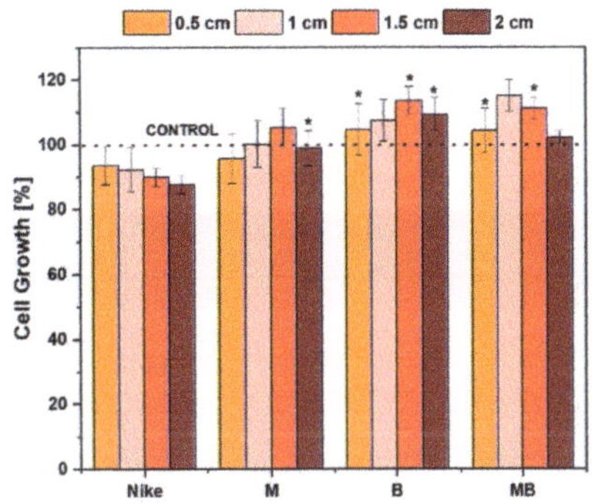

(B)

Figure 3. Cell proliferation of line V79 after 48 h of incubation with test flax fibers (**A**) and linen dressings (**B**) at four different concentrations and surfaces. The results represent means from 5 independent experiments ± SEM. Statistical significance of differences between results for test flax fabrics compared to the control (* $p < 0.05$).

2.3. Evaluation of the Intracellular Free Radical Level

The amount of free radicals increases with the increased cell proliferation due to improved metabolic processes. The highest values of the level of free radicals after placing flax fibers and fabrics on V79 cells occurred for fabrics. The highest values of free radicals were found for linen fabrics with a size of 0.5 cm. At the same time, the fabric made of unmodified NIKE linen (9791.49 FAU ± 1712.35) achieved the highest amount of free radicals. Among the modified linen fabrics, the highest reactive oxygen species (ROS) values occurred for the linen fabric M (7845.15 FAU ± 2020.14).

On the other hand, for fibers, the highest level of free radicals was also demonstrated for NIKE fibers with a sample of 10 mg (5370.82 FAU ± 555.25), and for modified fibers, it was for M (4885.08 FAU ± 648.35). The largest metabolic changes occur in NIKE fibers and fabrics and, to a lesser extent, for M-type fibers and fabrics. All tested flax fibers and fabrics reduced the level of free radicals compared to the control, which was treated with 100 μM H_2O_2 (Figure 4).

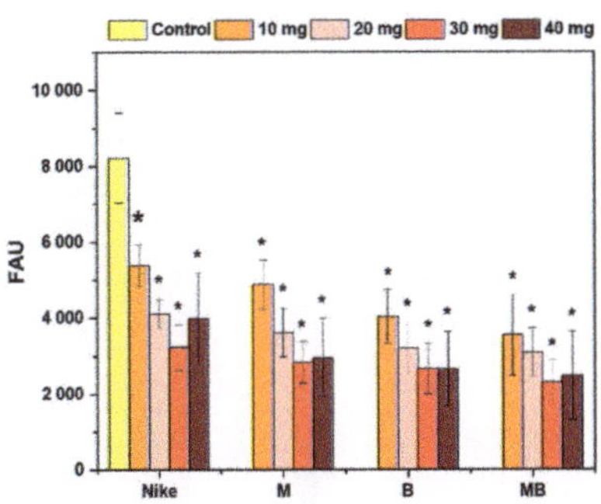

(A)

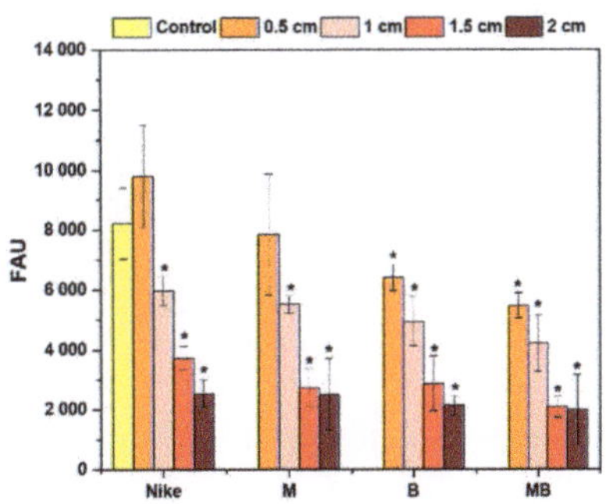

(B)

Figure 4. Influence of V79 cell incubation with the tested flax fiber (**A**) and linen dressing (**B**) on the levels of intracellular ROS induced by exposure to H_2O_2, as assessed with the 2′7′-dichlorofluorescein diacetate assay. Cell cultures were incubated for 48 h with flax fiber and linen dressing and then exposed to 100 μM H_2O_2. Control cultures were exposed to H_2O_2 without previous incubation with flax materials. Yhe fluorescence was read with a microspectrofluorimeter (λ ex = 485 nm, λ em = 535 nm). The results are presented as arbitrary fluorescence units (FAUs; mean ± SD, $n = 5$). The results (mean ± SD, $n = 5$) were compared to those for the control cultures, and statistically significant changes are marked with asterisks (* $p < 0.05$).

2.4. Genotoxicity Assessment

In the comet test for flax fibers and fabrics, an increase in the length of the tail is visible (Figures 5–7). A visible haze near the comet indicates the following apoptotic process. There is no reduction in the amount of DNA in the comet's head for fibers and fabrics. The comet head is a characteristic place where the test cells are located before lysis is carried out. The tails appear only when the cell is affected by a factor causing the degradation of the genetic material. The increase in tail length is caused by a small amount of badly damaged cells, which leads to apoptosis. The greatest increase in the tail length in the comet test was for flax fibers compared to flax fabrics. The longest tail was for the B fiber for the 20 and 30 mg samples, and for the dressings, it was for the B fiber fabric (0.5–1.5 cm), where cells disintegrate as a result of apoptosis. The tail length was similar to the control for the fibers and fabrics of the MB-type linen.

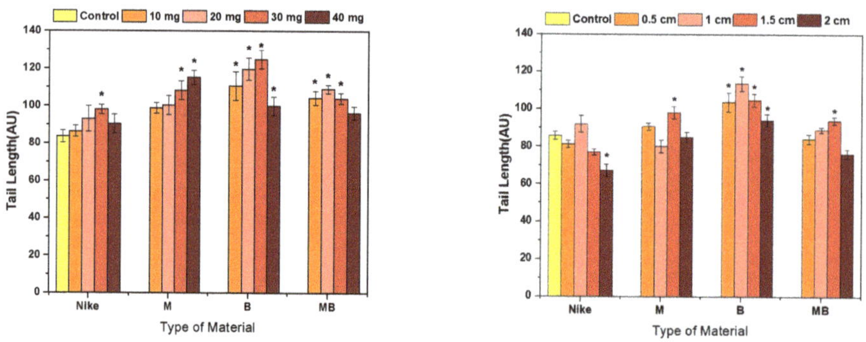

(A) (B)

Figure 5. Effect of incubation of fiber (**A**) and linen dressings (**B**) on the amount of DNA damage measured by the length of the comet tail in the comet assay (* $p = 0.05$).

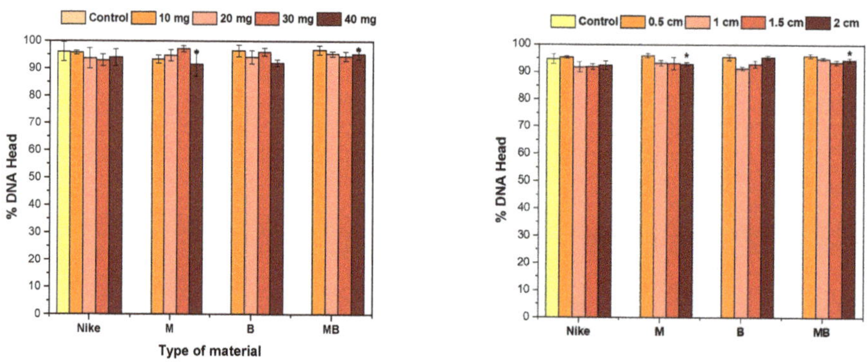

(A) (B)

Figure 6. Effect of fiber (**A**) and linen dressing (**B**) incubation on the amount of DNA damage measured by the DNA content in the comet head in the comet assay (* $p = 0.05$).

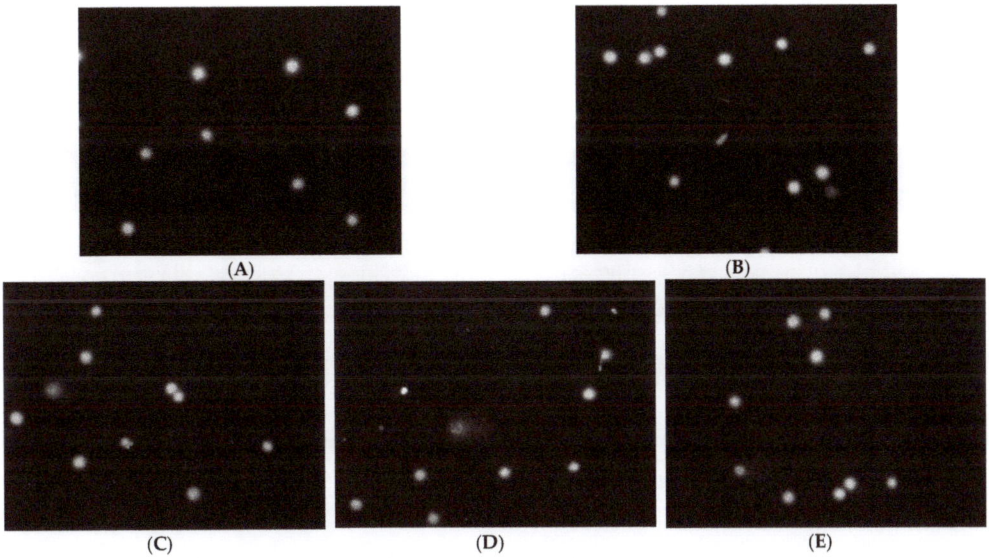

Figure 7. Effect of linseed dressings on the amount of DNA damage in cells in the comet assay. Lens magnification 20×, DNA staining with DAPI dye. (**A**) Control H_2O_2 100 μM, 20 min, 4 °C; (**B**) NIKE; (**C**) M; (**D**) B; and (**E**) MB.

2.5. Potential Wound Environment Response to Oxidative Stress

The culture exposed to H_2O_2 illustrates the linen dressing behavior in the wound environment, where DNA (ssb) damage is exacerbated by the action of H_2O_2. The M linen fabric presented the best properties—thanks to which, the amount of damaged DNA was significantly reduced. In the case of the remaining fabrics, there is no deterioration of the DNA damage. Comparing the influence of flax and flax fibers on the potential wound environment, it turns out that flax fabrics definitely have a clear advantage in this analysis over flax fibers (Figures 8 and 9). Of the fibers, the M and B fibers had the best properties in this test.

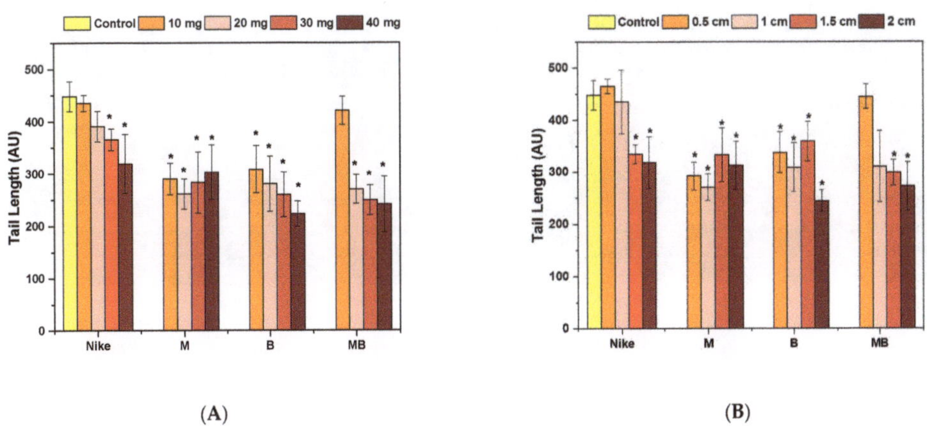

Figure 8. Protective effect of fiber (**A**) and linen dressing (**B**) incubation on the amount of DNA damage measured by the tail length in cells damaged with 100 μM H_2O_2 (20 min, 4 °C) in the comet assay (* $p = 0.05$). Control cells were incubated only with the damaging agent.

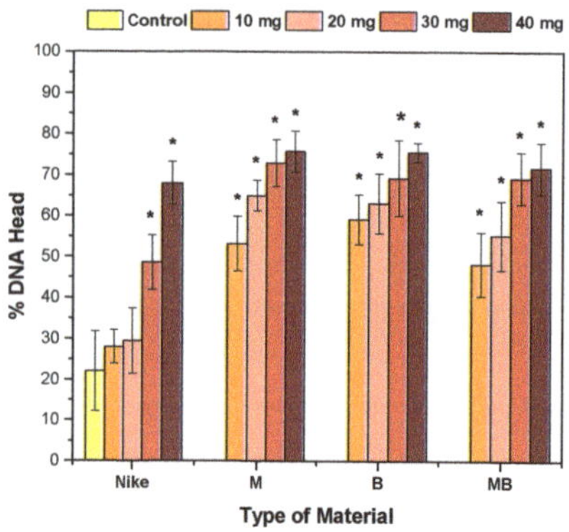

(A)

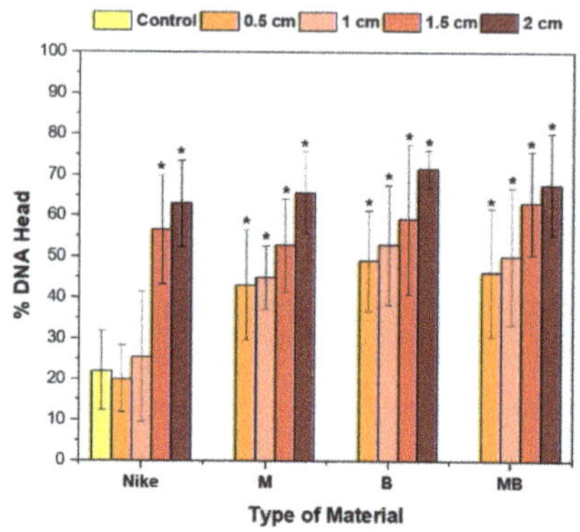

(B)

Figure 9. Protective effect of incubation with fiber (**A**) and linen dressings (**B**) on the amount of DNA damage measured by the DNA content in the nuclei of cells damaged with 100 µM H_2O_2 (20 min, 4 °C) in the comet assay (* $p = 0.05$). Control cells were incubated only with the damage agent.

The V79 cell culture exposed to H_2O_2 (without preincubation with flax fabrics), it demonstrated severe damage on all nucleoid (comets) undamaged DNA, but when it used linen dressing M, there was less damage (Figure 10).

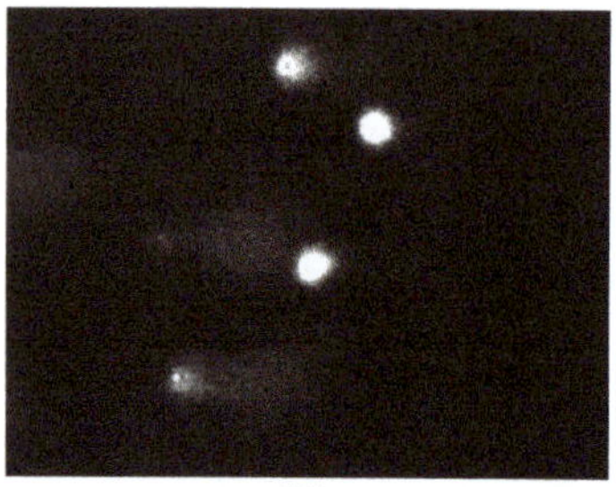

(A)

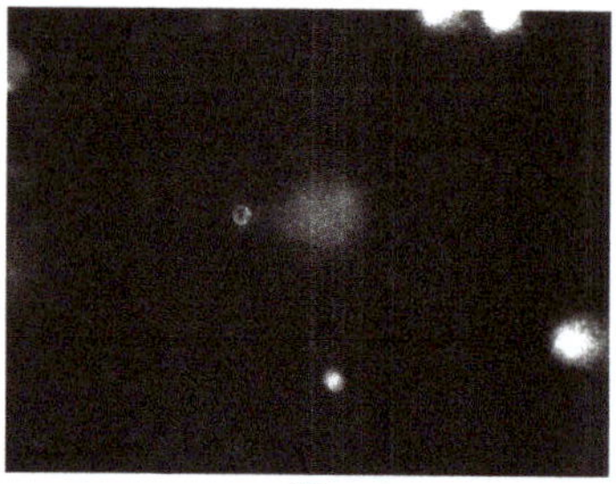

(B)

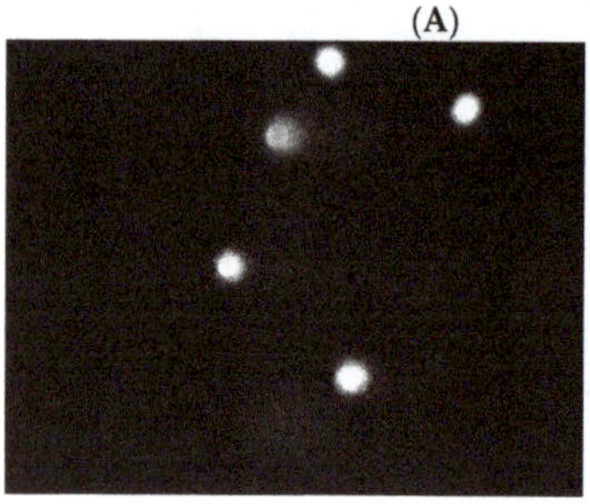

(C)

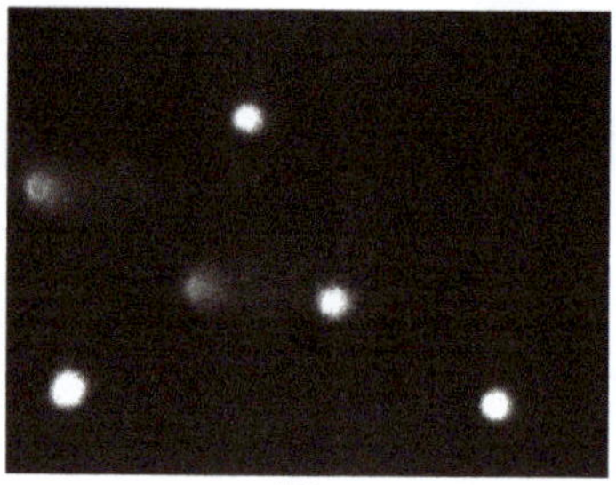

(D)

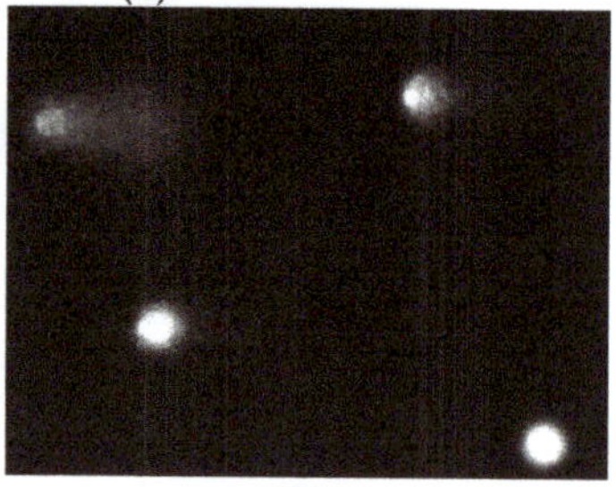

(E)

Figure 10. Protective effect of linen dressings on the amount of DNA damage to cells damaged by 100 µM H_2O_2 (20 min, 4C) in the comet assay. Magnification 20×, DNA staining with DAPI dye. (**A**) Control H_2O_2 100 µM, 20 min, 4 °C; (**B**) NIKE; (**C**) M; (**D**) B; and (**E**) MB.

2.6. Apoptotic and Necrotic Cells

Fluorescein isothiocyanate (FITC) staining with annexin and propidium iodide was performed to assess the number of apoptotic and necrotic cells. The vast majority of cells for all flax fibers and fabrics were in the state of apoptosis. The distribution of necrosis and apoptosis was similar for flax fibers and dressings. Still, flax fabrics achieved higher apoptosis rates (Figure 11). The fewest cells in the apoptotic phase were observed in cultures with traditional linen fabric and the largest with linen fabric B.

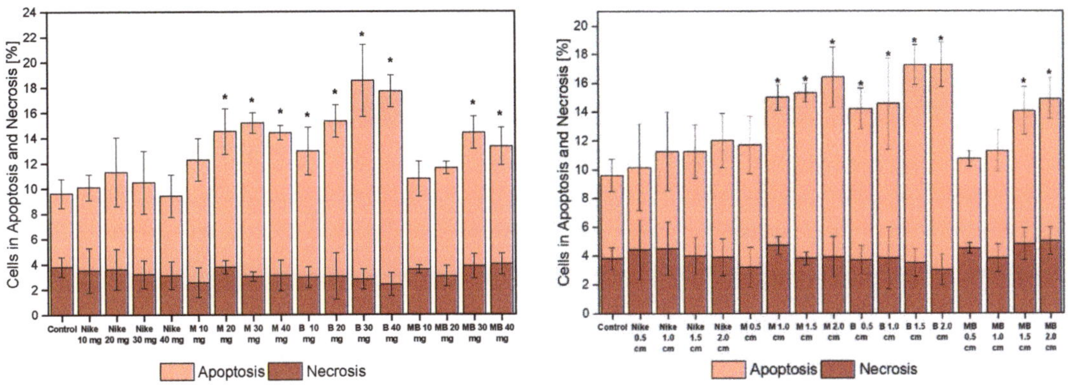

(A) (B)

Figure 11. Apoptosis and necrosis of the V79 cells after 48 h of incubation with the tested flax fiber (**A**) and linen dressing (**B**) on four different surfaces. The results are presented as the percentage of apoptotic cells. The results are the means of 5 independent experiments. The statistical significance of the differences between the results for the tested linen fabric is compared to the control (* $p < 0.05$).

2.7. Cell Cycle

A cell cycle analysis was performed to see if incubation of V79 cells with the test fibers and fabrics increased the number of cells in the proliferative phase (S phase) after 48-h incubation (Figure 12). For all fibers and fabrics from transgenic flax varieties, there were more cells in the S phase compared to the fibers and fabrics from traditional NIKE flax and an increase in the number of cells in the G_0/G_1 phase. For fibers and fabrics from transgenic variants, a similar number of cells is observed in the S phase, while the number of cells is different for the G_0/G_1 and G_2+M phases. For fibers of transgenic varieties of flax, the greatest number of cells in the G_0/G_1 phase occurs for the M fiber and the least for the MB fiber. In turn, the greatest number of cells in the G_2+M phase occurs for the MB fiber. On the other hand, for fabrics made of transgenic flax, the opposite is true. The greatest number of cells in the G_0/G_1 phase occurs for the MB linen fabric and the least for the M and B linen fabrics. The smallest number of cells in the G_2+M phase occurs for the MB linen fabric and the most for the B linen fabric. The G_1 phase in the cell, even before the S phase of the cycle, in which the duplication of abnormal genetic information may occur, occurs when various mutations and DNA damage appear. There may also be a cell cycle arrest in the G_2 phase, which prevents the formation of two defective daughter cells in the following M phase, hence the mitotic division phase. The obtained results indicate a favorable influence of the technological process of fiber on the obtained linen fabrics. Most preferably, it is directed to the programmed death of damaged cells at two cell cycle checkpoints, especially in the G_2 and M phases.

2.8. Scratch Assay

A scratch test was performed to assess the cell migration and, thus, wound-healing potential (Figure 13). As expected, the degree of soiling was presented to be slower when using flax fibers of the test compounds compared to flax fabrics. All the tested fabrics from transgenic flax varieties resulted in faster cell migration than the NIKE linen fabric. M linen fabric indicated the strongest cell migration, with MB slightly smaller. A similar distribution of results was obtained for the flax fibers. The strongest cell migration occurred for the M fiber and slightly weaker for the MB fiber.

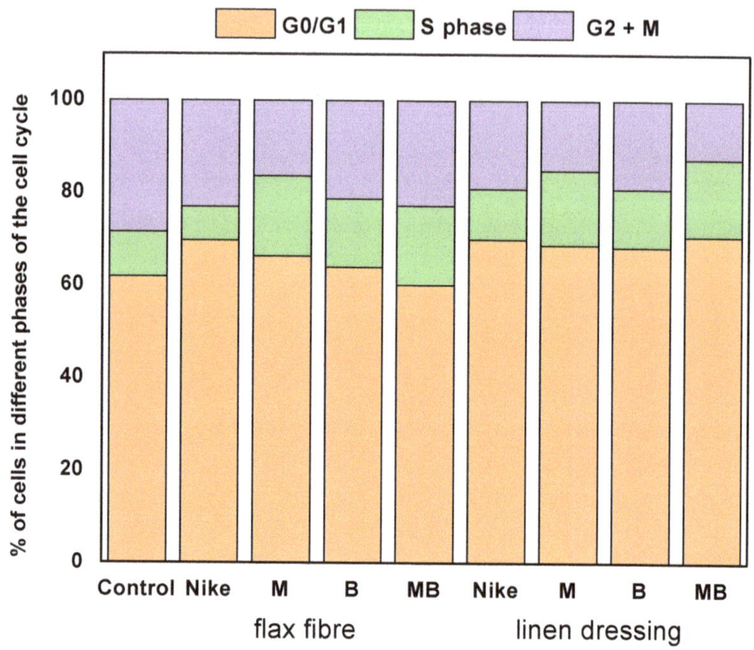

Figure 12. Cell cycle in V79 cells after 48-h incubation with the tested flax fibers and linen dressing. The results are presented as the percentage of cells in each phase. The results are the means of 5 independent experiments.

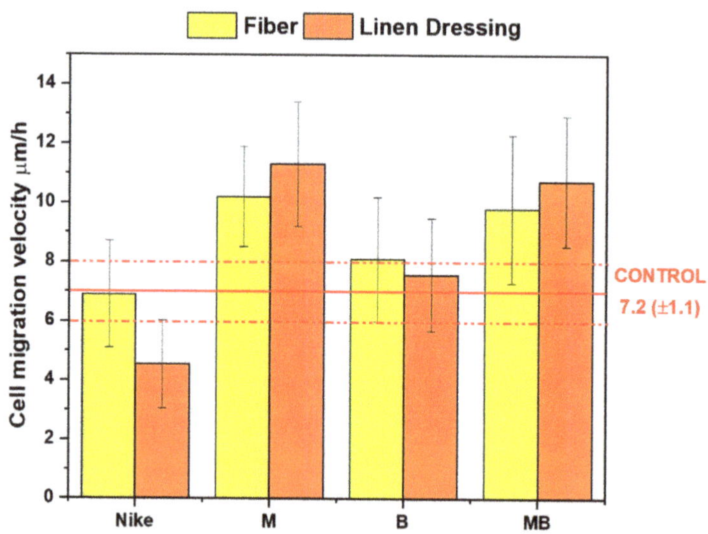

Figure 13. Average migration velocity of V79 lineage cells in um/h calculated after 20 h for flax fiber at a concentration of 20 mg/mL and a 1 cm^2 flax dressing compared to the control.

2.9. The Effect of Linen Fiber and Linen Dressing on Wound Healing in the V79 Cell Model

The effect of fiber and linen dressing on wound healing was determined in the V79 cell model by assessing the increase in the confluence of the culture area at the site of the injury. The test was carried out for 20 h for flax fiber at a concentration of 20 mg/mL and for a

1 cm^2 linen dressing compared to the control (Figures 14 and 15). The most physiological course of the wound healing process is in the form of a logarithmic plot. In a V79 cell model for linen fabrics, such a course of the granulation process occurs for B and M linen fabrics. In contrast, the healing process is characterized by constant growth without the plateau phase for other fabrics. The healing process proceeds most favorably for the M fabric, as there is a plateau phase but with a higher percentage of the wound healed than the B fabric. Additionally, the plateau phase for the M fiber occurs at higher wound-healing percentages. The results obtained in the model present that the most favorable properties for wound healing are found for M flax fiber and fabric.

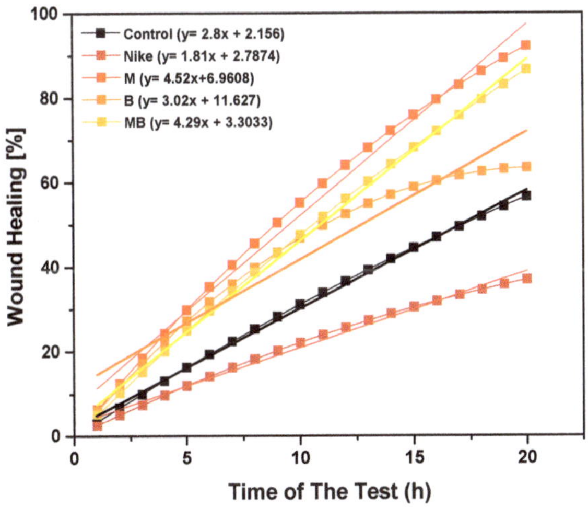

Figure 14. The effect of linen cloth on wound healing in a V79 cell model by assessing the increase in the confluence of the culture area at the injury site. The test was performed for a time of 20 h for linen fiber at a concentration of 20 mg/mL compared to the control.

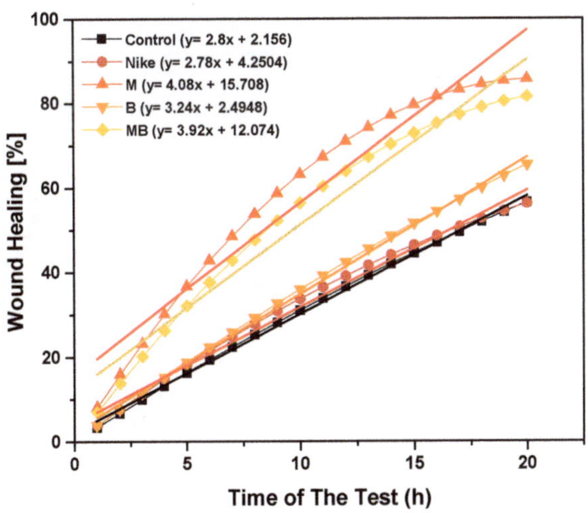

Figure 15. The effect of linen cloth on wound healing in a V79 cell model by assessing the increase in a confluence of the culture area at the site of injury. The test was performed for 20 h for a 1 cm^2 linen dressing compared to the control.

In the research carried out for this work, an attempt was made to determine the fiber and fabric with the best properties, summarized in Table 2. Furthermore, the correlation between apoptosis and the ROS assay and the genotoxicity test results is also determined in Table 3.

Table 2. The comparison of biological test results for flax fibers and fabrics.

Test	Fiber	Fabric
Cell viability	B	B
Cell proliferation	MB	MB
Free Radical Level	NIKE	NIKE
Genotoxic in the comet assay	MB	MB
Potential wound environment response to oxidative stress	M, B	MB
Apoptosis	B	B
Cell cycle	MB	MB
Scratch test—migration assay	M, MB	M, MB
The effect on wound healing in the V79 cell model	The first M, then MB	The first B, then M

Table 3. Designated correlations for apoptosis.

	* DCFDA (H_2O_2)/** Tail (H_2O_2)			
	*** NIKE	**** M	**** B	***** MB
fiber	0.699	−0.084	0.892	0.879
fabric	0.938	−0.686	0.452	0.874
	apoptosis/tail			
fiber	0.622095	0.678914	0.04192	−0.22859
fabric	−0.64786	0.00032	−0.68978	−0.17688

* DCFDA—Cellular ROS Assay/Reactive Oxygen Species Assay; ** tail—represents damaged DNA fragments in the comet assay; *** NIKE—fiber or linen without genetic modification; **** M and B—fiber or linen with genetic modification; and ***** MB—combination of M and B.

Based on the results of the tests performed, summarized in Table 2, it is difficult to select the fabric with the best properties unequivocally. However, it seems that the MB linen fabric presented the best properties.

Based on the presented results in Table 3, it is concluded that there is a strong correlation for the MB fiber and fabric, B fiber, and NIKE fabric between the level of free radicals and genotoxicity (the length of the tail) when the cell enters the apoptosis process and moderately strong for the NIKE fiber and B fabric. On the other hand, a moderately strong correlation between apoptosis and genotoxicity occurs for the NIKE and M fibers, and there is no correlation for the linen fabrics. The results indicate that the fiber strongly enhances damaged cell apoptosis. On the other hand, the dressing no longer exhibits such properties. There is a change in the properties between the fiber and the linen dressing, which indicates the influence of the technological process on the properties of the dressing, which induces more regenerative processes.

3. Discussion

Wounds have become one of the leading causes of death worldwide [20–23]. Chronic wounds are a problem for patients and the medical system in Poland and worldwide. Active or healed venous ulcers occur in 1% of the population, and pressure ulcers in 0.75% of the US [24,25]. In developed countries, up to 4% of the total expenditure is spent on treating chronic wounds [26]. A chronic wound is defined as a wound that does not heal within 3 months. The incidence of diabetes mellitus and other chronic diseases such as peripheral circulatory disorders and vascular diseases can impede wound healing [27–30]. Chronic wounds refer to damage to skin tissues caused by various causes. The healing process takes a long time, e.g., deep ulcers, including those formed after chemotherapy and radiotherapy, and in the course of a diabetic foot, as well as third to fourth-degree pressure ulcers [31]. With the aging of the population and the increasing number of comorbidities in the elderly, the problem of chronic wounds is increasing, and it is necessary to continue searching for new dressings with better healing properties [32,33].

However, the problem of difficult-to-heal wounds did not arise today. It has been accompanying people for millennia and is the subject of the search for effective methods of their treatment. Many natural methods have proved effective and have been used in natural medicine. Flax is an example of a natural raw material already used in antiquity [16]. The research subject was to compare the starting material, flax fiber, with the obtained dressing. Unfortunately, the industrial processing of even the best natural raw material often causes it to lose its health-promoting properties. Until now, unpublished studies presented that a linen dressing subjected to advanced industrial treatment, consisting of bleaching and improving the properties of the fabric itself by making it more elastic, caused its toxic effect on cell cultures. In the course of the research, the influence of the basic treatment of flax was checked in the context of its properties related to the wound-healing process.

The two main factors that are commonly thought of as common problems underlying nonhealing wounds are infection and wound inflammation. The hostile environment for wound healing creates inflammation. On the other hand, a difficult and slow-healing wound is more prone to infection. In turn, when a condition occurs, the inflammation of the wound is exacerbated [27,34]. However, wound healing is a complex process. In the first step, inflammation is induced, and the wound is debrided by finally removing dead cells from the wound. There will also be intense cell proliferation soon to restore the integrity of the damaged tissue. At the same time, a scarring process takes place in which the granulation tissue in the cell becomes fibrotic and hardened. At the same time, the excessive proliferation of fibroblasts may lead to excessive scarring and an impaired blood supply to the newly formed tissue [16,35,36].

During the application of the flax base, due to its properties, in the wet phase, due to the maintenance of optimal humidity and high hygroscopicity, flax slices can absorb exudate, which, in turn, significantly reduces the risk of infection and secondary infections. However, the patches have anti-inflammatory properties due to the enrichment of flax fibers with high concentrations of antioxidants, such as phenolic acids, vanillin, acetowanilone, and flavonoids. In contrast, the antioxidants are washed out of the wet dressing. Linen dressings support the natural stages of wound healing in all stages of healing.

Based on the conducted research, it was shown that the technological process of preparing linen dressings has a positive effect on their regenerative properties. It was observed that flax fibers induced a greater proliferation of V79 cells. However, a significantly increased proliferation of flax fiber mass (40 mg) already inhibited cell proliferation. The induction of cell proliferation in wound healing is indicated to restore the integrity of damaged tissue. However, the induction of cell proliferation in the wound healing process should occur after the first healing stage, which involves removing damaged cells from the wound. Initiating an intensive proliferation process too early may pose the risk of a faulty healing process. At the same time, the excessive proliferation process may lead to excessive scarring and impaired blood supply to the newly formed tissue. The wound-healing process is most favorable in the tested V79 cell model for the fabric of modified flax M, because the plateau phase is present. Therefore, dressings made of modified flax varieties are safe at every stage of wound healing and do not pose a risk of dangerous scarring. This work and the previous publication [16] showed that the fibers significantly increase the amount of total white in the cell cycle, which is only beneficial during the initial stage of wound healing. At the same time, the intensification of this process in the later stages is not advisable. At the same time, flax fibers are characterized by the ability to eliminate damaged cells. This is indicated by the presented studies on the apoptosis and necrosis of V79 cells. The fibers strongly induced apoptosis in injured V79 cells.

The flax dressings did not present any such properties. However, the linen dressings had stronger properties of controlled wound healing. This was indicated by the scratch tests performed, where modified linen fabrics intensified the migration of V79 cells on the scratch to a much greater extent than the fibers. The strongest migration of V79 cells was caused by a dressing made of M. According to the conducted research, the mechanism of wound healing of fibers and linen dressings is two-way, consisting of proapoptotic action of damaged cells and antioxidant activity. Flax fibers have a stronger proapoptotic effect compared to dressings, while linen dressings show stronger antioxidant properties and, at the same time, create a more favorable wound-healing environment. Linen dressings made of modified flax fibers induced a significant reduction in the number of free radicals, which allowed for the enhanced repair of DNA damage. This effect was observed for the M flax dressing. However, the remaining flax dressings did not increase the DNA damage in the cells.

Ideal wound dressings should have properties such as supporting tissue regeneration, enhancing cell proliferation and migration, and a biocombination. In addition, if there is wound exudate, it should be systematically removed from the wound environment by dressing [37,38]. Linen dressings made of modified flax varieties exhibit such properties.

The results indicate a strong fiber and linen dressing biological activity. The presented results indicate several mechanisms of action of the tested dressings. The tests confirmed the lack of toxicity for the cells of the V79 fibroblast line. Additionally, an acceleration of the cell growth was observed. The obtained results confirmed the results obtained in previous studies.

Research in a series of publications on linen dressings with chronic wound-healing properties indicated that all the obtained linen dressings did not lose their healing properties under technological processes. In contrast, none of the linen fabrics tested were cytotoxic for the NHDF, HMCEV, and THP-1 fibroblast cultures. What is more, the tested fabrics caused a significant decrease in the total protein content in skin cancer [17]. Moreover, the tested fabrics resulted in a statistically significant decrease in the total protein content in skin cancer [17]. During the technological processes, no chemicals are used that may have a negative effect in contact with the wound and may reduce the bactericidal properties of the fibers. Compared to the traditional flax fiber, genetically modified M, B, and MB flax fibers had a stronger effect on the proliferation activity of keratinocytes, fibroblasts, and microvascular endothelium [16].

The key advantage of linen fabric is its mechanical properties as a dressing and biological properties related to the substances contained in linen. This action manifests itself in reducing free radicals and protecting DNA against the effects of oxidative stress.

Skórkowska-Telichowska et al. presented the effects of woven fabrics from fibers derived from two types of transgenic plants were investigated: M-type plants, which produce the hydroxybutyrate polymer in their vascular bundles, and W92, which overproduce flavonoids. It was found that the incubation of V79 cells with these flax fabrics prevents ROS-induced chromatin instability and thus reduces DNA breakdown in the cells. The properties of the M fabric, which produces polyhydroxybutyrate, can also be compared to other linen fabrics from the transgenic plant W92, which overproduce phenylpropanoid compounds and are a source of antioxidants [13]. Wound healing is significantly improved by linseed dressings from plants containing more polyphenolic compounds [14]. Furthermore, the extracts containing phytosterols, cannabidiol (CBD), and flax fiber unsaturated fatty acids inhibited chronic inflammation and induced wound healing [39].

Similar effects were also obtained in patients during the clinical tests performed for the tested linen dressings. A 12-week pilot study of leg ulcer healing was also conducted by using a linseed dressing alone or in combination with seed extract and oil emulsion. Linen dressings show microbiological purity, are hypoallergenic, reduce the exudate and size of the wound, accelerate the healing process, and reduce the pain of the wound [11]. However, clinical trials have shown that they can be used on a diabetic foot with open varicose veins; severe thermal, chemical, and electrical burns; oozing wounds; bedsores; and mechanical damage to the body. In addition, they show very strong hygroscopic properties—they absorb exudate (deep, oozing wounds) and cleanse the tissue.

The mechanism of the action of linen dressings in wound healing is presented in Figure 16. The results of the in vitro and in vivo tests carried out so far, shown in Table 1, presented that the dressings obtained from the modified flax varieties do not indicate cytotoxicity in relation to all the cells and do not induce the progression of neoplastic cells. Moreover, linen dressings accelerate healing and reduce the exudation and wound size. Research conducted in 2017 presented that B and MB fabrics are the strongest activators of NHDF and are the most recommended dressings. On the other hand, the results of the research conducted on the V79 line so far show that the best properties are characteristic for dressings made of fabrics derived from modified MB flax. Moreover, the fibers are characterized by the ability to eliminate damaged cells in the elimination phase. However, the obtained fabrics acquire other properties during the technological processing of fibers into linen dressings. For example, linen fabrics have better regenerative properties for cells than fibers. Maintaining a sterile and moist wound microenvironment is a basic requirement for effective wound healing [40]. The current trends in dressing design focus on moistening the dressing with a linen oil emulsion, which should result in faster wound healing and additional antiviral properties. Natural phenolic acids are bactericidal and bacteriostatic [40–44]. Due to their properties, many metal nanoparticles, especially silver, have been used in medicine. Materials intended to be encapsulated into nanoparticles for medical applications must be nontoxic, chemically stable under various conditions, and biocompatible [45]. In further works, we want to focus on research on linen dressings containing silver nanoparticles, which will additionally increase the valence and use of linen dressings while extending the spectrum of their actions to dressings for infected wounds.

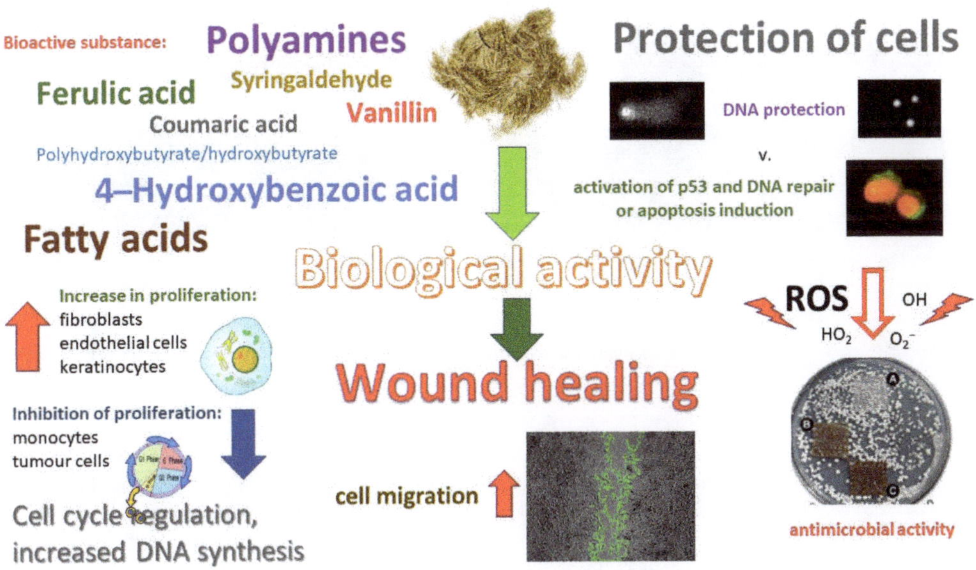

Figure 16. Mechanism of action of linen dressings (the microbiological evaluation was carried out by Kulma et al. [46]).

4. Materials and Methods

4.1. Plant Materials

The research used flax fibers and linen fabrics obtained from them, which come from the traditional variety of linen (NIKE) and transgenic types of linens (M50 and B14) and their combinations (M50 + B14) [16,47]. The transgenic plants are from NIKE. B14 plants defensively transformed the potato β-1,3-glucanase (PR-2) gene [5,17,48]. M50 plants were enriched with Ralstonia eutropha genes encoding acetoacetyl CoA reductase (phbB), β-ketothiolase (phbA), and PHB synthase (phbC) for poly-β-hydroxybutyrate (PHB) [16,17,49]. A combination of these two flax fibers was M50 + B14 [16,17,47].

The diagram presented pictures of flax fibers and the linen fabrics obtained from them, serving as dressings, which were used to conduct the experiments in this work (Figures 17 and 18).

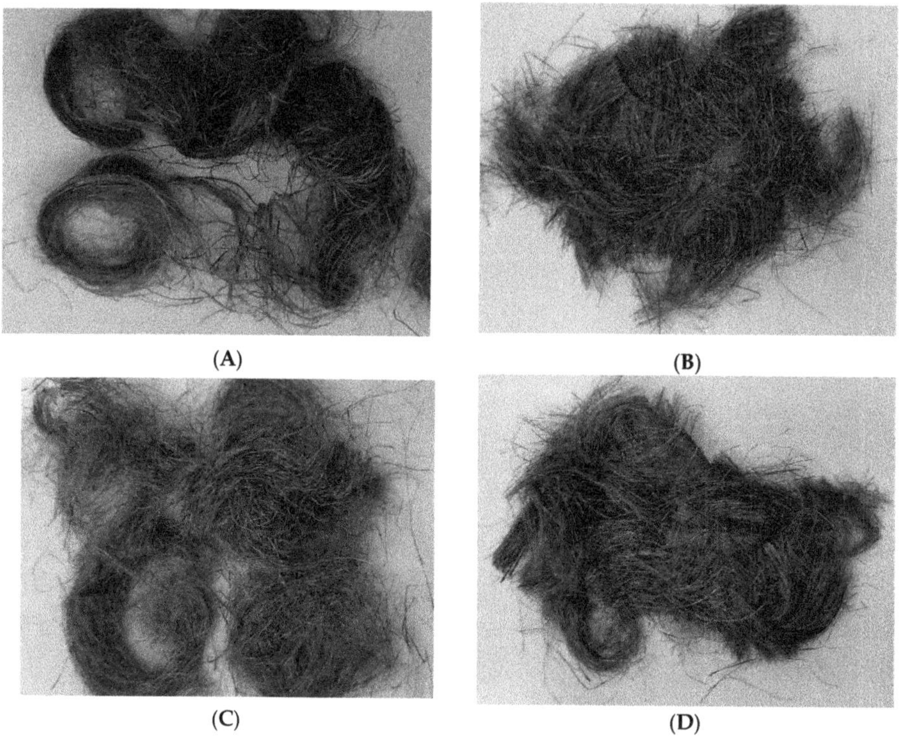

Figure 17. Flax fibers tested in the study: (**A**) NIKE plant fiber, (**B**) M plant fiber, (**C**) B plant fiber, and (**D**) MB plant fiber.

4.2. Reagents

Eagle's minimal essential medium (EMEM), fetal bovine serum (FBS), and trypsin/EDTA solution were obtained from Biological Industries (Beit-Haemek, Israel). The solution of antibiotics containing 10,000 U/mL penicillin, 10,000 µg/mL streptomycin, and 29.2 mg/mL L-glutamine (100×) was from Biological Industries (Beit-Haemek, Israel). Sulforhodamine B (SRB), 2,7′- dichlorodihydrofluorescein diacetate (DCFH-DA), 4′,6-diamidino-2-phenylindole (DAPI), dimethyl sulfoxide (DMSO), Trizma base, HEPES, Triton X-100, low melting point agarose (Sigma type VII), and regular agarose (Sigma type I-A) were purchased from Sigma-Aldrich (St. Louis, MO, USA). A fluorochrome mixture for detecting apoptosis (Alexa Fluor 488 Annexin V/Dead Cell Apoptosis Kit) was purchased from Invitrogen/Molecular Probes (Carlsbad, CA, USA). Phosphate-buffered saline (PBS), 0.4% trypan blue solution, NaOH,

NaCl, and hydrogen peroxide (H_2O_2; 30% solution in water) were obtained from POCH (Gliwice, Poland). Plastic 75-cm^2 growth area culture flasks and 24-well tissue culture-treated polystyrene culture plates for adherent cells were from SPL Life Sciences (Pochon, Korea). Disposable plastic pipettes and centrifuge tubes were from SPL Life Sciences (Korea).

Figure 18. Linen fabrics: (**A**) linen fabric from NIKE flax, (**B**) linen fabric from M flax, (**C**) linen fabric from B flax, and (**D**) linen fabric from MB flax.

4.3. Preparation of the Flax Fabric for Biological Tests

Four types of flax fibers (NIKE, M, B, and MB) were prepared and mixtures of 10–40 mg/mL in the culture medium. The fiber and culture medium mixture was then incubated for 48 h. Then, it was filtered. The extract obtained was added to the cell cultures for 48 h. The fibers were soaked in PBS, and the filtrate was collected for testing in the V79 cell culture. Linen fabrics were made out of four flax fibers (NIKE, M, B, and MB). The tested linen dressings were put into the culture medium (without PBS) for 10 min and placed in cell cultures on culture plates. The linen fabrics floated just below the surface of the growing medium, covered with a layer of substrate approximately 1 mm thick. The entire process of preparing linen fibers and fabrics for testing is presented in Figure 19.

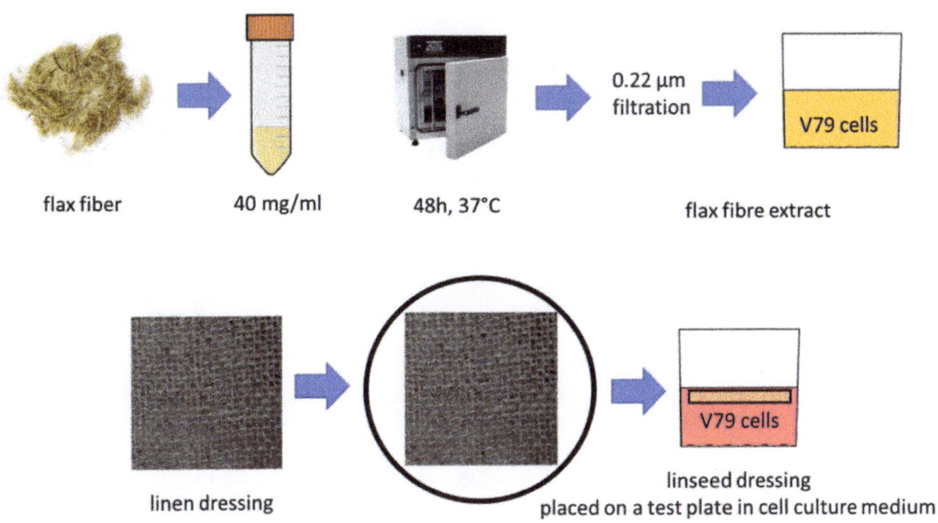

Figure 19. The process of preparing linen fibers for biological testing.

4.4. Cell Line and Cell Culture Conditions

Chinese hamster pulmonary fibroblasts (V79–379A cells) were obtained from ATCC (USA). Cells were grown at 37 °C in a CO_2 incubator in EMEM with 2 mM L-glutamine, 10% FBS, and a mixture of antibiotics: (0.1 mg/mL streptomycin and 100 U/mL penicillin). V79 cells were grown at 37 °C in a CO_2 incubator. Adherent cells were detached from culture plates with trypsin/EDTA solution, washed with PBS, spun out, counted, stained with a 0.4% solution of trypan blue, and inspected under a microscope for cell viability. The cells were plated on 1.5×10^5 cells per well in 24-well plates and 5×10^4 cells per well in 96-well plates. They were incubated for 24 h at 37 °C in a CO_2 incubator for cell adaptation after the reseeding procedure. The flax fabrics and linen dressing were added to the cell cultures, and the cultures were placed in a CO_2 incubator at 37 °C for 48 h.

4.5. Cell Viability

The influence of linen fibers and fabrics on vitality was assessed using the V79 cell line. After 24-h treatment, cells with tested fibers and fabrics were rinsed with PBS, which was collected into prepared centrifuge tubes. The culture supernatant was collected. Culture plates were washed with the TrypLe solution. The TrypLe solution was readded and culture plates were incubated for 2 min at 37 ° C. The solution with cells was collected and centrifuged at 600× *g* for 5 min. After the supernatant removal, cells were resuspended in PBS, and propidium iodide was added. After 5 min of incubation, the dark samples were analyzed on an Arthur image cytometer. In addition, live cell staining was performed using the LIVE/DEAD™ Cell Imaging Kit (488/570) (Life Technologies, Carlsbad, CA, USA). Stained cells were evaluated using an EVOS FL microscope (Thermo Fisher Scientific (Waltham, MA, USA) [50].

4.6. Cell Proliferation

The potential of the cells in the V79 line was assessed using the sulforhodamine B (SRB) test. Cell cultures with test fibers and fabrics were fixed with cold trichloroacetic acid (TCA) at 4–8 °C for 30 min after 48 h of incubation. The plates were washed five times under running water. After drying, the dye sulforhodamine B was added for 30 min. Unbound dye was removed through five rinses with 1% acetic acid and dried. Finally, the protein was dissolved in Trisma solution, and the absorbance at 555 nm was measured using a microplate reader (Victor2, PerkinElmer, Waltham, MA, USA).

4.7. Evaluation of the Intracellular Free Radical Level

According to the procedure [51], 2′7′-dichlorodihydrofluorescein diacetate (DCFH-DA) in a concentration of 25 µM was added for the last 2 h of culture and the V79 cells. It was incubated in the dark in the CO_2 incubator. Afterward, the cells were washed twice with PBS, and H_2O_2 (100 µM) was added to each culture for 30 min. The fluorescence of dichlorodihydrofluorescein was then read (λex = 485 nm, λem = 535 nm) with a Victor 2 microspectrophotometer (PerkinElmer, Waltham, MA, USA).

4.8. Comet Assay

Alkaline single-cell gel electrophoresis (comet test) was performed according to the procedure [52]. The cells were cultured in the presence of flax fibers and fabrics for 48 h. V79 cells were separated with trypsin/EDTA from the culture vessel, centrifuged, and washed in PBS chilled to 4 °C without Ca^{2+} or Mg^{2+} ions. Cells were incubated with PBS supplemented with H_2O_2 (100 µM) in an ice-water bath (4 °C) for 30 min. Incubation was terminated by dissolving the cells with an excess volume of chilled PBS, centrifugation, and resuspending the cell pellet in cold PBS containing Ca^{2+} and Mg^{2+} ions. The suspension cells were mixed with an equal volume of 1% low melting point agarose (Sigma VII) prewarmed in a 37 °C water bath. The suspensions were then placed on slides precoated with 0.5% plain agarose (Sigma I-A type). Coverslips were removed and slides kept carefully immersed in cold (4 °C) lysis solution (2.5M NaCl, 100 mM EDTA, 10 mM Tris, pH 10, 1% Triton X-100, and 10% DMSO) and held overnight. in the dark at 4 °C. The slides were then washed (five times for 5 min each) with alkaline electrophoresis buffer (300 mM NaOH and 1 mM EDTA, pH 13) and then placed in a horizontal gel electrophoresis unit filled with freshly prepared alkaline electrophoresis buffer. The slides were exposed to alkali for 45 min at 4 °C. Electrophoresis was performed (1.2 V/cm, 300 mA) for 20 min at 4–6 °C, and the slides were washed with neutralizing buffer (0.4 M Tris, pH 7.5) four times for 5 min. Finally, the slides were immersed in a fluorescent dye (DAPI, 1 µg/mL), covered with coverslips, and stained overnight in a refrigerator. All steps were performed in dim light. The slides were analyzed using a Nikon Eclipse E600 microscope in the Comet IV program.

4.9. Apoptotic and Necrotic Cells

V79 cells were separated from the culture plates, centrifuged, resuspended in binding buffer, and stained with a mixture of fluorochromes (Alexa Fluor 488 Annexin V and PI fluorescent dyes). After 15 min of incubation at room temperature in the dark, samples were taken on the IMAGE base cytometry Arthur cytometer. The fluorescence, granulation and size were measured for 40,000–10,000 cells. The percentage of viable, apoptotic, and necrotic (dead) cells was calculated from the scatter plots.

4.10. Cell Cycle

The V79 cell cycle was assessed after 24 h of treatment of the linen fibers and fabrics. After incubating, the cells were separated and centrifuged, and then, the pellet was fixed with cold ethanol (70%) for 10 min at room temperature and centrifuged again at 600× *g* for 5 min. The cell pellet was resuspended in propidium iodide solution and left in the dark for 10 min. Samples were transferred to chips and analyzed on an Arthur image-based cytometer (NanoEnTek Inc., Seoul, Korea).

4.11. Scratch Test

After inoculating the cells, they were incubated until they formed a monolayer over the entire surface of the well. The SPLScar kit (SPL Life Sciences, Korea) was used to perform the scratch test. A scratch of the same thickness and in the same place in each well of the plate covered with cells was made using a scratcher. Pictures were taken. The prepared linen fibers and fabrics were added to the monolayers scratched on the surface. The culture plates were incubated for 24 h. The micrographs and their analyses were made using Julia's microscope (Figure 20). The equipment took pictures showing the rate of fouling during 24 h of incubation in a CO_2 incubator. The use of a dedicated test system allowed for high repeatability of the test. The obtained scratch area was 33% of the photographed area (±1%).

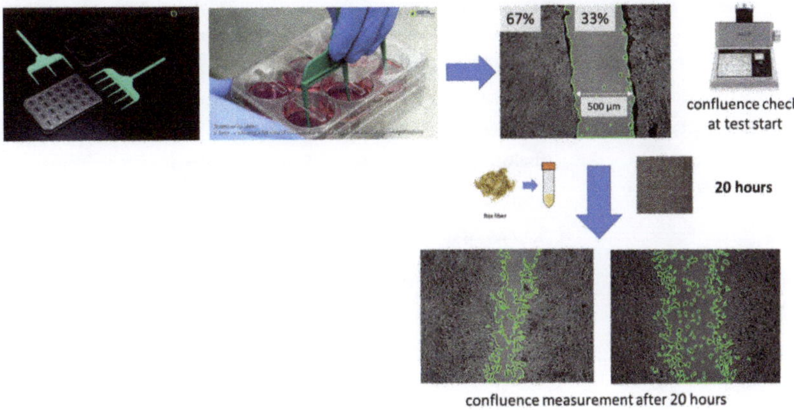

Figure 20. Scheme of the scratch test and microphotos.

4.12. Statistical Analysis

All biological tests were performed in five independent replicates. Due to the normal distribution and equal variance of the obtained results, statistical calculations were performed with parametric tests. Using Statistica v.13 software, the statistical significance was calculated using Tukey's post hoc test by using Statistica v.13 software. The significance point was set at * $p < 0.05$.

5. Conclusions

This conducted research confirms the knowledge known since antiquity that linen fabric has good properties that promote wound healing. The main aim of the research was to confirm that a very good raw material, which is linen fiber, does not lose its properties in the process of post-industrial processing. It is difficult to use the fiber directly in the treatment of wounds, so it was important to check the properties of the fabric obtained.Flax fabrics have the most favorable potential wound-healing properties compared to fibers. Better properties also characterize linen dressings made of modified varieties of linen compared to traditional linen fabric. Based on the tests performed, we indicated that the most advantageous properties have the dressings made of fabrics derived from modified MB flax. Linen dressings are made of woven fibers, which is why they help to cleanse wounds and ulcers and stimulate the growth of blood vessels. Thanks to the unsaturated fatty acids contained in the patches, the young tissue is strengthened and protected against drying out. The wound is protected against mechanical irritation or possible infection. In the epithelialization phase, linen dressings facilitate the epithelium's growth by maintaining an appropriate moisture level and thus protect the tissue against damage. Linen dressings are still subject to research and development processes. The tested flax fibers are characterized by a greater ability to eliminate damaged cells in potential wounds. However, during technological processing, linen dressings acquire more regenerative properties for damaged cells. Works on the genetic improvement of flax and its use in medicine or other industrial areas are still ongoing. The effectiveness of flax dressings has been confirmed by studies and clinical tests that have presented a reduction or disappearance of wounds. Most importantly, they are not prone to induce allergies, and so far, no side effects have been observed.

The obtained results indicate a two-way action consisting, on the one hand, of enhancing the process of tissue regeneration and protection and, on the other hand, of removing damaged cells through apoptosis.

Author Contributions: Conceptualization, T.G.; methodology, T.G.; validation, T.G.; formal analysis, T.G., I.J. and B.W.; investigation, T.G. and B.W.; data curation, T.G.; writing—original draft preparation, T.G., I.J. and B.W.; writing—review and editing, T.G., I.J. and B.W.; visualization, T.G.; supervision, B.W.; project administration, T.G.; and funding acquisition, T.G. All authors have read and agreed to the published version of the manuscript.

Funding: Applied Research Programme of the National Centre for Research and Development—PBS1/A9/17/2012.

Institutional Review Board Statement: Not applicable.

Informed Consent Statement: Not applicable.

Data Availability Statement: Raw data can be obtained after e-mail contact with the corresponding author.

Conflicts of Interest: The authors declare no conflict of interest.

References

1. Rasouli, M.; Rahimi, A.; Soleimani, M.; Keshel, S.H. The Interplay between Extracellular Matrix and Progenitor/Stem Cells during Wound Healing: Opportunities and Future Directions. *Acta Histochem.* **2021**, *123*, 151785. [CrossRef] [PubMed]
2. Abruzzo, A.; Cappadone, C.; Sallustio, V.; Picone, G.; Rossi, M.; Nicoletta, F.P.; Luppi, B.; Bigucci, F.; Cerchiara, T. Development of Spanish Broom and Flax Dressings with Glycyrrhetinic Acid-Loaded Films for Wound Healing: Characterization and Evaluation of Biological Properties. *Pharmaceutics* **2021**, *13*, 1192. [CrossRef] [PubMed]

3. Czemplik, M.; Kulma, A.; Bazela, K.; Szopa, J. The Biomedical Potential of Genetically Modified Flax Seeds Overexpressing the Glucosyltransferase Gene. *BMC Complement. Altern. Med.* **2012**, *12*, 251. [CrossRef] [PubMed]
4. Draganescu, D.; Ibanescu, C.; Tamba, B.I.; Andritoiu, C.V.; Dodi, G.; Popa, M.I. Flaxseed Lignan Wound Healing Formulation: Characterization and in Vivo Therapeutic Evaluation. *Int. J. Biol. Macromol.* **2015**, *72*, 614–623. [CrossRef]
5. Skórkowska-Telichowska, K.; Mierziak-Darecka, J.; Wrobel-Kwiatkowska, M.; Gebarowski, T.; Szopa, J.; Zuk, M. Wound Coverage by the Linen Dressing Accelerates Ulcer Healing. *Postep. Dermatol. Alergol.* **2021**, *38*, 827–841. [CrossRef]
6. Paul-Victor, C.; Dalle Vacche, S.; Sordo, F.; Fink, S.; Speck, T.; Michaud, V.; Speck, O. Effect of Mechanical Damage and Wound Healing on the Viscoelastic Properties of Stems of Flax Cultivars (*Linum Usitatissimum* L. Cv. Eden and Cv. Drakkar). *PLoS ONE* **2017**, *12*, e0185958. [CrossRef]
7. Satyanarayana, K.G.; Arizaga, G.G.C.; Wypych, F. Biodegradable Composites Based on Lignocellulosic Fibers-An Overview. *Prog. Polym. Sci.* **2009**, *34*, 982–1021. [CrossRef]
8. Charlet, K.; Eve, S.; Jernot, J.P.; Gomina, M.; Breard, J. Tensile Deformation of a Flax Fiber. *Procedia Eng.* **2009**, *1*, 233–236. [CrossRef]
9. Morvan, C.; Andème-Onzighi, C.; Girault, R.; Himmelsbach, D.S.; Driouich, A.; Akin, D.E. Building Flax Fibres: More than One Brick in the Walls. *Plant Physiol. Biochem.* **2003**, *41*, 935–944. [CrossRef]
10. Hughes, M. Defects in Natural Fibres: Their Origin, Characteristics and Implications for Natural Fibre-Reinforced Composites. *J. Mater. Sci.* **2012**, *47*, 599–609. [CrossRef]
11. Skórkowska-Telichowska, K.; Zuk, M.; Kulma, A.; Bugajska-Prusak, A.; Ratajczak, K.; Gasiorowski, K.; Kostyn, K.; Szopa, J. New Dressing Materials Derived from Transgenic Flax Products to Treat Long-Standing Venous Ulcers—A Pilot Study. *Wound Repair Regen.* **2010**, *18*, 168–179. [CrossRef]
12. Paladini, F.; Picca, R.A.; Sportelli, M.C.; Cioffi, N.; Sannino, A.; Pollini, M. Surface Chemical and Biological Characterization of Flax Fabrics Modified with Silver Nanoparticles for Biomedical Applications. *Mater. Sci. Eng. C* **2015**, *52*, 1–10. [CrossRef]
13. Skórkowska-Telichowska, K.; Kulma, A.; Gębarowski, T.; Wojtasik, W.; Kostyn, K.; Moreira, H.; Szyjka, A.; Boba, A.; Preisner, M.; Mierziak, J.; et al. V79 Fibroblasts Are Protected Against Reactive Oxygen Species by Flax Fabric. *Appl. Biochem. Biotechnol.* **2018**, *184*, 366–385. [CrossRef]
14. Gębarowski, T.; Moreira, H.; Szyjka, A.; Wiatrak, B.; Wojtasik, W.; Kulma, A.; Szopa, J.; Gasiorowski, K. Impact of Fabrics from Transgenic Flax Plant on Human Dermal Fibroblasts in Vitro Proliferation. *Acta Pol. Pharm. -Drug Res.* **2017**, *74*, 642–652.
15. Gąsiorowski, K.; Gębarowski, T.; Moreira, H.; Kulma, A.; Szatkowski, M.; Szopa, J. Impact of Fabrics from Transgenic Flax on Cultures of Skin Cells. *Adv. Clin. Exp. Med.* **2019**, *28*, 431–438. [CrossRef]
16. Gębarowski, T.; Wiatrak, B.; Janeczek, M.; Żuk, M.; Pistor, P.; Gąsiorowski, K. Were Our Ancestors Right in Using Flax Dressings? Research on the Properties of Flax Fibre and Its Usefulness in Wound Healing. *Oxid. Med. Cell. Longev.* **2020**, *2020*, 1682317. [CrossRef]
17. Gębarowski, T.; Jęśkowiak, I.; Janeczek, M.; Żuk, M.; Dobosz, A.; Wiatrak, B. The Technological Process of Obtaining New Linen Dressings Did Not Cause the Loss of Their Wound-Healing Properties. *Materials* **2021**, *14*, 7736. [CrossRef]
18. Chaung, W.; Mi, L.J.; Boorstein, R.J. The P53 Status of Chinese Hamster V79 Cells Frequently Used for Studies on DNA Damage and DNA Repair. *Nucleic Acids Res.* **1996**, *25*, 992–994. [CrossRef]
19. Sannino, A.; Zeni, O.; Romeo, S.; Massa, R.; Scarfi, M.R. Adverse and Beneficial Effects in Chinese Hamster Lung Fibroblast Cells Following Radiofrequency Exposure. *Bioelectromagnetics* **2017**, *38*, 245–254. [CrossRef]
20. Miao, F.; Li, Y.; Tai, Z.; Zhang, Y.; Gao, Y.; Hu, M.; Zhu, Q. Antimicrobial Peptides: The Promising Therapeutics for Cutaneous Wound Healing. *Macromol. Biosci.* **2021**, *21*, 2100103. [CrossRef]
21. Gould, L.J.; Orgill, D.P.; Armstrong, D.G.; Galiano, R.D.; Glat, P.M.; Zelen, C.M.; DiDomenico, L.A.; Carter, M.J.; Li, W.W. Improved Healing of Chronic Diabetic Foot Wounds in a Prospective Randomised Controlled Multi-Centre Clinical Trial with a Microvascular Tissue Allograft. *Int. Wound J.* **2022**, *19*, 811–825. [CrossRef] [PubMed]
22. Brega, C.; Calvi, S.; Albertini, A. Use of a Negative Pressure Wound Therapy System over Closed Incisions Option in Preventing Post-Sternotomy Wound Complications. *Wound Repair Regen.* **2021**, *29*, 848–852. [CrossRef]
23. Bieniek, E.; Skołucka-Szary, K.; Brzeziński, J.; Piaskowski, S.; Lewiński, A. Innovative Biodegradable Dibutyrylchitin Dressing for the Treatment of Ulcers Occurring during Chronic Venous Insufficiency in Patients with Type 2 Diabetes. *Int. J. Occup. Med. Environ. Health* **2021**, *34*, 563–573. [CrossRef] [PubMed]
24. Eriksson, E.; Liu, P.Y.; Schultz, G.S.; Martins-Green, M.M.; Tanaka, R.; Weir, D.; Gould, L.J.; Armstrong, D.G.; Gibbons, G.W.; Wolcott, R.; et al. Chronic Wounds: Treatment Consensus. *Wound Repair Regen.* **2022**, *30*, 156–171. [CrossRef] [PubMed]
25. Kaiser, P.; Wächter, J.; Windbergs, M. Therapy of Infected Wounds: Overcoming Clinical Challenges by Advanced Drug Delivery Systems. *Drug Deliv. Transl. Res.* **2021**, *11*, 1545–1567. [CrossRef] [PubMed]
26. Zahel, P.; Beekmann, U.; Eberlein, T.; Schmitz, M.; Werz, O.; Kralisch, D. Bacterial Cellulose—Adaptation of a Nature-Identical Material to the Needs of Advanced Chronic Wound Care. *Pharmaceuticals* **2022**, *15*, 683. [CrossRef]
27. Verdolino, D.V.; Thomason, H.A.; Fotticchia, A.; Cartmell, S. Wound Dressings: Curbing Inflammation in Chronic Wound Healing. *Emerg. Top. Life Sci.* **2021**, *5*, 523–537. [CrossRef]
28. Barrigah-Benissan, K.; Ory, J.; Sotto, A.; Salipante, F.; Lavigne, J.P.; Loubet, P. Antiseptic Agents for Chronic Wounds: A Systematic Review. *Antibiotics* **2022**, *11*, 350. [CrossRef]

29. Agostinis, C.; Spazzapan, M.; Vuerich, R.; Balduit, A.; Stocco, C.; Mangogna, A.; Ricci, G.; Papa, G.; Zacchigna, S.; Bulla, R. Differential Capability of Clinically Employed Dermal Regeneration Scaffolds to Support Vascularization for Tissue Bioengineering. *Biomedicines* **2021**, *9*, 1458. [CrossRef]
30. Del Amo, C.; Fern, X.; Cascajo-castresana, M.; Perez-valle, A.; Madarieta, I.; Olalde, B.; Andia, I. Wound-Microenvironment Engineering through Advanced-Dressing Bioprinting. *Int. J. Mol. Sci.* **2022**, *23*, 2836. [CrossRef]
31. Su, J.; Li, J.; Liang, J.; Zhang, K.; Li, J. Hydrogel Preparation Methods and Biomaterials for Wound Dressing. *Life* **2021**, *11*, 1016. [CrossRef]
32. Bray, E.R.; Oropallo, A.R.; Grande, D.A.; Kirsner, R.S.; Badiavas, E.V. Extracellular Vesicles as Therapeutic Tools for the Treatment of Chronic Wounds. *Pharmaceutics* **2021**, *13*, 1543. [CrossRef]
33. Chen, X.; Wu, J.; Cao, X.; Jiang, H.; Wu, Z.; Zeng, Z.; Chen, H.; Zhang, J. The Role of Gel Wound Dressings Loaded with Stem Cells in the Treatment of Diabetic Foot Ulcers. *Am. J. Transl Res.* **2021**, *13*, 13261–13272.
34. Derwin, R.; Patton, D.; Avsar, P.; Strapp, H.; Moore, Z. The Impact of Topical Agents and Dressing on PH and Temperature on Wound Healing: A Systematic, Narrative Review. *Int. Wound J.* **2021**. [CrossRef]
35. Wang, F.; Zhang, W.; Li, H.; Chen, X.; Feng, S.; Mei, Z. How Effective Are Nano-Based Dressings in Diabetic Wound Healing? A Comprehensive Review of Literature. *Int. J. Nanomed.* **2022**, *17*, 2097–2119. [CrossRef]
36. Aitcheson, S.M.; Frentiu, F.D.; Hurn, S.E.; Edwards, K.; Murray, R.Z. Skin Wound Healing: Normal Macrophage Function and Macrophage Dysfunction in Diabetic Wounds. *Molecules* **2021**, *26*, 4917. [CrossRef]
37. Li, Q.; Liu, K.; Jiang, T.; Ren, S.; Kang, Y.; Li, W.; Yao, H.; Yang, X.; Dai, H.; Chen, Z. Injectable and Self-Healing Chitosan-Based Hydrogel with MOF-Loaded α-Lipoic Acid Promotes Diabetic Wound Healing. *Mater. Sci. Eng. C* **2021**, *131*, 112519. [CrossRef]
38. Konop, M.; Rybka, M.; Drapała, A. Keratin Biomaterials in Skin Wound Healing, an Old Player in Modern Medicine: A Mini Review. *Pharmaceutics* **2021**, *13*, 2029. [CrossRef]
39. Styrczewska, M.; Kostyn, A.; Kulma, A.; Majkowska-Skrobek, G.; Augustyniak, D.; Prescha, A.; Czuj, T.; Szopa, J. Flax Fiber Hydrophobic Extract Inhibits Human Skin Cells Inflammation and Causes Remodeling of Extracellular Matrix and Wound Closure Activation. *Biomed. Res. Int.* **2015**, *2015*, 862391. [CrossRef]
40. He, C.; Liu, X.; Zhou, Z.; Liu, N.; Ning, X.; Miao, Y.; Long, Y.; Wu, T.; Leng, X. Harnessing Biocompatible Nanofibers and Silver Nanoparticles for Wound Healing: Sandwich Wound Dressing versus Commercial Silver Sulfadiazine Dressing. *Mater. Sci. Eng. C* **2021**, *128*, 112342. [CrossRef]
41. Shahzad, F. Management of Skin Graft Donor Site in Pediatric Patients with Tumescent Technique and AQUACEL® Ag Foam Dressing. *J. Plast. Surg. Hand Surg.* **2021**, *55*, 309–314. [CrossRef]
42. Yang, W.; Xu, F.; Ma, X.; Guo, J.; Li, C.; Shen, S.; Puglia, D.; Chen, J.; Xu, P.; Kenny, J.; et al. Highly-Toughened PVA/Nanocellulose Hydrogels with Anti-Oxidative and Antibacterial Properties Triggered by Lignin-Ag Nanoparticles. *Mater. Sci. Eng. C* **2021**, *129*, 112385. [CrossRef]
43. Ahmed, M.K.; Zayed, M.A.; El-dek, S.I.; Hady, M.A.; El Sherbiny, D.H.; Uskoković, V. Nanofibrous ε-Polycaprolactone Scaffolds Containing Ag-Doped Magnetite Nanoparticles: Physicochemical Characterization and Biological Testing for Wound Dressing Applications in Vitro and in Vivo. *Bioact. Mater.* **2021**, *6*, 2070–2088. [CrossRef]
44. Zhang, M.; Wang, D.; Ji, N.; Lee, S.; Wang, G.; Zheng, Y.; Zhang, X.; Yang, L.; Qin, Z.; Yang, Y. Bioinspired Design of Sericin/Chitosan/Ag@mof/Go Hydrogels for Efficiently Combating Resistant Bacteria, Rapid Hemostasis, and Wound Healing. *Polymers* **2021**, *13*, 2812. [CrossRef] [PubMed]
45. Farazin, A.; Mohammadimehr, M.; Ghasemi, A.H.; Naeimi, H. Design, Preparation, and Characterization of CS/PVA/SA Hydrogels Modified with Mesoporous Ag2O/SiO2and Curcumin Nanoparticles for Green, Biocompatible, and Antibacterial Biopolymer Film. *RSC Adv.* **2021**, *11*, 32775–32791. [CrossRef] [PubMed]
46. Kulma, A.; Skórkowska-Telichowska, K.; Kostyn, K.; Szatkowski, M.; Skała, J.; Drulis-Kawa, Z.; Preisner, M.; Zuk, M.; Szperlik, J.; Wang, Y.F.; et al. New Flax Producing Bioplastic Fibers for Medical Purposes. *Ind. Crops Prod.* **2015**, *68*, 80–89. [CrossRef]
47. Wróbel-Kwiatkowska, M.; Turnau, K.; Góralska, K.; Anielska, T.; Szopa, J. Effects of Genetic Modifications to Flax (Linum Usitatissimum) on Arbuscular Mycorrhiza and Plant Performance. *Mycorrhiza* **2012**, *22*, 493–499. [CrossRef]
48. Lukiw, W.J. Bacteroides Fragilis Lipopolysaccharide and Inflammatory Signaling in Alzheimer's Disease. *Front. Microbiol.* **2016**, *7*, 1544. [CrossRef]
49. Wróbel-Kwiatkowska, M.; Lorenz-Kukula, K.; Starzycki, M.; Oszmiański, J.; Kepczyńska, E.; Szopa, J. Expression of β-1,3-Glucanase in Flax Causes Increased Resistance to Fungi. *Physiol. Mol. Plant Pathol.* **2004**, *65*, 245–256. [CrossRef]
50. Arendt-Pindel, A.; Marszałek-Harych, A.; Gębarowska, E.; Gębarowski, T.; Jędrzkiewicz, D.; Plaskowska, E.; Zalewski, D.; Gulia, N.; Szafert, S.; Ejfler, J. Design and Functionalization of Bioactive Benzoxazines. An Unexpected Ortho-Substitution Effect. *New J. Chem.* **2019**, *43*, 12042–12053. [CrossRef]
51. Rhee, S.G.; Chang, T.S.; Jeong, W.; Kang, D. Methods for Detection and Measurement of Hydrogen Peroxide inside and Outside of Cells. *Mol. Cells* **2010**, *29*, 539–549. [CrossRef]
52. Collins, A.R. The Comet Assay for DNA Damage and Repair: Principles, Applications, and Limitations. *Appl. Biochem. Biotechnol. Part B Mol. Biotechnol.* **2004**, *26*, 249–261. [CrossRef]

International Journal of *Molecular Sciences*

MDPI

Article

Human Umbilical Cord Lining-Derived Epithelial Cells: A Potential Source of Non-Native Epithelial Cells That Accelerate Healing in a Porcine Cutaneous Wound Model

Jonah Ee Hsiang Kua [1], Chun Wei Siow [2], Wee Keng Lim [2], Jeyakumar Masilamani [3], Monica Suryana Tjin [4], Joe Yeong [5,6], Tony Kiat Hon Lim [6], Toan Thang Phan [3,7] and Alvin Wen Choong Chua [1,2,8,*]

1. Department of Plastic, Reconstructive and Aesthetic Surgery, Singapore General Hospital, 20 College Road, Singapore 169856, Singapore
2. Skin Bank Unit, Singapore General Hospital, Outram Road, Singapore 169608, Singapore
3. CellResearch Corporation Pte. Ltd., 137 Market Street, Grace Global Raffles #08-02, Singapore 048943, Singapore
4. Programme in Cardiovascular and Metabolic Disorders, Duke-NUS Medical School, 8 College Road, Singapore 169857, Singapore
5. Institute of Molecular and Cell Biology, Agency for Science, Technology and Research, 61 Biopolis, Proteos, Singapore 138673, Singapore
6. Department of Anatomical Pathology, Singapore General Hospital, 20 College Road, Singapore 169856, Singapore
7. Department of Surgery, Yong Loo Lin School of Medicine, National University of Singapore, Kent Ridge Road, Singapore 119228, Singapore
8. Musculoskeletal Sciences Academic Clinical Programme, Duke-NUS Medical School, 8 College Road, Singapore 169857, Singapore

* Correspondence: gmscwca@nus.edu.sg; Tel.: +65-6321-3807

Citation: Kua, J.E.H.; Siow, C.W.; Lim, W.K.; Masilamani, J.; Tjin, M.S.; Yeong, J.; Lim, T.K.H.; Phan, T.T.; Chua, A.W.C. Human Umbilical Cord Lining-Derived Epithelial Cells: A Potential Source of Non-Native Epithelial Cells That Accelerate Healing in a Porcine Cutaneous Wound Model. *Int. J. Mol. Sci.* **2022**, 23, 8918. https://doi.org/10.3390/ijms23168918

Academic Editors: César Viseras, Luana Perioli and Cinzia Pagano

Received: 30 June 2022
Accepted: 7 August 2022
Published: 10 August 2022

Abstract: Human umbilical cord lining epithelial cells [CLECs) are naïve in nature and can be ethically recovered from cords that are routinely discarded. The success of using oral mucosal epithelial cells for cornea defects hints at the feasibility of treating cutaneous wounds using non-native CLECs. Herein, we characterized CLECs using flow cytometry (FC) and skin organotypic cultures in direct comparison with skin keratinocytes (KCs). This was followed by wound healing study to compare the effects of CLEC application and the traditional use of human skin allografts (HSGs) in a porcine wound model. While CLECs were found to express all the epidermal cell markers probed, the major difference between CLECs and KCs lies in the level of expression (in FC analysis) as well as in the location of expression (of the epithelium in organotypic cultures) of some of the basal cell markers probed. On the pig wounds, CLEC application promoted accelerated healing with no adverse reaction compared to HSG use. Though CLECs, like HSGs, elicited high levels of local and systemic immune responses in the animals during the first week, these effects were tapered off more quickly in the CLEC-treated group. Overall, the in vivo porcine data point to the potential of CLECs as a non-native and safe source of cells to treat cutaneous wounds.

Keywords: umbilical cord; cord lining epithelial cells; skin keratinocytes; cutaneous wounds; wound healing; CLECs

1. Introduction

The success of autologous skin keratinocyte (KC) cultures that have been genetically modified to treat junctional epidermolysis bullosa (JEB) brought the spotlight back on cultured epithelial cell therapy in the field of regenerative medicine [1]. In 2017, De Luca and his team regenerated an entire human epidermis that is fully functional on a 7-year-old child whose devastating form of JEB affected 80% of his total body surface area. However, resurfacing critically large cutaneous wounds due to severe burns, diabetes, or genetic mutations remains a huge clinical challenge. In the current regenerative medicine landscape, one area that could be addressed is to identify an alternative source of epithelial cells that can be used effectively to treat extensive skin barrier defects in the clinics. There are known instances where suitable skin donor sites were not available for culture autologous KCs in life-saving procedures. In regions of tropical climate, high incidences of bacterial infection in severe and extensively burned patients have been reported [2–5] with limited donor sites available that were already highly colonized for any meaningful skin culture. Similarly, it is known that KCs isolated from mutated skin donor sites of EB patients are challenging to cultivate due to structural and functional abnormalities resulting in a lower growth rate compared to normal KCs [6,7]. Therefore, there is a need to look at non-native or alternative sources of epithelial cells with barrier function to resurface cutaneous wounds, especially those with large surface areas.

There is an emerging trend of using umbilical cord tissues to derive epithelial cells as a cost-effective option in regenerative medicine [8,9]. On top of having the advantages of a naive status and an abundant resource as medical waste, umbilical cords are collected without the need for any deliberate invasive procedures and with minimal ethical considerations [10,11]. The umbilical cord epithelium is known to display certain cytokeratin expressions similar to that of the human epidermis [12], and derived human umbilical cord lining epithelial cells (CLECs) were found to have common features with neonatal epidermal KCs at the morphological and molecular level [13]. In addition, CLECs were not only found to have a low immunogenicity and immunosuppressive function in vitro [14], these cells could also be maintained for extended periods in vivo as compared to KCs [8].

Interestingly, there is no known report to date on the safety, efficacy, and immunogenicity of CLECs used in cutaneous wound healing applications in vivo. Herein, we validated the phenotype of CLECs via flow cytometry and studied their behavior using ex vivo skin organotypic cultures in comparison to human skin KCs. This was followed by topical application of human CLECs on full thickness excisional wounds of immunocompetent pigs to study their wound healing efficacy and immunological effects.

2. Results

2.1. Immunophenotypic Profile of CLECs in Comparison to KCs

Analysis of the flow cytometry (FC) data found that isolated CLECs displayed some of the immunophenotypic profiles found in KCs with high expression levels of epidermal basal/adhesion cell markers of keratin 5, 14(KRT5, KRT14), and integrin alpha-6 (ITGA6). There were corresponding low levels of differentiated cell markers of keratin 1, 10(KRT1, KRT10), and involucrin (IVL) across all the three passages tested (Figure 1a–c, Supplementary Figure S1). While more than 50% of the overall CLECs expressed another set of basal/adhesion cell markers of KRT15 (Mean = 55.3%, SD = 4.64%, n = 18) and integrin beta-1 (ITGB1) (Mean = 60.0%, SD = 8.75%, n = 18) across the three passages tested, these numbers were significantly lower than that expressed by KCs for KRT15 (mean = 77.5%, SD = 8.90%, n = 18) and ITGB1 (mean = 80.8%, SD = 7.8%, n = 18).

2.2. Stratification of CLECs Compared to KCs in Organotypic Cultures

In organotypic cultures, CLECs were able to form stratified epithelium on skin fibroblast populated de-epithelialized dermis (DEDs), even though they were not as organized and mature as those formed by KCs after two weeks of air-liquid interface exposure (Figure 2a). This was reflected in the immunofluorescence (IF) staining data where basal markers of KRT14, KRT15, and p63 (Figure 2b) were found positive across the basal and suprabasal regions of CLEC-generated epithelia, while the same markers were restricted mainly at the basal area of KC-generated epithelia.

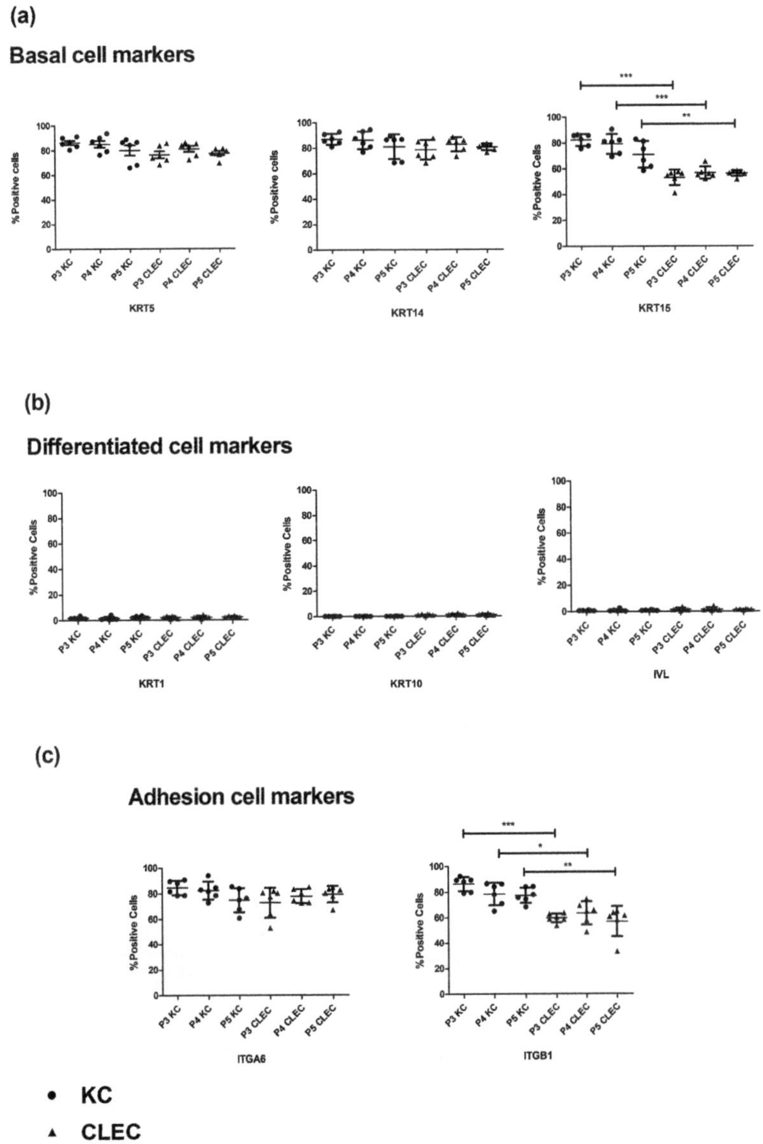

Figure 1. Dot plots based on flow cytometry analysis of passages three to five KCs and CLECs (three donors each cell type with two technical replicates), depicting the immunophenotypic expression levels of epidermal (**a**) basal cell markers using KRT5, KRT14, and KRT15; (**b**) differentiation cell markers using KRT1, KRT10, and IVL; and (**c**) adhesion cell markers using ITGA6 and ITGB1. Center line of the dot plots is the mean, and the whiskers represent standard deviation (SD). Statistical analysis was performed using one-way ANOVA—Bonferroni's Multiple Comparison Test (n = 6); * $p < 0.05$, ** $p < 0.001$, and *** $p < 0.0001$.

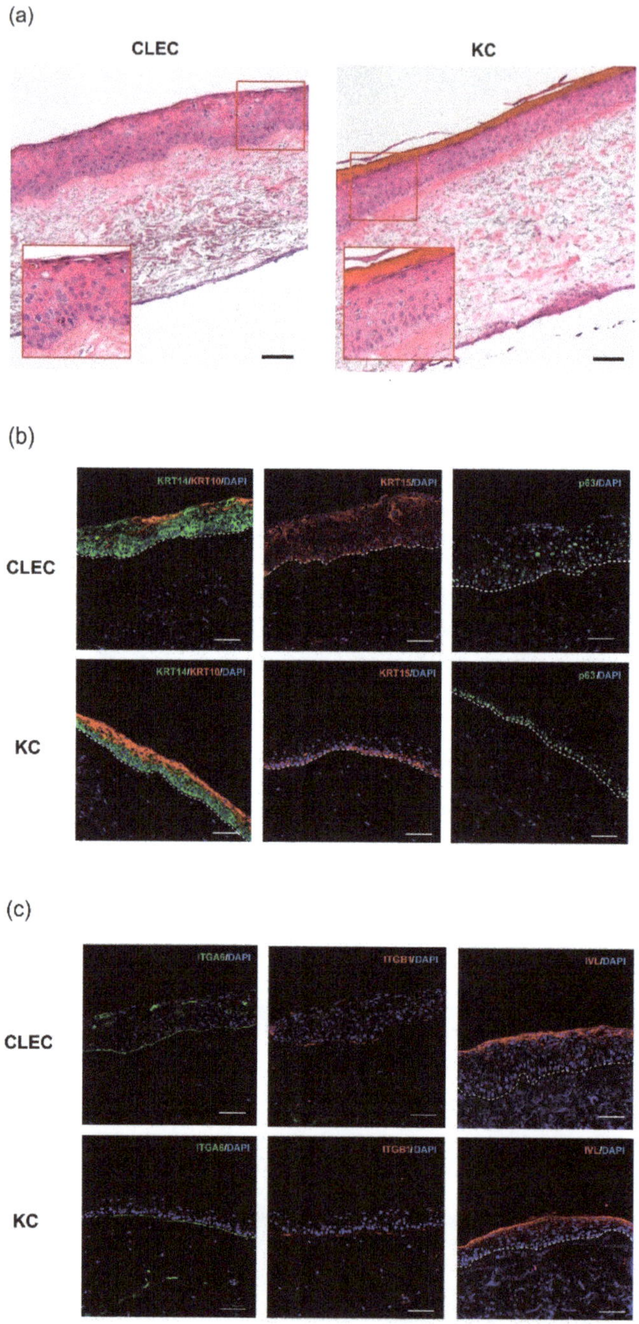

Figure 2. Epithelia formed by CLECs and KCs seeded on de-epithelialized dermis populated with human dermal fibroblasts. After 2 weeks of air-liquid interface exposure, these organotypic cultures were examined by (**a**) H&E stains; inset: higher magnification (20×) and IF stains of (**b**) KRT10, KRT14, KRT15, and p63; (**c**) ITGA6, ITGB1, and IVL. Scale bar = 100 μm.

However, differentiated cell markers of KRT10 and IVL (at the suprabasal region) as well as adhesion molecule markers of ITGA6 and ITGB1 (at the basement membrane) region were expressed in the CLEC-generated epithelia, similar to the marker profile/location of the KC-generated epithelia (Figure 2b,c). A further breakdown on the location and distribution of the various IF stained markers expressed within the entire epithelial layer of organotypic cultures formed by both CLECs and KCs were compared side by side in Table 1.

Table 1. Location and distribution of markers associated with human skin epidermis, basement membrane, and epidermal stem cells within the entire epithelia reconstituted by KCs or CLECs in organotypic cultures.

Protein Marker	CLEC	KC
Keratin 10 (KRT10)	sb (+)	sb (++)
Keratin 14 (KRT14)	bl (++), sb (++)	bl (++)
Keratin 15 (KRT15)	bl (++), sb (++)	bl (++)
Integrin alpha-6 (ITGA6)	bm (++)	bm (++)
Integrin beta-1 (ITGB1)	bm (++)	bm (++)
Involucrin (IVL)	usb (++)	usb (++)
p63	bl (+), sb (+)	bm (++)

usb: upper suprabasal layer, sb: suprabasal layer, bl: basal layer, bm: present in basement membrane, +: present in parts of layer or region, ++: present everywhere in layer or region.

2.3. *Wound Healing Performance of CLECs in Comparison to Human Skin Grafts (HSGs) in a Porcine Excisional Wound Model*

A total of eight pigs, matched for sex, age, and weight, were used for the above study. These large animals, each created with six full-thickness excisional wounds, were subjected to topical treatment of human CLECs as a fresh cell pellet layer (concentration at 10^5 cells/cm^2), cryopreserved human skin grafts (HSGs), and non-biological standard dressings ("untreated" control) for comparison. The various configurations of these wound treatments (Figure 3) are described in the Materials and Methods, Section 4.6 (Figure 4). In configuration 1 with a total of four wounds (n = 4) for each treatment arm that were performed across two pigs (Figure 4a), we found accelerated wound closure in the CLEC-treated group that was near significance ($p = 0.0518$) based on repeated measures two-way ANOVA over time (Figure 3a). Between Weeks 2 to 4, the percentage area of wound closure was found to be significantly higher with CLEC treatment compared to HSG and/or standard wound dressing treatment ("Untreated").

(a)

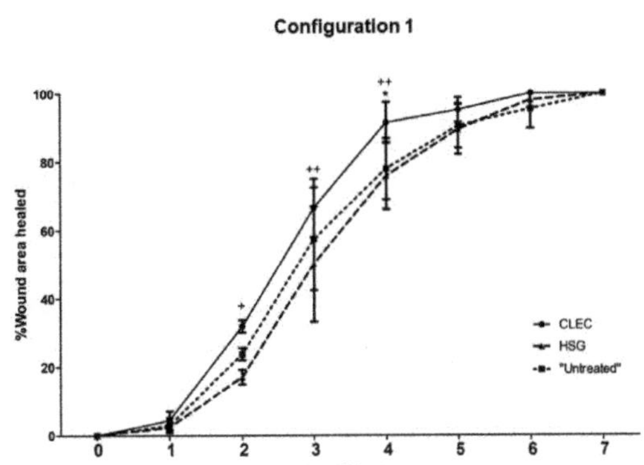

Figure 3. *Cont.*

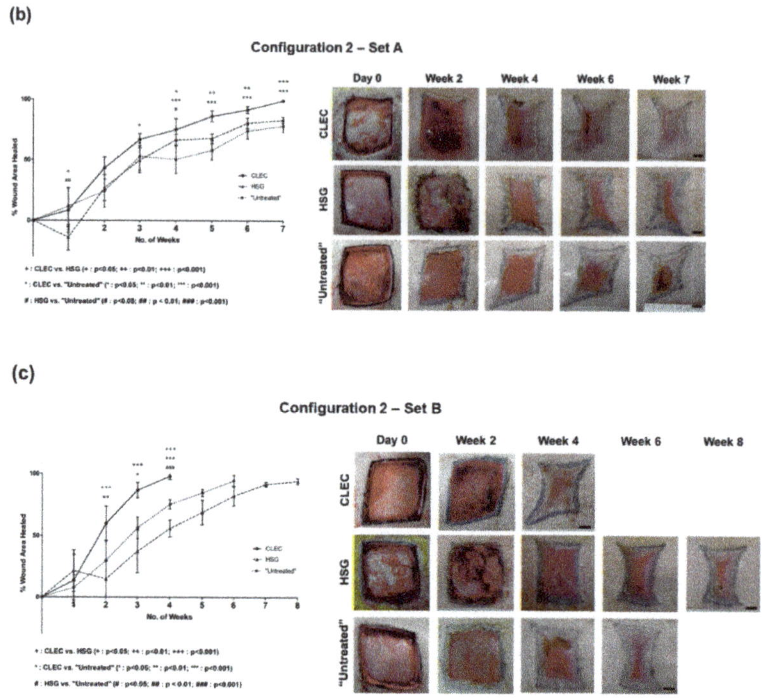

Figure 3. Percentage closure of weekly-measured wound area represented by mean ± SD based on (**a**) Configuration one with all the three treatment arms performed on a single pig (total pigs used: 2); (**b**) Configuration 2 Set A and (**c**) Configuration 2 Set B where only a single type of treatment was administered entirely to each pig (total pigs used: 6). The three treatment arms compared were CLEC, HSG, and standard dressings ("untreated"); n = 4 for configuration 1 and n = 5 for configuration 2. Statistical analysis was performed using one-way ANOVA—Bonferroni's Multiple Comparison Test. Representative images of the stages of wound closure were shown for Configuration 2 at different time points with scale bar = 1 cm.

In configuration 2—Set A (Figures 3b and 4b), each of the three pigs were subjected to a single type of treatment and compared across these pigs over a period of 7 weeks. The wounds (n = 5) of the CLEC-treated pig achieved the highest rate of healing, with 99% closure compared to 83% with the HSG-treated pig and 78% for the "untreated" pig just before sacrifice. The CLEC treatment provided an accelerated wound closure that was highly significant ($p < 0.0001$) over time compared to the other two treatment arms.

In configuration 2—Set B (Figures 3c and 4b), where the animals were sacrificed once the average closure of all wounds on the pig achieved 90% or above, we similarly found that the pig that received CLECs performed the best overall. The CLEC-treated pig achieved 98% wound closure (n = 5) at Week 4, while the "untreated" and HSG-treated pigs both achieved 94% wound closure at Week 6 and Week 8, respectively.

Throughout the entire wound inspection period, we observed no obvious signs of infection or severe adverse reaction to the animals in the CLEC and the "untreated groups, except for some swellings and sloughs that were found on the HSG-treated wound beds at Week 2 (Figure 3b,c).

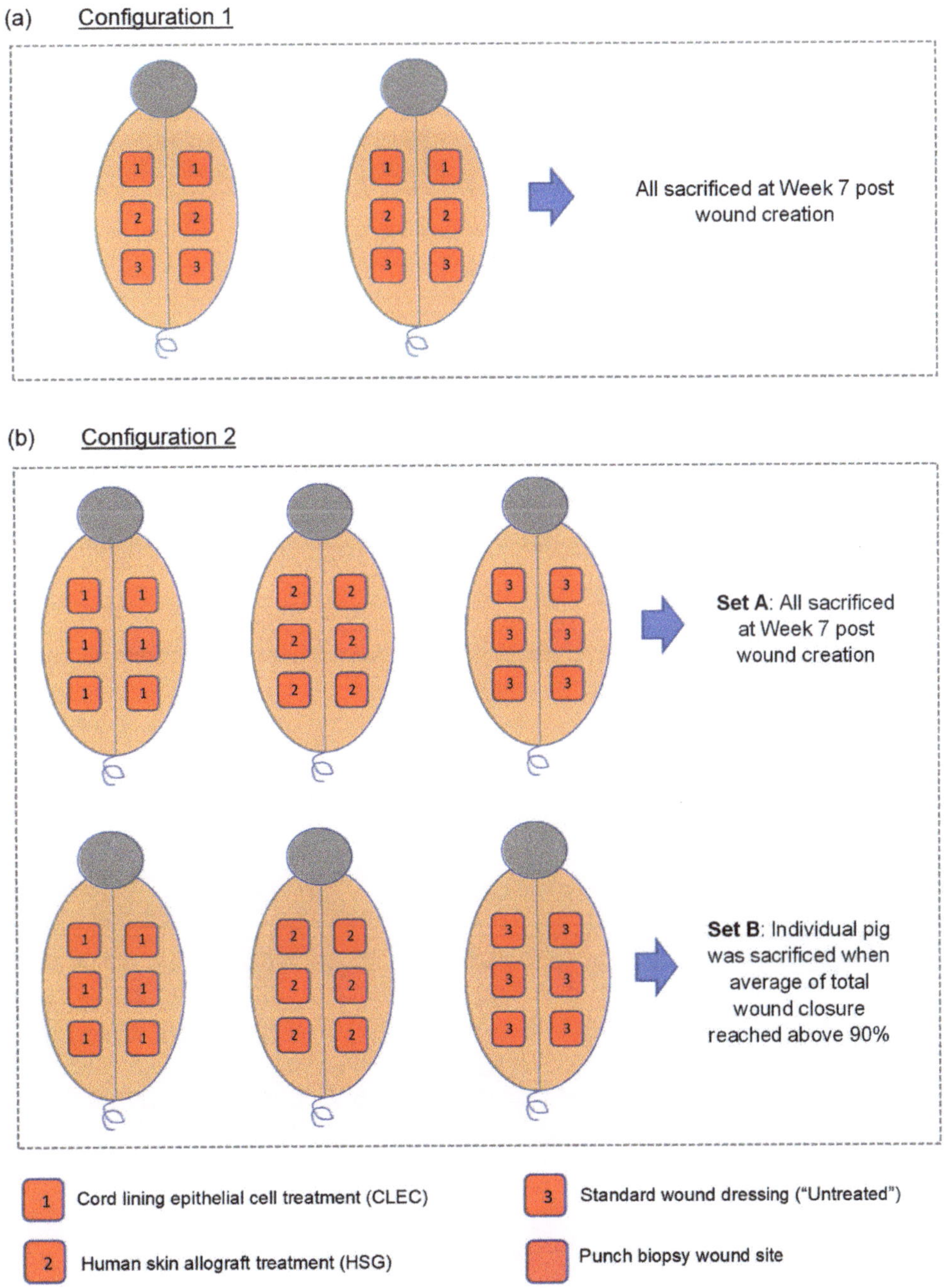

Figure 4. Wound treatment configurations for pigs created with full thickness excisional wounds. (**a**) Configuration 1 involved the use of multiple treatments on a single pig; (**b**) Configuration 2 involved the use of singular treatment on an entire pig.

2.4. Histological Assessment of the Wounds after Respective Treatments

In Masson's Trichome (MT) staining of representative wound tissue biopsies, we found the consistent presence of collagen (stained turquoise) with more mature and thicker epithelia formed on the wounds of the two CLEC-treated pigs: one at Week 6 in Configuration 2 Set A and the other at Week 3 in Set B. All of these time points were at one week before the animals were sacrificed (Figure 5a). Further analysis of the MT stains at a higher magnification (Figure 5b) using semi-quantitative scoring method [15] (Table 2) revealed that CLEC-treated skin stained with MT demonstrated strong blue staining indicating new collagen formation in the region of reticular dermis as early as at Week 3. In the Set B experiment, the blue staining could be found not only in the region of reticular dermis but also in the papillary dermis as early as at Week 3, whereas the HSG-treated skin as well as the untreated skin could only demonstrated the similar positive staining pattern at Week 6.

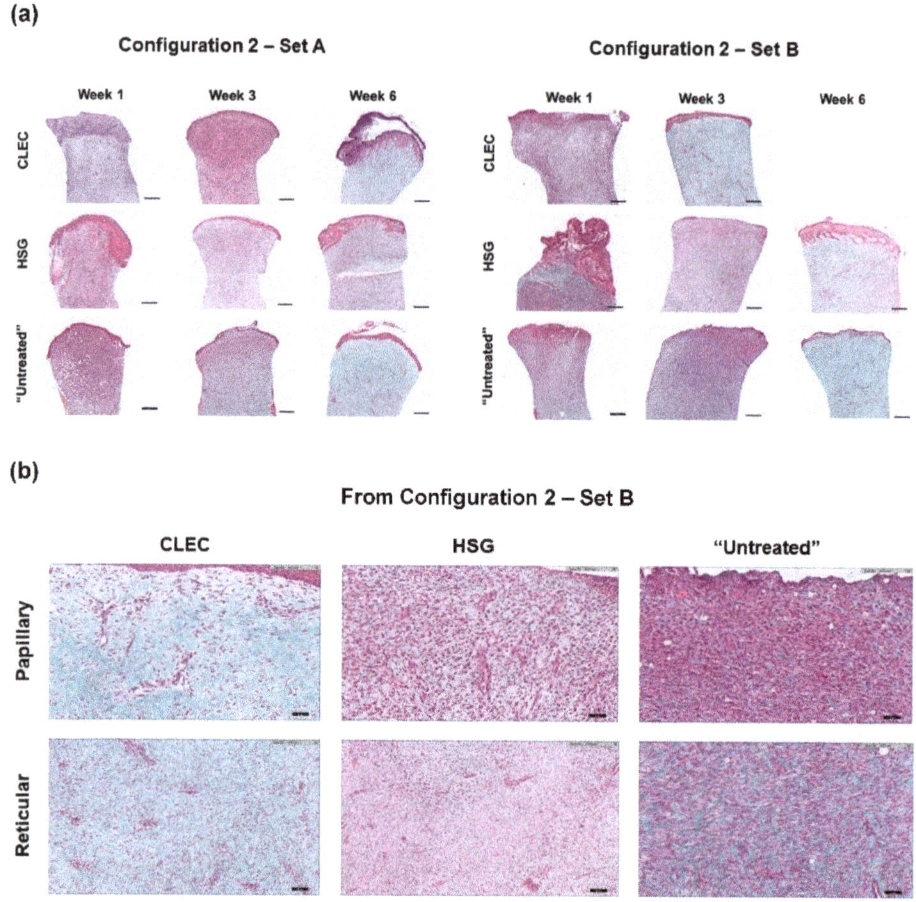

Figure 5. Week 3 tissue biopsies of pig cutaneous wounds treated with CLECs (CLEC), human skin grafts (HSG), and standard dressings ("Untreated") probed with Masson's Trichome (MT) stain (**a**) at 2× magnification for three time points in Configuration 2 Sets A and B with scale bar = 500 μm; (**b**) at 20× magnification based on Configuration 2 Set B with scale bar = 50 μm.

Table 2. Semi-quantitative scoring of Masson's Trichome (MT) stains at the papillary and recticular dermis of skin tissue biopsies shown in Figure 5a.

	Configuration 2—Set A			Configuration 2—Set B		
Week	**1**	**3**	**6**	**1**	**3**	**6**
CLEC treatment						
Papillary	-	-	+	-	+	NA
Recticular	-	+	+	+	+	NA
HSG treatment						
Papillary	-	-	+	-	-	+
Recticular	-	-	+	-	-	+
"Untreated"						
Papillary	-	-	+	-	-	+
Recticular	-	+	+	+	+	+

"+": Strong blue MT staining; "-", Negative MT staining; "NA": Not applicable.

Blinded assessment of immunohistochemistry (IHC) stains of representative wound tissue biopsies (Figure 6) to determine the inflammatory infiltration levels of CD4+ and CD8+ T lymphocytes [16] into the respective wound beds (treated by the three different treatments over time) were all compiled in Table 3. Differences in the CD4 and CD8 ratings between the two pigs treated with the same modality (comparing between Sets A and B) were observed and these could be attributed to pig-to-pig variation in the local immunological response of the wound bed. However, the overall trend seemed to suggest that while CLEC treatment elicited high levels of CD4+ T lymphocyte infiltration at the first week in the two pigs that were treated, and these levels subsequently subsided. This was unlike HSG treatment in which high levels of CD4+ T lymphocyte infiltration were still observable from Week 4/5 onward.

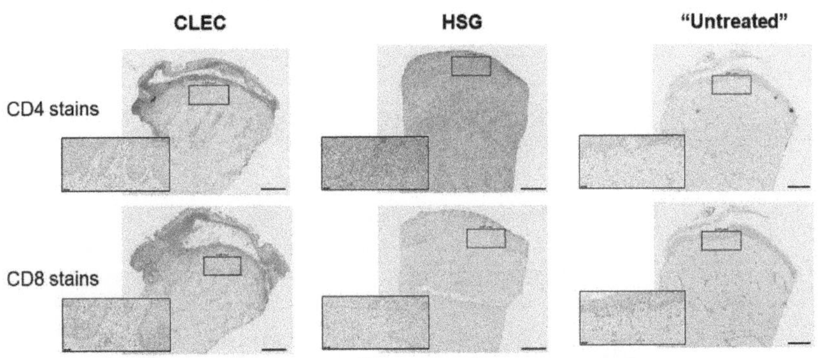

Figure 6. Immunohistochemical (IHC) stains of CD4 and CD8 on tissue biopsies from pig wounds treated with CLECs (CLEC), human skin grafts (HSG), and standard dressings ("Untreated"). Inset: higher magnification (20×). Main scale bar = 500 μm and inset scale bar = 50 μm.

Table 3. Distribution levels of CD4+- and CD8+-T lymphocytes infiltration into wound bed via representative tissue biopsies of each treated arm.

For CD4+ T cells								
					Week			
	1	**2**	**3**	**4**	**5**	**6**	**7**	**8**
CLEC treatment								
Set A	+++	+	+	++	-	+	+	NA
Set B	+++	+	-	-	NA	NA	NA	NA
HSG treatment								
Set A	+++	+	+	-	+	++	++	NA
Set B	++	++	+	++	++	++	-	-

Table 3. *Cont.*

For CD4+ T cells								
						Week		
	1	**2**	**3**	**4**	**5**	**6**	**7**	**8**
"Untreated"								
Set A	+	++	+	+	++	-	+	NA
Set B	+++	+	+	+	-	+	NA	NA
For CD8+ T cells								
						Week		
	1	**2**	**3**	**4**	**5**	**6**	**7**	**8**
CLEC treatment								
Set A	++	++	++	+	+	+	+	NA
Set B	++	++	++	++	NA	NA	NA	NA
HSG treatment								
Set A	++	++	++	++	++	+	+	NA
Set B	+	++	++	++	++	++	++	+
"Untreated"								
Set A	+	++	++	++	++	++	++	NA
Set B	++	++	++	++	+	+	NA	NA

"-": Absent, "+": Minimal or sparsely distributed, "++": Moderately distributed, "+++": Severe or densely populated, "NA": Not applicable.

2.5. Evaluation of Systemic Host Response through Time-Course Profiling of Probed Inflammatory Cytokines in Porcine Serum with Respective Wound Treatments

The profiling of pro- and anti-inflammatory cytokines present in the blood serum of the differently treated pigs (in Configuration 2 Set A where all pigs were tracked over a period of 7 weeks) revealed that there was an increase in the levels of IFN-γ, IL-8, and TNF-α, all pro-inflammatory cytokines of the CLEC-treated pig on Day 4, relative to the pre-procedure baseline level. The high level of IL-8 at this time point was especially pronounced with a fold increase in the range of 61 to 120. However, this observed increase in the IL-8 level completely subsided from Weeks 1 to 3, only to see its level rise again (fold increase of 31 to 60) on Week 4 (Table 4).

Table 4. Fold change increase of probed inflammatory cytokine concentrations in porcine blood serum from the pre-procedure baseline level; only cytokines with a fold change of two and above are reflected in the table.

CLEC treatment								
	Day 4	Week 1	Week 2	Week 3	Week 4	Week 5	Week 6	Week 7
IFN-γ	+							
IL-8	++++				+++			
TNF-α	+							
HSG treatment								
	Day 4	Week 1	Week 2	Week 3	Week 4	Week 5	Week 6	Week 7
IFN-γ	+							
IL-1β			++				+	
IL-2			+					
IL-6			+					
IL-8	++++			+++	++++	++++	+++	
IL-10			+	+				
IL-12			+		+			
IL-18			+		+			
TNF-α				+++	+++	+++	++	

Table 4. *Cont.*

"Untreated"								
	Day 4	Week 1	Week 2	Week 3	Week 4	Week 5	Week 6	Week 7
IL-10				+		+		+

+: 2 to 10 fold increase, ++: 11 to 30 fold increase, +++: 31 to 60 fold increase, ++++: 61 to 120 fold increase.

Similarly, the serum of an HSG-treated pig had a pronounced increase in the level of IL-8 on Day 4, which receded totally between Weeks 1 and 2, only to return at elevated levels from Weeks 3 to 6. There was also a substantial increase in the levels of TNF-α that were sustained from Weeks 3 to 6. Furthermore, the use of HSG also brought about sporadic increases in levels of other inflammatory cytokines—IFN-γ, IL-1β, IL-2, IL-6, Il-10, IL-12, and IL-18—at various time points, with most of them concentrated at Week 2. Finally, we found an increase in the level of only one anti-inflammatory cytokine, IL-10, in the pig serum that received standard dressings ("Untreated") on Weeks 3, 5, and 7 (Table 4).

3. Discussion

The concept of using a "non-native" source of cultured epithelial cells for healing and regeneration of different epithelial tissue type is not new. In 2004, the first-in-man corneal reconstruction with cultured cell sheets composed of autologous oral mucosal epithelium was described [17], and this technique is still being used in the clinic today [18]. Drawing on the same principle, we explored the possibility of using human CLECs as an alternative source to human KCs for the treatment of cutaneous wound injuries using Yorkshire pigs. This large-animal excisional wound model has been reported to closely resemble normal healing in humans with neither having excessive contraction nor forming hypercontracted scars [19].

3.1. Expression Levels of KRT15 and ITGB1 Were Found to Be Lower in CLECs Compared to KCs in Flow Cytometry

We first characterized CLECs by studying their phenotype in direct comparison to KCs via FC analysis. Isolated CLECs were found to have some immunophenotypical profiles similar to KCs (across all three passages) with high expression levels of epidermal basal keratin markers, KRT5 and KRT14, and the adhesion molecule marker, ITGA6, with correspondingly low levels of differentiated skin epithelial cell markers: KRT1, KRT10, and IVL. However, the expression levels of KRT15 and ITGB1 in CLECs were approximately 20% lower than that found in KCs (Figure 1a–c). The CLEC expression level for ITGB1 of 60% on average, differs from an earlier study, which reported higher expression levels at more than 90% [20]. As that study did not perform a direct comparison with KCs such as ours, the difference in ITGB1 expression levels in CLECs might be attributed to lab-to-lab variation in terms of protocols and reagent use, as well as biological variation from different donors.

3.2. Some Basal Cells Markers of the Human Epidermis Were Found to Be Expressed in Both the Basal and the Suprabasal Layers of CLEC-Generated Epithelium

In organotypic cultures, we found that seeded CLECs were able to form a fully stratified epithelium after 2 weeks of air-liquid interface exposure. IF staining showed that CLECs can generate an epithelium expressing basal-(KRT14, KRT15, p63, ITGA6, and ITGB1), suprabasal-(KRT10), and even upper suprabasal-(IVL) cell markers which are all typically found on the human skin epidermis (Figure 2b,c). While CLECs could form a stratified stratum corneum layer with the presence of IVL expression, known for its barrier function, the overall appearance of CLEC-generated epithelium appeared less mature and organized compared to that formed by KCs, as seen on the H&E stains (Figure 2a). Furthermore, differences were detected in the location within the layer of epithelia where these markers were expressed in the respective IF stains of CLEC- and

KC-organotypic cultures (Table 1). Essentially, KRT14, KRT15, and p63, known to be expressed in the basal KCs of the skin epidermis [21,22], were found to be more prevalent in the entire epithelium (up to the suprabasal layer) formed by CLECs. This observation correlates with a previous comparative study of umbilical cord and fetal skin tissues, where KRT14 expression was found in the whole epithelium of the cord tissue, while this expression was limited to the basal layer of the fetal skin epidermis [12]. Taken together, we postulate that the differentiation of seeded CLECs might not be as efficient as KCs during the 2-week stratification process. CLECs, being a non-native source cultured on skin dermis, might still be in their basal or naïve state in transit within the suprabasal region. These cells in transition might need more time for full maturation during the stratification process. Future studies and characterization would be needed to study this longer-term stratification process.

3.3. CLEC Treatment Accelerated Wound Closure Compared to HSG Treatment

Cutaneous wound healing in the pig is frequently used as a model for human cutaneous wound healing due to the anatomical and physiological similarities between the skin of these two species [19,23]. In our investigation to find out the suitability of human CLECs for cutaneous wound healing application, we tested these cells as a form of xenograft treatment [24] on a porcine full thickness excisional wound model and compared it with the use of cryopreserved human skin grafts (HSGs). Allogeneic HSGs are considered the off-the-shelf gold standard to treat severe wounds in extensive burns after wound excision [25]. In both configurations 1 and 2 (Figure 4), we found general improvement in percentage of wound closure in the pigs treated with CLECs (Figure 3a–c), and this remains so after discounting the effect of wound contraction, which was found to be on average close to 50% for all of the wounds regardless of treatment type at the point of sacrifice (Supplementary Figure S3). MT stains of collected tissue biopsies corroborate the observed improved wound healing in the CLEC-only-treated pigs with the presence of collagen in both Sets A and B, as well as having more mature and thicker epithelia one week before the animals were sacrificed (Figures 5a and 6). HSG-treated skin showed some positive MT staining only at Week 6, which demonstrated slower wound healing compared to the other groups. We speculate that the immunological response to the human xenograft might be one of the possible reasons.

The improvement in wound healing elicited by CLECs in configuration 1 was not as pronounced in the two pigs treated entirely by CLECs in configuration 2. Here, we hypothesized that there might be a confounding effect of the systemic response on wound healing performance over time due to multiple treatments administered onto a single pig used in configuration 1. And indeed, based on the pigs' serum evaluation, there were significant differences in the overall profile of the systemic inflammatory cytokines detected over time between the three treatment groups. The treatment arm that brought about the most immunogenic reaction might potentially affect the other more passive treatment arms (Table 4) on the same animal.

3.4. Use of CLECs and HSGs Elicited High Levels of Local and Systemic Immune Response in the Animals during the First Week but These Effects Tapered off More Quickly in the CLEC-Treated Group

Blinded IHC assessment of local inflammatory infiltrations of T lymphocytes in the wound biopsies to study immune rejection mediated by these cells [16] showed that treatment of both CLECs and HSGs brought high levels of CD4+ T cells into the wounds in the first week (Table 2). However, the CD4+ T cell distribution in the CLEC-treated group seemed to taper more over time compared to the HSG-treated group. Similarly, we also observed increased levels of pro-inflammatory cytokines detected in the pigs' serum at Day 4 of the CLEC- and HSG-treated group only to find that these were subsequently muted for the CLEC-treated group in the remaining weeks, save for the detection of IL-8 in Week 4. While we cannot fully explain the moderate presence of CD8+ T cells in almost all weeks of the different treatment arms, we can only postulate that these cells recruited into the wounds have reached a threshold regardless of the trigger that was due to the wounding itself, the immunogenic response to the foreign cells/tissues or a combination of both, and these CD8+ T cell levels were sustained during the entire wound healing process until the wounds were almost or completely epithelialized, quite similar to what was previously reported in mice wound healing [26].

The period of tapering in both the local and systemic immune response of CLEC-treated animals seemed to correspond to the period of improved wound healing compared to the HSG-treated animals. While it is not clear what causes this tapering effect, it might be attributed to the immunoregulatory effects mediated by CLECs as previously reported [8], or it might be due to the difference in the duration of CLECs and HSGs (along with their residues) that persisted on their respective wound bed after topical application. Based on clinical observation and assessment, we detected neither any adverse reaction nor overt immune rejection in animals of the CLEC and "untreated" groups. Swellings and sloughs were found only on the HSG-treated wound beds at Week 2.

4. Materials and Methods

4.1. Isolation and Culture of Human Cord Lining Epithelial Cells (CLECs)

Four lines of human CLECs were provided by CellResearch Corp, Singapore (see information in Supplementary Table S1). These cells were isolated from the lining membrane of human umbilical cords according to previously described protocols [8]. Briefly, human umbilical cord tissues were obtained after delivery of uncomplicated pregnancies with written informed consent from healthy donors based on the ethics approval given by the National University of Singapore. Dissection of the umbilical cord tissue was performed to separate the umbilical cord membrane from Wharton's jelly and other components. Sectioned small pieces of umbilical cord membrane were explanted on tissue culture dishes and the primary epithelial cells were allowed to grow out of these sections. Cultures of these CLECs were maintained in PTT-e3 medium (CellResearch Corp, Singapore) that is made up of medium 171 (Cascade Biologics, Portland, OR, USA) supplemented 2.5% fetal bovine serum (FBS), 50 μg/mL insulin-like growth factor-1 (IGF-1), 50 μg/mL platelet-derived growth factor-BB (PDGF-BB), 5 μg/mL transforming growth factor-β1 (TGF-β1), and 5 μg/mL insulin. CLECs from passages 2 to 6 were used for downstream in vitro and in vivo experiments.

4.2. Isolation and Culture of Human Skin Keratinocytes (KCs)

Four lines of human KCs (see information in Supplementary Table S1) were isolated from the waste foreskin of healthy subjects that were donated with informed consent and approved by the ethics review board of SingHealth. Briefly, the collected skin tissue was washed in phosphate-buffered saline (PBS, Lonza, Walkersville, MD, USA) and incubated in 10 mL of 2.5 $mgmL^{-1}$ Dispase II (Roche, Mannheim, Germany) in Dulbecco's modified Eagle medium (DMEM, Gibco, Thermo Fisher Scientific, Grand Island, NY, USA) and left overnight at 4 °C. The following day, epidermis was mechanically separated from dermis with fine forceps and incubated in 0.05% trypsin-EDTA solution (Gibco) for 15 min at 37 °C. Upon cellular dissociation, trypsin activity was reduced by diluting the solution with three volumes of fresh DMEM. KCs were then collected through centrifugation and resuspended in KGM-CD (Lonza) for downstream culture or cryopreservation. KCs were seeded at a density of 9×10^4 cells/cm^2 on 6-well plates (Corning, Sigma-Aldrich, New York, NY, USA) pre-coated with laminin 511 [27] and cultured in KGM-CD at 37 °C/7.5% CO_2 for further expansion. Cells between passages 2 to 6 were used for the in vitro experiments in this study.

4.3. Flow Cytometry (FC) and Analysis of Data

Isolated CLECs and KCs were collected from passages 3 to 5. Single-cell suspensions were fixed with Fixation Reagent (Medium A; Life Technologies, Thermo Fisher Scientific, Frederick, MD, USA) for 15 min at room temperature (RT), washed with FC buffer (0.5%

bovine serum albumin and 2 mM EDTA in 1× PBS), blocked with 5% goat serum in FC buffer and then immunostained with primary antibodies in Permeabilization Reagent (Medium B; Life Technologies) for 15 min at RT. Primary antibodies and their used dilution factor are shown in Supplementary Table S2. This would be followed by detection with secondary antibodies diluted with 1% goat serum in FACS buffer. Secondary antibodies used included rabbit anti-mouse FITC (1:1000, Dako, Glostrup, Denmark), Alexa Fluor 647-conjugated goat anti-rabbit (1:1000, Life Technologies, Carlsbad, CA, USA), and Alexa Fluor 647-conjugated goat anti-mouse (1:1000, Life Technologies). For fluorophore-conjugated antibodies, fixed cells were incubated with antibodies diluted in Medium B and human FcR blocking reagent (1:50, Miltenyi Biotec, Bergisch Gladbach, Germany) for 30 min at RT. Stained cells were resuspended in FC buffer and subjected to analysis (MACSQuant VYB, Miltenyi Biotec) with two technical duplicates for each cell type. FC data were analyzed using MACSQuantify (Miltenyi Biotec) software based on gated live cells.

4.4. Reconstruction of Epithelium on De-Epithelialized Dermis (Organotypic Culture)

The epidermis of glycerol-preserved split thickness allogeneic skin tissue (EURO SKIN BANK, EA Beverwijk, Netherland) was mechanically removed after several cycles of snap-freezing in liquid nitrogen and thawing. The remaining de-epithelialized dermis (DED) was cut into 2 × 2 cm squares and with the reticular side of the dermis facing up placed on a 6-well 0.4 µm pore size transparent PET membrane insert (Falcon, Corning, Durham, NC, USA). This insert was then placed within one well of a 6-deep well plate (Corning) and the dermal skin seeded with 5×10^5 human dermal fibroblasts (see information in Supplementary Table S1) in 50 µL of DMEM with 10% fetal bovine serum (FBS, Hyclone, Logan, UT, USA). After 30 min, the entire fibroblast-seeded skin was cultured submerged in DMEM with 10% FBS.

The following day, the DED was flipped over and 2×10^5 of fresh KCs or CLECs (in 50µL of medium) was seeded separately on individual DED. After 30 min, the entire organotypic culture was cultured in submerged medium for 7 days in complete F12 and DMEM (cFAD) medium that were changed every 2–3 days. Subsequently, these cultures were lifted to an air–liquid interface to stratify in the same cFAD medium for another 14 days as previously described [28]. Each sample was then processed and cryosectioned for both H&E and immunostaining.

4.5. Porcine Full Thickness Excisional Wound Model

Healthy, stress-free Yorkshire-Landrace (Sus scrofa) pigs matched for age (12 weeks old), weight, and sex (female) were obtained from the National Large Animal Research Facility, Singapore. The animal experiments were executed in accordance with the National Advisory Committee for Laboratory Animal Research. These immunocompetent pigs were intramuscularly pre-medicated with ketamine/diazepam and anesthesia maintained with 2% isoflurane. After removal of the dorsal hair at the thoracic region with hair clippers, the exposed skin region was cleaned with chlorhexidine and 70% isopropyl alcohol solution. A template was used to define a total of six wound sites—three bilateral wounds on each side of the back spine on the thoracic region. Each wound measured 5 cm × 5 cm was first tattooed followed by use of no.15 blade to excise each of the marked area to create a full thickness wound (Supplementary Figure S2).

Two configurations of treatment (Figure 4) were used to test the efficacy of fresh human CLECs applied topically to the six full thickness wounds created on each pig. The number of pigs used were worked out based on the 3 Rs principle in animal experimentation [29].

Configuration 1: As a form of screening, a total of two pigs with each of them subjected to three parallel arms of treatment were compared for wound healing performance over a period of 7 weeks (Figure 4a). The three treatment arms were: (a) fresh human CLECs applied topically as a cell pellet layer with a density of 10^5 cells/cm2, followed by coverage with standard wound dressings (CLEC); (b) cryopreserved human skin allografts (HSG) consented for research from the Singapore General Hospital Skin Bank [25] (Supplementary

Table S1), anchored with 4/0 Vicryl sutures followed by coverage with standard dressings; and (c) standard wound dressing coverage alone ("Untreated").

Configuration 2: Using a total of six pigs (separated into two sets of three pigs), each of the treatment arms mentioned in configuration 1 were used in its entirety on all six wounds per pig (Figure 4b). This was to eliminate the potential confounding effect to the systemic response on wound healing due to the multiple treatments on the same pig as used in configuration 1. In this configuration, one of the wounds was designated for skin punch biopsy samples to be collected for further histological analysis but would not be used in wound analysis. In Set A of configuration 2, the wounds were followed up for 7 weeks, while in Set B the pigs of the respective treatment arms were sacrificed once the average closure of all wounds on the pig achieved 90% or above.

In the two above-described configurations, all treatment arms were applied on the created wounds at Day 0. Analgesics (Carprofen 2–4 mg/kg) were given prior to all procedures that caused distress/pain and when necessary, based on the vet's discretion. The standard wound dressings consisted of Jelonet (Smith & Nephew, Hull, UK) sterile paraffin tulle gras dressing as the first layer applied to the wound with a secondary overlay of bulky dry gauze dressings to provide some degree of bolstering and a final layer of Opsite (Smith & Nephew) transparent adhesive film dressing. All wound dressings were further secured by crepe bandages wrapped around the torso of the animal, secured with an outer animal jacket, and changed weekly during wound inspections.

4.6. Wound Healing Analysis

During the weekly wound dressing changes and inspections, the wounds were gently washed with saline to remove any debris before digital images of the wounds were taken. These images were analyzed with an open-source digital imaging software, MacBiophotonics ImageJ^{TM} (National Institutes of Health, Bethesda, MD, USA) for the rate of wound closure across all of the three treatment arms over the assessment period. Complete wound closure was defined as 100% re-epithelization without drainage. The equation (original wound area—new wound area)/original wound area × 100% was used to calculate percentage of wound closure. For Masson's Trichome (MT) and immunohistochemistry (IHC) stainings, 5 mm punch skin biopsies were also taken weekly from a single designated wound of each pig, and these wounds were excluded for wound healing assessment.

4.7. Histological Staining and Analysis

Human organotypic cultures were embedded in OCT compound and snap-frozen in liquid nitrogen. The OCT blocks were sectioned into 7 μm sections onto a glass slide using CM1900 or CM1850 cryostat (Leica Biosystems, Wetzlar, Germany), stained with H&E on Autostainer XL (Leica Biosystems), according to standard protocol [30]. These sections were also immunostained to determine the presence of epithelial markers and adhesion molecules. Briefly, the sections were fixed in 4% paraformaldehyde in 1× PBS for 15 min and permeabilized in PBS/0.1% Triton X-100 solution for 5 min. Samples were washed three times with PBS, followed by blocking with 5% goat serum for 15 min and incubation with primary antibodies overnight at 4 °C. Primary antibodies and their used dilution factor are shown in Supplementary Table S2. Following washes with PBS, the samples were incubated with fluorescence-labeled secondary antibodies for 1 h at RT to visualize the antigens. Secondary antibodies used included Alexa-Fluor 647-conjugated goat anti-mouse (1:1000, Life Technologies), Alexa-Fluor 488-conjugated goat anti-mouse (1:1000, Life Technologies), and Alexa-Fluor 488-conjugated goat anti-rabbit (1:1000, Life Technologies). Thereafter, nuclei of the samples were counterstained and mounted with ProLong^{TM} Gold Antifade Reagent with DAPI (Life Technologies) and visualized under a Leica DMi8 fluorescent Microscope (Leica Biosystems).

Next, porcine skin punch biopsies were embedded in paraffin and sectioned into 4 μm slices onto glass slides using Microtome RM2235 (Leica Biosystems). Sections were processed according to the standard protocol for MT and IHC stainings. In the IHC stains, mouse anti-CD4 (1:50, Biorad, Hercules, CA, USA) and mouse anti-CD8 (1:100, Biorad) were used to stain the pig skin samples on Leica Bond III Automated Stainers (Leica Biosystems). The following were the default automated staining protocol (IHC DAB1 Leica Bond III): dewaxing at 72 °C, pre-treatment (unmasking) with Bond epitope retrieval solution 2 and wash steps using absolute alcohol and Bond Wash Solution, staining with primary antibodies, and detection using Bond™ Polymer Refine Detection. After staining, the slides were dehydrated in absolute alcohol, cleared with xylene, and finally mounted in depex. The stained slides were subsequently scanned using Ultra-Fast Scanner 1.6 (Philips, Amsterdam, The Netherlands).

Semi-quantitative analyses were respectively performed on the MT [15] and IHC [16] (blinded) stains by a pathologist.

4.8. Milliplex Cytokine Array

Porcine whole bloods were obtained weekly from pre-operation till Week 7 post excisional wound procedure. The bloods were centrifuged and the serum that was obtained was stored at −80 °C. Pre-operation serums were used as the baseline for the respective treatment groups. Anti-inflammatory and pro-inflammatory cytokines (GM-CSF, IFN-γ, IL-1α, IL-1β, IL-2, IL-4, IL-6, IL-8, IL-10, IL-12, IL-18, and TNFα) present in the porcine serum were detected through the use of Milliplex Porcine Cytokine/Chemokine Magnetic Bead Panel Kit (EMD Millipore Corporation, Burlington, MA, USA), performed in duplicates or triplicates according to the manufacturer's protocol with Luminex Sheath Fluid (Luminex Corporation, Austin, TX, USA) and handheld magnetic separation block (EMD Millipore Corporation). The detection of cytokines levels was subsequently analyzed using Luminex 200 software (Luminex Corporation).

4.9. Statistical Analysis

Statistical analysis using one-way ANOVA with Bonferroni's post-test was used for the comparison for the percentage of positively stained cells taken from three different donors for CLECs or KCs with two technical duplicates in flow cytometry analysis, as well as on tattooed wound contraction when the animals were sacrificed across the three treatment arms of CLEC, HSG, and standard dressings (no treatment). Two-way repeated measures ANOVA with Bonferroni's post-test was used to analyze and to compare the percentage of wound closure on the weekly inspected porcine wounds managed by the three treatment arms. All statistical analyses were performed using GraphPad Prism software (version 5.01) for Windows (GraphPad Software Inc., San Diego, CA, USA).

5. Conclusions

In summary, while CLECs were previously purported to have common features of KCs at the morphological, molecular, and functional level [13], as well as having stem cell-like properties [20], we found significantly lower expression levels of *ITGB1* and *KRT15* in CLECs based on flow cytometry analysis. These two markers were previously associated with the basal and the epidermal stem cell characteristics of KCs [22,31]. We further confirmed the capability of CLECs to fully stratify in skin organotypic cultures even though the generated epithelium appeared less mature compared to the one formed by KCs. In addition, the location of basal/epidermal stem cell markers of *KRT14*, *KRT15*, and *p63* were found to be expressed at both the basal and the suprabasal layers in the CLEC-generated epithelium, unlike in the KC-generated epithelium which was restricted mainly to the basal layer. Despite these discrepancies with KCs, CLECs administered topically on full thickness skin wounds in the pig, was able to accelerate healing with no observed adverse reaction and overt immune rejection. While further in vivo work is needed to delineate the mechanisms behind the improved healing and transplantation immunology, this first-in-porcine study using CLECs demonstrates the safety and the potential of these cells as a non-native source to provide an epithelial barrier and promote wound healing.

Supplementary Materials: The following supporting information can be downloaded at: https://www.mdpi.com/article/10.3390/ijms23168918/s1.

Author Contributions: Conceptualization, J.E.H.K., T.T.P. and A.W.C.C.; data curation, C.W.S. and W.K.L.; formal analysis, C.W.S., W.K.L. and J.Y.; investigation, J.E.H.K. and C.W.S.; methodology, J.E.H.K., M.S.T., J.Y. and J.M.; resources, T.T.P., T.K.H.L. and A.W.C.C.; validation, W.K.L.; supervision, T.K.H.L. and A.W.C.C.; writing—original draft preparation, J.E.H.K., C.W.S. and W.K.L.; writing—review and editing, J.E.H.K., M.S.T. and A.W.C.C. All authors have read and agreed to the published version of the manuscript.

Funding: This work was supported by grants from the National Medical Research Council, Ministry of Health, Singapore (NMRC/CNIG/1106/2013 and OFIRG20nov-0024).

Institutional Review Board Statement: The study was conducted in accordance with the Declaration of Helsinki and approved by the Institutional Review Board of the National University of Singapore (NUS-IRB Reference Code: 10-389) and SingHealth Centralised Institutional Review Board (CIRB#2014/283/D). The animal study was reviewed and approved by SingHealth Institutional Animal Care and Use Committee (IACUC Reference #: 2013/SHS/881).

Informed Consent Statement: Informed consent was obtained from all subjects involved in the study.

Data Availability Statement: The raw data supporting the conclusions of this article will be made available by the authors, without undue reservation.

Acknowledgments: The authors are grateful to Stephanie Fook-Chong from the Singapore General Hospital (SGH) Health Services Research Unit for her biostatistics advice; Jie Hua Loh and Xin Xiu Sam from SGH Anatomical Pathology for their assistance and coordination of the histology work; Chuan Han Ang from SGH Plastic, Reconstructive & Aesthetic Surgery, Sebastian Jose David and Irene Kee from the SingHealth Experimental Medical Centre for assistance and advice on animal surgical procedures. Finally, our sincere thanks to all the ex-interns attached to the SGH Skin Bank Unit for their support in animal handling, related laboratory procedures, and research efforts.

Conflicts of Interest: The following authors declare a potential conflict of interest. T.T.P. is a founder and a major shareholder of CellResearch Corp Pte. Ltd., Singapore; J.M. is an employee and AWCC was an external consultant to the same company.

References

1. Hirsch, T.; Rothoeft, T.; Teig, N.; Bauer, J.W.; Pellegrini, G.; De Rosa, L.; Scaglione, D.; Reichelt, J.; Klausegger, A.; Kneisz, D.; et al. Regeneration of the entire human epidermis using transgenic stem cells. *Nature* **2017**, *551*, 327–332. [CrossRef] [PubMed]
2. Williams, F.N.; Herndon, D.N.; Hawkins, H.K.; Lee, J.O.; Cox, R.A.; Kulp, G.A.; Finnerty, C.C.; Chinkes, D.L.; Jeschke, M.G. The leading causes of death after burn injury in a single pediatric burn center. *Crit. Care* **2009**, *13*, R183. [CrossRef] [PubMed]
3. D'Avignon, L.C.; Hogan, B.K.; Murray, C.K.; Loo, F.L.; Hospenthal, D.R.; Cancio, L.C.; Kim, S.H.; Renz, E.M.; Barillo, D.; Holcomb, J.B.; et al. Contribution of bacterial and viral infections to attributable mortality in patients with severe burns: An autopsy series. *Burn. J. Int. Soc. Burn Inj.* **2010**, *36*, 773–779. [CrossRef]
4. Chim, H.; Tan, B.H.; Song, C. Five-year review of infections in a burn intensive care unit: High incidence of Acinetobacter baumannii in a tropical climate. *Burn. J. Int. Soc. Burn Inj.* **2007**, *33*, 1008–1014. [CrossRef]
5. Song, C.T.; Hwee, J.; Song, C.; Tan, B.K.; Chong, S.J. Burns infection profile of Singapore: Prevalence of multidrug-resistant Acinetobacter baumannii and the role of blood cultures. *Burn. Trauma* **2016**, *4*, 13. [CrossRef] [PubMed]
6. Krueger, J.G.; Lin, A.N.; Leong, I.; Carter, D.M. Junctional epidermolysis bullosa keratinocytes in culture display adhesive, structural, and functional abnormalities. *J. Investig. Dermatol.* **1991**, *97*, 849–861. [CrossRef]
7. Morley, S.M.; D'Alessandro, M.; Sexton, C.; Rugg, E.L.; Navsaria, H.; Shemanko, C.S.; Huber, M.; Hohl, D.; Heagerty, A.I.; Leigh, I.M.; et al. Generation and characterization of epidermolysis bullosa simplex cell lines: Scratch assays show faster migration with disruptive keratin mutations. *Br. J. Dermatol.* **2003**, *149*, 46–58. [CrossRef]
8. Zhou, Y.; Gan, S.U.; Lin, G.; Lim, Y.T.; Masilamani, J.; Mustafa, F.B.; Phua, M.L.; Rivino, L.; Phan, T.T.; Lee, K.O.; et al. Characterization of human umbilical cord lining-derived epithelial cells and transplantation potential. *Cell Transplant.* **2011**, *20*, 1827–1841. [CrossRef]
9. Sivalingam, J.; Krishnan, S.; Ng, W.H.; Lee, S.S.; Phan, T.T.; Kon, O.L. Biosafety assessment of site-directed transgene integration in human umbilical cord-lining cells. *Mol. Ther. J. Am. Soc. Gene Ther.* **2010**, *18*, 1346–1356. [CrossRef]
10. Gubar, O.S.; Rodnichenko, A.E.; Vasyliev, R.G.; Zlatska, A.V.; Zubov, D.O. Postnatal extra-embryonic tissues as a source of multiple cell types for regenerative medicine applications. *Exp. Oncol.* **2017**, *39*, 186–190. [CrossRef]

11. Hayward, C.J.; Fradette, J.; Galbraith, T.; Remy, M.; Guignard, R.; Gauvin, R.; Germain, L.; Auger, F.A. Harvesting the potential of the human umbilical cord: Isolation and characterisation of four cell types for tissue engineering applications. *Cells Tissues Organs* **2013**, *197*, 37–54. [CrossRef] [PubMed]
12. Mizoguchi, M.; Ikeda, S.; Suga, Y.; Ogawa, H. Expression of cytokeratins and cornified cell envelope-associated proteins in umbilical cord epithelium: A comparative study of the umbilical cord, amniotic epithelia and fetal skin. *J. Investig. Dermatol.* **2000**, *115*, 133–134. [CrossRef] [PubMed]
13. Ruetze, M.; Gallinat, S.; Lim, I.J.; Chow, E.; Phan, T.T.; Staeb, F.; Wenck, H.; Deppert, W.; Knott, A. Common features of umbilical cord epithelial cells and epidermal keratinocytes. *J. Dermatol. Sci.* **2008**, *50*, 227–231. [CrossRef] [PubMed]
14. Cai, Y.J.; Huang, L.; Leung, T.Y.; Burd, A. A study of the immune properties of human umbilical cord lining epithelial cells. *Cytotherapy* **2014**, *16*, 631–639. [CrossRef] [PubMed]
15. Marcos-Garcés, V.; Harvat, M.; Molina Aguilar, P.; Ferrández Izquierdo, A.; Ruiz-Saurí, A. Comparative measurement of collagen bundle orientation by Fourier analysis and semiquantitative evaluation: Reliability and agreement in Masson's trichrome, Picrosirius red and confocal microscopy techniques. *J. Microsc.* **2017**, *267*, 130–142. [CrossRef]
16. Richters, C.D.; Hoekstra, M.J.; du Pont, J.S.; Kreis, R.W.; Kamperdijk, E.W. Immunology of skin transplantation. *Clin. Dermatol.* **2005**, *23*, 338–342. [CrossRef]
17. Nishida, K.; Yamato, M.; Hayashida, Y.; Watanabe, K.; Yamamoto, K.; Adachi, E.; Nagai, S.; Kikuchi, A.; Maeda, N.; Watanabe, H.; et al. Corneal reconstruction with tissue-engineered cell sheets composed of autologous oral mucosal epithelium. *N. Engl. J. Med.* **2004**, *351*, 1187–1196. [CrossRef]
18. Utheim, T.P.; Utheim, O.A.; Khan, Q.E.; Sehic, A. Culture of Oral Mucosal Epithelial Cells for the Purpose of Treating Limbal Stem Cell Deficiency. *J. Funct. Biomater.* **2016**, *7*, 5. [CrossRef]
19. Gallant-Behm, C.L.; Hart, D.A. Genetic analysis of skin wound healing and scarring in a porcine model. *Wound Repair Regen. Off. Publ. Wound Heal. Soc. Eur. Tissue Repair Soc.* **2006**, *14*, 46–54. [CrossRef]
20. Huang, L.; Wong, Y.P.; Gu, H.; Cai, Y.J.; Ho, Y.; Wang, C.C.; Leung, T.Y.; Burd, A. Stem cell-like properties of human umbilical cord lining epithelial cells and the potential for epidermal reconstitution. *Cytotherapy* **2011**, *13*, 145–155. [CrossRef]
21. Webb, A.; Li, A.; Kaur, P. Location and phenotype of human adult keratinocyte stem cells of the skin. *Differ. Res. Biol. Divers.* **2004**, *72*, 387–395. [CrossRef] [PubMed]
22. Bose, A.; Teh, M.T.; Mackenzie, I.C.; Waseem, A. Keratin k15 as a biomarker of epidermal stem cells. *Int. J. Mol. Sci.* **2013**, *14*, 19385–19398. [CrossRef] [PubMed]
23. Seaton, M.; Hocking, A.; Gibran, N.S. Porcine models of cutaneous wound healing. *ILAR J.* **2015**, *56*, 127–138. [CrossRef] [PubMed]
24. Chiu, T.; Burd, A. "Xenograft" dressing in the treatment of burns. *Clin. Dermatol.* **2005**, *23*, 419–423. [CrossRef]
25. Chua, A.; Song, C.; Chai, A.; Chan, L.; Tan, K.C. The impact of skin banking and the use of its cadaveric skin allografts for severe burn victims in Singapore. *Burn. J. Int. Soc. Burn Inj.* **2004**, *30*, 696–700. [CrossRef] [PubMed]
26. Chen, L.; Mehta, N.D.; Zhao, Y.; DiPietro, L.A. Absence of CD4 or CD8 lymphocytes changes infiltration of inflammatory cells and profiles of cytokine expression in skin wounds, but does not impair healing. *Exp Derm.* **2014**, *23*, 189–194. [CrossRef]
27. Tjin, M.S.; Chua, A.W.C.; Tryggvason, K. Chemically defined and xenogeneic-free culture method for human epidermal keratinocytes on laminin-based matrices. *Nat. Protoc.* **2020**, *15*, 694–711. [CrossRef]
28. Tjin, M.S.; Chua, A.W.C.; Moreno-Moral, A.; Chong, L.Y.; Tang, P.Y.; Harmston, N.P.; Cai, Z.; Petretto, E.; Tan, B.K.; Tryggvason, K. Biologically relevant laminin as chemically defined and fully human platform for human epidermal keratinocyte culture. *Nat. Commun.* **2018**, *9*, 4432. [CrossRef]
29. Kirk, R.G.W. Recovering The Principles of Humane Experimental Technique: The 3Rs and the Human Essence of Animal Research. *Sci. Technol. Hum. Values* **2018**, *43*, 622–648. [CrossRef]
30. Fischer, A.H.; Jacobson, K.A.; Rose, J.; Zeller, R. Hematoxylin and eosin staining of tissue and cell sections. *CSH Protoc.* **2008**, *2008*, pdb.prot4986. [CrossRef]
31. Jones, P.H.; Watt, F.M. Separation of human epidermal stem cells from transit amplifying cells on the basis of differences in integrin function and expression. *Cell* **1993**, *73*, 713–724. [CrossRef]

International Journal of
Molecular Sciences

MDPI

Article

In Vitro Wound Healing Properties of Novel Acidic Treatment Regimen in Enhancing Metabolic Activity and Migration of Skin Cells

Pivian Sim [1], Yunmei Song [1], Gink N. Yang [2], Allison J. Cowin [2] and Sanjay Garg [1,*]

1 Centre for Pharmaceutical Innovation (CPI)Clinical and Health Sciences, University of South Australia, Adelaide, SA 5000, Australia; simpy010@mymail.unisa.edu.au (P.S.); may.song@unisa.edu.au (Y.S.)
2 Regenerative Medicine, Future Industries Institute, University of South Australia, Adelaide, SA 5095, Australia; gink.yang@mymail.unisa.edu.au (G.N.Y.); allison.cowin@unisa.edu.au (A.J.C.)
* Correspondence: sanjay.garg@unisa.edu.au; Tel.: +61-883021575

Abstract: Strategies that alter the pH of wounds to improve healing outcomes are an emerging area of interest. Currently, there is limited understanding of the effect of hydrogen (H^+) on the functionality of skin cells during proliferation and migration, highlighting the need for research to determine the effect of pH during wound healing. This study aimed to determine the effect of acidification on the metabolic activity and migration of human immortalized keratinocytes (HaCaT) and human foreskin fibroblasts (HFF). In vitro models were used with phosphoric and citric acid buffers at a pH range between 3 and 7. Our results showed that cells were more viable in buffers with low rather than high ionic strength. A time-dependent effect of the acidification treatment was also observed with cell metabolic activity varying with treatment duration and frequency. Our results showed that a 24 h treatment and subsequent resting phase significantly improved cell proliferation and migration. This in vitro study is the first to establish a correlation between the role of acidic pH, molarity and treatment regimen in cellular activity. Our data demonstrated a positive effect of acidic pH on cell metabolic activity and migration rate, suggesting a clinical potential in indications such as wound healing.

Keywords: acidic; buffer; ionic strength; pH; proliferation; metabolic activity; migration; skin; treatment; wound healing

Citation: Sim, P.; Song, Y.; Yang, G.N.; Cowin, A.J.; Garg, S. In Vitro Wound Healing Properties of Novel Acidic Treatment Regimen in Enhancing Metabolic Activity and Migration of Skin Cells. *Int. J. Mol. Sci.* **2022**, *23*, 7188. https://doi.org/10.3390/ijms23137188

Academic Editors: Cinzia Pagano, César Viseras and Luana Perioli

Received: 22 May 2022
Accepted: 24 June 2022
Published: 28 June 2022

Publisher's Note: MDPI stays neutral with regard to jurisdictional claims in published maps and institutional affiliations.

1. Introduction

Under normal conditions, the outer environment of the skin maintains an acidic pH in the range of 4 to 6. When the skin barrier is damaged, the natural acidic pH of the skin is disrupted by the physiological pH of the underlying tissue. This change in microenvironment from acidic to physiological pH has been shown to affect wound healing [1,2]. Understanding how the acidification of the wound microenvironment affects different processes of healing is an emerging area of interest.

Studies have shown that decreasing wound pH by acidification improves the dynamic regeneration of wounds by supporting cellular processes within the healing cascade. Ascorbic acid, commonly known as vitamin C, has been proven to enhance dermal fibroblast proliferation and migration in vitro [3]. Retinoic acid, an active metabolite of vitamin A, has been found to elevate collagen synthesis in vitro [4]. Treatment using folic acid and its derivatives show increased DNA synthesis and repair, whilst hyaluronic acid has been reported to support extracellular matrix (ECM) synthesis by stimulating angiogenesis [5–8]. Cell migration, a key factor during re-epithelization and wound closure, is enhanced when treated with usnic acid, and this correlates to faster cellular repair in vitro [9,10]. Abietic acid shows a similar effect, presenting stimulatory effects on the migration of endothelial cells [11,12]. Syringic acid has been reported to accelerate wound regeneration by increasing cell re-epithelialization and collagen synthesis in diabetic wounds [13,14]. Additionally, fumaric acid can enhance fibroblast proliferation, granulation tissue formation, collagen synthesis and angiogenesis in vivo [15,16].

An acidic microenvironment can influence microbial growth in skin wounds by imparting an inhospitable environment for bacterial growth that neutralizes ammonia toxicity produced by skin microorganisms such as *Pseudomonas aeruginosa*, commonly present in chronic wounds [17,18]. Furthermore, the stimulative effect of acidification on wound healing has been correlated to increased oxygenation at the wound site. Reduction in wound pH by 0.6 units using chemical acidification has been shown to increase the amount of oxygen released from oxyhemoglobin by an additional 50%. Higher wound oxygen saturation is known to promote fibroblast growth, collagen synthesis and epithelialization [17]. Inducing an alkaline microenvironment in wounded tissues causes a paradoxical effect, lowering wound oxygen concentration and tension, resulting in an increase in ammonia toxicity that delays the process of epithelialization and wound closure [17,18]. Whilst acidification of the wound microenvironment is known to promote wound regeneration, there is little understanding of how different types of acids, pH values and ionic strength affect the wound healing process.

The present study utilized in vitro methods to determine the effect of acidic culturing conditions on cell proliferation and migration in keratinocytes and fibroblasts. This study aimed to establish the effect of acidic pH, molarity (ionic strength) and dosing regimen on cellular functions. The tetrazolium MTT metabolic assay and scratch migration assay were used to investigate the effect of phosphoric and citric acids, with different pH values and treatment durations, on cell viability and migration.

2. Results

2.1. Low Ionic Strength Increases Metabolic Activity of Keratinocytes

The effect of acids' ionic strength (molarity) on the metabolic activity of primary keratinocyte (HaCaT) cells was investigated using an MTT assay following treatment regimen A (Table 1). A 24 h acidification process over a 3 day treatment period was used to study the effect of high- (0.1 M) and low-ionic-strength (0.01 M) phosphoric acid at pH 4 (PA-4), as shown in Figure 1. The study showed that initial (Day 1) HaCaT cells remained viable in buffers with both high- and low-ionic-strength phosphoric acid, and acidification had a positive effect on cell metabolic activity (approximately 30% and 20%, respectively) in comparison to that of the control group (DMEM-7). Subsequent treatment (Day 2 to Day 3) with low-ionic-strength phosphoric acid (0.01 M) had little effect on cell viability. However, HaCaT cells treated with high-ionic-strength (0.1 M) phosphoric acid showed a significant decrease in cell viability after Day 1 treatment, from 118% to 50% (Day 2) and subsequently to 21% (Day 3). The results showed that a decrease in percentage viability of the treatment groups were not due to the treatment protocol. These findings suggest that HaCaT cells did not tolerate a high-ionic-strength acidic buffer.

Table 1. Summary of treatment regimens.

Treatment Regimen	Protocol	
	Treatment Period (Hour)	**Resting Period (Hour)**
A	24	-
B	12	24
C	24	24

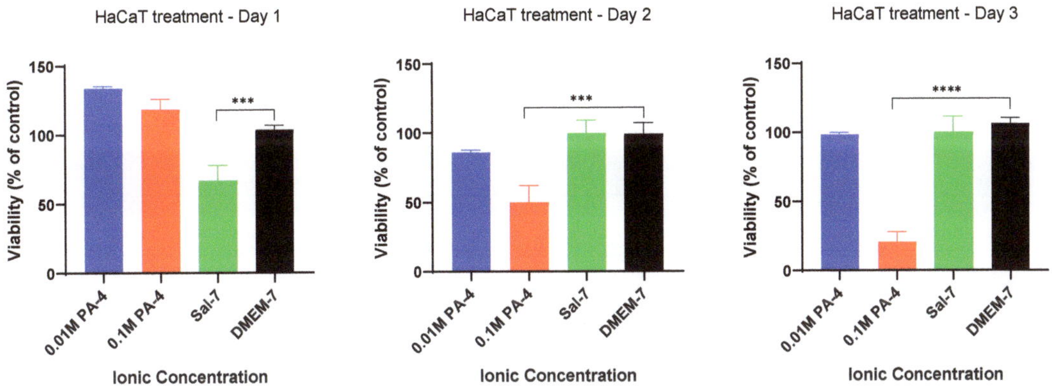

Figure 1. HaCaT cells metabolized well at low ionic strength and acid molarity of 0.01 M. The metabolism rate was significantly reduced with increased acid molarity to 0.1 M. Each bar represents the mean ± standard deviation. *** $p < 0.005$ and **** $p < 0.001$ indicates that the results obtained were statistically significant from those of the control group (DMEM-7).

2.2. Acidification Enhances Metabolic Activity of Keratinocytes and Fibroblasts

The metabolic activity of acidified keratinocytes (HaCaT) and fibroblasts (HFF) were studied following treatment by acidification per regimen A (Table 1). This regimen consisted of continuous acidification with low-ionic-strength (0.01 M) phosphoric and citric acid buffers at a pH ranging from 3 to 7. As shown in Figure 2a, a significant increase in cellular metabolic activity for the initial 24 h treatment (Day 1) was observed in HaCaT cells when treated with phosphoric acid buffers. The rate of metabolism was measured to be significantly higher ($p < 0.05$) in all treatment groups when compared to that of the control group (DMEM-7). However, cells in media treated with further PA-3 to PA-7 acidification (Day 2) showed a decrease in metabolic activity (Figure 2a). In contrast, cells subsequently treated (Day 2) with citric acid buffers remained viable in buffers with pH 5 and 6 and showed a significant increase in metabolic activity on Day 2 (Figure 2b).

This treatment regimen was also investigated on fibroblasts (HFF) following a similar protocol. Similarly, HFF cells remained viable when treated with acidic buffers at pH ranging from 3 to 6 for the first 24 h (Day 1) (Figure 3). The results also demonstrated an increase in metabolic activity by a further 29%, 39% and 30%, respectively, when media were added with phosphoric acid with a pH adjusted to 4, 5 and 7, as shown in Figure 4a. HFF cells tolerated the change in pH and showed little changes in overall metabolic activity on subsequent citric acid treatment (Day 2) at all pH ranges from CA-3 to CA-7 (Figure 4b). Contrasting results were obtained for Day 2 treatment by both acidic buffers in both HaCaT and HFF cells.

2.3. Metabolic Activity Influenced by pH and Time-Dependent Acidification

To investigate if cell metabolic activity was affected by the duration of acidification, a different treatment regimen (treatment regimen B) was tested. Treatment regimen B consisted of an acidic buffer treatment for 12 h, followed by a 24 h resting interval involving replacing the acidified medium with a DMEM solution. Metabolic activity was then assessed after 72 h as described in Table 1. The results demonstrated that acidification following treatment regimen B showed that HaCaT cells did not tolerate acidification treatment with low pH 3–6 of phosphoric and citric acid buffers, demonstrating low percentage cell viability in comparison to that of the control group (DMEM-7) throughout the treatment period, as shown in Figure 4. However, better tolerance and higher viability of HaCaT cells were observed when treated with phosphoric acid (PA-6 and PA-7) and citric acid (CA-6 and CA-7) buffers at a pH range closer to physiological pH, in comparison to lower-acidic-pH-treated cells. Percentage cell viability higher by 50%was observed in HaCaT cells when treated with a phosphoric acid pH 7 buffer (PA-7) in comparison to that of control (DMEM-7), as shown in Figure 4a. An increase in metabolic activity of approximately 20% to 40% (p-value < 0.001) was also observed in HaCaT cells following treatment with citric acid at pH 7 (CA-7) (Figure 4b). These findings indicate that shorter treatment intervals of 12 h in the treatment protocol were not effective in increasing cell growth.

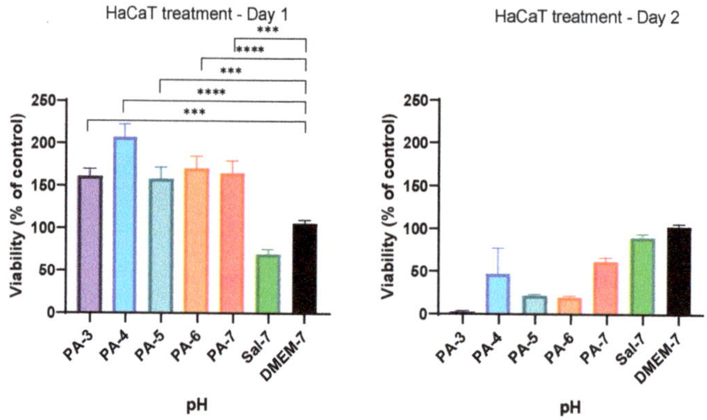

(a)

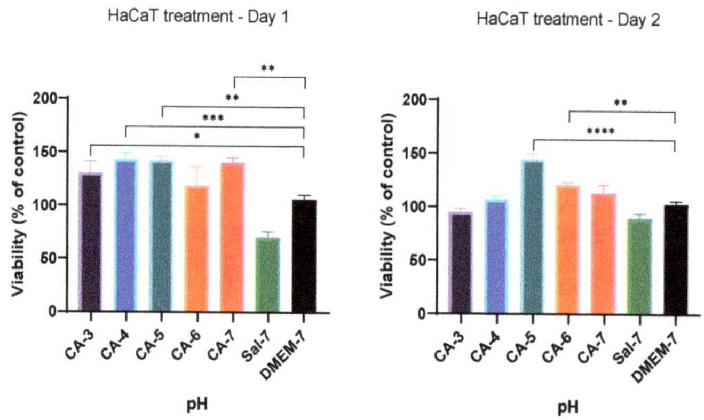

(b)

Figure 2. Percentage viability of HaCaT cells when treated with (**a**) 0.01 M phosphoric acid (PA) buffer solutions, with pH ranges from 3 to 7 and (**b**) 0.01 M citric acid (CA) buffer solutions, with pH adjusted to 3, 4, 5, 6 and 7. HaCaT cells tolerated well within an acidic pH range of 3 to 7 for 24 h. Each bar represents the mean ± standard deviation. * $p < 0.05$, ** $p < 0.01$, *** $p < 0.005$ and **** $p < 0.001$ indicates that the results obtained were statistically significant from those of the control group (DMEM-7).

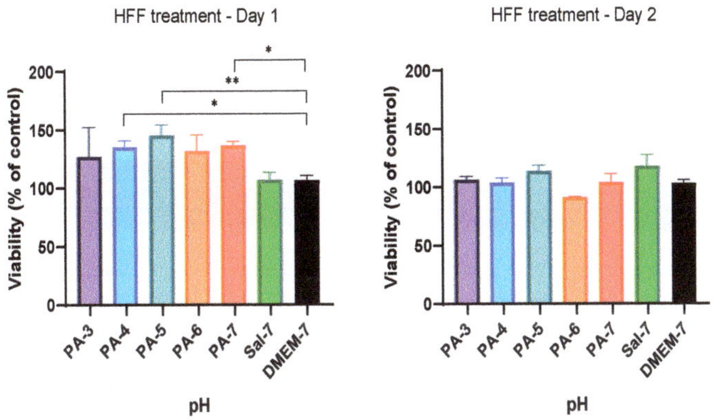

(a)

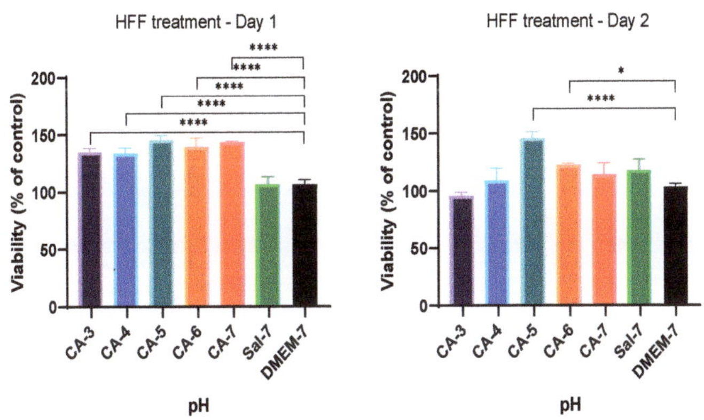

(b)

Figure 3. Percentage viability of HFF cells when treated with (**a**) 0.01 M phosphoric acid (PA) buffers with pH ranges from 3 to 7 and (**b**) 0.01 M citric acid (CA) buffers with pH values of 3, 4, 5, 6 and 7 utilizing the standardized MTT protocol of 24 h continuous treatment without a resting period. HFF cells metabolized well with phosphoric acid buffer treatments of pH 4, 5 and 7, while the metabolic rates of HFF cells were all statistically significant when treated with citric acid buffers at T = 24 h (Day 1). Each bar represents the mean ± standard deviation. * $p < 0.05$, ** $p < 0.01$ and **** $p < 0.001$ indicates that the results obtained were statistically significant from those of the control group (DMEM-7).

2.4. Treatment Regimen C Improves the Proliferation Rate

Based on the previous findings, a new treatment regimen was employed to study if cell metabolic activity was affected by the different duration of acidification treatment and the resting interval following treatment regimen C as described in Table 1. In summary, the treatment regimen employed a 24 h acidification treatment period before a subsequent 24 h standard culture medium replacement (resting period), and the metabolic activity was measured after every incubation period (24 h). The alteration in the treatment duration for both phosphoric (PA-3 to PA-7) and citric (CA-3 to CA-7) acidic buffers showed a significant improvement of the metabolic activity of HaCaT cells in comparison to that of DMEM-cultured cells (Figure 5). HaCaT cells tolerated the change in pH and showed increases in percentage cell viability of 15.72%, 10.51% and 8.82% at pH 4, 5 and 6 (PA-4 to PA-6) treatments when compared to that of HaCaT cells cultured in DMEM, respectively

(Figure 5a). Similarly, increases of 32.79%, 25.21% and 31.72% in percentage cell viability were observed in HaCaT cells when treated with citric acid buffers adjusted to pH 4, 5 and 6 (CA-4 to CA-6), respectively, indicating higher metabolic activity in these treatment groups (Figure 5b). Furthermore, HaCaT cells treated with both phosphoric and citric acid buffers with a 24 h resting period further improved the metabolic activity and percentage cell viability. Phosphoric acid treatment significantly increased cell viability by 44.00%, 45.02 and 25.08% for PA-4, PA-5 and PA-6, and citric acid treatment increased cell viability by 41.28%, 31.98 and 30.80% for CA-4, CA-5 and CA-6, respectively.

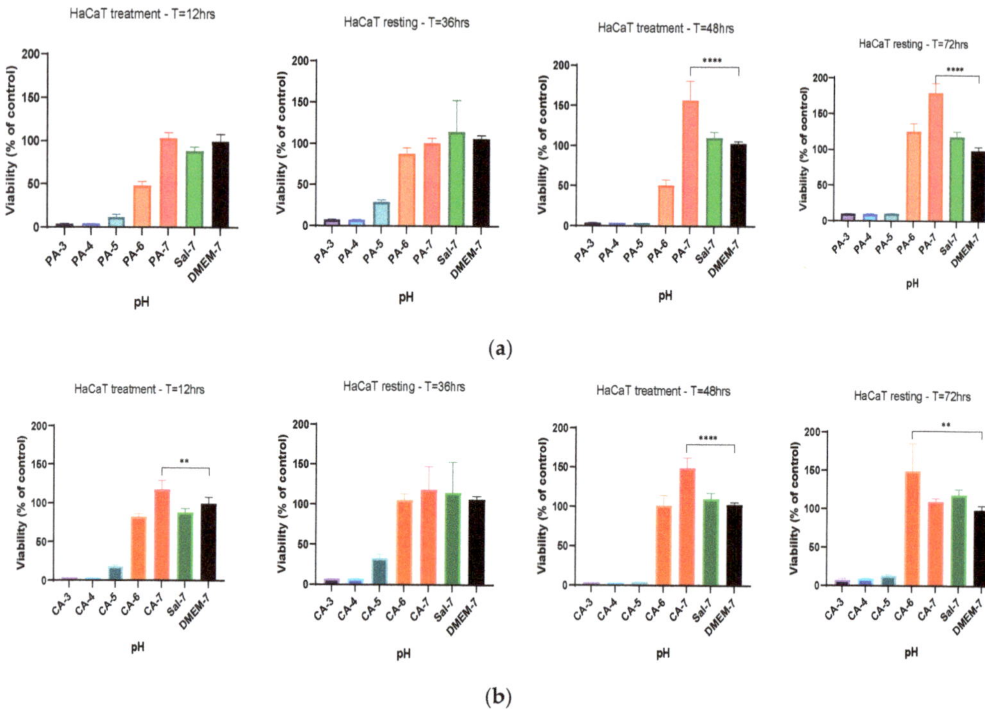

Figure 4. Percentage viability of HaCaT keratinocytes at different time points when treated with (**a**) 0.01 M phosphoric acid (PA) and (**b**) citric acid (CA) buffers, with pH adjusted to 3, 4, 5, 6 and 7. Each bar represents the mean ± standard deviation. ** $p < 0.01$ and **** $p < 0.001$ indicates that the results obtained were statistically significant from those of the control group (DMEM-7).

This treatment regimen was repeated on fibroblast (HFF) cells. A similar increment in percentage cell viability of HFF cells was observed when treated with both phosphoric and citric acid buffers. Similarly, initial 24 h acidification treatment with phosphoric acid showed higher-percentage HFF viability of 36.18%, 34.5% and 21.56% at pH 4–6, as shown in Figure 6a. Citric acid also improved the metabolic activity of HFF cells at pH 4, 5 and 6, showing increases of 37.66%, 23.17% and 8.19%, respectively (Figure 6b). After implementing a resting period, significant increases in percentage viability of 73.51%, 149.84% and 180.07% were observed in HFF cells when treated with phosphoric acid buffers with pH adjusted to 3, 4 and 5, respectively, in comparison to that of DMEM-cultured HFF cells (Figure 6a). After a replacement of the culture medium (resting period) and resting interval of 24 h, similarly significant increases of 96.9%, 152.3% and 71.06% were also observed in the metabolic rate of HFF cells when treated with citric acid buffers with pH adjusted to 3, 4 and 5, respectively, as depicted in Figure 6b. These findings demonstrated a time-dependence correlation between metabolic activity of HaCaT and HFF cells and duration of resting interval following the initial treatment. This increased metabolic activity at Day 2 in comparison to that of Day 1 treatment and control group indicated an increase in cell proliferation rate by acidification, influenced by a time-dependent regimen.

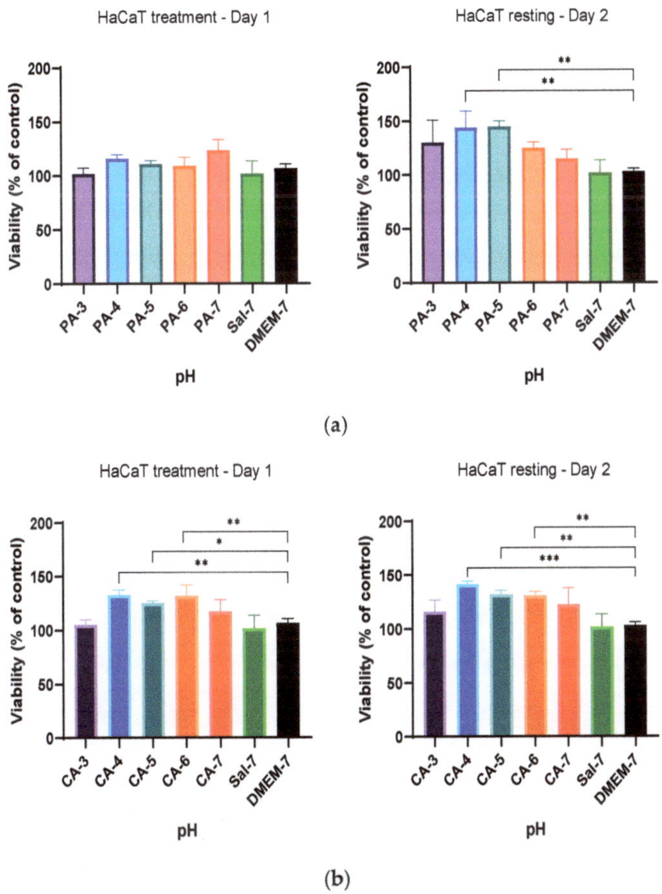

Figure 5. Percentage viability of HaCaT cells with a 24 h treatment with (**a**) 0.01 M phosphoric acid (PA) and (**b**) 0.01 M citric acid (CA), with pH ranges from 3 to 7, followed by a 24 h resting period with DMEM-7 replacement. The viability of HaCaT cells was significantly higher after treatment with 0.01 M phosphoric acid pH 4 and 5 (PA-4 and PA-5). The percentage viability of HaCaT cells was also observed to be statistically significant after treatment of 0.01 M citric acid buffers with pH values of 4, 5 and 6 (CA-4, CA-5 and CA-6). Each bar represents the mean ± standard deviation. * $p < 0.05$, ** $p < 0.01$ and *** $p < 0.001$ indicates that the results obtained were statistically significant from those of the control group (DMEM-7).

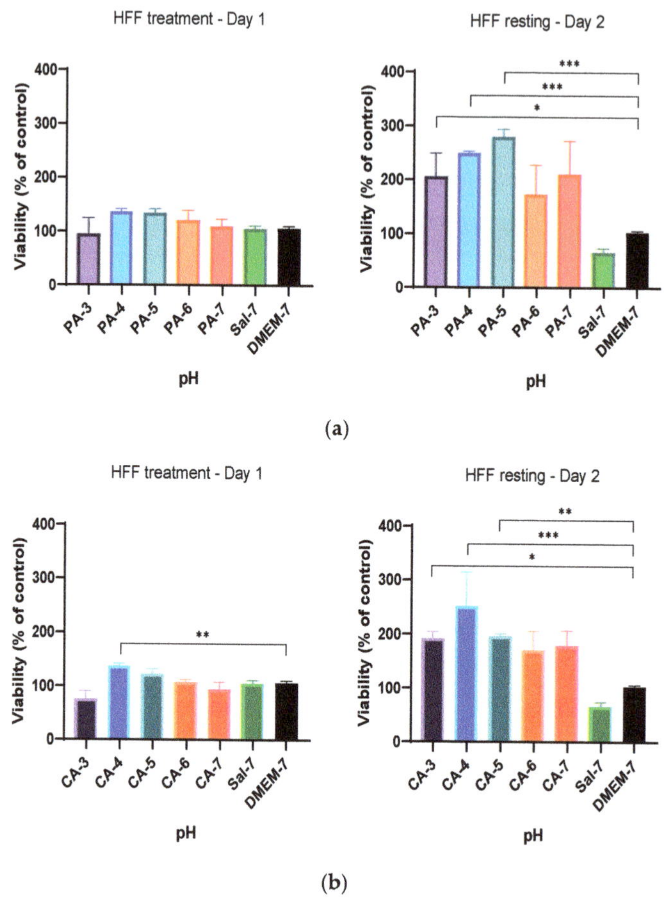

Figure 6. The effect of acidic pH buffers on the metabolism rate of HFF fibroblast cells. HFF cells were cultured in DMEM growth media with the treatment of acidic buffers for a duration of 24 h, followed by aspiration and replacement of fresh DMEM media for another 24 h. (**a**) Percentage viability of HFF cells when treated with 0.01 M phosphoric acid (PA), with pH adjusted to 3, 4, 5, 6 and 7 and (**b**) treatment with 0.01 M citric acid (CA) buffer solutions (pH 3 to pH 7). The results are expressed as mean ± standard deviation. Statistical significance (* $p < 0.05$, ** $p < 0.01$ and *** $p < 0.001$) when compared with the percentage viability of HFF cells in the control group (DMEM-7).

2.5. Acidification Increases Migration Rate of Keratinocytes and Fibroblasts

The effect of both acidic buffers with pH adjusted to 3–7 following treatment regimen C (Table 1) on the rate of migration of keratinocytes (HaCaT) and fibroblasts (HFF) was investigated using a scratch migration assay as described in Section 4.5 (Figure 7a). As shown in Figure 7b, the rate of migration of HaCaT cells was enhanced following treatment with low-ionic-strength (0.01 M) phosphoric and citric acid buffers in comparison to DMEM-cultured cells (DMEM-7). The phosphoric acidic buffer at pH 4 (PA-4) was found to induce the highest cell density (confluency) in the artificial wound gap, which showed 50% cell confluency at T = 12 h followed by 80% confluency at T= 20 h. Other pH showed 50% cell confluency at T = 13–22 h with 80% confluency at T = 22–39 h in comparison to DMEM-cultured cells that reached 80% by T = 50 h. Citric-acid-buffer treatments from pH 3 to 7 induced similar migration of HaCaT cells (Figure 7c), especially pH 5 buffer (CA-5), which achieved 50% HaCaT cell confluency by T = 16 h, with other pH achieving 50%

confluency at T = 17–20 h. All pH for citric acidic buffers showed similar 80% confluency at T = 24–28 h.

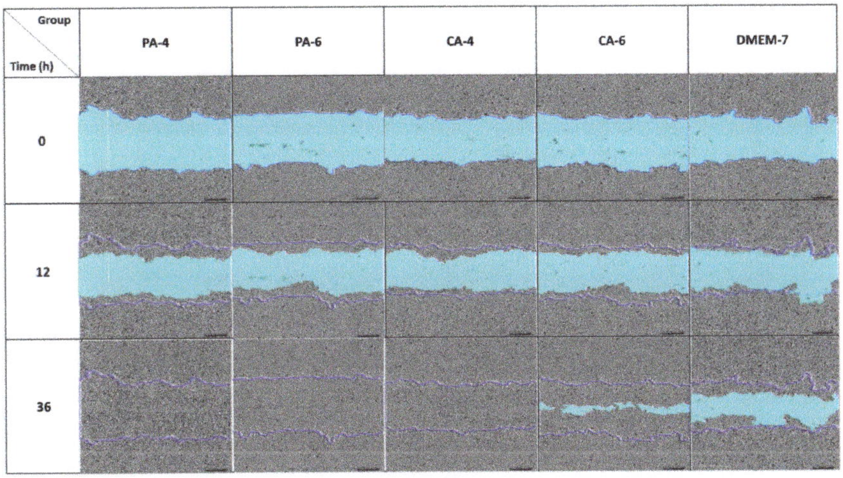

(a)

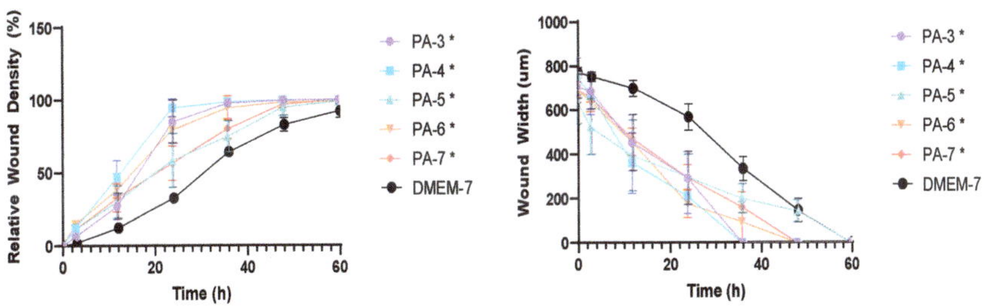

(b)

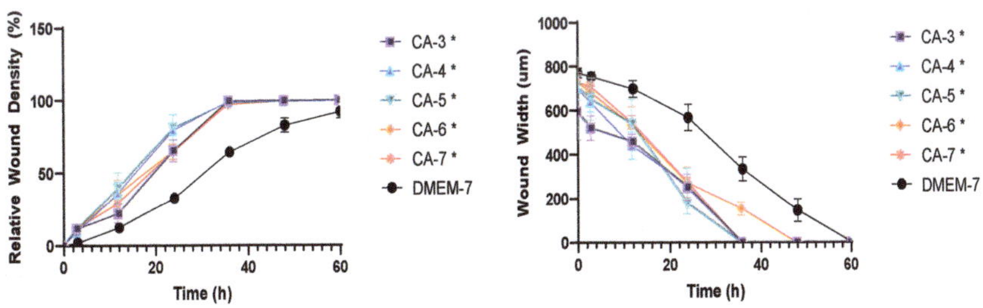

(c)

Figure 7. (**a**) Representative contrast images illustrating the migration rate of keratinocyte cells (HaCaT) following acidification treatment regimen C. (**b**) Relative wound density and wound width measured after treatment with 0.01 M phosphoric acid (PA) buffers with pH values of 3, 4, 5, 6 and 7. (**c**) Relative wound density and wound width obtained after incubation with 0.01 M citric acid (CA) buffers. Each error bar represents the mean ± standard deviation. * $p < 0.05$ indicates that the results obtained were statistically significant from those of the control group (DMEM-7).

The effect of acidification using phosphoric and citric acid buffers on migration rate was also investigated with HFF fibroblast cells (Figure 8a). A low-ionic-strength phosphoric acid (0.01 M) buffer at pH 4 (PA-4) induced the fastest rate of HFF cell migration, reaching 50% confluency at the wound gap by T = 10 h, and other pH showing it at T = 11–13 h (Figure 8b). In contrast, all pH phosphoric acidic buffers induced a similar migration rate, achieving 80% confluency at T = 21–30 h, whilst the DMEM control group took between T = 42–48 h to achieve 80% confluency for HFF cells. With citric acid, pH 4 (CA-4) was found to show the fastest 50% confluency by T = 13 h, while other pH did it at T = 13–26 h, as shown in Figure 8c. HFF cell confluency of 80% by all pH treatments was obtained beat T = 32–52 h in comparison to that of DMEM-cultured HFF cells that reached 100% confluency after T > 60 h (data not shown).

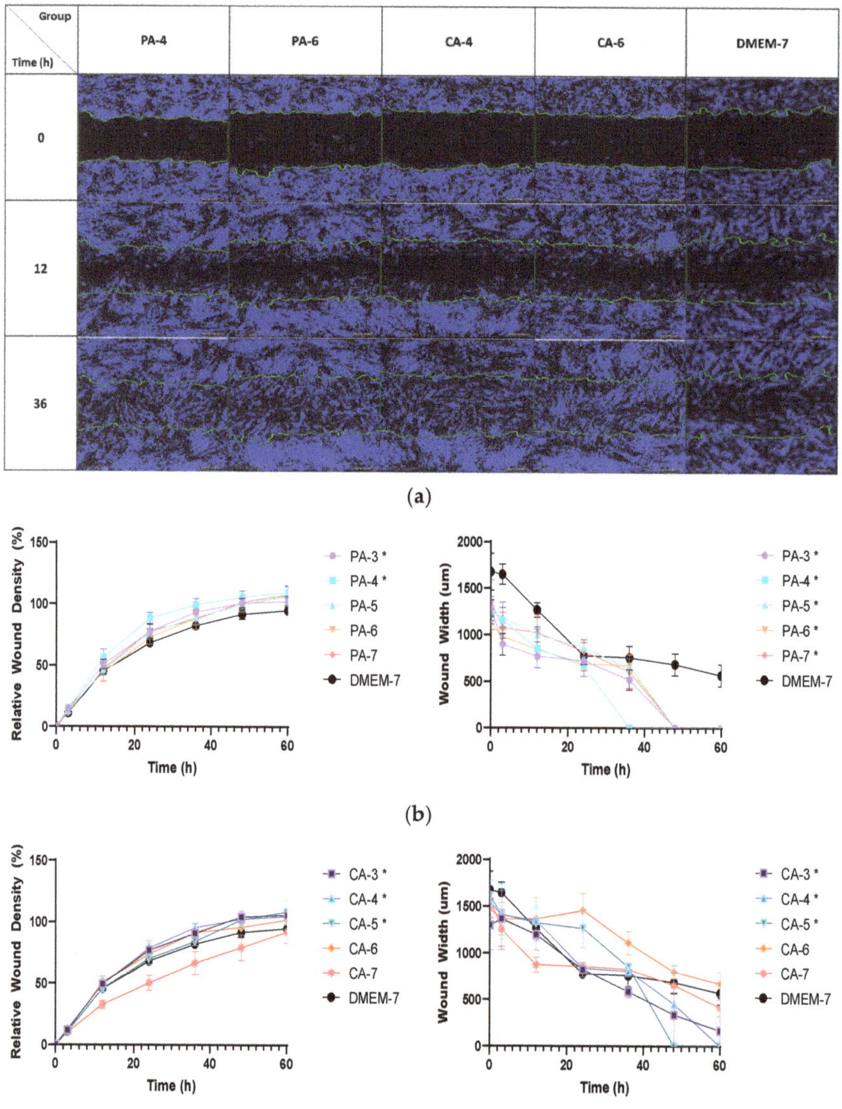

Figure 8. (**a**) The duration taken for HFF fibroblasts to migrate across an artificial open wound when

treated with acidic buffer solutions prepared from phosphoric acid and citric acid. (**b**) The percentage relative wound density and wound width measured after a treatment with 0.01 M phosphoric acid (PA) buffers with pH ranges from 3 to 7. (**c**) The percentage relative wound density and wound width of an HFF cell monolayer after incubation with 0.01 M citric acid (CA) buffers with pH adjusted to 3, 4, 5, 6 and 7. Each error bar represents the mean ± standard deviation. * $p < 0.05$ indicates that the results obtained were statistically significant from those of the control group (DMEM-7).

3. Discussion

In this study, phosphoric and citric acids were chosen as model acidic buffers to investigate the effect of acidification of the cell microenvironment on the metabolic activity and migration rate of human immortalized keratinocytes (HaCaT) and human foreskin fibroblasts (HFF). Phosphoric acid was chosen for its important phosphorous constituent that plays a vital role in cell division, growth and development [19,20]. Citric acid is a natural organic acid that acts as an intermediary in the regulation of the tricarboxylic acid cycle (TCA) and plays an important role in the oxidation of carbohydrates, fats and proteins to yield energy for cell proliferation and metabolism [21,22].

A preliminary study of cell viability in HaCaT cells showed that treatment with high-ionic-strength acidic buffers leads to premature apoptosis. Schreml et al. (2014) and Lönnqvist et al. (2015) reported that a short exposure to strong acidic pH reduced cell migration and proliferation by inducing cell apoptosis [23,24]. A similar study by Kruse et al. (2017) found that acidification of a culture medium with high-ionic-strength 0.1 M acetic acid and 1 M potassium hydroxide buffer reduced the proliferation and migration rate of primary keratinocytes and fibroblasts in vitro and reduced the effectiveness of wound re-epithelization and closure in vivo [25]. The findings of cell apoptosis with a high-ionic-strength buffer are consistent with those of other studies reporting a disruption of ions in the culture medium by aggregation-forming crystals [26]. Crystallization can cause structural alterations of triglycerides and free fatty acids in the culture medium and reduction of lipids necessary for the differentiation and proliferation of cells, resulting in cell cycle arrest at the resting phase (G0/G1). Interestingly, our results showed HaCaT cells treated with low-ionic-strength acidic buffers displayed good tolerance and further increased metabolic activity after an initial 24 h acidic treatment (Figure 1), indicating that a low-ionic-strength acid may enhance cell growth.

Different treatment regimens were used to investigate the effect of acidification on cell functions. Regimen A treatment (24 h acidification treatment with no resting period) highlighted the importance of acidifying the cell microenvironment to improve cell metabolic activity. Acidification with phosphoric and citric acid buffers significantly improved the metabolic activity of HaCaT and HFF cells after the initial 24 h acidification treatment at all pH ranges 3–7. However, implementing regimen B treatment, which was a 12 h acidification treatment and a subsequent 24 h resting period, to HaCaT cells showed significantly lower cell viability at low acidic pH 3–5, while both cell lines were unaffected by higher acidic pH of 6 and 7, which were closer to physiological pH (Figure 3). This finding indicates that pH plays an important role in regulating cellular metabolism and growth. Such behavior was reported by a study using manuka honey dressing at acidic pH on chronic wounds. This study showed that reducing wound pH by 0.1 units stimulated wound healing by 8.1%, with dressings at higher pH of 7.8 demonstrating minimal epithelialization and patients with wound pH above 8.0 experiencing increased wound size [27]. Another clinical study by Kaufman et al. (1985) also reported that topical acidification of wounds to pH 3.5 significantly enhanced epithelialization and the closure of burn wounds, whilst alkalinization retarded wound closure and increased the thickness of scar tissues [1]. Other studies have also shown a significant improvement in wound healing properties, including myofibroblasts contraction, fibroblasts migration and DNA synthesis, when the pH of the wound was lowered to an acidic condition [2,28].

Our results showed that changes in treatment duration and resting period affected the metabolic activity of both HaCaT and HFF cells. Employing treatment regimen C, which was a 24 h acidification treatment and a subsequent 24 h resting period, showed not only a significant increase in cell metabolism after the first 24 h treatment (Day 1) but a further increase in metabolic activity than that in the control group after the resting interval (Day 2). This indicated that cell proliferation also increased following this treatment regimen. The importance of treatment duration and a resting interval was further demonstrated with regimen C enabling a significantly faster cell migration rate in both keratinocytes (HaCaT) and fibroblasts (HFF). The ionic strength or molar concentration of hydrogen ions (H^+) of acid is hypothesized to improve cell proliferation and migration by affecting cell polarity and epithelial potential. Clinical studies showed that acidification of the wound by increasing H^+ concentration showed improved wound regeneration. This difference in polarity due to H^+ and epithelial potentials (EP) between wounded and unwounded tissues promoted cellular migration during the tissue proliferation stage [2,29,30].

4. Materials and Methods

4.1. Chemicals

Dimethyl sulfoxide (DMSO), phosphoric acid, citric acid and sodium hydroxide were purchased from Sigma-Aldrich (Castle Hill, NSW, AUS). Dulbecco Modified Eagle Medium (DMEM), fetal bovine serum (FBS), penicillin–streptomycin, trypsin-EDTA and phosphate-buffered saline (PBS) were purchased from Gibco, ThermoFisher Scientific (Scoresby, VIC, Australia).

4.2. Buffer Preparation

Phosphoric acid solutions (H_3PO_4, 0.01 M and 0.1 M) were prepared by gently pipetting 0.068 mL and 0.68 mL of 85% w/w phosphoric acid to 25 mL of sterile Milli-Q water, respectively. A mixture of solutions was mixed thoroughly using a magnetic stirrer, and the final volume was adjusted to 100 mL with sterile Milli-Q water.

Citric acid solutions ($C_6H_8O_7$, 0.01 M and 0.1 M) were prepared by adding 100 mL of sterilized Milli-Q water to crystalline citric acid powders weighing 0.19 g and 1.9 g, respectively. Sodium hydroxide solutions (NaOH, 0.01 M and 0.1 M) were prepared by adding 100 mL of sterilized Milli-Q water to 0.4 g and 4.0 g crystalline sodium hydroxide powders, respectively. All mixtures were mixed thoroughly by sonication before experimentation.

Both phosphoric acid and citric acid buffers were prepared by adjusting pH values of phosphoric acid (0.01 M and 0.1 M) and citric acid (0.01 M and 0.1 M) with 0.01 M and 0.1 M sodium hydroxide solutions to pH values of 3, 4, 5, 6 and 7, respectively. All acidic buffer solutions were incubated for 24 h at room temperature, and the pH values of all the prepared buffers were confirmed with an Orion Star A321 portable pH meter (ThermoFisher Scientific, Scoresby, VIC, Australia) prior to experimentation.

4.3. Cell Culture

Human immortalized keratinocytes (HaCaT) and human foreskin fibroblasts (HFF) were purchased from ThermoFisher Scientific (Scoresby, VIC, Australia) and ATCC (Noble Park North, VIC, Australia), respectively. HaCaT and HFF cells were cultured in Dulbecco Modified Eagle Medium (DMEM) supplemented with 10% fetal bovine serum (FBS) and 1% penicillin–streptomycin and incubated at 37 °C with 5% CO_2. The cells were seeded in T75 flasks at a concentration of 1×10^4 cells/mL. Passaged cells were split 1 in 5 every 3 to 4 days. The cells were collected by trypsinization with a 1× trypsin-EDTA solution (company and country) following final culturing of 7 days.

4.4. Cell Viability Assay

The cell viability assay that indicated the metabolic activity, cytotoxicity and proliferation of viable cells was determined using an MTT assay. The cells were plated at a density of 1×10^4 cells/well in a 96-well plate and incubated overnight at 37 °C in 5% CO_2. Following method as described in Figure 9, the growth medium was replaced with fresh DMEM at T = 24 h before the addition of different acidic buffers with various pH values (phosphoric acid pH 3–7 and citric acid pH 3–7). HaCaT and HFF cells were seeded in triplicates and incubated for 24 h. At T = 48 h, the growth media with various pH buffers were aspirated from each well and replaced with fresh DMEM (resting period). At T = 72 h, DMEM was aspirated and replaced with new DMEM with acidic buffers (treatment period). Replacement of DMEM and acidic buffers was carried out for 3 days, during which cell viability was assessed at an interval of 24 h. At a concentration of 2 mg/mL, 50 µL of MTT/PBS solution was added to each well and incubated for 4 h at 37 °C in 5% CO_2. The wells were replaced with 150 µL of dimethyl sulfoxide (DMSO) to dissolve MTT crystals formed for 10 min at room temperature. The percentage viability of cells was measured by the absorbance of the MTT crystals formed during the experiment at a wavelength of 540 nm in an EnSpire Plate Reader (PerkinElmer, Waltham, MA, USA).

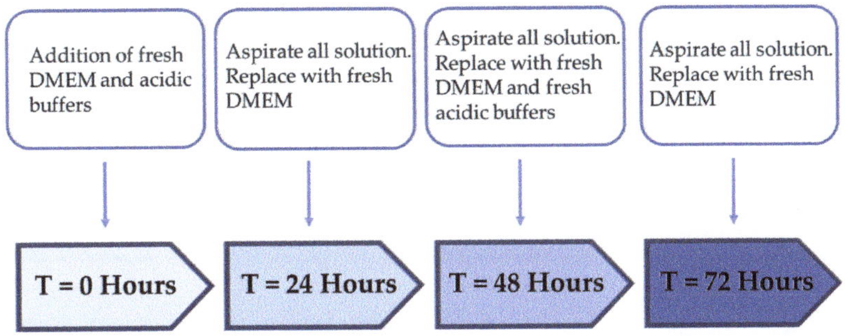

Figure 9. An example of the experimental protocol for treatment regimen C, indicating 24 h of treatment followed by a 24 h resting period.

4.5. Cell Migration Assay

The cell migration assay assessing the rate of wound coverage in a monolayer of 90% confluent cells was performed in IncuCyte® ZOOM (Essen BioScience, QLD, Australia). The cells were plated at 1×10^4 cells/well in a 96-well flat-bottom ImageLock plate and incubated overnight at 37 °C in 5% CO_2. Following 24 h of incubation, an artificial scratch wound measuring 700 to 800 µm was applied to the monolayer of 90% confluent cells in each well using a WoundMaker (Essen BioScience, QLD, Australia). The media were aspirated from the wells to remove debris and washed with sterile PBS. A volume of 100 µL of DMEM with 20 µL of acidic buffer solutions was added as treatment and incubated at 37 °C in 5% CO_2. Live cells were imaged using a phase-contrast microscope with a ×10 objective (Zeiss Axiovert 200; Carl Zeiss, Jena, Germany). Microscopic images were captured at an interval of 3 h for 72 h following the initial scratch (Prior, Cambridge, UK).

4.6. Data Analysis

Continuous variables are displayed as the mean ± standard deviation, and categorical variables—as percentages. Statistical analysis between treatment and control groups was carried out using two-way analysis of variance (ANOVA) for multiple comparisons and Dunnett's multiple comparisons test for independent groups' comparison. The level of statistical significance was set at less than 5%.

5. Conclusions

Our study showed that cell acidification with phosphoric and citric acid buffers enhanced cell proliferation and improved directional cell migration in HaCaT and HFF cells. There was little effect of acidic buffer treatment at low ionic strength (0.01 M) and pH ranges of 4–5, however, a high-ionic-strength acid resulted in reduced metabolic activity and migration, particularly after a subsequent acidification treatment. A time-dependent treatment effect was demonstrated by the inclusion of a resting period after a 24 h treatment with further improvements in cell proliferation and migration observed. This highlights the importance of treatment frequency and duration. Changes in pH and ionic strength suggest that cell proliferation and migration are strongly correlated to the concentration of hydrogen ions (H^+), which governs the intrinsic activity of cellular activities.

Author Contributions: Conceptualization, P.S., Y.S., A.J.C. and S.G.; methodology, P.S. and Y.S.; validation, P.S. and Y.S.; formal analysis, P.S.; investigation, P.S.; resources, A.J.C. and S.G.; data curation, P.S., Y.S. and A.J.C.; writing—original draft preparation, P.S.; writing—review and editing, P.S., S.G., Y.S., G.N.Y. and A.J.C.; visualization, P.S., Y.S. and A.J.C.; supervision, Y.S., S.G. and A.J.C.; project administration, S.G. and A.J.C.; funding acquisition, S.G. and A.J.C. All authors have read and agreed to the published version of the manuscript.

Funding: This research was funded by Wound Management Innovation Cooperative Research Center (WMI CRC), grant number SP39-2.

Institutional Review Board Statement: Not applicable.

Informed Consent Statement: Not applicable.

Data Availability Statement: Data is contained within the article.

Conflicts of Interest: The authors declare no conflict of interest.

References

1. Kaufman, T.; Eichenlaub, E.H.; Angel, M.F.; Levin, M.; Futrell, J.W. Topical acidification promotes healing of experimental deep partial thickness skin burns: A ran-domized double-blind preliminary study. *Burns* **1985**, *12*, 84–90. [CrossRef]
2. Lengheden, A.; Jansson, L. PH effects on experimental wound healing of human fibroblasts in vitro. *Eur. J. Oral Sci.* **1995**, *103*, 148–155. [CrossRef] [PubMed]
3. Ohgoda, O.; Sakai, A.; Koga, H.; Kanai, K.; Miyazaki, T.; Niwano, Y. Fibroblast-migration in a wound model of ascorbic acid-supplemented three-dimensional culture system: The effects of cytokines and malotilate, a new wound healing stimulant, on cell-migration. *J. Dermatol. Sci.* **1998**, *17*, 123–131. [CrossRef]
4. Demetriou, A.A.; Levenson, S.M.; Rettura, G.; Seifter, E. Vitamin A and retinoic acid: Induced fibroblast differentiation in vitro. *Surgery* **1985**, *98*, 931–934.
5. Duman, N.; Duman, R.; Tosun, M.; Akıcı, M.; Göksel, E.; Gökçe, B.; Alagöz, O. Topical folinic acid enhances wound healing in rat model. *Adv. Med. Sci.* **2018**, *63*, 347–352. [CrossRef]
6. Makvandi, P.; Ali, G.W.; Della Sala, F.; Abdel-Fattah, W.I.; Borzacchiello, A. Biosynthesis and characterization of antibacterial thermosensitive hydrogels based on corn silk extract, hyaluronic acid and nanosilver for potential wound healing. *Carbohydr. Polym.* **2019**, *223*, 115023. [CrossRef]
7. Hsu, Y.-Y.; Liu, K.-L.; Yeh, H.-H.; Lin, H.-R.; Wu, H.-L.; Tsai, J.-C. Sustained release of recombinant thrombomodulin from cross-linked gelatin/hyaluronic acid hydrogels potentiate wound healing in diabetic mice. *Eur. J. Pharm. Biopharm.* **2019**, *135*, 61–71. [CrossRef]
8. Ying, H.; Zhou, J.; Wang, M.; Su, D.; Ma, Q.; Lv, G.; Chen, J. In situ formed collagen-hyaluronic acid hydrogel as biomimetic dressing for promoting spontaneous wound healing. *Mater. Sci. Eng. C* **2019**, *101*, 487–498. [CrossRef]
9. Baier, R. Surface Chemistry in Epidermal Repair. In *Epidermal Wound Healing*; Year Book Medical Publishers, Inc.: Chicago, IL, USA, 1972; pp. 27–48.
10. Bruno, M.; Trucchi, B.; Burlando, B.; Ranzato, E.; Martinotti, S.; Akkol, E.K.; Süntar, I.; Keleş, H.; Verotta, L. (+)-Usnic acid enamines with remarkable cicatrizing properties. *Bioorg. Med. Chem.* **2013**, *21*, 1834–1843. [CrossRef]
11. Gao, Y.; Zhaoyu, L.; Xiangming, F.; Chunyi, L.; Jiayu, P.; Lu, S.; Jitao, C.; Liangcai, C.; Jifang, L. Abietic acid attenuates allergic airway inflammation in a mouse allergic asthma model. *Int. Immunopharmacol.* **2016**, *38*, 261–266. [CrossRef]
12. González, M.A.; Pérez-Guaita, D.; Correa-Royero, J.; Zapata, B.; Agudelo, L.; Mesa-Arango, A.; Betancur-Galvis, L. Synthesis and biological evaluation of dehydroabietic acid derivatives. *Eur. J. Med. Chem.* **2010**, *45*, 811–816. [CrossRef] [PubMed]
13. Ren, J.; Yang, M.; Xu, F.; Chen, J.; Ma, S. Acceleration of wound healing activity with syringic acid in streptozotocin induced diabetic rats. *Life Sci.* **2019**, *233*, 116728. [CrossRef] [PubMed]
14. Srinivasulu, C.; Ramgopal, M.; Ramanjaneyulu, G.; Anuradha, C.M.; Kumar, C.S. Syringic acid (SA)—A Review of Its Occurrence, Biosynthesis, Pharmacological and Industrial Importance. *Biomed. Pharmacother.* **2018**, *108*, 547–557. [CrossRef] [PubMed]
15. Kumar, V. Efficacies of fumaric acid and its mono and di-methyl esters in rodent models for analgesics and an-ti-inflammatory agents. *EC Pharm. Sci.* **2015**, *1*, 73–85.
16. Basha, S.; Ghosh, S.; Vinothkumar, K.; Ramesh, B.; Kumari, P.H.P.; Mohan, K.M.; Sukumar, E. Fumaric acid incorporated Ag/agar-agar hybrid hydrogel: A multifunctional avenue to tackle wound healing. *Mater. Sci. Eng. C* **2020**, *111*, 110743. [CrossRef] [PubMed]

17. Leveen, H.H.; Falk, G.E.R.A.L.D.; Borek, B.; Diaz, C.A.R.L.O.S.; Lynfield, Y.; Wynkoop, B.J.; Mabunda, G.A.; Rubricius, J.L.; Christoudias, G.C. Chemical acidification of wounds. An adjuvant to healing and the unfavorable action of alkalinity and ammonia. *Ann. Surg.* **1973**, *178*, 745. [CrossRef]
18. Jeong, H.S.; Lee, B.H.; Lee, H.K.; Kim, H.S.; Moon, M.S.; Suh, I.S. Negative Pressure Wound Therapy of Chronically Infected Wounds Using 1% Acetic Acid Irrigation. *Arch. Plast. Surg.* **2015**, *42*, 59–67. [CrossRef]
19. Yang, Q.; Liang, H.; Maulu, S.; Ge, X.; Ren, M.; Xie, J.; Xi, B. Dietary phosphorus affects growth, glucolipid metabolism, antioxidant activity and immune status of juvenile blunt snout bream (*Megalobrama amblycephala*). *Anim. Feed Sci. Technol.* **2021**, *274*, 114896. [CrossRef]
20. Zhou, Q.C.; Liu, Y.J.; Mai, K.S.; Tian, L.X. Effect of dietary phosphorus levels on growth, body composition, muscle and bone mineral concen-trations for orange-spotted grouper *Epinephelus coioides* reared in floating cages. *J. World Aquac. Soc.* **2004**, *35*, 427–435. [CrossRef]
21. Chen, X.; Lv, Q.; Liu, Y.; Deng, W. Effect of Food Additive Citric Acid on The Growth of Human Esophageal Carcinoma Cell Line EC109. *Cell J.* **2016**, *18*, 493–502. [CrossRef]
22. Bodner, G.M. Metabolism Part II: The tricarboxylic acid (TCA), citric acid, or Krebs cycle. *J. Chem. Educ.* **1986**, *63*, 673. [CrossRef]
23. Schreml, S.; Meier, R.J.; Kirschbaum, M.; Kong, S.C.; Gehmert, S.; Felthaus, O.; Küchler, S.; Sharpe, J.R.; Wöltje, K.; Weiß, K.T.; et al. Luminescent dual sensors reveal extracellular pH-gradients and hypoxia on chronic wounds that disrupt epidermal repair. *Theranostics* **2014**, *4*, 721. [CrossRef] [PubMed]
24. Lönnqvist, S.; Emanuelsson, P.; Kratz, G. Influence of acidic pH on keratinocyte function and re-epithelialisation of human in vitro wounds. *J. Plast. Surg. Hand Surg.* **2015**, *49*, 346–352. [CrossRef] [PubMed]
25. Kruse, C.R.; Singh, M.; Targosinski, S.; Sinha, I.; Sørensen, J.A.; Eriksson, E.; Nuutila, K. The effect of pH on cell viability, cell migration, cell proliferation, wound closure, and wound reep-ithelialization: In vitro and in vivo study. *Wound Repair Regen.* **2017**, *25*, 260–269. [CrossRef]
26. Li, N.-B.; Xu, W.-H.; Zhao, J.-H.; Xiao, G.-Y.; Lu, Y.-P. The significant influence of ionic concentrations and immersion temperatures on deposition behaviors of hydroxyapatite on alkali- and heat-treated titanium in simulated body fluid. *Thin Solid Film.* **2018**, *646*, 163–172. [CrossRef]
27. Gethin, G.T.; Cowman, S.; Conroy, R.M. The impact of Manuka honey dressings on the surface pH of chronic wounds. *Int. Wound J.* **2008**, *5*, 185–194. [CrossRef]
28. Pipelzadeh, M.H.; Naylor, I.L. The in vitro enhancement of rat myofibroblast contractility by alterations to the pH of the physiological solution. *Eur. J. Pharmacol.* **1998**, *357*, 257–259. [CrossRef]
29. Chang, P.C.; Sulik, G.I.; Soong, H.K.; Parkinson, W.C. Galvanotropic and galvanotaxic responses of corneal endothelial cells. *J. Formos. Med. Assoc.* **1996**, *95*, 623–627.
30. Soong, H.K.; Parkinson, W.C.; Bafna, S.; Sulik, G.L.; Huang, S.C. Movements of cultured corneal epithelial cells and stromal fibroblasts in electric fields. *Investig. Ophthalmol. Vis. Sci.* **1990**, *31*, 2278–2282.

International Journal of
Molecular Sciences

MDPI

Article

Antimicrobial Combined Action of Graphene Oxide and Light Emitting Diodes for Chronic Wound Management

Silvia Di Lodovico [1], Firas Diban [1], Paola Di Fermo [1], Morena Petrini [2], Antonella Fontana [1], Mara Di Giulio [1], Adriano Piattelli [3,4,5,6], Simonetta D'Ercole [2,*] and Luigina Cellini [1]

1 Department of Pharmacy, University of "G. d'Annunzio" Chieti-Pescara, 66100 Chieti, Italy; silvia.dilodovico@unich.it (S.D.L.); firas.diban@unich.it (F.D.); paola.difermo@unich.it (P.D.F.); antonella.fontana@unich.it (A.F.); mara.digiulio@unich.it (M.D.G.); l.cellini@unich.it (L.C.)
2 Department of Medical, Oral and Biotechnological Sciences, University of "G. d'Annunzio" Chieti-Pescara, 66100 Chieti, Italy; morena.petrini@unich.it
3 School of Dentistry, Saint Camillus International University of Health and Medical Sciences, Via di Sant'Alessandro 8, 00131 Rome, Italy; apiatteli51@gmail.com
4 Faculty of Dental Medicine, University of Belgrade, 11000 Belgrade, Serbia
5 Fondazione Villa Serena per la Ricerca, 65013 Città Sant'Angelo, Italy
6 Casa di Cura Villa Serena del Dott. L. Petruzzi, 65013 Città Sant'Angelo, Italy
* Correspondence: simonetta.dercole@unich.it; Tel.: +39-0871-3554017

Abstract: Innovative non-antibiotic compounds such as graphene oxide (GO) and light-emitting diodes (LEDs) may represent a valid strategy for managing chronic wound infections related to resistant pathogens. This study aimed to evaluate 630 nm LED and 880 nm LED ability to enhance the GO antimicrobial activity against *Staphylococcus aureus*- and *Pseudomonas aeruginosa*-resistant strains in a dual-species biofilm in the Lubbock chronic wound biofilm (LCWB) model. The effect of a 630 nm LED, alone or plus 5-aminolevulinic acid (ALAD)-mediated photodynamic therapy (PDT) (ALAD-PDT), or an 880 nm LED on the GO (50 mg/l) action was evaluated by determining the CFU/mg reductions, live/dead analysis, scanning electron microscope observation, and reactive oxygen species assay. Among the LCWBs, the best effect was obtained with GO irradiated with ALAD-PDT, with percentages of CFU/mg reduction up to 78.96% ± 0.21 and 95.17% ± 2.56 for *S. aureus* and *P. aeruginosa*, respectively. The microscope images showed a reduction in the cell number and viability when treated with GO + ALAD-PDT. In addition, increased ROS production was detected. No differences were recorded when GO was irradiated with an 880 nm LED versus GO alone. The obtained results suggest that treatment with GO irradiated with ALAD-PDT represents a valid, sustainable strategy to counteract the polymicrobial colonization of chronic wounds.

Keywords: chronic wounds; *Staphylococcus aureus*; *Pseudomonas aeruginosa*; graphene oxide; light emitting diodes; Lubbock chronic wound biofilm model; polymicrobial biofilm; antimicrobial resistance

Citation: Di Lodovico, S.; Diban, F.; Di Fermo, P.; Petrini, M.; Fontana, A.; Di Giulio, M.; Piattelli, A.; D'Ercole, S.; Cellini, L. Antimicrobial Combined Action of Graphene Oxide and Light Emitting Diodes for Chronic Wound Management. *Int. J. Mol. Sci.* **2022**, *23*, 6942. https://doi.org/10.3390/ijms23136942

Academic Editors: Cinzia Pagano, César Viseras and Luana Perioli

Received: 1 June 2022
Accepted: 20 June 2022
Published: 22 June 2022

1. Introduction

Chronic wounds are defined as those that do not heal in an orderly and timely way within three months, representing an important challenge worldwide. They are characterized by excessive levels of pro-inflammatory cytokines, proteases, reactive oxygen species (ROS), and senescent cells, as well as the existence of persistent infections [1].

In a chronic wound, polymicrobial biofilms play a pivotal role in the pathogenesis of wounds, impairing cutaneous healing [2]. In particular, in the polymicrobial sessile growth mode, different bacterial species communicate, cooperate, or compete with each other. Wounds' microbial colonization involves different aerobic and anaerobic pathogenic microorganisms including bacteria and yeasts. *Staphylococcus aureus* and *Pseudomonas aeruginosa* are the main pathogens isolated in chronic polymicrobial infections [3]. In an early phase of colonization, an antagonistic interaction occurs and *P. aeruginosa* tries to kill

S. aureus; then, a synergistic interaction occurs with an increasing tolerance of traditional treatments [4]. Polymicrobial infections are more persistent than mono-microbial ones. In fact, Orazi et al. [5] reported that the *P. aeruginosa* exoproducts decrease the susceptibility of *S. aureus* to vancomycin and tobramycin due to *P. aeruginosa* 4-hydroxy-2-heptylquinoline-N-oxide (HQNO) production. Moreover, the release of N-acetyl glucosamine (GlcNAc) by *S. aureus* stimulates the *P. aeruginosa* quinolone signal (PQS), which controls the extracellular virulence factors' production (e.g., pyocyanin, elastase, rhamnolipids, and HQNO) and quorum sensing [5,6]. In a typical chronic wound, *P. aeruginosa* colonizes the deep wound and *S. aureus* is found at the surface. *Pseudomonas aeruginosa* can colonize the deeper region of the chronic wound thanks to its capability to migrate via type-IV pili and flagellum-mediated motility in biofilms [7].

A suitable in vitro model to study the effect of novel solutions to counteract chronic wound infections is the Lubbock chronic wound biofilm (LCWB) model. Since the media used contains red blood cells, plasma, and nutrients in a typical 3D gradient, this model mimics the microbial distribution and environment of a real chronic wound [8–10]. In particular, *S. aureus* produces a fibrin network that represents a scaffold on which bacteria can adhere, forming a biofilm. The LCWB is a well-recognized model for evaluating the interactions among microorganisms from a chronic wound, including aerobic and anaerobic microorganisms. Consequently, before conducting in vivo studies, this complex model is used to evaluate the effects of different antimicrobials on microorganisms in a complex chronic wound-resembling environment [11].

Different treatments are proposed to prevent the bacterial infection of skin wounds, such as iodine, silver, zinc oxide, and polyhexamethylene, but they have certain levels of cytotoxicity [6]. Moreover, the increasing number of multidrug-resistant strains strongly suggests the need for new and more effective antimicrobials for clinical application. We previously demonstrated the effect of graphene oxide (GO) in an LCWB model against clinical *S. aureus* and *P. aeruginosa* strains. Graphene oxide reduces the growth of *S. aureus* and *P. aeruginosa* by wrapping up the microorganisms and increasing the fluidity of the fibrin network in LCWBs [3]. Moreover, GO has been recognized as a smart and cheap material with wide application potential [12]. In the literature, it has been reported that GO is activated by light-emitting diodes (LEDs) [13]. In this regard, the LEDs, semiconductors that convert electrical current into incoherent narrow-spectrum light, represent a new treatment against microorganisms that are difficult to treat. In fact, LEDs show good antimicrobial action against Gram-positive and -negative bacteria, alone or combined with chemical antimicrobials such as sodium hypochlorite and chlorhexidine [14]. Light-emitting diodes are widely used in clinical therapy for pain attenuation, wound healing, skin rejuvenation, and repair [15]. Light-emitting diodes, emitting red light with wavelengths between 610 and 760 nm, are made up of semiconductors of different materials: aluminum gallium arsenide, gallium arsenide phosphide (GaAsP), aluminum gallium indium phosphide (AlGaInP), gallium phosphide (GaP), or aluminum gallium arsenide (AlGaAs). In terms of clinical applications, red LEDs are widely used in dentistry, algaculture, and wound healing [16]. Infrared light (>760 nm) LEDs are used for home-entertainment remotes, night-vision cameras, security systems and medical devices for promoting tissue regeneration and healing. Nowadays, the use of photodynamic therapy represents an eco-sustainable and efficacious therapy to counteract the worrying phenomenon of infections related to resistant microorganisms [17]. Yang et al. [18] demonstrated the efficacy of the synergistic combination of the photodynamic/photothermal properties of diketopyrrolopyrrole and fluconazole against resistant *Candida albicans* infections. Moreover, LEDs are characterized by an antibacterial activity given they can excite endogenous photosensitive compounds, e.g., porphyrins, present in the bacterial cells, causing the production of ROS such as hydroxyl radicals, hydrogen peroxide and singlet oxygen ($^1O_2$). Reactive oxygen species further react with cellular components, causing cell death [19]. Aminolevulinic acid (ala), a precursor of the natural photosensitizer protoporphyrin IX (PpIX), can be administered exogenously to reduce the accumulation of the molecules and cytotoxic effects of irradiation. An increase in photoactive porphyrin products (PAPs) produces a bacteria-killing action [20].

Based on these considerations, this work aimed to study the antimicrobial combined effect of GO and 630 nm LEDs, alone or with ala (ALAD-PDT), and at 880 nm in the double-species *S. aureus* and *P. aeruginosa* LCWB model.

The experimental plan was organized as follows (Figure 1).

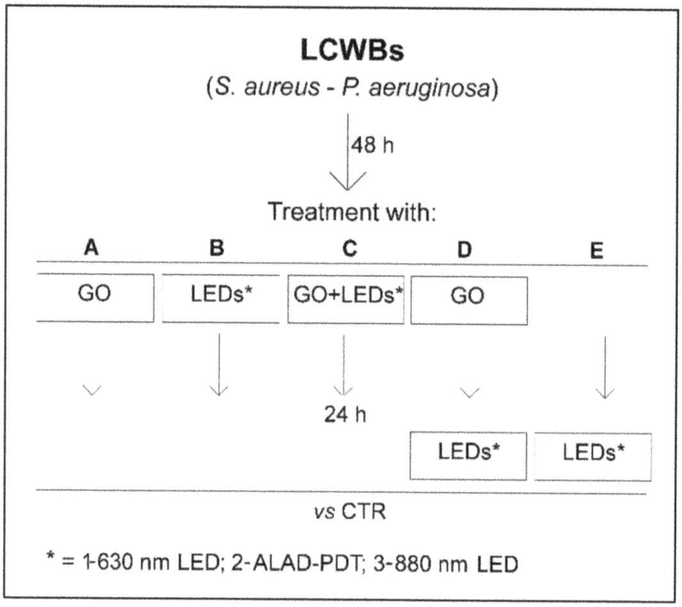

Figure 1. Experimental plan of the study. The mature LCWBs, obtained after 48 h of incubation, were placed on a "wound bed" and treated as follows: A = with GO (50 mg/mL) and incubated for 24 h; B1 = with 630 nm LED for 17 min and incubated for 24 h; B2 = with ALAD-PDT for 17 min and incubated for 24 h; B3 = with 880 nm LED for 17 min and incubated for 24 h; C1 = with GO (50 mg/mL) irradiated with 630 nm LED for 17 min and incubated for 24 h; C2 = with GO (50 mg/mL) irradiated with ALAD-PDT for 17 min and incubated for 24 h; C3 = with GO (50 mg/mL) irradiated with 880 nm LED for 17 min and incubated for 24 h; D1 = with GO (50 mg/mL) incubated for 24 h and then irradiated with 630 nm LED for 17 min; D2 = with GO (50 mg/mL) incubated for 24 h and then irradiated with ALAD-PDT for 17 min; D3 = with GO (50 mg/mL) incubated for 24 h and then irradiated with 880 nm LED for 17 min; E1 = with 630 nm LED for 17 min after 24 h of incubation; E2 = with ALAD-PDT for 17 min after 24 h of incubation; E3 = with 880 nm LED for 17 min after 24 h of incubation. The untreated mature LCWBs (CTRs), after 48 h of incubation, were placed on a "wound bed" and incubated for 24 h in the same time and temperature conditions as all experimental LCWBs.

2. Results

The combined effect of GO and LEDs was evaluated on *S. aureus* and *P. aeruginosa* growth in the LCWB model. The resistant *S. aureus* and *P. aeruginosa* clinical strains used for the experiments were characterized for their main virulence factors (Supplementary Table S1).

Figure 2 shows the percentages of CFU/mg reduction of *S. aureus* and *P. aeruginosa* in the LCWB model after treatment with GO and LEDs.

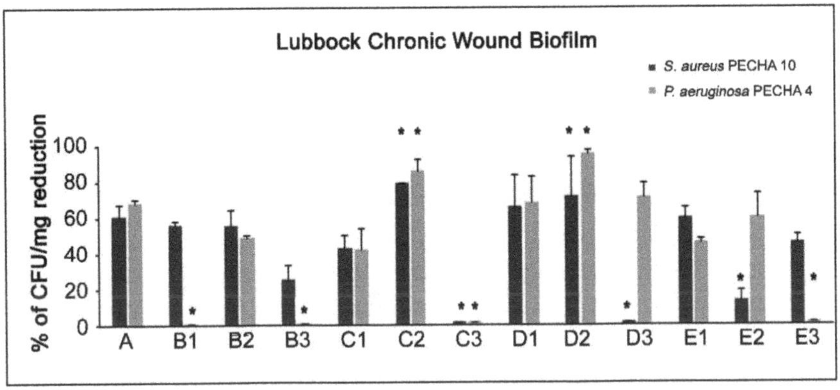

Figure 2. Percentages of CFU/mg reduction of *S. aureus* and *P. aeruginosa* in treated LCWB model versus the control. For the experimental points, see Figure 1 and the Section 4, paragraph 5. * Statistically significant difference ($p < 0.05$) for each strain in respect to A condition.

In the B1 condition, a remarkable *S. aureus* CFU/mg reduction versus the control ($p < 0.05$) was generated without affecting *P. aeruginosa*. A CFU/mg reduction was produced for both tested strains in the B2 condition, meanwhile, with a significant effect versus the control ($p < 0.05$) but not versus GO. When the LCWB was treated in the B3 condition, weak *S. aureus* growth reduction was noted.

As shown in Figure 2, in the C1 combination, an antimicrobial on the growth of *S. aureus* and *P. aeruginosa* was observed in the LCWB model without a statistically significant ($p > 0.05$) effect versus GO. When the LCWB was treated under the C2 combination, significant ($p < 0.05$) CFU/mg reductions for *S. aureus* (78.96% ± 0.21) and *P. aeruginosa* (85.67% ± 6.56) were detected versus the control and the A condition. On the contrary, the LCWB treated under the C3 combination showed an antagonist effect, without CFU/mg reductions for any tested strain.

The LCWB treated with the D1 combination showed greater antimicrobial efficacy than the C1 combination and a similar trend to the A condition. The treatment with the D2 combination increased the *P. aeruginosa* growth effect with significant ($p < 0.05$) CFU/mg reduction (95.17% ± 2.66) versus the control and the A condition. For *S. aureus*, a slightly greater CFU/mg reduction was produced versus the other combinations, with a statistically significant difference ($p < 0.05$) versus the control.

The treatment with the D3 combination displayed an effect only against *P. aeruginosa* growth, with significant differences ($p < 0.05$) when compared to the control, B3 condition, and C3 combination.

A similar effect to the A condition was obtained under the E1 condition, with 60.10% ± 5.81 and 45.82% ± 1.81 reductions in *S. aureus* and *P. aeruginosa*, respectively. In E2, a similar trend to the A condition was recorded only for *P. aeruginosa*. A good *S. aureus* CFU/mg reduction was detected in the E3 condition with no significant difference compared to the A condition.

Considering all tested conditions, the best enhancement of GO antimicrobial action was obtained via irradiation with ALAD-PDT (C2 and D2 combinations).

No reduction in the cell number and viability versus the control were detected with 630 nm and 880 nm LEDs in the B1 and B3 conditions. A remarkable number of red cells was recorded in the B2 condition with the ALAD application. In general, the cell viability in the presence of GO was influenced by the LEDs. In particular, in the C1 and C2 combinations, the cell clusters appeared more disaggregated and there were more dead cells compared to the control and the A condition. In the presence of ALAD (C2, D2, E2), the cells were blocked by the gel and most were dead (red). The images obtained with the

C3 and D3 combinations confirmed the CFU/mg results, with more green cells versus the A condition and C1 and C2 combinations. In the D1 and D2 conditions, the number of damaged cells increased and their number was fewer than in both the control and other conditions. In E1 and E3, the treatment with LEDs did not affect the cell viability (Figure 3).

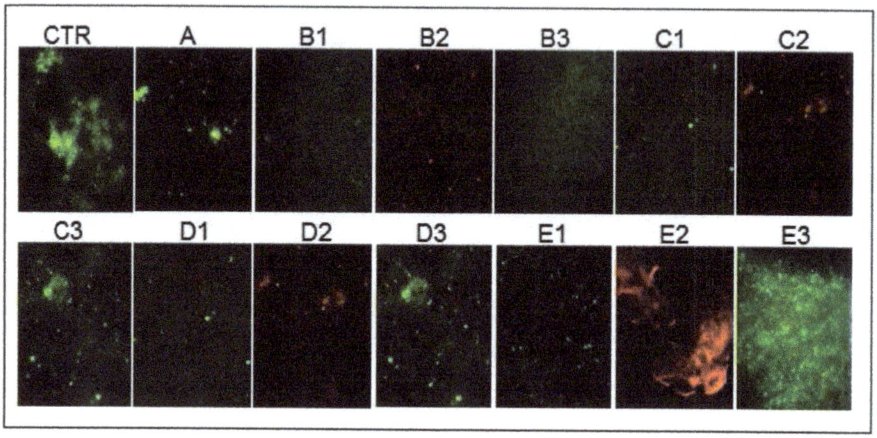

Figure 3. Representative live/dead images of untreated (CTR) and treated LCWBs. For the experimental points, see Figure 1 and the Section 4, paragraph 5.

The representative SEM images (Figure 4) showed non-mixed bacteria in the untreated LCWB (CTR) with a prevalence of bacillary *P. aeruginosa* cells. In the C1 combination, a weak bacterial reduction was detected with cleavage plans of the biomass biofilm versus the control. A remarkable strain reduction was displayed in the LCWB treated with the C2 combination, confirming a significantly greater antimicrobial potentiating effect of 630 nm LEDs toward GO. No difference in terms of microbial reduction was noted for the LCWB treated with C3.

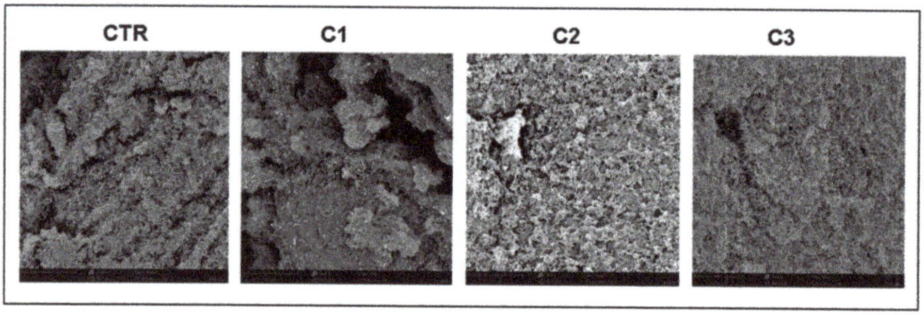

Figure 4. Representative SEM images of untreated (CTR) and treated LCWBs treated with C1, C2, and C3 combinations. For the experimental points, see Figure 1 and the Section 4, paragraph 5.

The ROS production was normalized based on the weight of the LCWBs. As can be seen in Figure 5, the ROS evaluation showed significant ($p < 0.05$) ROS production in presence of GO plus ALAD-PDT, confirming the strong antimicrobial action of this combination. No statistical significance ($p > 0.05$) was obtained with GO and 630 nm LEDs alone, either in respect to the control or each other.

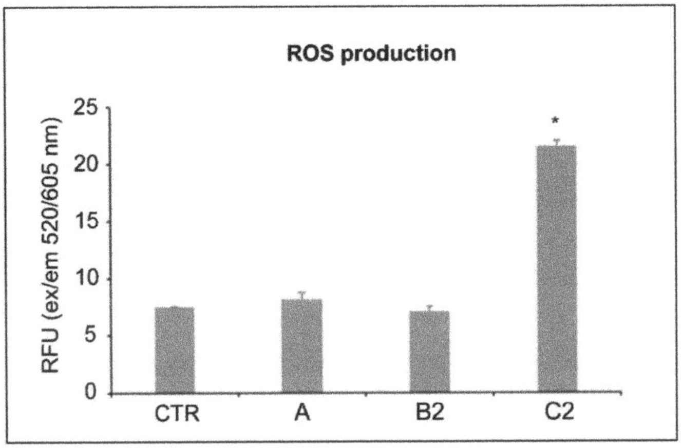

Figure 5. ROS production for the LCWBs: untreated (CTR), treated with the A condition, and treated with the B2 and C2 combinations. For the experimental points, see Figure 1 and the Section 4, paragraph 5. * Statistically significant difference from the CTR ($p < 0.05$).

3. Discussion

Uncovering new non-antibiotic strategies to counteract microbial proliferation in chronic wounds was the pivotal aim of this study. The use of antibiotics for chronic wound management is not ideal and the search for new non-antibiotic strategies has been well considered by the WHO [21]. The failure of standard therapies can be associated with an increase in the resistant/tolerant microorganisms in polymicrobial biofilms. The co-infection of multiple strains in the biofilm environment leads to suppression of the immune response and wound healing activities, contributing to enhancements of both the antibiotic resistance/tolerance and virulence factors' production. Hence, it is essential to identify novel solutions to overcome this issue [22].

In the present study, we evaluated the antimicrobial/antibiofilm/antivirulence action of GO on the polymicrobial LCWB model when irradiated with LEDs in different experimental conditions. Graphene oxide's unique structure gives it several important properties. Graphene oxide is a one-atom-thick carbon-based nanomaterial with several oxygen-containing groups, a large surface area, and high near-infrared absorbance [17]. Generally, LED therapy relies on photosensitizer material being excited by irradiation, followed by an interaction with oxygen-containing functionalities in situ, causing cell death with different mechanisms [23]. Several applications of this interesting technology have been studied thoroughly, starting with tumor therapy and targeting, immune system response modulation, tissue regeneration, periodontal diseases, and wound infections [24–26]. In particular, in the present work, enhanced GO action was obtained when it was combined with ALAD-PDT. The microbial CFU/mg reduction in the presence of GO plus ALAD-PDT could be justified by the expected activation of GO through irradiation, leading to stimulated ROS production (especially oxygen singlet $^1O_2$) [13]. This hypothesis is demonstrated by an increase in ROS production versus the control and versus GO and 630 nm LED alone. The same results obtained with GO plus ALAD-PDT at the two exposure times show a double application of the LEDs: an immediate enhancement of the antimicrobial GO effect and preservation of the GO effect over time. As such, if immediate antimicrobial action is required, the 630 nm LED can be irradiated immediately after GO treatment; if preservation of the GO effect over time is required, after the treatment with GO, it is possible to apply the 630 nm LED. This major killing effect compared to the other setups is due to the activation of both GO and ALAD by irradiation. Greater activation products were available in the biofilm model, creating a stressful environment that promotes cells' death. Aladent, as a photosensitizer, acts as an exogenous prodrug that inters the bacterial cells, causing accumulation in 5-aminolevulinic acid, which overwhelms the enzymatic capacity in the heme synthesis pathway, resulting in protoporphyrin IX (PpIX) accumulation. Finally, PpIX, under irradiation, serves as an in situ photosensitizer, leading to bacterial inactivation [27]. In an *in vitro* study, Petrini et al. [28] demonstrated the increase in fluorescence of PpIX after the addition of ALAD gel to *E. faecalis* solution and after the LED irradiation, the endogenous PpIX produced remarkable cell death.

Several studies mentioned the LED therapy impact in different conditions against biofilm-forming microorganisms associated with chronic wound infections.

Elias et al. [29] indicated the remarkable effect of LED therapy (up to 3 h of application) after GO treatment against methicillin-resistant *S. aureus* without using a photosensitizer. Mahmoudi et al. [30] found an important reduction in the expression of biofilm-associated *S. aureus* genes after applying 630 nm LED irradiation with a photosensitizer (toluidine blue O).

Similar results were obtained in Tan et al.'s study [31], in which ALAD-PDT application caused the destruction of the biofilm structure and reduced the expression of quorum-sensing genes in *P. aeruginosa*. Meanwhile, our study outcomes provided interesting results about this effect in the LCWB model, confirming that irradiation acted on the complex biofilm, taking into consideration the mutual interaction between bacteria in the biofilm and the bacterial distribution in the artificial wound model.

In presence of infrared LEDs and GO, there was an antagonistic action in a dual-species polymicrobial biofilm compared to the treatment with 880 nm LED and GO alone. This finding could seem to contradict those of Petrini et al. [32], but we must consider that the LCWB is a complex 3D polymicrobial biofilm in which the synergistic interaction of *S. aureus* and *P. aeruginosa* increases tolerance. LED treatment can produce oxidative stress, protein damage, and inhibition or delay of growth, without killing the microorganisms that were irradiated, which remained viable (green) [33]. The microbial population decreased, indicating a growth inhibition effect versus the control, without a killing action. Instead, remarkable cell death was detected in presence of ala. As demonstrated by Petrini et al. [28], the gel could englobe and suffocate the cells most susceptible to the treatment.

Through SEM analysis, in the samples treated with GO plus ALAD-PDT, more areas free of bacteria were observed than in the control. These SEM results were in agreement with Li et al., who demonstrated the effect of ALAD-PDT in reducing adherent and aggregated bacteria, suggesting that ALAD-PDT could cause cell detachment, and consequently, inhibition of biofilm formation [34].

The interesting antibacterial results obtained with GO activated by LEDs are of particular importance considering the action of LEDs on regeneration. In fact, as demonstrated by Yang et al. [35], irradiation with ALAD-PDT significantly increased the re-epithelialization of the wound in mice, with a reduction of the NF-κB signaling pathway involved in acute and chronic inflammatory responses.

Future studies should be performed on epithelial cells to confirm these results, including GO.

In conclusion, GO treatment with ALAD-PDT irradiation could represent a valid strategy to counteract the microbial proliferation of chronic wound microorganisms. Furthermore, this therapy represents a valid ecofriendly strategy with a low environmental impact in terms of the manufacturing, transport, and disposal for each production cycle. In terms of application, for the treatment of microbial proliferation in the LCWB, we suggest applying GO irradiated immediately with 630 nm LED and reprocessed with 630 nm LED after another 24 h, to increase the effectiveness of the GO. The results suggest the creation of advanced medicaments consisting of GO and 630 nm LED or only with GO and then treated with 630 nm LED devices. Noteworthy is the low cost of both GO and the 630 nm LED, giving this research a great economic and public health impact.

4. Materials and Methods

4.1. Bacterial Cultures

Anonymized clinical strains *S. aureus* PECHA 10 and *P. aeruginosa* PECHA 4, isolated from patients with chronic wounds, were used in this study (Inter-Institutional Ethic Committee of University "G. d'Annunzio" Chieti-Pescara, Chieti, Italy, ID n. richycnvw). These bacteria, coming from the private collection of the Bacteriological Laboratory of the Pharmacy Department, University "G. d'Annunzio" Chieti-Pescara, were cultured on Mannitol Salt Agar (MSA, Oxoid, Milan, Italy) and Cetrimide Agar (CET, Oxoid, Milan, Italy), respectively. The bacteria were previously characterized for their resistance profiles [36]. In this study, *S. aureus* PECHA 10 was characterized for its hemolytic activity, detection of *agr* allels and *icaA/icaD* genes, and biofilm production [37]. Briefly, for the hemolytic activity, 5 μL of refreshed *S. aureus* PECHA 10 broth cultures in Tryticase Soy Broth (TSB, Oxoid, Milan, Italy) (OD_{600} = 0.04–0.05) were spotted onto Trypticase Soy Agar (TSA, Oxoid, Milan, Italy) plus 5% sheep sterile blood (Biomerieux, Florence, Italy) and incubated for 48 h at 37 °C, then chilled at 4 °C for 1 h for the evaluation. For the *agr* genotyping, a multiplex polymerase chain reaction (PCR) was performed according to Di Stefano et al. [38], and the presence of *icaA* and *icaD* was detected by PCR according to Zhou et al. [39]. *Pseudomonas aeruginosa* was characterized for the *lasB* gene according to Lanotte et al. [40], and for its capability to form a biofilm.

For the study, the bacteria were cultured in TSB and incubated at 37 °C overnight in an aerobic condition, and then refreshed for 2 h at 37 °C in an orbital shaker in an aerobic condition. The cultures were standardized to an optical density at 600 nm (OD_{600}) = 0.125 and diluted 1:10 for *S. aureus* PECHA 10 and 1:100 for *P. aeruginosa* PECHA 4, to obtain 10^6 and 10^5 CFU/mL, respectively [3].

4.2. Substances

4.2.1. Preparation of Graphene Oxide Aqueous Dispersion

Graphene oxide (GO) in an aqueous solution of 4 g/L (Graphenea, Donostia San Sebastian, Spain) was added to PBS (Merk, KGaA, Darmstadt, Germany) to obtain the desired concentration, bath ultrasonicated for 10 min (37 kHz, 180 W; Elmasonic P60H; Elma), and sterilized for 2 h under a UV lamp (6 W, 50 Hz, 0.17 A; Spectroline EF 160/C FE; Spectronics). The GO concentration was standardized spectrophotometrically at λmax 230 nm. Graphene oxide flakes' dimensions (dimension: 670 ± 50 nm at 37 °C; polydispersity: 0.25 ± 0.02) were checked using dynamic laser light scattering (DLS) (90Plus/BI-MAS ZetaPlus multi-angle particle size analyzer; Brookhaven Instruments Corp.) [3]. For the study, GO was used at the non-toxic concentration of 50 mg/L [41].

4.2.2. Aladent Gel

Aladent (ALAD) (Alpha strumenti, Melzo, Milan, Italy) is a gel containing 5% of 5-aminolevulinic acid (ala), as previously described. ALAD is covered by a patent (PCT/IB2018/060368, 12.19.2018) where the object is a "pharmaceutical preparation comprising a topically released active ingredient and a heat-sensitive carrier, method of obtaining same, and use of same in the treatment of skin and mucosal infections". The full text is registered on patentscope/WIPO.int with pub. no. WO2019123332 [20,28,42].

4.3. Light-Emitting Diode (LED) Devices

In this experiment, two different devices emitting light at different wavelengths were applied for 17 min, a time included in the previously evaluated time ranges (from 5 to 20 min) and recommended by the manufacturer (TR-LUX, Errevi group, Bergamo, Italy). The following instruments were used:

- An AlGaAs power LED device (TL-01), characterized by a 630 nm ± 10 nm FHWM nm wavelength, was used as light source (Alpha strumenti, Melzo, Milan, Italy). The handpiece constituted by one LED with a 6-mm diameter at the exit and a surface irradiance of 380 mW/cm^2. During the experiments, the LED handpiece was mounted perpendicularly to the LCWB sample at a 0.5-mm distance. Irradiation was performed under a laminar flow hood in the dark, under aseptic conditions [20,28,42]. For the tests, 630 nm LED alone and plus ALAD (ALAD-PDT) were used.

- A NIR-LED device characterized by an 880 nm wavelength was used as the light source TR-LUX (Errevi, Bergamo, Italy). The handpiece constituted six LEDs (12 mm diameter) disposed in two lines. Each of the by six LEDs was used for irradiation, emitting a power output of 2.37 mW [14,25].

For both devices, light irradiation was performed by keeping the light sources stationary, in a perpendicular position, and at 0.5 mm from the samples.

4.4. Lubbock Chronic Wound Biofilm (LCWB) Model

The LCWB model was prepared according to Di Giulio et al. (2020) [3]. In brief, 5 mL of medium containing Brucella Broth (BB, Oxoid, Milan, Italy) with 0.1% agar bacteriological, 50% porcine plasma (Sigma Aldrich, Milan, Italy), 5% horse erythrocytes (BBL, Microbiology System, Milan, Italy) and 2% fetal calf serum (Biolife Italiana, Milan, Italy) were distributed in sterile glass tubes. For the LCWB preparation, 10 μL of each diluted broth culture were inoculated in glass tubes with sterile pipette tips. After 48 h of incubation, the mature biofilm was harvested from the glass tubes, the pipette tip was removed, the biofilm biomass was washed two times with sterile PBS, and the LCWB volumes were determined [3]. The LCWBs were placed on a "wound bed", an artificial home-made oval-shaped wound bed created with sterile 1.5 mL Eppendorf tubes on the surface of a nutrient medium containing Bolton Broth (Oxoid, Milan, Italy) with 1.5% agar, to reproduce an in vitro chronic wound biofilm and to allow for the treatment [3].

4.5. Effect of GO Alone and Combined with LEDs on LCWB Model

The effect of GO alone and combined with LEDs was evaluated following the experimental plan displayed in Figure 1. In detail, the mature LCWBs, incubated for 48 h at 37 °C in an aerobic condition, were differentiated as follows:

A = treated with:

GO (50 mg/L) and incubated for 24 h at 37 °C in an aerobic condition and then analyzed vs. the control;

B = irradiated for 17 min with:

- B1: 630 nm LED
- B2: ALAD-PDT
- B3: 880 nm LED

and incubated for 24 h at 37 °C in an aerobic condition and then analyzed vs. the control;

C = treated with:

GO (50 mg/L) and irradiated for 17 min with:

- C1: 630 nm LED
- C2: ALAD-PDT
- C3: 880 nm LED

then incubated for 24 h at 37 °C in an aerobic condition and then analyzed vs. the control;

D = treated with:

GO (50 mg/L), incubated for 24 h at 37 °C in an aerobic condition and then irradiated for 17 min with:

- D1: 630 nm LED
- D2: ALAD-PDT
- D3: 880 nm LED

then analyzed vs. the control;

E = incubated for 24 h at 37 °C in an aerobic condition and then irradiated for 17 min with:

- E1: 630 nm LED
- E2: ALAD-PDT
- E3: 880 nm LED

then analyzed vs. the control.

All experimental points (A–E) were analyzed after 72 h (48 h for the mature LCWB preparation plus 24 h for the treatments).

The effect of GO alone and combined with LEDs was evaluated in terms of: (i) *S. aureus* PECHA 10 and *P. aeruginosa* PECHA 4 CFU/mg reduction; (ii) live/dead analysis; (iii) scanning electron microscope (SEM) evaluation; iv) ROS production.

For CFU/mg determination, after treatment and incubation, the biofilm was harvested from the artificial "wound bed", washed twice with sterile PBS, and the weight was measured. Subsequently, the biofilm was vortexed for 2 min, sonicated for 3 min (with ultrasound bath), vortexed for other 2 min and diluted in PBS for the microbial enumeration. Live/dead staining was used to confirm the effect of this procedure in terms of disaggregating action and cell viability retention. The CFU/mL was determined by spreading on MSA for *S. aureus* PECHA 10 and on CET for *P. aeruginosa* PECHA 4 and the plates were incubated at 37 °C for 24–48 h. Data were expressed as percentage of CFU/mg reduction versus the control.

For the cell viability, observation under fluorescence Leica 4000 DM microscopy after live/dead staining was performed according to Di Giulio et al. (2020) [3].

The SEM observation was carried out according to Di Fermo et al. [43]. Briefly, the untreated and treated LCWBs were fixed with glutaraldehyde, dehydrated with ascending concentrations of ethanol and then immersed in hexamethyldisilazane (HMDS, Sigma-Aldrich, Milan, Italy) for 10 min, twice. Hexamethyldisilazane was decanted from the specimen vial and the tissues were left to air dry at room temperature. The dried samples were subjected to the gold-sputtering with a Desk Sputter Coater (Phenom-World B.V., Dillenburgstraat 97 Eindhoven, 5652,AM, Netherlands) and then observed under SEM (Phenom-World B.V., Dillenburgstraat 97 Eindhoven, 5652,AM, Netherlands) at different magnifications.

The best-performing combinations were analyzed for ROS production to define a possible mechanism of action. The ROS production in cells was detected using a Cellular Reactive Oxygen Species Detection Assay Kit (ab186027, Abcam, Cambridge, UK), following the manufacturer's instructions. Briefly, after treating LCWBs with the best-performing GO and LED combinations, the cells were seeded into a 96-well plate × cells per well. We added 100 µL/well of ROS Red Working Solution to the plate. Then, we incubated the cell plate at 37 °C for 1 h and we detected the fluorescence signal using a microplate reader (Synergy H1 BioTek, Santa Clara, CA 95051, USA) after the treatments.

4.6. Statistical Analysis

Data were obtained from at least three independent experiments performed in duplicate. Data were shown as the means ± standard deviation. Differences between groups were assessed with one-way analysis of variance (ANOVA). *P*-values $\leq$0.05 were considered statistically significant.

5. Conclusions

The present study underlines the notable action of non-antibiotic compounds against resistant pathogens mainly growing in polymicrobial biofilms, involved in chronic wound infections. The combined use of GO plus ALAD-PDT represents a valid suggestion for chronic wound management. An added value of these promising results relates to the eco-sustainability of the proposed non-antibiotic combinations: the evolutionary smart low-cost of GO and the low environmental impact of the LED technology.

6. Patents

ALAD is covered by a patent (PCT/IB2018/060368, 12.19.2018) where the object is a "pharmaceutical preparation comprising a topically released active ingredient and a heat-sensitive carrier, method of obtaining same, and use of same in the treatment of skin and mucosal infections". The full text is registered on patentscope/WIPO.int with pub. no. WO2019123332.

Supplementary Materials: The following supporting information can be downloaded at: https://www.mdpi.com/article/10.3390/ijms23136942/s1. (Reference [37] is cited in the Supplementary Materials).

Author Contributions: Conceptualization, S.D.L., F.D., L.C. and S.D.; methodology, S.D.L., F.D., P.D.F. and M.P.; software, M.P. and S.D.L.; validation, M.D.G., A.F., L.C. and S.D.; formal analysis, S.D.L., F.D. and P.D.F.; investigation, S.D.L.; resources, M.D.G., L.C. and S.D.; writing—original draft preparation, S.D.L., F.D. and L.C.; writing—review and editing, L.C. and A.P.; supervision, A.F., A.P. and S.D.; project administration, S.D.; funding acquisition, M.D.G., L.C. and S.D. All authors have read and agreed to the published version of the manuscript.

Funding: This research was funded by: FAR 2021 CELLINI/DI GIULIO and FAR 2020-21 D'ERCOLE.

Institutional Review Board Statement: Not applicable.

Informed Consent Statement: Not applicable.

Data Availability Statement: Not applicable.

Acknowledgments: The authors are grateful to Sara D'Arcangelo and Morena Pinti for their support molecular microbiological characterization and cultural media preparation. In addition, the authors thank Tania Pierfelice and Emira D'Amico for their support in ROS detection.

Conflicts of Interest: The authors declare no conflict of interest.

References

1. Frykberg, R.G.; Banks, J. Challenges in the Treatment of Chronic Wounds. *Adv. Wound Care* **2015**, *4*, 560–582. [CrossRef] [PubMed]
2. Johnson, T.; Gómez, B.; McIntyre, M.; Dubick, M.; Christy, R.; Nicholson, S.; Burmeister, D. The Cutaneous Microbiome and Wounds: New Molecular Targets to Promote Wound Healing. *Int. J. Mol. Sci.* **2018**, *19*, 2699. [CrossRef] [PubMed]
3. Di Giulio, M.; Di Lodovico, S.; Fontana, A.; Traini, T.; Di Campli, E.; Pilato, S.; D'Ercole, S.; Cellini, L. Graphene Oxide Affects *Staphylococcus aureus* and *Pseudomonas aeruginosa* Dual Species Biofilm in Lubbock Chronic Wound Biofilm Model. *Sci. Rep.* **2020**, *10*, 18525. [CrossRef] [PubMed]
4. DeLeon, S.; Clinton, A.; Fowler, H.; Everett, J.; Horswill, A.R.; Rumbaugh, K.P. Synergistic Interactions of *Pseudomonas aeruginosa* and *Staphylococcus aureus* in an in vitro Wound Model. *Infect. Immun.* **2014**, *82*, 4718–4728. [CrossRef] [PubMed]
5. Orazi, G.; O'Toole, G.A. *Pseudomonas aeruginosa* Alters *Staphylococcus aureus* Sensitivity to Vancomycin in a Biofilm Model of Cystic Fibrosis Infection. *mBio* **2017**, *8*. [CrossRef] [PubMed]
6. Batoni, G.; Maisetta, G.; Esin, S. Therapeutic Potential of Antimicrobial Peptides in Polymicrobial Biofilm-Associated Infections. *Int. J. Mol. Sci.* **2021**, *22*, 482. [CrossRef]
7. Fazli, M.; Bjarnsholt, T.; Kirketerp-Møller, K.; Jørgensen, B.; Andersen, A.S.; Krogfelt, K.A.; Givskov, M.; Tolker-Nielsen, T. Nonrandom Distribution of *Pseudomonas aeruginosa* and *Staphylococcus aureus* in Chronic Wounds. *J. Clin. Microbiol.* **2009**, *47*, 4084–4089. [CrossRef]
8. Sun, Y.; Dowd, S.E.; Smith, E.; Rhoads, D.D.; Wolcott, R.D. In Vitro Multispecies Lubbock Chronic Wound Biofilm Model. *Wound Rep. Regen.* **2008**, *16*, 805–813. [CrossRef]
9. Kucera, J.; Sojka, M.; Pavlik, V.; Szuszkiewicz, K.; Velebny, V.; Klein, P. Multispecies Biofilm in an Artificial Wound Bed—A Novel Model for in Vitro Assessment of Solid Antimicrobial Dressings. *J. Microbiol. Methods* **2014**, *103*, 18–24. [CrossRef]
10. Thaarup, I.C.; Bjarnsholt, T. Current in Vitro Biofilm-Infected Chronic Wound Models for Developing New Treatment Possibilities. *Adv. Wound Care* **2020**. [CrossRef]
11. Ganesh, K.; Sinha, M.; Mathew-Steiner, S.S.; Das, A.; Roy, S.; Sen, C.K. Chronic Wound Biofilm Model. *Adv. Wound Care* **2015**, *4*, 382–388. [CrossRef] [PubMed]
12. Patil, T.V.; Patel, D.K.; Dutta, S.D.; Ganguly, K.; Lim, K.T. Graphene Oxide-Based Stimuli-Responsive Platforms for Biomedical Applications. *Molecules* **2021**, *26*, 2797. [CrossRef] [PubMed]
13. Romero, M.P.; Marangoni, V.S.; de Faria, C.G.; Leite, I.S.; Silva, C.d.C.C.E.; Maroneze, C.M.; Pereira-da-Silva, M.A.; Bagnato, V.S.; Inada, N.M. Graphene Oxide Mediated Broad-Spectrum Antibacterial Based on Bimodal Action of Photodynamic and Photothermal Effects. *Front. Microbiol.* **2020**, *10*, 2995. [CrossRef] [PubMed]
14. D'Ercole, S.; Di Fermo, P.; Di Giulio, M.; Di Lodovico, S.; Di Campli, E.; Scarano, A.; Tripodi, D.; Cellini, L.; Petrini, M. Near-infrared NIR Irradiation and Sodium Hypochlorite: An Efficacious Association to Counteract the *Enterococcus faecalis* Biofilm in Endodontic Infections. *J. Photochem. Photobiol. B* **2020**, *210*, 111989. [CrossRef] [PubMed]
15. Kim, W.-S.; Calderhead, R.G. Is Light-Emitting Diode Phototherapy (LED-LLLT) Really Effective? *Laser Ther.* **2011**, *20*, 205–215. [CrossRef] [PubMed]

16. Prasad, A.; Du, L.; Zubair, M.; Subedi, S.; Ullah, A.; Roopesh, M.S. Applications of Light-Emitting Diodes (LEDs) in Food Processing and Water Treatment. *Food Eng. Rev.* **2020**, *12*, 268–289. [CrossRef]
17. Bekmukhametova, A.; Ruprai, H.; Hook, J.M.; Mawad, D.; Houang, J.; Lauto, A. Photodynamic Therapy With Nanoparticles to Combat Microbial Infection and Resistance. *Nanoscale* **2020**, *12*, 21034–21059. [CrossRef]
18. Yang, D.; Lv, X.; Xue, L.; Yang, N.; Hu, Y.; Weng, L.; Fu, N.; Wang, L.; Dong, X. A Lipase-Responsive Antifungal Nanoplatform for Synergistic Photodynamic/Photothermal/Pharmaco-Therapy of Azole-Resistant *Candida albicans* Infections. *Chem. Commun.* **2019**, *55*, 15145–15148. [CrossRef]
19. Ghate, V.; Leong, A.L.; Kumar, A.; Bang, W.S.; Zhou, W.; Yuk, H.-G. Enhancing the Antibacterial Effect of 461 and 521 Nm Light Emitting Diodes on Selected Foodborne Pathogens in Trypticase Soy Broth by Acidic and Alkaline PH Conditions. *Food Microbiol.* **2015**, *48*, 49–57. [CrossRef]
20. Radunović, M.; Petrini, M.; Vlajic, T.; Iezzi, G.; Di Lodovico, S.; Piattelli, A.; D'Ercole, S. Effects of a Novel Gel Containing 5-Aminolevulinic Acid and Red LED against Bacteria Involved in Peri-Implantitis and Other Oral Infections. *J. Photochem. Photobiol. B* **2020**, *205*, 111826. [CrossRef]
21. W.H.O.; Traditional Medicine Programme. Regulatory Situation of Herbal Medicines : A Worldwide Review. apps.who.int. 1998.
22. Maslova, E.; Eisaiankhongi, L.; Sjöberg, F.; McCarthy, R.R. Burns and Biofilms: Priority Pathogens and *In Vivo* Models. *NPJ Biofilms Microbiomes* **2021**, *7*, 73. [CrossRef] [PubMed]
23. Chilakamarthi, U.; Giribabu, L. Photodynamic Therapy: Past, Present and Future. *Chem. Rec.* **2017**, *17*, 775–802. [CrossRef] [PubMed]
24. Amos-Tautua, B.; Songca, S.; Oluwafemi, O. Application of Porphyrins in Antibacterial Photodynamic Therapy. *Molecules* **2019**, *24*, 2456. [CrossRef]
25. Gunaydin, G.; Gedik, M.E.; Ayan, S. Photodynamic Therapy—Current Limitations and Novel Approaches. *Front. Chem.* **2021**, *9*, 691697. [CrossRef]
26. D'Ercole, S.; Spoto, G.; Trentini, P.; Tripodi, D.; Petrini, M. In Vitro Inactivation of *Enterococcus faecalis* with a Led Device. *J. Photochem. Photobiol. B* **2016**, *160*, 172–177. [CrossRef]
27. Harris, F.; Pierpoint, L. Photodynamic Therapy Based on 5-Aminolevulinic Acid and Its Use as an Antimicrobial Agent. *Med. Res. Rev.* **2011**, *32*, 1292–1327. [CrossRef]
28. Petrini, M.; Pierfelice, T.V.; D'Amico, E.; Carlesi, T.; Iezzi, G.; D'Arcangelo, C.; Di Lodovico, S.; Piattelli, A.; D'Ercole, S. Comparison Between Single and Multi-LED Emitters for Photodynamic Therapy: An in vitro Study on *Enterococcus Faecalis* and Human Gingival Fibroblasts. *Int. J. Environ. Res.* **2022**, *19*, 3048. [CrossRef]
29. Elias, L.; Taengua, R.; Frígols, B.; Salesa, B.; Serrano-Aroca, Á. Carbon Nanomaterials and LED Irradiation as Antibacterial Strategies against Gram-Positive Multidrug-Resistant Pathogens. *Int. J. Mol. Sci.* **2019**, *20*, 3603. [CrossRef]
30. Mahmoudi, H.; Pourhajibagher, M.; Alikhani, M.Y.; Bahador, A. The Effect of Antimicrobial Photodynamic Therapy on the Expression of Biofilm Associated Genes in *Staphylococcus aureus* Strains Isolated from Wound Infections in Burn Patients. *Photodiagn. Photodyn. Ther.* **2019**, *25*, 406–413. [CrossRef]
31. Tan, Y.; Cheng, Q.; Yang, H.; Li, H.; Gong, N.; Liu, D.; Wu, J.; Lei, X. Effects of ALA-PDT on Biofilm Structure, Virulence Factor Secretion, and QS in *Pseudomonas aeruginosa*. *Photodiagn. Photodyn. Ther.* **2018**, *24*, 88–94. [CrossRef] [PubMed]
32. Petrini, M.; Trentini, P.; Tripodi, D.; Spoto, G.; D'Ercole, S. In Vitro Antimicrobial Activity of LED Irradiation on *Pseudomonas aeruginosa*. *J. Photochem. Photobiol. B* **2017**, *168*, 25–29. [CrossRef] [PubMed]
33. Probst-Rüd, S.; McNeill, K.; Ackermann, M. Thiouridine Residues in TRNAs Are Responsible for a Synergistic Effect of UVA and UVB Light in Photoinactivation of *Escherichia coli*. *Environ. Microbiol.* **2016**, *19*, 434–442. [CrossRef] [PubMed]
34. Li, X.; Guo, H.; Tian, Q.; Zheng, G.; Hu, Y.; Fu, Y.; Tan, H. Effects of 5-Aminolevulinic Acid–Mediated Photodynamic Therapy on Antibiotic-Resistant Staphylococcal Biofilm: An in Vitro Study. *J. Surg. Res.* **2013**, *184*, 1013–1021. [CrossRef] [PubMed]
35. Yang, T.; Tan, Y.; Zhang, W.; Yang, W.; Luo, J.; Chen, L.; Liu, H.; Yang, G.; Lei, X. Effects of ALA-PDT on the Healing of Mouse Skin Wounds Infected With *Pseudomonas aeruginosa* and Its Related Mechanisms. *Front. Cell Dev. Biol.* **2020**, *8*, 585132. [CrossRef]
36. Di Lodovico, S.; Bacchetti, T.; D'Ercole, S.; Covone, S.; Petrini, M.; Di Giulio, M.; Di Fermo, P.; Diban, F.; Ferretti, G.; Cellini, L. Complex Chronic Wound Biofilms Are Inhibited in Vitro by the Natural Extract of *Capparis Spinose*. *Front. Microbiol.* **2022**, *13*, 832919. [CrossRef]
37. Stepanović, S.; Vuković, D.; Dakić, I.; Savić, B.; Švabić-Vlahović, M. A Modified Microtiter-Plate Test for Quantification of Staphylococcal Biofilm Formation. *J. Microbiol. Methods* **2000**, *40*, 175–179. [CrossRef]
38. Di Stefano, A.; D'Aurizio, E.; Trubiani, O.; Grande, R.; Di Campli, E.; Di Giulio, M.; Di Bartolomeo, S.; Sozio, P.; Iannitelli, A.; Nostro, A.; et al. Viscoelastic Properties Of *Staphylococcus aureus* and *Staphylococcus epidermidis* mono-Microbial Biofilms. *Microb. Biotechnol.* **2009**, *2*, 634–641. [CrossRef]
39. Zhou, S.; Chao, X.; Fei, M.; Dai, Y.; Liu, B. Analysis of *S. epidermidis IcaA* and *IcaD* Genes by Polymerase Chain Reaction and Slime Production: A Case Control Study. *BMC Infect. Dis.* **2013**, *13*, 242. [CrossRef]
40. Lanotte, P. Genetic Features of *Pseudomonas aeruginosa* Isolates from Cystic Fibrosis Patients Compared with Those of Isolates from Other Origins. *J. Med. Microbiol.* **2004**, *53*, 73–81. [CrossRef]
41. Fusco, L.; Garrido, M.; Martín, C.; Sosa, S.; Ponti, C.; Centeno, A.; Alonso, B.; Zurutuza, A.; Vázquez, E.; Tubaro, A.; et al. Skin Irritation Potential of Graphene-Based Materials Using a Non-Animal Test. *Nanoscale* **2020**, *12*, 610–622. [CrossRef] [PubMed]

42. Petrini, M.; Di Lodovico, S.; Iezzi, G.; Cellini, L.; Tripodi, D.; Piattelli, A.; D'Ercole, S. Photodynamic Antibiofilm and Antibacterial Activity of a New Gel with 5-Aminolevulinic Acid on Infected Titanium Surfaces. *Biomedicines* **2022**, *10*, 572. [CrossRef] [PubMed]
43. Di Fermo, P.; Ciociola, T.; Di Lodovico, S.; D'Ercole, S.; Petrini, M.; Giovati, L.; Conti, S.; Di Giulio, M.; Cellini, L. Antimicrobial Peptide L18R Displays a Modulating Action against Inter-Kingdom Biofilms in the Lubbock Chronic Wound Biofilm Model. *Microorganisms* **2021**, *9*, 1779. [CrossRef] [PubMed]

MDPI
St. Alban-Anlage 66
4052 Basel
Switzerland
www.mdpi.com

International Journal of Molecular Sciences Editorial Office
E-mail: ijms@mdpi.com
www.mdpi.com/journal/ijms

www.ingramcontent.com/pod-product-compliance
Lightning Source LLC
Chambersburg PA
CBHW061552210926
51850CB00009B/2078
* 9 7 8 3 0 3 6 5 8 6 9 7 7 *